A Guide to Practicum and Internship for School Counselors-in-Training

"The new edition of *A Guide to Practicum and Internship for School Counselors-in-Training* is the definitive text and guide for pre-service practicum and internship students. The new features, especially the expanded sections on supervision and the ASCA National Model, bring theory alive in practical school-based applications, from working with special populations to the politics and culture climate of today's schools. Since this text was first published, it has helped shaped the direction of our internship program."

Carol Dahir, EdD, is professor and chair of the school counseling program in the school of education at New York Institute of Technology.

"Where was this gem of a book when I was doing my practicum and internship? It is comprehensive and up-to-date, full of practical examples and conceptual activities. It provides students with the knowledge and tools essential to maximizing their practicum and internship experience. As a school counselor educator, this book is now a staple of my training program."

Deborah K. Buchanan, PhD, is a counselor educator at Austin Peay State University.

A Guide to Practicum and Internship for School Counselors-in-Training, second edition, covers all aspects of the practicum and internship experience, from the initial contact with supervisors to detailed descriptions of students' different roles. Readers will gain both an awareness of the school culture and the understanding needed to develop an individualized philosophy of school counseling. Specific topics covered include popular counseling theories used by school counselors, strategies for working with special populations of students, understanding the school counselor's role in utilizing the 2012 National Model of the American School Counselor Association (ASCA), including the inherent elements and themes, putting the ASCA Ethical Standards into practice, and administration of day-to-day tasks. Each chapter contains activities, case studies, worksheets, and images to facilitate understanding, and all material presented is consistent with both the accreditation standards of the Council for Accreditation of Counseling and Related Educational Programs (CACREP) and the school counselor standards identified by the ASCA.

Jeannine R. Studer, Ed.D, is a professor emerita from the University of Tennessee, Knoxville.

A Guide to Practicum and Internship for School Counselors-in-Training

Second Edition

Edited by Jeannine R. Studer

Routledge
Taylor & Francis Group

NEW YORK AND LONDON

Second edition published 2016
by Routledge
711 Third Avenue, New York, NY 10017

and by Routledge
27 Church Road, Hove, East Sussex BN3 2FA

Routledge is an imprint of the Taylor & Francis Group, an informa business

First edition published by Routledge 2010

Library of Congress Cataloging-in-Publication Data
Studer, Jeannine R.
  A guide to practicum and internship for school counselors-in-training/
by Jeannine R. Studer.—Second edition.
     pages cm
  Includes bibliographical references and index.
  1. Educational counseling.   2. Student counselors—Training of.   3. Internship programs.
I. Title.
  LB1027.5.S85315 2015
  371.4071′55—dc23
  2014043123

ISBN: 978-1-138-79055-1 (hbk)
ISBN: 978-1-138-79056-8 (pbk)
ISBN: 978-1-315-76412-2 (ebk)

Typeset in Galliard
by ApexCoVantage, LLC

Printed and bound in the United States of America by
Edwards Brothers Malloy on sustainably sourced paper

This book is dedicated to all of my former school counseling students, the dedicated school counselors who have volunteered their time and expertise to supervise school counselors-in-training, and future students who will carry on the tradition of the school counseling profession.

Contents

Preface   xi
Acknowledgements   xv
About the Editor   xvi
About the Contributors   xvii

SECTION I
The Practicum and Internship Journey   1

**1 Getting Started in Your Clinical Experiences as a School
     Counselor-in-Training**   3
   JEANNINE R. STUDER
   Introduction 3
   Conclusion 15
   Websites 16
   References 16

2 Understanding the School Culture as a School Counselor-in-Training 17
   AMY KRONINGER AND JEANNINE R. STUDER
   Introduction 17
   Federal and State Initiatives and the Role of the Professional School Counselor 18
   Communicating Responsibilities, Duties, and Tasks to Stakeholders 23
   Building Relationships for Enhancing Student Growth 26
   Interaction With Other Professionals 33
   Conclusion 36
   Websites 36
   References 36

3 Applying Counseling Theories During the Clinical Experiences   38
   CYNTHIA CRAWFORD AND JEANNINE R. STUDER
   Introduction 38
   Individual Counseling Theories 41
   Creative Counseling Approaches 48
   Conclusion 56
   Websites 56
   References 57

4 An Overview of Supervisory Practices for School Counselors-in-Training 59
   JEANNINE R. STUDER
   Introduction 59

Conclusion 73
Websites 73
References 74

5 Supervision as a Developmental Passage   **75**
KRISTI A. GIBBS AND VIRGINIA A. MAGNUS
Introduction 75
Supervisory Relationship and Supervision Challenges 83
Other Challenges 84
Conclusion 88
Websites 88
References 88

SECTION II
The American School Counselor Association (ASCA)
National Model as a Structure for Understanding the
Role of the Professional School Counselor   **91**

6 The ASCA National Model as a Supervisory Guide   **93**
JEANNINE R. STUDER
Introduction 93
A Summary of the Development of the ASCA National Standards
   (now ASCA Student Standards) 94
Studies Supporting the Benefits of a Comprehensive,
   Developmental School Counseling Program 97
The Professional School Counselor Standards:
   School Counselor Competencies 99
Recommended Percentage of Time Performing School
   Counseling Activities 108
Conclusion 110
Websites 110
References 110

7 The ASCA National Model Themes and the Clinical Experiences   **112**
JEANNINE R. STUDER
Introduction 112
Systemic Change 113
Leadership 115
Advocacy 119
Collaboration 122
Conclusion 125
Websites 125
References 125

8 Understanding the Foundation Component of the ASCA
National Model as a School Counselor-in-Training   **127**
CAROLINE A. BAKER AND SIBYL CATO WEST
Introduction 127
Program Focus 128

*ASCA Mindsets and Behaviors for Student Success: K–12 College- and
Career-Readiness Standards for Every Student 131*
School Counselor Professional Competencies 132
Values, Ethical Standards, and Laws 132
Conclusion 135
Websites 135
References 135

9 **Understanding the Management Component of the ASCA
National Model as a School Counselor-in-Training**   136
  JEANNINE R. STUDER
  Introduction 136
  Assessments 138
  Tools 140
  Conclusion 149
  Websites 149
  References 149

10 **Understanding the Delivery System Component of the
ASCA National Model as a School Counselor-in-Training**   150
  JEANNINE R. STUDER
  Introduction 150
  Direct Student Services 151
  Indirect Student Services 162
  Conclusion 164
  Websites 164
  References 164

11 **Understanding the Accountability Component of the ASCA
National Model as a School Counselor-in-Training**   166
  AARON H. OBERMAN
  Introduction 166
  Data Analysis 167
  Program Results 168
  MEASURE 170
  Evaluation and Improvement 176
  Conclusion 181
  Websites 182
  References 182

12 **Applying the American School Counselor Association (ASCA)
Ethical Standards to Clinical Experiences**   183
  MELINDA M. GIBBONS AND SHAWN L. SPURGEON
  Introduction 183
  The ASCA Ethical Standards 187
  Conclusion 194
  Websites 194
  References 194
  Appendix A: Ethical Standards for School Counselors 196

SECTION III
Diversity and Developmental Issues Among School-Aged Youth:
Guidelines for the School Counselor-in-Training   **207**

13 Understanding Differences in the Schools   209
    JOLIE ZIOMEK-DAIGLE AND MICHAEL JAY MANALO
    Introduction 210
    Assessment of School Counselor-in-Training Awareness, Knowledge, and Skills 210
    Assessment of School Site and Developing a School Profile 213
    Conclusion 229
    Websites 229
    References 230

14 Developmental Issues of Students   233
    ROBIN WILBOURN LEE AND JENNIFER JORDAN
    Introduction 233
    Theories of Development 234
    Basic Forces in Human Development 245
    Elementary School–Aged Children and Developmental Issues (Grades K–5) 245
    Adolescents and Developmental Issues (Grades 6–12) 249
    Conclusion 255
    Websites 255
    References 255

SECTION IV
Completing the Clinical Experiences   **257**

15 Transitioning Forward: From Clinical Experiences to
    a Professional School Counselor   259
    MICHAEL BUNDY
    Introduction 259
    Self-assessment as a Transition Activity 263
    The Application Process 264
    Professional Credentials 269
    Membership in Professional Organizations 272
    Conclusion 273
    Websites 273
    References 273

Index   275

Preface

Since the inception of the school counseling profession, the role of the school counselor has been a source of confusion among parents, students, teachers, administrators, and even school counselors themselves. Although various school counseling models and role descriptions have been proposed throughout its brief history, it was not until the American School Counselor Association (ASCA) took a vigorous stance and developed the ASCA National Standards (later renamed Student Standards, and now retitled Mindsets and Behaviors for Student Success) and then the ASCA National Model that school counselors were able to understand more thoroughly their role in a comprehensive, developmental school counseling (CDSC) program. These prototypes serve as a foundation for the creation of a template for school counselors to create a program that harmonizes with the philosophy and beliefs of the professional organization. The ASCA continues to vocalize and validate the growth of students who participate in a CDSC program, which has led to stakeholders having a more thorough understanding of the school counselor's role and enriched student growth.

In line with this systematic change was an endorsement to standardize the title from that of "guidance counselor" to "professional school counselor" to express more aggressively our role in the schools. These endeavors have been instrumental in assisting school counselors to provide tasks that are more reflective of our education and training, rather than engaging in quasi-administrative or clerical activities.

FOR THE SCHOOL COUNSELOR-IN-TRAINING

This text is designed to help you understand the clinical experiences of practicum and internship. These are pivotal field-based opportunities in which you will be supervised under the vigilant eyes of a school site counselor supervisor and program supervisor. I encourage you to take advantage of the supervision you receive, take risks, and explore new areas of personal and professional growth. The guidance and advice you receive from your supervisors at this time are especially critical, as this will probably be the last time you will receive feedback on your clinical skills before you completely transition into the profession. As you read the information in the chapters and engage in the Conceptual Application Activities and student activities that are provided in the text, you will have opportunities to appreciate your role as a leader of a CDSC program.

As the school counseling profession undergoes a renewal in perspective, you as a school counselor-in-training are instrumental in clarifying this new era of school counseling. With your newly acquired skills and knowledge, you will be an influential voice for communicating our role, building on the foundations established by our predecessors, and acting as a change agent who more directly contributes to greater student development.

FOR SCHOOL COUNSELOR SITE SUPERVISORS

A "dirty little secret" of the profession is that most school counselor training programs do not offer information about supervision, which leads to a gap for school counselors entering the profession without this knowledge or skill. Ironically, an ASCA ethical responsibility is to provide supervision to students entering the profession. The question then becomes, "How do I receive training in supervision?" School counselor training programs often offer classes in supervision, and this information can also be found through books, conferences, and/or workshops. However, professional development workshops that focus on supervision of school counselors are sometimes difficult to find, particularly for school counselors who are located in remote areas. The materials in this text will assist you in gaining information regarding your role in supervision, issues surrounding this practice, models of supervision, and activities to help your supervisee learn about the school counselor's leadership role in the ASCA National Model.

FOR FACULTY PROGRAM SUPERVISORS

This text provides students with information about the clinical experiences of practicum and internship. Standards of the Council for Accreditation of Counseling and Related Educational Programs (CACREP) are specified to address student learning, and strategies for gaining experiential understanding of the ASCA National Model are included within these chapters. Through my experience as a clinical instructor, students in these classes often struggle to apply concepts, theories, and techniques they may have already acquired in previous classes, or those they will obtain in future classes. Although school counseling curricula often require specific courses in professional orientation and ethical practice, social and cultural diversity, human growth and development, and helping relationships, additional knowledge surrounding these areas is included in this text to facilitate students' conceptual application in their clinical classes.

This text is divided into four sections with designated CACREP standards to help you negotiate your way through the clinical experiences and transition into the role of a professional school counselor. The chapters contain hypothetical situations, activities, case studies, and worksheets that are intended to facilitate your understanding of the profession and your responsibilities, knowledge, and skills as a school counselor. Conceptual application activities are intended to facilitate your professional development, and student activities are presented as interventions that can be adapted in work with students. As our society changes as a result of various social, political, and economic issues, so does the role of the school counselor under the auspices of the ASCA. For instance, the ASCA National Standards were renamed the ASCA Student Standards with the newest revision of the ASCA National Model. More recently, these Student Standards were renamed the Mindsets and Behaviors for Student Success. Furthermore, the personal/social domain was retitled the social/emotional domain. As you progress through your clinical experiences, keep in mind that these are exciting times for our profession, and throughout your career you will have numerous opportunities to advocate for the profession and for your students.

Section I, "The Practicum and Internship Journey," is divided into five chapters. Chapter 1, "Getting Started in Your Clinical Experiences as a School Counselor-in-Training," includes a glossary of supervisory terms, various perspectives surrounding school counselor identity, practical views of the clinical experiences of practicum and internship, professional counseling organizations, what to expect from supervision, materials that will be needed for supervision, factors to consider in working with a site supervisor, and concrete activities that are designed for you to think about your personal identity in the profession. As you engage in a rudimentary grasp of the supervisory process, understanding the educational milieu is the next step.

Practicing professional school counselors at various grade levels authored Chapter 2, "Understanding the School Culture as a School Counselor-in-Training." Essential topics to facilitate your understanding of the school environment include explanations of the school culture and climate, federal and state initiatives, and responsibilities to stakeholders and other professionals. After you have had an opportunity to get a basic appreciation for school-related concepts, your attention is then turned to a review of theories most frequently used by school counselors.

Chapter 3, "Applying Counseling Theories During the Clinical Experiences," provides a summarization of the more widespread approaches for counseling students in schools. Although you have probably already had a class in counseling theories, clinical school counseling students often express a need to review some of the more popular theories that are used in working with children and adolescents. This need becomes particularly relevant because the nature of the clinical experiences requires application of theory to actual counselees with real concerns. In addition, creative counseling strategies such as art, play, and music as well as additional considerations for working with school-aged youth are found in this chapter.

Chapter 4, "An Overview of Supervisory Practices for School Counselors-in-Training," describes rudimentary clinical initial considerations such as making an initial contact with your school site supervisor, appropriate dress, school policies and procedures, introducing yourself to stakeholders within the boundaries of the school policies, and considerations for making a contribution to the school site and the profession. Furthermore, wellness as an integral, philosophical, professional component with attention to self-care is described. As you are apprised of the logistics surrounding supervision, your next step is to have an awareness of how supervision works.

The information in Chapter 5, "Supervision as a Developmental Passage," provides insight into developmental models of supervision with examples of supervisor roles and expectations of your role as a supervisee. In this chapter you will read about some of the more typical processes and stages to which you will likely be able to relate. At times, supervision is not always a smooth progression, as there are various challenges such as multicultural issues, anxiety and resistance, parallel process, and dual roles that could impair the process. As a student training for the school counseling profession (and later on, when you are an experienced member of the profession), an awareness of these issues can assist in preparation for supervision. From here, the next section provides a more thorough appreciation of your role within a comprehensive, developmental school counseling (CDSC) program.

Section II, "The American School Counselor Association (ASCA) National Model as a Structure for Understanding the Role of the Professional School Counselor," contains six chapters. The information is written to assist you in understanding how the tasks you will be performing at your school site correlate to the essential activities within a developmental program as outlined by the ASCA National Model. Five of these chapters are devoted to a specific component of the National Model, with a final chapter on the ASCA Ethical Standards.

Chapter 6, "The ASCA National Model as a Supervisory Guide," summarizes the ASCA National Model and the school counselor's role in leading a comprehensive, developmental program. Although it is likely that you have already been introduced to the ASCA National Model, the model is summarized, and empirically based studies that support this type of programming are described. Furthermore, a discussion of the professional school counselor standards and recommended percentage of time that school counselors are to spend in various direct and indirect activities are outlined.

Chapter 7, "The ASCA National Model Themes and the Clinical Experiences," provides an explanation of systemic change, transformational leaders, advocacy skills, collaboration with others, and attention to confidentiality with stakeholders.

Chapter 8, "Understanding the Foundation Component of the ASCA National Model as a School Counselor-in-Training," provides activities designed to help you think about your beliefs in regard to school counseling as a base for developing a program vision/mission and goals. The ASCA Student and School Counselor Standards and Competencies are explained and a discussion of personal values and ethical and legal standards is included.

Chapter 9, "Understanding the Management Component of the ASCA National Model as a School Counselor-in-Training," contains practical suggestions for organizing and administering school counseling tasks throughout the academic year. Considerations such as the school counselor's office arrangement and space, assessments, and tools that facilitate these tasks such as management agreements, the advisory council, the use of data, action and lesson plans, and calendars are discussed to aid in your understanding of how the school counseling program can be best organized.

Chapter 10, "Understanding the Delivery System Component of the ASCA National Model as a School Counselor-in-Training," reviews direct student services in the form of the school counseling core curriculum, individual student planning, and responsive services. Indirect student services in the form of referrals, consultation, and collaboration are included in addition to specific techniques and exercises that will be beneficial to you personally, as well as those that you can use with students in grades pre-K–12. The next chapter will introduce you to specific strategies that are helpful in assessing your effectiveness in delivering your services.

Chapter 11, "Understanding the Accountability Component of the ASCA National Model as a School Counselor-in-Training," includes a discussion of program evaluation and procedures for applying process, perception, and outcome data. Types of research, a summary of the MEASURE program, specific types of assessment instruments, and evaluation and counselor performance assessment strategies are discussed in this chapter.

Central to the practice of school counseling and the ASCA National Model are ethical standards. Chapter 12, "Applying the American School Counselor Association (ASCA) Ethical Standards to Clinical Experiences," reviews the principles of counseling ethics and provides a model for making ethical decisions. In addition, your ethical responsibilities to various stakeholders with specific scenarios for applying the ethical standards are outlined, and the complete ASCA Ethical Standards are given for use as a resource.

Section III, "Diversity and Developmental Issues Among School-Aged Youth: Guidelines for the School Counselor-in-Training," includes two chapters that are written to assist with your understanding of unique student needs in the school setting. School counselors have a responsibility to work with *all* students in a school setting, yet too often counselors have not received the training or education to work with students with specific needs.

Chapter 13, "Understanding Differences in the Schools," provides information related to working with different groups of school-aged youth. A self-assessment of awareness, knowledge, and skills in relation to working with diverse populations while in your training program is summarized. Highlighted in the chapter are culturally and ethnically diverse students, those with special needs, gifted students, gender differences among youth, students who are lesbian, gay, bisexual, transgender, and queer (LGBTQ), English Language Learners, socioeconomic differences among students, and students with multiple exceptionalities. School counselor responsibilities in working with these students are also discussed.

Chapter 14, "Developmental Issues of Students," provides school counseling students with a summarization of the cognitive, physical, affective, and behavioral issues of students at various grade levels. Discussions of childhood obesity, asthma, autism spectrum disorder, attention-deficit hyperactivity disorder, learning disabilities, and the role of the school counselor are also provided.

The concluding section, "Completing the Clinical Experiences," includes information for your journey as a professional school counselor. Chapter 15, "Transitioning Forward: From Clinical Experiences to a Professional School Counselor," provides suggestions for terminating your internship experiences. At this stage in your professional development you will have mixed feelings of sadness and anticipation. Useful strategies for terminating relationships with the individuals with whom you worked are included, as are considerations for taking the next step in your professional journey as you apply for a position as a professional school counselor.

Acknowledgements

This book could not have been possible without the work of many talented individuals. Due to the expertise of the chapter contributors, school counselors-in-training perform with success during their clinical experiences, armed with practical strategies and ideas. I am grateful to Amy Kroninger, Cynthia Crawford, Kristi Gibbs, Virginia Magnus, Caroline Baker, Sibyl West, Aaron Oberman, Melinda Gibbons, Shawn Spurgeon, Jolie Ziomek-Daigle, Jay Manalo, Robin Wilbourn Lee, Jennifer Jordan, and Mike Bundy.

I am exceptionally grateful for the support and encouragement from the accomplished individuals at Taylor & Francis Publishing Group for bringing this book to completion. In particular, I would like to thank Anna Moore, senior editor, Elizabeth Graber, editorial assistant, and Sheri Sipka, project manager.

Finally, a special appreciation goes to Maggie, my Cavalier King Charles.

About the Editor

Jeannine R. Studer, Ed.D, received her master's degree from Bowling Green State University and her specialist and doctorate from the University of Toledo. Dr. Studer was previously a high school counselor in Sandusky, Ohio, as well as an assistant/associate professor at Heidelberg University in Tiffin, Ohio, and California State University, Stanislaus. She formerly served as a professor of counselor education, as the school counseling program and clinical experiences coordinator at the University of Tennessee. She is now a professor emerita. Dr. Studer has made numerous presentations at the regional, state, national, and international levels. In addition, she has written numerous articles and has published four texts on school counseling issues.

About the Contributors

Caroline A. Baker, PhD, is an assistant professor of school counseling at the University of Wisconsin–River Falls. With an emphasis on diversity in counseling, Baker has completed 11 publications, including peer-reviewed journal articles, book chapters, and newsletters, and has presented at the national and state levels. Her additional research interests include culture and counseling, career counseling, and the scholarship of teaching and learning in counselor education. Baker has also served as postsecondary vice president for the Wisconsin School Counseling Association and is committed to preparing graduate students to become excellent professional school counselors.

Michael Bundy, PhD, NCC, CPC, is director of the school counseling program at Carson-Newman University, where he is responsible for the internship program. Previously, he was an elementary school counselor for more than 20 years in Oak Ridge, Tennessee, where he also served as site supervisor for many interns and practicum students. In addition, he was an adjunct instructor of school counseling practicum and internship at the University of Tennessee. Bundy has numerous publications and has conducted presentations on a variety of issues related to working with children and young people.

Cynthia Crawford, PhD, LPC, NCC, has served as a counselor educator at the Citadel Graduate School in Charleston, South Carolina, as well as Appalachian State University, located in Boone, North Carolina. She has also worked in private practice as a child and adolescent therapist. Crawford currently works for Capella and Webster Universities.

Melinda M. Gibbons, PhD, NCC, is currently an associate professor of counselor education at the University of Tennessee, where she coordinates the doctoral program in counselor education and supervision. Before earning her doctorate in counseling and counselor education from the University of North Carolina at Greensboro, she worked as a school counselor, primarily at the high school level. Gibbons' research interests include career development for underserved populations, prospective first-generation college students, and school counseling best practices. She also helps coordinate a postsecondary education program for students with intellectual disabilities called FUTURE.

Kristi A. Gibbs, PhD, LPC/MHSP, RPT-S, previously worked as a professional counselor in both community and school settings. She has provided clinical supervision for counselors-in-training both on-site and as a university supervisor. Gibbs has also supervised post-master's interns pursuing licensure or specialized training in play therapy. She is presently the director of counselor education at the University of Tennessee at Chattanooga. Gibbs has presented at regional, state, national, and international levels. She has published one additional book chapter on supervision.

Jennifer Jordan, PhD, LPC, NCC, specializes in counseling skill development, supervision, and overseeing on-site practicum experiences. Jordan's interests include evaluating and determining appropriate intervention strategies for children and adolescents with a variety of problems utilizing play therapy and other creative techniques.

Amy Kroninger, MS, is a school counselor for grades 3–5 at a school of over 1000 students in Knoxville, Tennessee. She is also on the advisory board for elementary school counselors, and is a lead counselor evaluator in Knox County Schools. She has served as a site supervisor for practicum and internship students and is actively involved in the Smoky Mountain Counseling Association (SMCA), the local chapter of the Tennessee Counseling Association, in which she served as president.

Robin Wilbourn Lee, PhD, LPC, earned a PhD in counselor education and supervision from Mississippi State University. Lee teaches in the professional counseling program of the Womack Educational Leadership Department at Middle Tennessee State University, specializing in mental health counseling. Prior to joining MTSU, she held faculty positions in counseling programs at the University of Tennessee at Chattanooga and Columbus State University in Columbus, Georgia. Lee has served as president and secretary of the Association for Counselor Education and Supervision (ACES); president and secretary of the Southern Association for Counselor Education and Supervision (SACES); and president and treasurer of the Tennessee Association for Counselor Education and Supervision (TACES). She is a founding member of the Tennessee Licensed Professional Counselors Association (TLPCA) and serves as the Legislative/Public Policy Chair. Lee received the 2011–2012 President's Outstanding Service Award from ACES, the 2011 Dr. Susan Hammonds-White Leadership Award from TLPCA, the 2009–2010 Dr. Charles Thompson Counselor Educator of the Year from TACES, the 2009 Outstanding Alumni from the College of Education at Delta State University, the 2009–2010 President's Service Award, the 2008 Counselor Educator of the Year from TLPCA, and the 2008 President's Outstanding Service Award from SACES.

Virginia A. Magnus, PhD, LPC, CSC, is the school counseling coordinator at the University of Tennessee–Chattanooga. She was previously a school counselor and substance abuse counselor. Magnus presents at various professional conferences at the local, regional, state, and national levels. She is currently conducting research at a magnet middle school.

Michael Jay Manalo, PhD, HSP-P, NCC, completed a PhD in counseling psychology from the University of Georgia in 2011 and holds an additional certificate in interdisciplinary qualitative studies. He is the associate director of training at Western Carolina University's office of counseling and psychological services and is licensed as a psychologist in both Georgia and North Carolina.

Aaron H. Oberman, PhD, NCC, is an associate professor at the Citadel and program coordinator for the division of counselor education. Oberman's research interests include the implementation of the ASCA National Model, school counselor accountability, and creative teaching methods.

Shawn L. Spurgeon, PhD, serves as the coordinator of the clinical mental health counseling program at the University of Tennessee at Knoxville. His primary courses include professional orientation, formal measurement, psychopathology, and human development. He has made numerous state, regional, and national presentations. Spurgeon's current research interests include African American male identity development over the life span and counselor identity development.

Sibyl Cato West, PhD, is an associate professor in the department of counseling at Indiana University of Pennsylvania. She received her doctorate at The Ohio State University and previously worked as a school counselor for the Tucson Unified School District.

Jolie Ziomek-Daigle, PhD, holds a doctoral degree in counselor education from the University of Georgia and is an associate professor in the department of counseling and human development services. Ziomek-Daigle has published extensively on remediation and retention issues in counselor education, the clinical development of school counselors, school counseling interventions, and school-based play therapy services in the following journals: *Journal of Counseling and Development, Professional School Counseling, Guidance and Counselling, Middle School Journal,* and the *Family Journal,* among others. Ziomek-Daigle is a member of several counseling organizations, such as the ACA, ASCA, ACES, SACES, and GSCA. She has contributed book chapters and case studies to several texts published by the American Counseling Association, Routledge, and Insight Media and currently has a textbook under contract with Sage.

Section I

The Practicum and Internship Journey

1 Getting Started in Your Clinical Experiences as a School Counselor-in-Training

Jeannine R. Studer

CACREP Standards

Foundations

B. Skills and Practices

2. Demonstrates the ability to articulate, model, and advocate for an appropriate school counselor identity and program.

The purpose of this chapter is to:

*   provide an understanding of the school counseling practicum and internship experiences,
*   describe clinical supervision and what to expect in these experiences,
*   provide you with opportunities to self-reflect on your reasons for entering the profession.

INTRODUCTION

This chapter is written to assist you in understanding the *what* of the clinical experiences. In other words, as you read this chapter you will hopefully have a better understanding of what the school counselor clinical experiences entail, what the expectations are, and what factors need to be considered during the supervisory process. You have undoubtedly already taken several courses that have provided you with a perspective of the historical developments that have impacted the professional school counselor's role and how the American School Counselor Association (ASCA) has shaped policy to address societal concerns. If you have not taken the time to reflect on your reasons for entering this profession prior to now, take time to do so. Have you had certain experiences that have led you to this career? Were school counselors that you had as a pre-K–12 student part of this decision? Or, do you have special talents that are compatible with those of people who are successful in this profession?

As a counselor educator I meet with prospective school counseling students, and when I question them regarding the reasons they are interested in this profession, I have had a few inquiring students state, "I want to have time off in the summer and I know I do not want to teach, so I think this would be a good alternative." If this is one of your reasons for your career decision, perhaps you need to think in terms of whether this is the best profession for you and for those with whom you will be working. The professional school counselor requires skill, dedication, and energy, and as you enter the clinical experiences you are provided with an extraordinary opportunity to scrutinize your readiness for this profession. For those of you who have already taken courses within the school counseling curriculum, you are probably already familiar with some phraseology related to supervision. Others may not have had these foundation courses and are in the process of learning professional terminology. Table 1.1 is a glossary of terms that serve as a review or introduction to the phrases common to the profession.

Table 1.1 Glossary of Common Supervisory Terms

American Counseling Association (ACA)	Counseling association that represents counselors in various settings
American School Counselor Association (ASCA)	Promotes school counseling professionals and activities that support student development
ASCA National Model	A framework developed by ASCA for comprehensive school counseling programs that are preventive and developmental
Council for Accreditation of Counseling and Related Educational Programs (CACREP)	Independent organization that develops standards for counseling training programs
Comprehensive, developmental school counseling (CDSC) programs	A data-driven program based on standards that enhance student growth (ASCA, 2012)
Mindsets and Behaviors for Student Success	Term replacing the ASCA National Standards that were later retitled ASCA Student Standards
Supervision	A process by which novice professionals acquire skills under the direction of an experienced member of the profession (Bernard & Goodyear, 2004)
Triadic supervision	Occurs between an experienced member of the counseling profession and two counselors-in-training
Individual supervision	Occurs between a counselor-in-training and an experienced member of the counseling profession
Group supervision	Takes place between experienced members of the counseling profession and more than two counselors-in-training
Transforming School Counseling Initiative (TSCI)	A national agenda to reshape school counseling that emphasizes the use of data to promote student achievement
Site supervisor	A counseling professional in the pre-K–12 school setting with credentials in school counseling, a minimum of 2 years of experience in the school, and training in supervision
Program faculty supervisor	A practicum or internship instructor who is a member of the counselor education program and has appropriate training and experiences
Program placement coordinator	An individual who is usually associated with the school counseling training program who serves as a liaison between the program and the school sites. This person coordinates the practicum and internship placements.

As you begin your clinical training you will probably have conflicting feelings and thoughts. Not only will you be feeling a sense of excitement about putting the textbook concepts into practice, you may also be feeling anxious about beginning these new experiences. The school counseling program in which you are enrolled will provide you with specific details regarding the program requirements and policies for these experiences in a program handbook. However, this chapter will provide you with additional ideas and information about school counselor identity, the clinical experiences, and your responsibilities as a school counselor-in-training.

What Is Meant by a Counselor Identity?

The formation of a professional identity is a process that starts from the beginning of your course-work and continues throughout your professional career. As you navigate your way through the profession, you may find it disconcerting when some school counselors still refer to themselves as "guidance counselors" rather than using the title "professional school counselor" as endorsed by the American School Counselor Association (ASCA). Furthermore, it may be disheartening to learn that not all school counselors operate under a comprehensive, developmental paradigm that is supported by the ASCA, but rather one that is more traditional in structure. And you may be confused when the school administrator assigns tasks to the school counselor that often have little resemblance to the counselor's education and training.

Throughout the decades, counseling professionals have made concerted efforts to define this profession. The American Counseling Association (ACA) initiated an effort known as the 20/20 Vision for the Future of Counseling, in which counseling was defined as . . . a professional relationship that empowers diverse individuals, families, and groups to accomplish mental health, wellness, education, and career goals (American Counseling Association, n.d.) with the intention that this definition would be broad enough to encompass the "whole" of the profession, yet specific enough to describe the unique settings in which school counselors work. The ASCA professionals did not endorse this definition, using the rationale that the definition did not fully represent counseling in schools. The definition as provided by the ASCA identifies the school counselor as "professional *educators* with a mental health perspective who understand and respond to the challenges presented by today's diverse population" (ASCA, n.d., para. 3). A major goal of the ASCA is to have all professional school counselors speak with one voice regarding the definition of school counseling and to perform tasks that are consistent with the mission of the organization that represents school counselors in all settings.

Today's professional school counselors evolved from what were formerly known as guidance counselors. These "guidance counselors" were trained under a traditional, reactive approach to counseling with an emphasis on counselor-initiated services and tasks rather than student outcomes. Today, due to the Transforming School Counseling Initiative (TSCI) and the ASCA National Model, the emphasis is on training school counselors as leaders of a comprehensive, developmental school counseling (CDSC) program based on measurable student outcomes.

An unfortunate truth, despite the efforts of the ASCA and many state departments of education, is that many school counseling programs have still not made the shift to a CDSC program—for such reasons as too few resources, external barriers, and lack of administrative support (Lambie & Williamson, 2004). In addition, there is debate regarding as to whether the school counselor is a practitioner responsible for the mental health of students or an educator with the responsibility of assisting teachers and other educators in the learning process. However, as future school counselors advocate for their profession through the collection, analysis, and distribution of meaningful data, support for a professional school counselor identity will eventually be an outcome. The application of knowledge to authentic school settings begins through the clinical experiences.

What Is Meant by the Clinical Experiences?

The Council for Accreditation of Counseling and Related Educational Programs (CACREP) was created to standardize counselor education programs, including the clinical experiences of practicum and internship.

Not all school counselor programs are CACREP accredited. At the time of this writing, there are 247 nationally accredited CACREP school counseling programs (CACREP, 2014). Programs that do not have this accreditation follow other standards, such as those mandated by their state board of education. Other CACREP-like programs follow the recommendations of the council and may offer clinical programs in a different format, such as combining clinical work into one experience, or in some cases even use different terms, such as *fieldwork*. Be certain that you are aware of your program training requirements and terminology.

What Is the Difference Between Practicum and Internship?

The *practicum* provides an opportunity for counselors-in-training to work with pre-K–12 students for the express purpose of improving counseling skills with individuals and groups of students. During weekly individual or group supervision sessions, you will review your tapes to discuss counseling techniques and theory, and self-reflect while receiving feedback on your skills. In addition, you will have an opportunity to share case conceptualizations, receive feedback, have questions answered, and plan future sessions.

Although direct learning occurs in group supervision, vicarious learning is more prevalent. A breadth of experiences are shared, reviewed, and thoughtfully considered, which provide greater insight from a broad perspective and help you see the bigger picture of the school counseling profession.

For programs that are CACREP accredited, the student will complete a minimum of 100 clock hours that include at least 40 hours of direct service in individual counseling and group experiences. The remaining 60 or more hours are considered indirect hours. You will have weekly interactions of at least 1 hour per week by your site supervisor and a minimum of 1½ hours per week in group supervision, most likely by a program faculty member or a doctoral-level counseling student.

The *internship* is taken after the completion of the practicum and is designed to help you become familiar with a variety of professional tasks that are a normal part of the professional school counselor's regular responsibilities. The internship consists of a minimum of 600 clock hours, of which at least 240 are spent providing direct service to students. As in the practicum, the remaining hours are considered indirect.

Some of the experiences that may be part of the supervision include:

- Role-play
- Case study conceptualization
- Counseling technique demonstrations
- Listening to previously recorded counseling sessions
- Providing feedback to peers regarding taped sessions
- Discussing theory and techniques
- Sharing site concerns
- Brainstorming solutions to dilemmas encountered at the school.

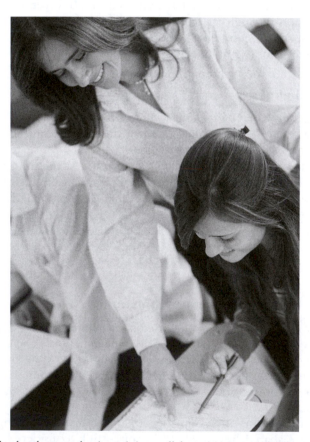

Figure 1.1 Supervisor and school counselor-in-training collaborating on a project.

Source: Shutterstock

What Are Direct and Indirect Hours?

Students are often confused about the differences between direct and indirect service hours. How these hours are defined may vary from program to program, but generally *direct hours* refer to the activities in which there is face-to-face interaction with students, such as in group and individual counseling, classroom lessons, individual student planning, and responsive services. *Indirect hours* are those activities that are provided on behalf of students, such as referrals, consultation, and collaboration (ASCA, 2012). Examples of indirect hours include such experiences as creating a calendar, examining school data, identifying program goals, and developing action plans. These hours are discussed in more detail in Chapter 10, which addresses the delivery system component of the ASCA National Model.

Conceptual Application Activity 1.1

From the following list, identify those professional school counselor practicum and internship tasks, responsibilities, or activities you consider to be indirect or direct. Mark those you think are indirect with an *I* and direct with a *D*.

Planning the school-wide academic calendar for the year	Making phone calls to identify an appropriate community referral for a student who is learning to speak English as a second language
Reviewing career assessment results and postsecondary school plans with a student in your office	Chatting with a student in the hall between classes
Conducting a parent workshop focused on study skill improvement	Eating lunch in the cafeteria surrounded by singing third graders
Performing a puppet show to newly arrived first graders to help them transfer to your school	Facilitating a group for eight students whose parents recently divorced
Accompanying a student and her parents to a nearby college to discuss scholarship offers	Composing thank-you letters to parents who shared information about their careers with the fifth-grade classes
Assessing the academic performance of seventh graders across subjects for the previous year	Conducting a faculty meeting to share the results from a parent/student survey
Meeting with your principal to evaluate your performance	Conducting a suicide assessment with a distraught ninth-grade boy
Formulating a Mission and Vision Statement	Making copies of flyers for an upcoming new student orientation
Monitoring detention hall while assisting students with homework	Calling a student's guardian grandparents to inform them that their granddaughter missed school again
Entering grades into the database and analyzing results to determine player eligibility for athletic competition	Reviewing the school policy manual to determine if a moment of silence due to the death of a student is permissible

What is it that makes some activities clear and others more ambiguous? Which of these activities do you feel are congruent with a CDSC program?

You are not entering these experiences by yourself. During the practicum and internship, you will be receiving supervision from both your program and school counselor supervisors at the school setting where you have been placed for the clinical experiences. These individuals will provide you with direction, assist in identifying tasks to accomplish, and offer feedback and suggestions.

What Is Meant by Supervision?

According to CACREP standards, the supervisor at the school site must have at least 2 years of experience as a professional school counselor, with training in supervision. This person is often referred to as a *site supervisor*. You will also have a supervisor who is a faculty member, often referred to as a *program faculty supervisor*, or in some cases you may be supervised by a doctoral-level counseling student who is also receiving supervision on his/her supervision with you by a counselor education faculty member. In this book, the students with whom you will be working will be referred to as *counselees* to avoid confusion between the student counselors-in-training and the pre-K–12 student.

Box 1.1

On-site supervision is crucial in the growth and development of school counseling students (Swank & Tyson, 2012).

The supervisors are experienced members of the counseling profession, and their main priority is to create a trustful environment for you to learn the profession of school counseling while providing feedback. In addition to supervising you, they are aware of the counseling concerns of the counselees with whom you will be working (Lizzio, Stokes, & Wilson, 2005), which requires the supervisor to be attentive of your needs as well as those of your counselees. As an example, one of my counselors-in-training was assigned to a site supervisor who was well known for implementing many counseling groups and creating numerous activities and programs to address the identified competencies of the school. My graduate student was placed with this experienced professional during the internship, but after several weeks she expressed frustration at not being able to work with counselees on her own. She explained that whenever a counselee came to see her, she was not allowed to work individually with this person, but instead had to notify her site supervisor, who in turn would counsel the counselee while the counselor-in-training observed. When we spoke with the supervisor, she explained that she was concerned about the type of care the counselee was receiving and thought the counselee was not getting the same quality of care when she was not involved. The supervisor had difficulty allowing the supervisee to work independently, and even though she was an excellent counselor, our graduate student was not provided with the opportunity to work independently. Under the supervision of your site supervisor, you will be moving from a stance in which you will need and desire more direction to one in which you will be more autonomous. These changes are part of the supervisory developmental process that you will learn more about in Chapter 5.

During your practicum, you will meet with the program faculty supervisor or doctoral-level supervisor for an average of 1 hour each week either individually or in triadic supervision, and an additional 1.5 hours each week in which all the school counselors-in-training enrolled in the practicum will meet for group supervision. *Triadic supervision* is that in which two counselors-in-training meet with their supervisor. You will not have more than twelve students in your group practicum class if your program follows CACREP standards.

Box 1.2

You will receive individual, triadic, and/or group supervision during your clinical experiences. Each of these types of supervision brings benefits. Supervisees stated that greater self-awareness and confidence and a focus on self were some of the advantages of individual supervision. In triadic supervision, greater knowledge about peers' supervisees, opportunities to learn from peers, and vicarious learning were the benefits of this type of supervision. However, group supervision provided greater educational opportunities and normalized experiences (Borders et al., 2012).

In internship, if CACREP standards are followed, there will be no more than 12 individuals in your class. Each counselor-in-training will meet an average of 1 hour each week for individual or triadic supervision with the on-site supervisor. The purpose of this supervisory experience is to discuss concerns, the school counselor's role, the counseling process, accomplishments, theoretical approach, and so forth. In addition, you will meet for an average of 1.5 hours each week of group supervision, usually with the faculty supervisor. School counselors-in-training often wonder how supervision works. The questions in Conceptual Application Activity 1.2 are designed for you to ask your site supervisor in order to get a better understanding of the expectations.

Conceptual Application Activity 1.2

When you meet with your site supervisor, ask the following questions and write down the information for future reference.

1. When will we meet? _____

2. How often will we meet? _____

3. How long will we meet? _____

4. Where will we meet? _____

5. How will the meetings be structured and what do I need to bring? _____

6. Who else will be present when we meet? _____

7. What are some of the issues that we will discuss? _____

8. What are the procedures I need to follow when you are absent? _____

9. What is the dress code? _____

10. What is the school schedule? _____

11. What are the school policies and rules? _____

12. Who do I contact when I am ill? _____

13. Who do I contact if I am going to be late? _____

14. What contact information do I need? _____

15. What contact information do you need? _____

16. Is there a copy of the faculty handbook that I could have? _____

17. Is there a crisis plan that I can study? _____

During the clinical experiences, you will be asked to create a contract that outlines your personal and professional goals. This contract will be based on the course objectives, the site and program supervisors' requirements, and your own needs. A sample contract and guidelines for creating a contract is in Chapter 4.

Too often, students training for the school counseling profession treat the clinical courses as if they were voluntary experiences. You are not a volunteer, because you have specific learning goals and objectives, receive supervision from both an on-site supervisor and a faculty supervisor, and are evaluated formally and regularly. Unfortunately, there are some occasions when counselors-in-training believe that since they are not being paid to work in the schools, they can attend the school site whenever they feel like it if they have other competing responsibilities. *You need to be aware that the practicum and internship experiences are not only a course requirement, but are also professional responsibilities and are to be treated as if you were working in a professional career.* It is not only the site supervisor who relies on your attendance: Students, teachers, administrators, and parents also depend upon you. Imagine what it would be like for a fifth grader who is anxiously waiting to continue counseling sessions with you, and you do not take the time to notify anyone at the school that you will be absent. Or, think about the teacher who is planning to team-teach a school counseling lesson with you and you do not put in an appearance. Your decision disappoints the fifth grader, disrupts the teacher's plans, and leaves an entire class let down.

Your attitude, motivation, and willingness to learn at these sites can make a huge difference when you are seeking employment as a school counselor. It is not uncommon for employers to contact your supervisors, principals, and any other references at the schools in which you have trained. In fact, you may be applying for full-time employment at the school where you were placed in practicum or internship.

In some cases, counselors-in-training receive payment for their services before matriculating from their school counseling program. For instance, when schools face a shortage of school counselors, or a school counselor needs to take a leave of absence, it is sometimes necessary to hire an individual who has not yet finished with his/her school counseling program. In this situation, each state has certain criteria for working under these circumstances. Each state uses a different term, such as *alternative, transitional,* or *interim school counselor license,* for this arrangement, with various stipulations under which the school system is able to hire this individual. If you are interested in learning more about this type of license, check the Department of Education in the state in which you are interested.

What Materials Are Needed?

Since audio and/or video recordings are requirements in most school counseling programs, you will need access to taping equipment. If you do not have this equipment, first check with your college or university, or ask at the school where you are conducting practicum or internship if the required equipment is available. Some schools will allow you to sign out this equipment during the academic term, but other sites may not have these devices readily available. Some recording devices are in the form of tapes, others are in the form of discs, and some seemingly use nothing. Some of these recording devices can be erased and reused, whereas others cannot. Some supervisors require audio recording, while others mandate video recording, and still others require both. Be sure to check with all parties before choosing recording equipment, size, and format. The format depends on the equipment your supervisor uses to listen to or view the recordings.

It is also possible that technology-mediated supervision may be conducted. This type of technology may take place in real time, also called *synchronous supervision*, and could include Skype, Google Voice and Video, or Facetime. Some computers already have a built-in camera for communication ease, whereas others require a separate camera that is attached to the computer. Or instant messaging, wikis, YouTube, or email may also be a type of technology-mediated supervision, also known as *asynchronous supervision*, and occurs without the constraints of time. Asynchronous supervision allows feedback without the supervisor having to be in the room, increased availability of supervisors, and more flexibility in supervising. Some of the disadvantages of technology-mediated supervision include security and confidentiality concerns (regardless of the type of equipment needed for supervision), equipment malfunction, and limited sharing due to questionable skill regarding technology.

Because you will be recording counseling sessions, a private room will be needed to provide a quiet environment and ensure student confidentiality. In schools where space is a problem, school counselors-in-training are sometimes placed in a classroom that is vacant when the teacher is not teaching a class or in other spaces that are less private. Using a teacher's classroom can jeopardize confidentiality, especially if the teacher needs access to the room while you are counseling students. If you have difficulty finding a secluded place for counseling, discuss this issue with your on-site supervisor.

Issues With Taping Counseling Sessions

During the clinical experiences, and the practicum class in particular, assessing your counseling skills is a primary focus with traditional methods such as video and audio recording. Yet, with increased concern for privacy and individual rights, these as well as more sophisticated technological methods are becoming more problematic due to regulations by the Federal Education Rights and Privacy Act (FERPA) and the Health Insurance Portability and Accountability Act (HIPAA).

FERPA, also known as the Buckley Amendment, protects the privacy of student records and limits parental/guardian access to all student records, files, and documents maintained by school personnel. Record keeping permits school counselors to refresh memory and to increase counseling effectiveness by keeping personal notes about individual counseling sessions. Many school counselors believe that they are FERPA compliant if the notes they take are sole possession notes and remain confidential. However, the US Department of Education maintained that these notes are to be considered a part of the educational record. Yet, according to the US Family Policy Compliance Office, various notes that serve as memory aids are exempt (Wheeler & Bertram, 2012). These contradictory opinions create confusion, and at some point a final decision will be needed for clarification. However, anytime notes are shared, they are no longer considered confidential. This is where confidentiality regarding taping and note taking becomes an issue; individual sessions are shared during supervision.

Box 1.3

Are case notes truly my own or do I have to share them if lawyers get involved? Do I have to testify? According to the ASCA, state statutes influence the sharing of notes. Privileged communication is recognized in some states, but in the majority of states school counselors are mandated to testify in court. Discuss your concerns about testifying with the attorney if you believe that your information will not be helpful, and explain your responsibilities to students, including the importance of confidentiality and ethical standards. If the student does not have privileged communication, then you are compelled to testify (Stone, Herman, & Williams, 2012).

Although not every counseling setting is HIPAA related, HIPAA (Pub. L. 104–191) protects health information (including mental health) held by an educational institute from becoming education records unless a state law mandates differently. Counseling notes, also known as process notes, are used to help counselors recall information, and are protected by HIPAA as long as they are kept in a separate file.

Parents/guardians need to be informed about the purpose of the counseling sessions and the importance of this activity for the counselor-in-training's education. Some institutions will only allow digital recording if the counselee's identity remains unknown, such as focusing the camera on the counselee's back. Erasing tapes on a regular schedule, such as at the end of the semester, can also maintain program integrity and assist with student anonymity. Check with your program supervisor regarding tape erasure protocol.

Some training institutions respond to the taping issue by providing on-site observation in which the program or site supervisor observes a live counseling session and provides feedback immediately following the session. However, this strategy may create other concerns, such as the counselee's discomfort with the presence of another individual, the amount of time that is required, and the trainee feeling not completely autonomous in conducting the counseling session. An informed consent form and professional disclosure statement facilitate communication with parents, teachers, and administrators regarding your work with students.

Informed Consent Form and Professional Disclosure Statement

As a new, yet temporary member of your educational community, it is often difficult to get permission to work with school-aged youth. Because you will be taping your counseling sessions with children and adolescents, written permission from parents or guardians to tape their child during counseling sessions is necessary. Not surprisingly, this could create a problem, since parents/guardians may have difficulty with their child working with someone they do not know. An *informed consent* form is an ethical, legal, and clinical document that is used to explain the counseling relationship (Wheeler & Bertram, 2012) and the purpose of the counseling session, including expectations during the clinical experiences. A *professional disclosure statement* describes who you are, your education, training qualifications, and how you will be supervised. When this information is provided to parents/guardians, they are usually more willing to provide consent. An example of a consent form is found in Figure 1.2, and an example of a professional disclosure statement is found in Chapter 4.

How Do I Choose a School Site for Supervision?

Location and proximity to home, the college or university, and school site are the most common motives for selecting a placement for the clinical experiences. Although these reasons are practical and understandable, they are not always the best considerations in making this choice. For instance, the potential supervisor may not have had training in supervision, may have a different philosophy regarding the school counselor's role, operate under a program that does not support a CDSC program, or may not have time to provide a quality supervisory experience. Furthermore, the school may have a homogeneous population of students and may not provide an opportunity to work with a diverse student body. You want to work with a supervisor in a school that will give you the best experience possible. To assist you with this decision, Conceptual Application Activity 1.3 is designed to help you think about this process.

RELEASE FORM/PERMISSION TO TAPE

Hello. My name is_____, and I am a graduate student in the school counseling program at _____. Your son/daughter is participating in counseling interviews with me as I train to be a school counselor under the direction of the Counseling Department faculty at _____. These interviews will either be videotaped or audiotaped, and portions of the interview will be used for evaluation and/or supervision purposes only.

- Precautions will be taken to protect your child's identity.
- The taping will be used for supervision purposes only.
- After the student trainee and supervisor have met to critique the trainee's counseling skills, the tape will be erased.
- The tape/video recorder will be turned off at any time and/or any portion of the tape will be erased if requested.

If you are willing to give permission for your child to assist with this training, please sign below. If you have additional questions, you can contact my site supervisor at _____.

_____   _____
Parent/Guardian Signature   Date

_____   _____
Student Signature   Date

Figure 1.2 Release form/permission to tape.

Conceptual Application Activity 1.3

1. With which age or group of students would you be most interested in working? Explain.

   _____

   _____

   _____

2. With what age or group of students would you feel most uncomfortable working? Write down those things that make you uncomfortable.

   _____

   _____

   _____

3. School counselors have the responsibility to work with all students, including those in special education and those who have been identified as "gifted." Identify the students with whom you feel you need additional knowledge and experiences.

   _____

   _____

How Do I Choose a Site Supervisor?

There are several methods of matching a supervisor with a counselor-in-training. Some institutions provide flexibility in allowing their students to select a supervisor based on reputation, school system, or other special characteristics. In these cases, the program placement coordinator will probably determine if this selection is appropriate before the assignment is made. It could be that the placement coordinator is aware of the strengths and weaknesses of area supervisors and may believe that a certain placement you desire may not be the best match for various reasons. For instance, I was serving as a faculty supervisor for the practicum class, and when making a visit with a middle school site supervisor, the supervisor stated, "We teach what school counselors really need to know—not the stuff they teach at the university." This remark indicated that there was an absence of similar program goals as well as a lack of communication regarding site and academic program expectations. At the university, the benefits of a comprehensive, developmental approach to school counseling are taught, as opposed to the reactive, traditional model under which some school counselors still operate. The latter was the type of program in which this particular supervisor was working. In another situation, a motivated practicum student who was excited about the opportunity to work with school-aged youth was placed with a site supervisor who showed little interest in her middle school students. The site supervisor would flippantly dismiss the practicum student's concerns about students by stating, "That's just the way they are, and we really don't have the time to help them." As a result of this experience, this practicum counselor-in-training left the experience disappointed and disillusioned with the profession.

In post-graduation surveys conducted by training institutions for the purpose of evaluating program needs, many graduates of school counselor programs indicate that supervision was the most important aspect of their clinical experiences. Therefore, it is important that supervisors are chosen carefully.

Regardless of whether you are placed in a setting by your placement coordinator or you choose a supervisor, be certain that you have thought in terms of the specific supervisor characteristics that you feel may best meet your needs. Consider the list of questions found in Conceptual Application Activity 1.4.

Conceptual Application Activity 1.4

- What is the experience and training of the site supervisor? _____

- What are the grade level and ages of students with whom the supervisor works? _____

- Is equipment available for taping? _____

- What are the procedures to check out this equipment? _____

- Is there an office or room available to conduct individual or group counseling? _____ _____

- What is the philosophy and mission of the school counseling program? _____ _____

- Will the supervisor be available to meet for supervision at least one hour per week? _____

- What are the greatest student needs? _____

- What are the procedures to dismiss students from class for individual and/or group counseling? _____

- How receptive are parents/guardians to allowing their children to work with a practicum/intern student? _____

- Will there be opportunities to work with students representative of diverse ethnic, cultural, and gender groups? _____

- Will there be opportunities to work with students of different abilities? _____

- What is the administrator's view of counseling students in the schools? _____ _____

- Does this individual have the time to supervise me? _____

- When does the supervisor expect me to be at the school? _____

- Will I have the opportunity to attend such events as in-service meetings or parent conferences? _____

- Will I need to make a safety plan? _____

- Will I be expected to stay after the school day is over? _____

The presence of *nonprofessional interactions or relationships* (formerly known as dual relationships) is a fundamental consideration in selecting a supervisor (Note: The ACA uses the term nonprofessional interactions or relationships in reference to what was formerly known as dual relationships. However, the ASCA continues to use the term dual relationships, and for this reason this term will be used in this text.). These interactions emerge as a result of family, social, community, school, or work exchanges (Wheeler & Bertram, 2012). They often occur through unanticipated circumstances such as attending a community meeting, exercising at the same gym, meeting at a book club, and so on. In fact, according to a study by Bodenhorn (2006), school counselors reported that dual relationships were one of the most common ethical dilemmas they have encountered. This type of conflicting relationship is more common than many practicum and internship students realize.

Box 1.4

If a dual relationship is unavoidable, and the benefits outweigh the risks, consider the following steps:

- Discuss the benefits and risks with your supervisors.
- Engage in ongoing communication with your supervisors to ensure that the relationship is being managed appropriately.
- Self-monitor.

Source: Adapted from Wheeler & Bertram (2012)

In the case of supervision, a dual relationship may be a supervisor whom you know in a different context, such as a friend, relative, or even a parent of your child's friend. Dual relationships could also be in relation to teachers, parents, administrators, or even a counselor-in-training's spouse employed in that school setting. In one situation, a difficult counselor-in-training was placed in an internship site without the placement coordinator knowing that this individual's spouse worked in the super-intendent's office. The site supervisor was also unaware of this situation until the superintendent questioned the counselor-in-training's poor evaluation completed by the supervisor. The school site supervisor felt personally offended that her judgment was being questioned when the superintendent asked about the negative evaluation. There are numerous considerations in beginning the supervisory journey, and it is up to you to learn as much as you can about the expectations for this experience and to take opportunities that are available so that you can feel competent and successful when you are a fully licensed member of the profession.

CONCLUSION

You are starting your professional journey by working in a school as a counselor during your clinical experiences, often known as the practicum and internship. These experiences are not to be taken lightly, as they are superb opportunities to get "hands-on" experience in a school counseling setting. Practicum and internship may also be the last time that you will receive formal feedback on your counseling skills because the building administrator is generally the person who supervises school counselors, and frequently this individual has no training in counseling skills and process. Therefore, it is important that your school and site supervisor are chosen wisely. This choice requires self-reflection and an understanding of both the potential supervisor's philosophy and the types of experiences that you desire for a comprehensive foundation of the school counseling profession.

WEBSITES

- American Counseling Association (ACA): www.counseling.org/

  This website provides resources for counseling practitioners and students in addition to giving recent legislative information concerning the counseling profession. The salary calculator resource available from this organization provides a tool for determining salaries in various parts of the United States.

- American School Counselor Association (ASCA): www.schoolcounselor.org/

  This division of ACA focuses on the counseling specialty of school counseling. Numerous resources are available, as well as position papers and documents that provide timely information on numerous topics commonly impacting the profession and the stakeholders.

- Council for Accreditation of Counseling and Related Educational Programs (CACREP) www.cacrep.org/template/index.cfm

  This accreditation body sets standards for master's and doctoral degree programs in counseling.

- National Center for Transforming School Counseling, www.edtrust.org/dc/tsc

  The NCTSC is dedicated to training school counselors to focus on academics and to raise achievement among all students.

REFERENCES

American Counseling Association. (n.d.). *20/20: Consensus definition of counseling.* Retrieved from www.counseling.org/knowledge-center/20–20-a-vision-for-the-future-of-counseling/consensus-definition-of-counseling

ASCA [American School Counselor Association]. (n.d.). Why middle school counselors. Retrieved from http://schoolcounselor.org/school-counselors-members/careers-roles/why-middle-school-counselors

ASCA. (2012). *The ASCA national model: A framework for school counseling programs* (3rd ed.). Alexandria, VA: Author.

Bernard, J.M., & Goodyear, R.K. (2004). *Fundamentals of clinical supervision* (3rd ed.). New York: Pearson.

Bodenhorn, N. (2006). Exploratory study of common and challenging ethical dilemmas experienced by professional school counselors. *Professional School Counseling, 10*, 195–202.

Borders, L.D., Welfare, L.E. Greason, P.B., Paladino, D.A., Mobley, A.K., Villalba, J.A., & Wester, K.L. (2012). Individual and triadic and group: Supervisee and supervisor perceptions of each modality. *Counselor Education and Supervision, 51*, 281–295. doi: 10.1002/j.1556–6978.2012.00021.x

CACREP [Council for Accreditation of Counseling and Related Educational Programs]. (2014). *Directory of accredited programs.* Retrieved from www.cacrep.org/directory/?state=&dl=M&pt_id=27&keywords=&submitthis=

Lambie, G.W., & Williamson, L.L. (2004). The challenge to change from guidance counseling to professional school counseling: A historical proposition. *Professional School Counseling, 8,* 124–131.

Lizzio, A., Stokes, L., & Wilson, K. (2005). Approaches to learning in professional supervision: Supervisee perceptions of processes and outcome. *Studies in Continuing Education, 27,* 239–256.

Stone, C., Herman, M., & Williams, R. (2012, May). Asked and answered. *ASCA School Counselor.* Retrieved from www.schoolcounselor.org/magazine/blogs/may-june-2012/asked-and-answered

Swank, J.M., & Tyson, L. (2012). School counseling site supervisor training: A web-based approach. *Professional School Counseling, 16*, 40–48. doi: 10.5330/PSC.n.2012–16.40.

Wheeler, M., & Bertram, B. (2012). *The counselor and the law: A guide to legal and ethical practice* (6th ed.). Alexandria, VA: American Counseling Association.

2 Understanding the School Culture as a School Counselor-in-Training

Amy Kroninger and Jeannine R. Studer

CACREP Standards

Foundations

A. Knowledge

3. Knows roles, functions, settings, and professional identity of the school counselor in relation to the roles of other professionals and support personnel in the school.

Academic Development

K. Knowledge

1. Understands the relationship of the school counseling program to the academic mission of the school.

The purpose of this chapter is to:

- discuss school culture and climate and differences among settings,
- provide information regarding federal and state initiatives such as School-Wide Positive Interventions and Behavioral Supports, Response to Intervention, and No Child Left Behind, including the School Safety Initiative,
- share the integral role of the school counselor in developing a positive school culture.

INTRODUCTION

> I was at least five years into my job as a school counselor before I felt I had a grip on my job description even though my yearlong practicum/internship experience in a diverse high school concluded a very positive graduate school experience. I thought I was very prepared for the next step. What I soon realized, however, was I had barely skimmed the surface in my learning experience. Having said that, every situation is different, every school is different, every principal has different expectations, etc. Learning and understanding the school culture takes time but is critical for finding your place and gaining a vision as to where and how the counseling program functions within the school. What do I wish I had known as an intern or first year counselor? The clinical experiences include a variety of learning experiences that should be entered with an open mind, and with knowledge that flexibility and initiative are valued.
>
> **Anne Troutman, Secondary School Counselor Coach**

The School Culture and Climate

When you think about a school culture, what comes to mind? What about the school climate? Although these terms are often interchangeable, there are distinct differences. The culture generally refers to such things as unwritten rules, traditions, language, diversity, and school vision. Climate, on the other hand, refers to the atmosphere and expressed morale of the students and educational personnel (Peterson & Deal, 2002) and can be considered as the personality of the school (Abrams, Karvonen, Nasar-McMillan, & Perez, 2009). People are the most important element in a respectful, invitational climate, but the physical atmosphere is also a contributing factor, and creating a pleasant environment is one method to show concern for others (Smith, 2005).

Each school culture is multifaceted and unique and is influenced by the socioeconomic status of the community, cultural groups, and school size (Phillips & Wagner, 2003). Whenever I enter a school, the climate is often readily apparent from the way I am greeted when I report into the school office, the treatment of students as they change classes, to the general attitude that is expressed by the school personnel. School counselors are key personnel to create a positive school culture and climate and are particularly influential due to the multiple individuals with whom they have interactions.

The focus of this chapter is to assist you in understanding the school counselor's role as this position influences and is influenced by the school culture. Federal and state initiatives such as No Child Left Behind (NCLB), including School Improvement Plans, School Wide Positive Interventions and Behavioral Supports, Response to Intervention, and the Common Core, also impact the school culture and climate. In addition, understanding and negotiating responsibilities such as discipline, testing, special education, and the never-ending debate regarding whether school counselors should have an education background with teaching experience is discussed. Finally, collaboration with stakeholders including Professional Learning Communities is highlighted.

FEDERAL AND STATE INITIATIVES AND THE ROLE OF THE PROFESSIONAL SCHOOL COUNSELOR

No Child Left Behind and Implications for School Counselors

No Child Left Behind was signed into law on January 8, 2002 (Ed.Gov., n.d.). This standards-based education reform package is based on the belief that high expectations and measurable goals can improve student achievement. Schools must make adequate yearly progress (AYP) in reading/language arts, mathematics, and science test scores (i.e., each year, fourth graders must do better on standardized tests than the previous years), attendance, and graduation rate. If a school fails to make AYP toward the state benchmarks for 2 consecutive years, then it is put on a "high priority" list and will be restructured by the state to improve achievement.

No Child Left Behind requires that each state measure every child's progress at least once in grades 3–8 in reading/language arts and math, and at least once in the grade span of 10–12; once in science in the grade span of 3–5, once in the grade span of 6–9, and once in grades 10–12. Because NCLB requires schools and districts to focus attention on the academic achievement of traditionally underserved groups such as students from low-income families, students with disabilities, and those from racial and ethnic subgroups, the school counselor can help by monitoring how these students are performing and offer their services when appropriate. For example, a high school counselor could work closely with students who are behind on their academic credits.

NCLB also considers graduation rates as a secondary indicator of AYP, and according to this law, a graduate is considered as an individual who has received a high school diploma in a specified number of years (usually 4 years). This would obviously exclude students with disabilities who leave school with a certificate of attendance or those students who were held back a year and took longer to receive a diploma. These incidents impact the schools' graduation rate. Be aware of the implications of NCLB and ask your supervisor for suggestions on how you might conduct activities that will improve academic achievement as indicated by the data from the school report card.

School Improvement Plans are another requirement of NCLB that includes assessing specific objectives and strategies through evidence-based practices. With educational institutions under pressure to perform and to show program effectiveness, this is an opportunity for you to engage in tasks that will assist the educational mission.

School Improvement Plans

State and federal laws require each school to submit a School Improvement Plan (SIP) every 2 years for the purpose of helping educators use data to set student improvement goals. With the demands of NCLB, each school develops a plan that serves as the accountability document for measuring adequate yearly progress. Components of the school improvement process include school profile and collaborative process; academic and nonacademic data analysis; beliefs, mission, and vision; curricular, instructional, assessment, and organizational effectiveness; action plan development; and improvement plan and process evaluation. The school counselor is an integral person able to assist with this plan by providing data regarding their efforts in improving student growth.

Safe School Initiatives

School counselors want to create an environment in which all students feel safe and emotionally secure. Bullying, harassment, and intimidation typically include verbal, physical, relational, and cyber attacks that take place on school property, at school-sponsored functions, and on school buses. Bullying policies frequently require that schools implement specific practices to achieve safer, less violent schools, with ongoing professional education for school employees to learn about methods to prevent harassment, intimidation, and bullying. Many schools have adopted policies to prevent school violence known as *zero-tolerance* policies. These policies are usually in regard to illegal drug possession, firearms, or the commission of battery with full punishment as the consequence for any individual on the school grounds not following the policies established. Furthermore, when planning classroom school counseling lessons, consider multicultural and non-stereotypical curricula. For elementary schools, *Second Step* is an effective multicultural, nonviolence curriculum that includes empathy, impulse control, and anger management within its framework.

Box 2.1

A Phi Delta Kappa/Gallup poll was conducted in 2013 to determine attitudes toward public schools. By a large margin, public school parents (59%) supported providing more mental health service in school than more security guards (35%). In this same study, parents were more concerned about the actions of other students in the schools than intruders.

Source: ASCA School Counselor, 2013

Conceptual Application Activity 2.1

Ask your site supervisor to show you how services and activities that are integral to the school improvement initiative are documented and how the school counseling program standards are aligned with those of academic course objectives. You can use information highlighted in Chapter 10 that outlines study skills strategies to assist in promoting achievement among students struggling academically.

_____

_____

Positive Behavior Intervention Supports

Positive Behavior Intervention Supports (PBIS) is a multilevel framework with a focus on interventions for creating and maintaining a positive school culture (Shepard, Shahidullah, & Carlson, 2013) and ensuring that the needs of all students are met by improving student outcomes. This approach is positive, data driven, and evidence based and is associated with improved behavior and achievement. PBIS consists of agreed-upon school rules that are stated positively, reinforced, and understood by all. When acceptable behavior is followed, improved academic achievement is a result. School-wide PBIS consists of three tiers of prevention. Tier 1 is a universal school-wide intervention based on reinforcing

Figure 2.1 School counselors are instrumental in enhancing students' academic, career, and social/emotional growth. High school graduation as an outcome for all students is a goal of all educators.

Source: Steve Martin Photography

positive behaviors. Tier 2 is a more intense intervention that targets small groups of students, and Tier 3 is an individualized, focused intervention for frequent or intense behavior problems (Farkas et al., 2012) (see Figure 2.2). School counselors may be involved at each of the levels through such activities as training school personnel in crisis management, teaching behavioral modification strategies, assisting with transitions, engaging in parent collaboration, or serving as behavioral consults.

A rural K–5 elementary school located in western North Carolina implemented and assessed its school-wide positive behavioral support program. Data were collected for 5 consecutive academic years and as a result of the school-wide plan, behavioral referrals, extended timeouts, out-of-school suspensions and instructional days students lost for poor behavior decreased. In this school the principal and school counselor regularly collaborated and informed the faculty and staff about problems that were addressed (Curtis, Van Horne, Robertson, & Karvonen, 2010).

Conceptual Application Activity 2.2

Discuss the Positive Intervention Prevention Support format that has been adapted by the school site in which you are training. Share the interventions in which your supervisor is involved with those of your peers. Are there similarities? Differences?

_____

_____

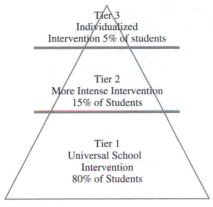

Figure 2.2 Students supported by PBIS.

Response to Intervention

The *Response to Intervention* (RTI) is a multi-tiered framework that brings together all educational personnel for the purpose of providing a format to meet the needs of ALL students to improve student outcomes. Because the main goal of this system is to increase academic achievement, students are monitored at each tier (Sabella & Clements, 2010). The steps include:

- Tier 1: Interventions that are preventive and proactive are provided, and universal screening for all students is conducted with careful monitoring and documentation. The school counselor may provide classroom lessons for all students to address identified goals.
- Tier 2: Students who are not making AYP in Tier 1 are given additional support in Tier 2. Although the student continues to receive instruction in Tier 1, additional support is given at this stage, usually in the form of small group counseling. Some counselors use the *Voyager Learning* intervention that is designed as supplemental assistance. More information about this series can be found at www.voyagerlearning.com/about/intervention. If the student is still not making adequate progress, he/she will move to Tier 3.
- Tier 3: Students are provided intense individual, long-term interventions with designated individuals. The school counselor may provide individual counseling as a type of intervention, or make referrals to community personnel if the student has more serious concerns. If adequate progress is still not reached, the student may be eligible for special education services.

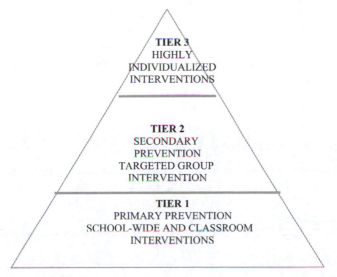

Figure 2.3 Illustration of the RTI tiers.

Conceptual Application Activity 2.3

With your school counselor supervisor, discuss his/her role with RTI. Share your supervisor's responses with your peers. Are there similarities? Differences?

The Common Core State Standards Initiative

There is much discussion and debate regarding the Common Core standards. This initiative was developed in 2009 by the National Governors' Association (NGA) Center for Best Practices and the Council of Chief State School Officers (CCSSO) for the purpose of identifying consistent learning goals to ensure that all students graduate career/college (Common Core, n.d.). This set of standards was developed as a result of educational inconsistencies among states, which led to great disparity in educational ability among students. For instance, a student successfully passing algebra in Ohio could move to Pennsylvania and flunk the course.

At the present time 43 states, the District of Columbia, and four U.S. territories have adopted the Common Core, which identifies what students should be able to know and when these competencies are to be achieved in English and math.

Box 2.2

With the Common Core standards, the demonstration of an understanding of the concepts is as important as getting the correct answer. This view has been labeled "fuzzy math," and parents report being frustrated and unable to help their child with math. For example, one problem students are to solve is: "Use number bonds to help you skip-count by seven by making ten or adding to the ones (i.e., $7 + 7 = 10 + 4 = ?$)."

Source: The Week (2014, June 6), *The Core's 'fuzzy math'* p. 13

Proponents of the standards state that students need to understand concepts before they are able to solve problems in the traditional way and that the standards are research based and developmentally appropriate. Critics, however, state that the standards fail to stress basic computational skills, leaving students unprepared for higher mathematics. Furthermore, teachers are largely unprepared to teach the standards and parents are frustrated with unfamiliar terms and their inability to assist their child with homework (Rubinkam, 2014).

Conceptual Application Activity 2.4

Interview your school counselor supervisor, English or language arts teacher, and mathematics teacher. Ask them about their impression of the Common Core and their role in this initiative. Share their responses with your peers. What are some of the common themes?

Hopefully, you have had an opportunity to learn about some of the federal educational initiatives and their impact on the education of students and responsibilities of school personnel, predominantly school counselors. As you have probably observed, principals and other decision makers often ask school counselors to engage in activities that are distinct from their training and education. These requests can be difficult, since we are members of a school team that works together for the benefit of our students. What would be your response if a teacher suddenly gets sick and has to leave for the remainder of the day and your principal asks you to serve as a replacement in the classroom until a substitute can be found? Or, if teachers are required to serve on bus duty or playground duty, what is your responsibility as a collaborative member of the school team?

COMMUNICATING RESPONSIBILITIES, DUTIES, AND TASKS TO STAKEHOLDERS

Through your graduate program, you have learned about the responsibilities of a school counselor as they relate to national, state, and local standards. The challenge is to integrate these guidelines with the culture and expectations of your school. There may be principals, teachers, parents, other counselors, and various staff whose expectations of your role vary greatly from your training and education. When this occurs, others define your identity for you. Instead, find a professional means for communicating your role and concretely revealing where you spend your time and how you contribute to the academic educational mission through concrete data. This conversation could possibly assist in changes to your job description.

At all levels, communication is crucial. Returning phone calls and emails promptly will help promote a positive image for your office, and a solid reputation will be built through your ability to provide answers or solutions in a timely manner. As a school counselor-in-training, start this communication process now so that it is a regular part of your routine while in training, and continue this practice during your professional career. Parents of students who are failing courses or behind on their credits for graduation (high school) should be notified on a regular basis by their teachers and counselor, or by you as a supervisee if this is one of your designated duties. In addition, regularly updating school counseling websites with information such as SAT and ACT registration deadlines, college admission deadlines, scholarships, parent meetings, and progress report distribution dates is a method of sharing essential dates. It is possible that your supervisor does not have the skills to design a website, and if this is the case and you have the skills to create a website for the school counseling department, you are able to offer an essential service that could be a lasting contribution to the school site.

Next, we turn to additional issues that impact school counselors, such as how students are assigned to counselors, the school counselor's role in discipline, testing, and how special education assignments are determined.

School Counselors' Division of Responsibilities

Factors such as the school system's budget, the school's enrollment, the needs of the particular school, and the priorities of the school district all contribute to the number of school counselors that are placed in each school. As you begin your clinical experiences, you may find counselors in elementary schools assigned to more than one school and those who split time between schools. Other schools may have one full-time counselor, and still others may have two or more. If you are working in a program with more than one counselor, you will need to blend philosophies, work styles, and various personalities, which requires compromise, communication, and cooperation in order to effectively address the needs of ALL students. Learning collaborative strategies while you are a supervisee will assist you when you begin your first school counseling position.

Middle schools and high schools with more than one counselor have different methods of assigning responsibility. Some of the more common methods of dividing responsibilities include: (a) grade-level classification in which each counselor is assigned to a particular grade level year after year, with students having a different counselor each year; (b) alphabetically, in which students have the same counselor all 4 years; (c) by specialty area such as college and career, special education, or mental health; and (d) by academies. There are several kinds of academy structures. Schools with different career academies such as health and sciences or technology may have one counselor per academy, and all students in this academy have the same counselor every year.

Conceptual Application Activity 2.5

Make note of the division of responsibility at the school to which you are assigned, and discuss the advantages and disadvantages of this arrangement with your site supervisor. Discuss your perceptions with your classmates.

_____

_____

The School Counselor's Role in Discipline

A counselor's role with regard to discipline is, for the most part, unlike any other person's in the building. Teachers will write up students for misconduct and either discipline the students themselves or, for serious matters, send the students to a principal or assistant principal. The school counselor's role should not be one of meting out discipline, because this has the potential to jeopardize the counseling relationship. As stated in the ASCA position statement, "the professional school counselor is not a disciplinarian but should be a resource for school personnel as they develop individual and school-wide discipline positions" (American School Counselor Association, 2013a). Instead, the counselor can help the counselee recognize the consequences for behaviors and provide support for the counselee to remediate his/her behavior. Each school will have its own set of expectations for student conduct based on the ages of the student body as well as the school culture.

As a school counselor-in-training, be sure to implement a classroom management plan when you teach lessons. Or, it may be that a teacher prefers that you use his or her own management plan when you are in a particular class. In either case, have an effective plan ready. Take advantage of your supervisor's assistance and expertise in classroom management, and take every opportunity to practice teaching classroom school counseling lessons before you have a job of your own. Principals and other educators will want to know that a potential school counselor can teach and manage a class with confidence and skill after graduate training has ended. Refer to Chapter 10 for behavior management techniques in conducting small groups or providing classroom lessons.

Peer mediation is one effective technique that may help improve the school culture. Peer mediation can be used to resolve small issues between two students that, if left alone, might snowball into much bigger issues. The counselor often takes a leadership role in this program, including selecting and training peer mediators, identifying situations where mediation could be used effectively, and scheduling mediations. If the school to which you are assigned has already implemented a peer mediation program, become involved with this plan. If not, talk with your site supervisor about instituting one as a part of your clinical experiences.

Conceptual Application Activity 2.6

Read and respond to the following scenarios and compare your responses with those of your peers.

It is your first day as an elementary school counseling intern. Your site supervisor has informed you that you are to share your office with the speech therapist and are to counsel students in the hallway. You have been taught about confidentiality and privacy, yet you are also keenly aware that school space is very limited. Keeping in mind your values, professional ethics, and responsibilities in addition to the school's inadequate space, how would you respond to your site supervisor?

_____

_____

Clerical duties, testing responsibilities, and administrative tasks are often some of the biggest obstacles to overcome. Sometimes there is a fine line between the school counselor's job and some of these roles. For example, as we move into the age of electronic transcripts, high school counselors in particular have a responsibility to maintain and ensure accuracy of student records. If you are lucky enough to have a secretary, this individual is able to handle this task, yet needs to be educated about confidential materials and information that may and may not be released. For instance, a concerned aunt called about her niece's grades, and an uninformed secretary gave this information to her, a violation of the Family Educational Rights and Privacy Act (FERPA).

Testing

With accountability and evidence-based interventions, schools have become centers for continual testing and assessment. Unfortunately, many school districts simply name one of the counselors to assume this position, and rely on that counselor to make all the testing arrangements or to allocate responsibilities to other individuals. With high stakes testing a norm in our schools, we have a responsibility to communicate how we support and boost student achievement, but we should not be in the role of a test facilitator. This is a time-consuming task that takes counselors away from providing direct service to our students. Due to the enormous responsibility that accompanies year-end tests, some systems hire a test coordinator whose sole responsibility is to be accountable for the testing program.

Some of the tests of which you should be familiar are ACT and SAT, PLAN and PSAT, AP exams, and writing assessments, as well as local and state end-of-course exams. Once test results are returned to the school, a plan is necessary to disseminate and explain the results to parents/guardians and students. This is an opportunity for you to utilize the knowledge you have acquired in your courses that addressed testing and measurement. Test orientation and interpretation are activities that you may consider including in your clinical contract and are instrumental for individual planning and goal setting.

Conceptual Application Activity 2.7

Read and respond to the following scenarios and compare your responses with those of your peers.

All teachers in your school are scheduled for bus duty throughout the year. When you began as a counselor-in-training, you were asked and agreed to help with lunch duty 2 days a week even though you are aware of limiting your noncounseling duties. Today your site supervisor asked you to perform bus duty. How do you reconcile these multiple noncounseling-related requests with your university program requirements? What factors will influence your decision and how will you proceed?

_____

_____

Special Education

Although Chapter 13 contains a more comprehensive discussion concerning the role of the counselor with students with disabilities, this is a population that is often overlooked by many professional school counselors. Assisting these students and their families may even be more difficult for individuals who do not have a background in education or have not taken coursework that addresses some of the legislative issues and concerns that accompany these individuals. As stated by the American School Counselor Association (2013b):

> Professional school counselors encourage and support the academic, career and personal/social [renamed social/emotional] development for all students through comprehensive school counseling programs. Professional school counselors are committed to helping all students realize their potential and meet or exceed academic standards regardless of challenges resulting from disabilities and other special needs.
>
> (para. 1)

The elementary school counselor may include counselees with special needs in such areas as conducting group lessons, leading small groups, providing individual counseling, assisting with peer relationships, mediating problems among students, and improving self-confidence. Middle and high school counselors work closely with the resource teachers as students approach high school registration to assist in developing a transition plan for the students as they matriculate to high school and beyond.

BUILDING RELATIONSHIPS FOR ENHANCING STUDENT GROWTH

Professional Learning Communities (PLCs) were developed as a strategy for building relationships with others. The school board, school administrators, teachers, students, parents/guardians, other counseling professionals, and other school-related personnel are all integral to the school counseling program. As a school counselor-in-training, it is essential to understand how you can collaborate effectively with these individuals in the school milieu.

Figure 2.4 Students benefit when teachers collaborate with counselors to improve achievement.

Source: Shutterstock

The Professional Learning Community

The PLC is one systematic method in which educational personnel partner to share expertise with the intention of improving the academic achievement of students through research-based practices. PLCs are an intentional school-improvement strategy to reduce professional isolation and to encourage the insights and ideas of all involved. PLCs are built around shared goals or responsibilities such as fifth-grade teachers or teachers of a certain subject who meet on a regular basis to address learning best practices and commit to engaging and analyzing effective research practices. Likewise, school counselors within the district may meet to discuss such topics as new counseling strategies or identifying student standards that address district competencies from pre-K–12.

The work of Richard DuFour guides PLCs, but this collaborative is not without controversy. Some individuals question whether these groups are able to make a positive impact due to the difficulty in attributing student performance improvements to one particular initiative. Proponents, however, emphasize that as teachers develop more professional relationships, more effective, evidence-based practices will ensue.

Box 2.3

Advantages to school counselors participating in PLCs:

1. Collaboration with teachers and others to identify student needs.
2. Suggestions for quality solutions to problems.
3. Provision of resources for referrals to appropriate interventions for students.
4. Suggestions to improve student behavior and attendance.
5. Gathering information about social/emotional or developmental needs of students.
6. Sharing information about activities and programs within the school counseling program that are available to address student needs.
7. Facilitation of communication between PLC members.

The School Board

School systems are governed by a group of individuals who form a school board, and as a school counselor-in-training, it would be an educational opportunity to study your school system's website to view the structure of the school board, the members composing this board, responsibilities of the members, and when and where meetings are held. Board members are typically elected to terms consisting of a predetermined number of years, although some school districts may have board members who are appointed to the position. School boards set policies under which school systems operate, and either appoint a superintendent or hold an election. In turn, with the approval of the school board members, superintendents hire other school personnel, including building-level administrators, and depending on the size of the school system, assistant and/or deputy assistant superintendents may be hired. The responsibilities of the school district are divided among a variety of department directors, supervisors, and specialists.

School board policies affect all school staff, faculty, and the community. Some districts hire a director of counseling who is responsible exclusively to the school counselors in the district and often works closely with school counselor training programs in placing students in their clinical sites. Or, this person may be assigned duties that encompass supervising school counselors in addition to a broader array of responsibilities. It is also possible that since this person serves as a supervisor of school counselors, an administration degree is required for this responsibility. To address this issue, this person could be given a title such as "coach," which does not reflect an administrative role. Smaller systems may not have a person specifically identified to supervise counselors, and in these instances this task would probably belong to the building administrator.

Getting to know the school board members who represent your school or district helps build a relationship and allows the counselor to educate board members about the importance of school counseling, advocate for counseling needs in areas such as staffing, money, and materials, and communicate the counselor's education and training. In fact, once you are hired as a professional school counselor, consider speaking to the school board at least once a year so that the activities of the school counseling program are better understood. This occasion also provides an opportunity to show appreciation to the board member who advocates for the school counseling program.

Conceptual Application Activity 2.8

Attend a school board meeting and take notes on the topics that were discussed. Share your impressions and notes with your peers. What were your impressions of this meeting? What group dynamics did you observe?

_____

_____

School Administrators

Part of a positive work culture and climate involves administrators and counselors working closely together with mutual trust, and therefore it is essential that you inform your site supervisor and principal of your activities without burdening him or her with minor details. You will be receiving supervision in which you will share your concerns with your site supervisor on a regular basis, and you may want to consider getting principal approval for topics you plan on discussing in class or small groups. It is easy to venture into controversial territory with young adolescents, and it is possible that you will need the principal's support if a parent/guardian disapproves of a topic that is discussed. If there is any possibility that a discussion area might generate controversy in the community, talk to your supervisor about sending a letter home prior to the discussion explaining what you plan to do and offer parents/guardians the option of providing alternative activities for their child if they do not want their child to participate in the activity. Any time you have a discussion with a parent that is not resolved in the way the parent/guardian hoped, inform your supervisor and principal of what transpired so that he/she has advance knowledge of the problem and is better able to assist with the issue.

Box 2.4

As stated by an elementary school counselor:

"I am so frustrated! I work in a very poor county school district and am assigned to two elementary schools. Neither school has art or music classes. The principal views my job as that of conducting classroom lessons while teachers are on their planning period. I teach seven 45-minute classes 2 days each week, and six 45-minute classes 3 days each week. With this schedule, I only have 40 minutes at one school each week to meet with students and parents/guardians, and 60 minutes each week at the second school I am assigned. Yet, the administrators still expect me to see students and families as well as handle typical school counselor duties. I try to meet with as many students and parents/guardians as possible but am doing so during my lunch time and before and after school. I have a long waiting list of students who would like to meet with me. This isn't what I thought this job would be like!"

Conceptual Application Activity 2.9

Read and respond to the following scenarios and discuss your answers with your peers.

A father of one of your students makes an appointment to see you about his son's grades. He indicates that he is divorced from the child's mother (the custodial parent), and he does not approve of the mother's lack of discipline. He is planning on going to court to get custody, and he wants you to testify to the child's lack of progress academically. He feels that the teachers as well as your site supervisor do not keep him as informed as they should. As he talks, he gets visibly more upset. How do you handle this?

_____

_____

Conceptual Application Activity 2.10

You are leading a lesson session on suicide that is integral to your internship contract and the expectations of your school counseling training program. Your principal receives an emotional call from a parent. There has been a recent suicide in the family and the discussion in class has opened some deep wounds. As a result, the parent is angry that this topic is being discussed in school. How would you handle this situation?

_____

_____

Teachers

A school counselor's relationship with faculty and staff is vital to the success of the school counseling program, and through good communication teachers are aware of the work you do in your school. Posting your schedule outside your door in addition to displaying information on the school staff bulletin board, PTA newsletter, and school website are helpful methods to communicate the types of activities in which you are engaged in the school.

It may also be beneficial to present a short orientation for teachers about your role as a school counselor-in-training and provide them with a professional disclosure statement that outlines your contact information, education, training, philosophy, and so forth. Furthermore, when meeting with teachers, they can give you an idea of student concerns that need to be addressed, such as bullying, divorce, child or sexual abuse, substance abuse, basic friendship skills, self-esteem, study skills, and peer pressure. Or, these educators may suggest a particular school or community problem on which to focus your attention. Be certain that you set up a schedule of dates and times with teachers in advance for when you are coming to their classrooms for any reason.

Collaborating with teachers on ASCA Mindsets and Behaviors for Student Success that coordinate with Common Core standards is an additional strategy for revealing your contributions to student achievement. Furthermore, career readiness is an essential concept that is necessary to begin in elementary school, and school counselors are aware of and trained to address career and college readiness for all students, and the skills and knowledge that are needed to address career goals.

You need to make an effort to be seen around the school. At times school counselors are involved in a myriad of activities in their offices, and teachers may be uncertain of who you are and how you are involved in the school. Therefore, whenever possible, try to eat lunch with different groups of teachers to build rapport with the faculty, or visit teachers during their planning time just to say hello and ask how they are doing. This attention will help tremendously in getting referrals and support for calling students from classes when you need to see them.

When you need to meet with students, stop by the teachers' classrooms to briefly speak with the teachers regarding individual students you plan to meet with that day. Early morning or teacher planning times are good opportunities to do this. Exchange any relevant information, staying within the bounds of confidentiality, and ask if the teacher has any specific incidents that need to be addressed with the student when scheduling your day.

School counselors and teachers often compete for time with students, and scheduling times to see counselees is challenging. You may alleviate this problem by calling students to your office before or after school or during their elective classes, class change time, homeroom periods, study halls, lunch, or other times that do not interfere with academics. However, if the situation is an emergency, teachers are usually understanding about interruptions; you will just need to talk with the teacher as to the importance of seeing the student at that time.

It is not uncommon for a student to see you to avoid going to a class, and a common mistake of many counselors-in-training is to allow students to see them without checking whether he or she has permission to be out of class. You will create much ill will if teachers think you are allowing students to cut classes to come see you, even though this situation could happen inadvertently. If it does happen, be sure to see the teacher as soon as possible to explain or apologize.

When a teacher refers a student to you, acknowledge this referral and follow up with the teacher. If you will be seeing the student regularly, discuss this with the teacher and be sure to let him/her know that you will be checking to see if the student has made any attitudinal or behavioral changes. Even though you cannot ethically share confidential information about a student, providing general information or suggestions for how the teacher may facilitate counseling goals will be appreciated and teachers will be more likely to make accommodations for students.

Conceptual Application Activity 2.11

Read and respond to the following situation and discuss your response with your peers.

A critical incident happened in a classroom in which a student seriously harmed another, and you have been involved with counseling the victim. Staff and parents are concerned about the actions taken regarding this incident and ask you to tell them specifics about the incident and how it is being handled. How do you respond?

_____

_____

Students

A student is the most important resource in the school. Being responsible for numerous students can seem overwhelming at times, especially given the high student to low counselor ratio in many schools. Remember that you cannot be all things to all people, but you can be an effective presence and participant in the lives of your students. Try to get to each classroom within the first 2 weeks of school, either for a brief visit or for a regular classroom lesson to introduce yourself and tell the students why you are there and how they can contact you.

Discuss with your supervisor how students can make an appointment to see you. Having students place a note on your desk or putting a mailbox outside your counseling office are typical strategies.

In addition, try to familiarize yourself with a variety of individual counseling techniques. In an elementary setting these strategies might include bibliotherapy, puppetry, writing stories, playing games, art activities, and the use of props and charts.

Be a visible presence around the school whenever possible. If you have a few extra minutes, visit the lunchroom or playground, simply walk the halls, or attend students' musicals, plays, sporting events, and school festivals. However, there are certain limits that should be placed on interaction with students. As professional adults, counselors should never be involved with students inappropriately or in ways that would disrupt integrity. Counselors and counselors-in-training alike should not be "friends" with students on social networks such as Facebook and MySpace. There have been some incidents in which the counselor-in-training was unable to maintain appropriate boundaries with students due to unethical fraternization, which resulted in dismissal from the school counseling program.

Parents/Guardians

As a supervisee, learn how to collaborate with parents/guardians by holding informational meetings or workshops on relevant issues. Teaching parenting classes, providing information on bullying, discussing the effects of divorce, helping children with study skills, or discussing your role as a school counselor trainee are all topics that will help you get experience in working with parents/guardians while under supervision. Supplying handouts may also help the learning process, and offering snacks can add a festive mood to the meeting.

Herbert and Sergent (2006) suggest inviting parents/guardians and their children to view a movie with a school counseling theme and then discuss the movie and its relevance to their lives. *Monster University, Frozen,* or *Saving Mr. Banks* are appropriate movies that are rated G or PG with a message to share. To make movie night more enticing and fun, popcorn could be served.

When having parent/guardian conferences, be very careful with words and try to start and end every conference with something positive about the child. Keep the following suggestions in mind:

- When problem areas are being discussed, link any words of criticism to the fact that the goal is to get the student back on track so that he or she can be happy and successful.
- Be respectful and tactful about giving advice, especially if you are not a parent yourself.
- Never give the impression that you know more about the child than the parent/guardian does. Allow these caregivers to share valuable information that can help you better understand their son or daughter. They are to be considered experts of their own children.
- Affirm the fact that parenting is an important and difficult job and that you want to do your part to help with any concerns.
- Use the technique of *joining*, which means establishing rapport by making small talk with the parents/guardians, matching your communication style with theirs, and using appropriate self-disclosure to relate to their experiences. If the conference concerns grades in a particular subject, the teacher of that class should be involved.
- Stay with the facts and observations that you have gathered in your interaction with the student and look for ways to incorporate the child's strengths into the discussion with his or her parents/guardians.

Other suggestions for working with parents/guardians include normalizing children's problems through *reframing*, which means to change the negative label attributed to the child. For instance, if a young boy is described as being "bossy," you could refer to this behavior as "likes to express himself." Or, you could consider establishing a library of helpful information for caregivers such as handouts, pamphlets, books, audiovisual materials, or links to informative websites. This effort is something that you can begin as a school counselor trainee and continue throughout the entire span of your career.

Conceptual Application Activity 2.12

Read and respond to the following scenario and discuss your answers with your peers.

Parents have called you to request a conference regarding their son. According to his parents, his grades are dropping, he seems unfocused, and his behavior in the classroom and with his peers is becoming a concern. They are adamant that you are aware of how much he disrupts their family life and that you "fix" him. How would you prepare for this conference?

_____

_____

Conceptual Application Activity 2.13

Read and respond to the following scenario and discuss your answers with your peers.

It is Monday morning, and you are speaking with a student's mother who is requesting that you see her child for school anxiety issues. You continue to explore with the mother what her specific concerns are about the student, and what she would like to see happen as you agree to work with the student. At the end of the conversation, the student's mother adds, "I would like you to call me each week to let me know what she is talking about with you." What do you do?

_____

_____

One challenging issue particularly for school counselors-in-training is how to balance the student's right to confidentiality without alienating the parent or guardian, who has a legitimate interest in the well-being of his or her child. Minors' ethical rights to confidentiality in the counseling relationship are often misunderstood or ignored altogether, and the demands of parents to be informed of the specific content of counseling sessions sometimes overshadow the child's right to privacy. School counselors who develop a reputation for arbitrarily sharing students' information with others may find students reluctant to seek counseling (Glosoff & Pate, 2002). Yet, communicating the value of confidentiality as a cornerstone to the counseling relationship to parents/guardians is a major consideration in collaborating with these stakeholders.

Technology has improved methods of communicating with parents/guardians. Counselor websites can be updated regularly with information parents/guardians need to know. For example, parent/teacher conferences, ACT and SAT dates, college admission deadlines, scholarships, year-end exams, and other opportunities for students allow parents to be aware of special dates that impact their child.

Conceptual Application Activity 2.14

Read and respond to the following scenario and discuss your responses with those of your peers.

You are part of a parent conference in which the language arts teacher mentions that the student has written something in a journal that alludes to the fact that the student seems to be afraid of someone at home. The parent gets very angry and leans across the table in a threatening manner when the journal entry is mentioned, and menacingly states that you are no longer allowed to work with the child. You, your site supervisor, and the teacher are the only ones in the room with this parent. How do you handle this situation?

_____

_____

INTERACTION WITH OTHER PROFESSIONALS

Maintaining positive relationships with counselors at neighboring schools or community counselors has obvious benefits. For instance, students often transfer schools, and counselors need to communicate with one another about transfer students' academic records, guardianship issues, grades, special placements, behavior, and so forth. In other cases, when registering eighth-grade students for high school, it is helpful for counselors from all feeder schools to meet, plan, and prepare for the occasion. Talk with your site supervisor about the opportunity to observe and assist with registration so that you can learn about this responsibility firsthand. It is also an opportune time to provide career counseling by discussing how certain classes provide a foundation for identified career plans. Furthermore, although time for collaboration or idea exchange among school counselors is scarce, counselors within a system may want to make an effort to meet together. It may be helpful to you as a school counselor-in-training to talk and observe counselors in neighboring systems to learn how they conduct their program.

In addition, students may require more intense counseling than you are able to provide. In these cases, a referral to a community counselor who has the skill and expertise may be in the best interests of the student. When a referral is needed, a network of resources is desirable. Providing at least three experts in a particular area allows parents/guardians to make their own decision about the professional they feel is best equipped to work with their child. A signed parent/guardian consent form allows all parties to communicate about the student's progress. In these cases, knowledge of terminology and diagnoses, collaborative plans for working with the student, and services to facilitate academic achievement aid in a smooth transition.

Box 2.5

School counselors are able to create a positive school climate by treating others with dignity and respect. There will be more support for a comprehensive, developmental school counseling (CDSC) program when the value of others is recognized and acknowledged and school counselors follow through on commitments (Mason, 2011).

Other School-Related Personnel

A school counselor's role also intersects with the duties of other school personnel, such as secretaries, social workers, nurses, school psychologists, custodians, bookkeepers, and school resource officers. Each of these individuals is a valuable resource for learning about collaborative relationships that impact the school culture and students. The following sections summarize the roles these personnel play in the school.

Secretaries

School secretaries are critical in establishing a welcoming climate, as they are often the first contact with people who enter the building or call the school. The role of a secretary can be very stressful, as office personnel are extremely busy and constantly interrupted. There are some school counseling departments that are fortunate to have a clerical assistant assigned exclusively to the school counselors, whereas other schools do not have this privilege and the clerical help is restricted to one or two individuals for the entire school. As a person new to the school, you will have lots of questions, so be careful about interrupting these secretaries and do not ask them to do small things for you that you can do yourself.

School Social Workers

Social workers are a liaison between home and school. School attendance and graduation rates are two regulations under NCLB in which school performance is scrutinized. School social workers can help with these issues by making home visits and assisting with attendance and tardiness issues. Furthermore, they are instrumental resources in connecting families with community agencies that provide such needs as clothing, food, shelter, community mental health counseling, and medical assistance.

School Nurses

Nurses range from being at a school on a full-time basis to traveling from school site to school site throughout the school day or week. If a student requires immediate medications or procedures that are complicated, a nurse will likely be assigned to administer the necessary treatment. Furthermore, in the course of providing assistance, nurses often hear students talk about troublesome issues. For example, a child may have a stomachache and tell the nurse that his or her parents had a fight that morning. Children's complaints are often expressed through physical symptoms rather than through a verbalizing of thoughts and emotions, and are therefore often clues to more serious emotional concerns. As a school counselor-in-training, make a point to talk with the school nurse about any concerns you have about counselees with whom you are working.

School Psychologists

In some school systems there is confusion between the role of the school psychologist and that of the counselor, and in other schools the roles are more clearly understood. For example, in some schools, counselors process student referrals, help with testing, and attend all or most IEP (Individualized Education Plan) meetings. In other schools, this is the role of the school psychologist. The school psychologist and school counselor can form a collaborative relationship in which each clearly understands the training and education of the other so that duties are not duplicated. As a school counselor-in-training, take time to interview the school psychologist to obtain a better understanding of his or her responsibilities, and how the two of you are able to assist one another.

Custodians

Custodians work long, hard hours for relatively low pay, and many are quite dedicated to the school staff and students. As a new person in the school, introduce yourself and show your appreciation for their assistance. As with the office staff, do not ask them to do minor things for you that you could do yourself. However, when you need to arrange a room or transport large materials, they can be a great help. Also, remember that custodians get to know the students on a regular basis and can be helpful resources in understanding your students better.

Bookkeeper/Treasurer

Not all school counseling programs are provided with funds to assist with purchases for counseling-related needs. Talk with your supervisor about the monies that are provided to the school counseling department and how these funds are budgeted. Hopefully, you will be given some funds to spend on your school counseling program once you are a fully credentialed member of the profession, but if not, organizations such as the PTO (parent/teacher organization) may provide needed funds, or grants may be a resource. These funding opportunities will not only give you needed resources, they will also generate publicity for your program. As a supervisee, you may want to investigate the types of grants that are available and complete a grant application for essentials that your school site can use. In some school systems, your expenditures will be processed through the school bookkeeper. These individuals have critically important jobs that require compliance with both state and district guidelines for spending and collecting money. As a school counselor trainee, familiarize yourself with the particular bookkeeping procedures in your school and ask questions regarding funding, expenditures, and procuring funds so that you can have a better idea of how monies may be obtained for your program.

Security/School Resource Officer (SRO)

Most schools today have a security officer in the building on a full-time basis or on call when needed. These individuals are often members of local law enforcement agencies with specialty training to work in schools. The security officer's role is to protect students and school personnel from harm, prevent dangerous situations from occurring, and de-escalate situations that have the potential to become violent. A security officer on the premises acts as a deterrent to anyone seeking to inflict harm on school grounds, and often serves as a confidant to students. SROs establish rapport with students, serve as a resource for the staff, and are significant personnel with whom the school counselor should collaborate. For instance, you may be aware of a volatile situation that is to be reported as outlined in school policy, or the school security office may provide support with runaway students, contentious custody issues, or topics such as bullying and harassment. Be sure to learn about this individual's role in the school, particularly as the job relates to working with the school counselors.

Conceptual Application Activity 2.15

Interview the SRO assigned to your building. What are some of his/her responsibilities? Share your findings with your classmates.

_____

_____

Community Agencies

When making referrals for community services, some school counselors seek much outside assistance for students and families, while other counselors only occasionally seek help from outside agencies. Examples of referral sources used by school counselors include services for the homeless, extra clothing, investigation into suspected child abuse, mentoring relationships for children in single-parent homes, and assistance with medical or physical needs such as eyeglasses and dental care.

In addition, agencies can assist counselors by working with students who have special counseling needs. Mental health agencies facilitate groups for at-risk students, or health agencies may talk to students about issues such as pregnancy prevention or other health issues like anorexia and bulimia, weight problems, and handling diabetes.

Conceptual Application Activity 2.16

Learn about the various agencies in your community and make a list of these resources for referral sources. And, if you decide to stay in the community after graduation, you can expand this list of helpful community services.

_____

_____

CONCLUSION

This chapter provides information to help you understand the school culture and climate and how the school counselor is a contributing person to the school milieu. In learning about the role of the school counselor, it is essential that you be knowledgeable of the various school-based initiatives and projects that contribute to the school atmosphere. For instance, No Child Left Behind and the Safe School Initiative, Positive Interventions and Behavioral Supports, Response to Intervention, and the Common Core are discussed. In addition, from reading this chapter you will have a deeper appreciation for the educational personnel as you familiarize yourself with the roles of these integral school and community members.

WEBSITES

- More information about Professional Learning Communities and the work of Richard DuFour can be accessed at: www.ascd.org/publications/educational-leadership/may04/vol61/num08/What-Is-a-Professional-Learning-Community%C2%A2.aspx
- For more information on the Safe School Initiative, you can access www2.ed.gov/admins/lead/safety/preventingattacksreport.pdf
- The article "School Context: Bridge or Barrier to Change" provides helpful information on attitudes and beliefs, attitudes toward change, and cultural norms that facilitate school improvement. This information can be accessed at: www.sedl.org/change/school/culture.html

REFERENCES

Abrams, L.P., Karvonen, M., Nassar-McMillan, S.C., & Perez, T.R. (2009). Identity development and school climate: The role of the school counselor. *Journal of Humanistic Counseling, Education and Development, 48*, 195–214.

ASCA School Counselor. (2013, Nov./Dec.). What does the public think? Retrieved from http://schoolcounselor.org/asca/media/asca/Magazine/Archives/NovDec2013.pdf

American School Counselor Association. (2013a). *The professional school counselor and discipline.* Retrieved from http://schoolcounselor.org/asca/media/asca/home/position%20statements/PS_Discipline-%281%29.pdf

American School Counselor Association. (2013b). *The professional school counselor and students with disabilities.* Position statement. Retrieved from www.schoolcounselor.org/asca/media/asca/PositionStatements/PS_Disabilities.pd

Common Core. (n.d.). *Common Core state standards initiative: Preparing America's students for college & career.* Retrieved from www.corestandards.org/about-the-standards/development-process/

Curtis, R., Van Horne, J.W. Robertson, P., & Karvonen, M. (2010). Outcomes of a school-wide positive behavioral support program. *Professional School counseling, 13,* 159–164. doi: 10.5330/PSC.n.2010–13.159

Ed.Gov. (n.d.). *A capsule view of the history of federal education legislation.* Retrieved from www.ed.gov/policy/gen/leg/edpicks.jhtml?src=ln

Farkas, M.S., Simonsen, B., Migdole, S., Donovan, M.E., Clemens, K., & Cicchese, V. (2012). Schoolwide positive behavior support in an alternative school setting: An evaluation of fidelity outcomes and social validity of Tier 1 implementation. *Journal of Emotional and Behavioral Disorders, 20,* 275–288.

Glosoff, H.L., & Pate, R.H. (2002). Privacy and confidentiality in school counseling. *Professional School Counseling, 6,* 20–27.

Herbert, T.P., & Sergent, D. (2006). Using movies to guide: Teachers and counselors collaborating to support gifted students. *Gifted Child Today, 4,* 14–25.

Mason, E. (2011). Leadership practices of school counselors and counseling program implementation. *NASSP Bulletin, 94,* 274–285. doi: 10.1177/0192636510395012

Peterson, K.D., & Deal, T.E. (2002). *The shaping school culture fieldbook.* San Francisco: Jossey-Bass.

Phillips, G., & Wagner, C. (2003). *School culture assessment.* Vancouver, British Columbia: Agent 5 Design.

Rubinkam, M. (2014, May 18). Parents rail against common core math. *The Knoxville Sentinel,* p. 6A.

Sabella, R.A., & Clements, K.D. (2010, May/June). Response to intervention: Make it work. *ASCA School Counselor.*

Shepard, J.M., Shahidullah, J.D., & Carlson, J.S. (2013). *Counseling students in levels 2 and 3: A PBIS/RTI guide.* Thousand Oaks, CA: Corwin.

Smith, K.H. (2005). The Inviting School Survey Revised (ISS-R): A survey for measuring the invitational qualities (I.Q.) of the total school climate. *Journal of Invitational Theory and Practice, 11,* 35–53.

3 Applying Counseling Theories During the Clinical Experiences

Cynthia Crawford and Jeannine R. Studer

CACREP Standards

Counseling, Prevention, and Intervention

C. Knowledge

1. Knows the theories and processes of effective counseling and wellness programs for individual students and groups of students.
2. Provides individual and group counseling and classroom guidance to promote the academic career, and personal/social (renamed social/emotional) development of students.

The purpose of this chapter is to:

- summarize the most commonly used counseling theories used in schools,
- reflect on one's personal theory of counseling as a school counselor-in-training,
- apply theory to school-related case studies.

INTRODUCTION

The school counselor's approach to counseling is influenced by one or more theoretical orientations. There are a myriad of theoretical approaches within the counseling field, some representing an extension of preexisting theories of personality development and others expressing a reaction against earlier systems of thought. Overall, counseling theories explain (a) why people live productive or unproductive lives and (b) how to assist people in changing aspects within themselves that seem counterproductive (Hackney & Cormier, 2009). Regardless of one's theoretical orientation, knowledge of counseling theory is critical in accurately assessing and conceptualizing a counselee's case. Choosing a theoretical foundation is guided by the counselor's phenomenological and philosophical views from affective, cognitive, behavioral, and relational perspectives (Hackney & Cormier, 2009).

Both the counselee and counselor come to the counseling situation with a unique background of cultural experiences that influence the counselor–counselee relationship, the counseling process, and interventions that may therapeutically meet the needs of the counselee. Because no one particular theory is best suited for all counselees, it is incumbent upon the counselor to choose a theoretical approach that best fits the needs of the counselee in terms of personality factors, background experiences, and cultural milieu (Corey, 2009).

Although you undoubtedly have a separate counseling theories class within your training program curriculum, this chapter is not intended to replace the information that you will receive within this class. Instead, a general overview of the unique differences found in individual schools that often influence theoretical counseling orientation is given. In addition, we introduce motivational interviewing, a "front-loaded" approach that is used with all counseling theories, and summarize the more commonly used counseling theories, including person-centered counseling, reality therapy, cognitive behavioral approaches, solution-focused brief counseling, and narrative therapy. Finally, the creative counseling approaches such as art, play, and music are discussed.

Contextual Aspects of Schools

Schools provide a unique environment in which to provide counseling. Although some of the aspects unique to schools are more thoroughly discussed in Chapter 2, it is important to consider the distinct aspects of the school environment that impact school counselors' choice of theoretical orientation. Some of these aspects include the developmental age of children and adolescents as counselees, the scope of school counselor responsibilities, students' time availability, and the school mission and philosophy. First, the primary goal of school personnel is to educate children. Because school counselors focus their counseling energies primarily on children and adolescents, developmental issues influence choice of theoretical orientation. Second, school counselors are responsible for many tasks and activities which often limit the amount of energy and time the school counselor has available for counseling. As a result, school counselors may not have the resources or time to adequately counsel students who present significant mental health issues or who require unavailable resources or intensive ongoing counseling. The third aspect is the students' time availability. Students are in school to be educated. Excessive time spent in the school counseling office can take away from time spent in the classroom. Furthermore, based on the mission and vision statement of the school, certain topics may not be addressed in counseling. For example, there is debate regarding the appropriate age to discuss sexuality issues. In fact, the state of Tennessee once considered legislation known as the "Don't Say Gay Bill" that would disallow talk about sexual orientation in public schools (Shahid, 2011). This short-sighted approach prevents school-aged youth from discussing concerns regarding their sexual orientation. In other schools, school counselors are forbidden from discussing birth control or abortion. Awareness of the school policies and state legal and ethical issues may prevent costly mistakes that you could inadvertently cause. Furthermore, awareness of your personal beliefs and philosophical counseling approach assists in establishing a foundation for directing the counseling relationship.

Box 3.1

Youth needing mental health services are more likely to access those services in a school setting than in a community-based mental health environment. However, in a study by Carlson and Kees (2013), school counselors reported uneasiness when counseling with students diagnosed with a mental health disorder. Understanding the numerous mental disorders, and being able to understand the *Diagnostic and Statistical Manual of Mental Disorders*, 5th edition (DSM-V) is helpful for working with students with diagnoses and communicating with their clinical mental health therapist.

The following theoretical counseling descriptions are not intended to exhaustively explain the tenets of any one particular theory but are designed to serve as references when counseling with school-aged youth. Regardless of the theoretical approach that you choose, motivational interviewing (MI) serves as a structure for determining a counselee's desire for change.

Motivational Interviewing

Motivational interviewing focuses on an individual's readiness for change (Sheldon, 2010) and the belief that interpersonal interactions have a significant impact on intrinsic motivation (Frey et al., 2011). As an initial stage in the counseling process, the counselor and student are able to build rapport that facilitates change The pre-commitment phase and the post-commitment phase are two stages identified within this approach (Frey et al., 2011). In the pre-commitment phase an attempt is made to promote intrinsic motivation, whereas the post-commitment phase utilizes collaboration to reach an identified goal.

Pre-commitment Phase

The counselor uses basic counseling skills to influence the counselee's ambivalence to change and to establish the importance of change. The OARS acronym, as identified in Table 3.1, is used to focus on appropriate responses to the student's concerns.

Post-commitment Phase

A central belief behind motivational interviewing is to avoid getting stuck on issues while keeping a positive momentum (Sheldon, 2010). During this phase, measureable, achievable, specific goals are established. The acronym FRAMES, as identified in Table 3.2, can be implemented to increase the probability of change.

A scale is used to monitor the student's motivation to change and confidence in ability to reach a goal. For instance, the counselor can ask, "On a scale of 1–10, with 1 meaning little motivation and 10 meaning high motivation, how enthusiastic are you to make your goal happen?" Or, "On a scale of 1–10, how confident are you that you can reach your goal?" If the student answers with a 6,

Table 3.1 The OARS Acronym in Determining the Student's Ambivalence to Change

Acronym	Explanation	Example
Open-ended questions	Questions that require a response other than a yes or a no. More information is generated by these queries. Use "what" and "how" to elicit an enhanced response.	"What is your biggest concern?"
Affirmations	Affirmations are based on implanting a positive, encouraging thought or goal	"You came to school every day this week. Way to go!"
Reflective listening	Restatement of the counselee's words reveals that the counselor is listening	"You are concerned about your mom's reaction to your teacher's report and you are not sure how to talk with her."
Summary statements	Summarizing the conversation is often done at the end of the counseling session to remind the student what was discussed.	"We discussed your grades in English and you decided to talk with Mrs. Smith after class."

Table 3.2 The FRAMES Acronym for Assessing the Probability of Change

Acronym	Explanation	Example
Feedback	Providing nonjudgmental feedback as facts to articulate discrepancies in what was said or done	"You are saying you want to get better grades, yet you are also telling me you don't have time to study."
Responsibility	Accepting personal accountability for actions	"What was your role in the class disruption?"
Advice	Providing information that can be used to solve a problem	"I am wondering if you have tried to speak in an assertive manner?"
Menus	Presenting a list of options as solutions to a problem	"You have tried talking, emailing, and texting your friend to explain the situation. Is there anything else to consider?"
Empathy	Building rapport by acknowledging that change is difficult	"I can imagine how uncomfortable it will be to take this first step."
Self-efficacy	Promoting autonomy and a belief in the ability to change	"This is a plan that I think makes sense and I have confidence in your ability to carry these plans out."

the counselor then asks the student what he/she needs to do to move up to a 7. The response serves as a basis for assigning homework as a step toward change. From here, the counselor is able to select a counseling theory in work with the counselee.

INDIVIDUAL COUNSELING THEORIES

Person-Centered Counseling

Dr. Carl Rogers, the founder of person-centered counseling, developed his nondirective approach in reaction to the prevailing direct method of counseling. Rogers' approach challenged the assumption that "the counselor knows best" and the prevailing attitude that counselees are unable to understand and resolve their problems without direct help on the part of a counselor. Instead, he believed that all individuals have an innate ability to feel in control with the skills to solve his/her personal problems (Seligman & Reichenberg, 2014).

Rogers believed the focus of counseling should be on the person rather than the problem, and that the ultimate goal of counseling is to achieve congruence between the person's true inner self and his or her perceived self. On the part of the counselor, Rogers advocated for unconditional positive regard or nonjudgmental acceptance of the counselee; a genuine, unpretentious presentation of congruence; and accurate empathic understanding. When the counselee experiences these conditions, he/she is able to work toward meaningful goals leading to personal change (Corey, 2012). Overall, the counselor strives to provide a warm, respectful, genuine, and caring environment in which self-actualization, or as stated in the former Army slogan, "to be all you can be," may occur.

Person-centered counseling has been applied in a number of countries and in numerous multicultural settings. The role a counselor takes in setting aside personal values, thus completely identifying with those of the counselee, enhances the applicability of the approach with diverse populations (Sharf, 2008). The person-centered approach is widely applicable and has been used with individuals, groups, and families and employed in educational settings from elementary to graduate school. With its emphasis on a warm, caring counselor–counselee connection, the approach is particularly applicable in crisis intervention, including traumatic disasters, extreme illness, unplanned pregnancies, and grief (Corsini & Wedding, 2005). Although person-centered counseling is considered a "way of being" in the counseling relationship, techniques are generally not associated with this theory. However, experiential learning facilitates self-esteem development, with success and achievement used as stepping-stones to develop a greater sense of self-worth (Seligman & Reichenberg, 2014). Student Activity 3.1 can be adapted to promote self-esteem with students.

Student Activity 3.1 I Can, Can

Directions: Cut paper into strips. Brainstorm with the student about his/her successes, positive traits, and accomplishments, and write these down on the strips of paper. Place the completed strips of paper into a can, and whenever the student is feeling anxious or upset about him/herself, instruct the student to pull a strip of paper out of the can to read and reflect upon.

Conceptual Application Activity 3.1

Conduct a role-play using the following scenario with a partner. One person will play the role of a person-centered counselor using the philosophical approach described earlier, and the other person will role-play the counselee described in the vignette.

Ella is a fourth-grade student in a rural school that has few resources, poorly paid personnel, and no mental health agencies. The closest facility that provides counseling is in a city located nearly one hour away. Ella arrives in the counselor's office upset, crying, and incapable of talking about the issue that brought her to the office. It seems that her mother, her primary caregiver, was arrested the night before due to charges of drug use and abuse. Ella was sent to live with her grandparents, a few blocks away, until her mother is arraigned. Ella's grandparents care about Ella but have physical difficulties that prevent them from caring for her appropriately.

a. Discuss what it was like to role-play the counselor and some of the challenges in using this approach. What aspects of this theory seemed to facilitate the counseling relationship?
b. Discuss what it was like to role-play Ella. What were some of the aspects of this counseling approach that you think assisted the counseling process? What aspects detracted from the counseling process?

_____

_____

Reality Therapy or Choice Theory

William Glasser developed reality therapy in the early 1960s as a result of his work with institutionalized delinquent adolescent girls. Glasser emphasized the importance of taking responsibility for oneself, meeting basic needs without interfering with the lives of others, and maintaining relationships (Seligman & Reichenberg, 2014). Glasser identified the five interrelated and mutually dependent needs of survival, belonging, power, freedom, and fun that all individuals attempt to accomplish (Archer & McCarthy, 2007). According to Glasser, individuals choose their behaviors to meet perceived needs in response to the quality of relationships they experience. Glasser frequently converts diagnostic descriptors such as depression, anxiety, and phobia into verb forms, expressed as *depressing, anxietizing,* and *phobicing*, thus implying that the individual chooses the behavioral symptom and enacts it within his or her life (Sharf, 2008).

Reality therapy suggests that the underlying issue for a troubled counselee is an absence or lack of satisfaction with a significant interpersonal relationship. Therefore, as a counselor, you can facilitate a significant relationship with your student counselee, in fact in some cases *you* may be the only reliable person the student is able to trust. In treating counselees for emotional disturbance, Glasser stated that psychiatric symptoms emerge in an attempt to meet needs stemming from an ineffective relationship. The goals of reality therapy, therefore, are to create a trustful environment in which the counselee is able to meet his/her needs by taking control of life choices.

In assessing the counselee's status in meeting his or her needs in a realistic manner, the reality counselor may use the WDEP system (Wubbolding, 2004):

W = Wants: What do you want to be and do? Your mental picture of yourself.
D = Doing and direction: What are you doing? Where do you want to go?
E = Evaluation: Is what you are doing now working for you? Is it getting you what you want?
P = Planning: A plan to get you where you want to be, often represented by the acronym SAMI^{2}C^3 (Seligman & Reichenberg, 2014)

S = Simple, specific, and understandable
A = Attainable by the student
M = Measurable through the use of recording methods
I = Implemented immediately
    Involving the counselor for feedback
C = Controlled by the student
    Commitment to change
    Consistent changes in behavior

Glasser believed that reality therapy is successful with individuals from all cultural groups due to the universal nature of the five basic needs. However, there is little empirical evidence that it is effective with different cultural groups. For instance, the excessive use of questions may be considered offensive by some Asian cultures, and individuals who are disenfranchised may face negative social barriers. Therefore, counselors have a responsibility to communicate that each person is responsible for his/her reactions and the consequences of these behaviors (Archer & McCarthy, 2007).

Reality therapy is quite popular in middle and high school settings but may be used across all grade levels by teachers, administrators, and school counselors. Questioning, optimism, humor, confrontation, and paradoxical techniques are a few of the strategies that reality therapists use to bring about change. Activity 3.2 is a student activity that can be implemented.

Student Activity 3.2   My Basic Needs

Glasser identified the basic needs of survival, belonging, power, freedom, and fun as catalysts to behavior. In the squares below, ask the student to draw, write, or cut out pictures from magazines to represent how each of his/her basic needs is met.

Survival	Belonging	Power
Freedom	Fun	

Conceptual Application Activity 3.2

Using the WDEP system (Wubbolding, 2004) with a partner, conduct a role-play including a counselor and a counselee using the following scenarios.

- A 12th-grade student who is having difficulty with career plans
- A 7th-grade male who is being bullied by his peers
- A 3rd-grade female who is having problems getting along with her sister

a. Discuss what it was like to role-play the counselor and some of the challenges in using this approach. What aspects of this theory seemed to facilitate the counseling relationship?
b. Discuss what it was like to role-play the student counselee. What were some of the aspects of this counseling approach that assisted the counseling process? What aspects detracted from the counseling process?

Rational Emotive Behavior Therapy

Albert Ellis (2004a, 2004b) developed rational emotive behavior therapy (REBT) in which principles from cognitive and behavioral theories are integrated into short-term counseling approaches; this approach is popular among counselors in all settings (Corey, 2009). REBT is based on the concept that how a person thinks influences behavior and emotions (Archer & McCarthy, 2007). Therefore, by changing the interpretation or the way we think about life situations, we also change how we feel and what we do in response to this thinking. Common cognitive distortions include all-or-nothing thinking typically represented by the words *must*, *ought*, and *should*; mind reading; catastrophizing; overgeneralization; labeling and mislabeling; magnification and minimization; and personalization; among others (Sharf, 2008). He contended that emotional problems are largely a result of mistaken beliefs and may be rectified by recognizing the irrational nature of one's thinking, disputing such irrational cognitions, and replacing these thoughts with more rational and effective thinking.

Rational emotive behavior therapy is directive and educational in nature, with an emphasis on thinking, judging, deciding, analyzing, and doing (Corey, 2009; Sharf, 2008). The counselor's role in REBT is to help the counselee realize the irrationality of mistaken beliefs, which will later be replaced by more functional thoughts and behaviors through experiential activities and behavioral homework assignments to reinforce the newly acquired behaviors. The ABCDE approach is used to modify irrational beliefs (Seligman & Reichenberg, 2014).

A = *A*ctivating event, or the source that initiated the irrational thinking
B = *B*elief and evaluation of the event, whether it is viewed as positive, negative, or neutral
C = *C*onsequences of the belief that may be helpful or harmful. Rational beliefs usually lead to healthier outcomes, whereas irrational beliefs often lead to destructive outcomes.
D = *D*ispute (or debate) of beliefs and whether they are rational or irrational
E = *E*ffect of new belief, and hopefully a new perspective

Once cognitive distortions are recognized, students are able to continue collaborative work with their counselor to restructure their thinking and improve their problem-solving and coping skills (Corey, 2009; Sharf, 2008). Treatment strategies include behavioral rehearsal, role-play, and homework assignments for continued practice of positive cognitions and behaviors (Corsini & Wedding, 2005).

From a multicultural perspective, REBT has been criticized because it doesn't take into account the context in which the irrational thoughts occur; nor is there attention given to gender differences (Archer & McCarthy, 2007). Therefore, counselors need to use caution when using this approach with those from non-Western backgrounds, and to consider the situation from a gender perspective (Seligman & Reichenberg, 2014).

Student Activity 3.3   Using REBT to Recognize Irrational Thoughts

Use the REBT approach with a student who is expressing irrational beliefs. Use the following worksheet to identify irrational thoughts and to assist the student to dispute the statements.

A	B	C	D	E
Identify an event that you found upsetting.	What was your belief?	What were the consequences of the belief?	What is the evidence for this belief?	What is the consequence of this new belief?

Conceptual Application Activity 3.3

With a partner, conduct a role-play of the following situation using a cognitive behavioral approach.

A parent of one of your fifth graders comes to see you because she is concerned that her son, Kyle, is gay. According to Kyle's mom, he is not interested in sports or any type of physical activity typical for boys his age. Kyle, according to his mother, is quiet and prefers to play with dolls with his sister. Kyle's mom further states that it is her fault because she divorced his father when he was baby and as a result of not having a male figure in the home, Kyle is suffering the consequences.

a.   Discuss what it was like to role-play the counselor and some of the challenges in using this approach. What aspects of this theory seemed to facilitate the counseling relationship?

b. Discuss what it was like to role-play Kyle's mom. What were some of the aspects of this counseling approach that assisted the counseling process? What aspects detracted from the counseling process?

_____

_____

Solution-Focused Brief Counseling

Solution-focused brief counseling (SFBC) was initially influenced by the work of Milton Erickson (deShazer, 1985). The premise behind SFBC is that change is always happening and that things cannot *not* change (Seligman & Reichenberg, 2014). This approach is similar to person-centered counseling due to the premise that each individual is capable of solving his/her own problems (Guterman, 2013). SFBC conceptualizes a collaborative approach in that the focus is on what the counselee would like to see happen rather than on problem-saturated talk. According to counselors who adhere to this approach, primary principles include: (a) The primary task of the counselor is to help the counselee do something different; (b) a shift should occur from attending to the problem itself to a solution that may already be present within the counselee's life; (c) change, even in small increments, is productive in creating the medium for further change; and (d) goals stated in positive terms create expectations for change (Seligman & Reichenberg, 2014).

In SFBC, problems are viewed as being maintained by the counselee's belief that the problem is always happening and may have intensified as a result of the individual repeatedly applying the same solutions to each area of difficulty (Archer & McCarthy, 2007). Using a solution-focused approach, the counselor will co-construct a solvable problem for counseling, or in other words, a goal for how life would be without the problem (Guterman, 2013). From here, the counselor explores *exceptions* to the problem, or times when the problem doesn't occur. For instance, the counselor may ask the question, "Is there a time when you didn't have the problem?" Or, "Has there been a time when you were able to cope with the problem?"

At times, the counselee is unable to recognize a time when the problem has not occurred, and if this is the case, the counselor then asks what is known as the *miracle question*. This question serves to help the counselee imagine the future without the trouble that brought him/her into counseling. The miracle question is generally stated as, "Suppose you went to bed this evening and while you were sleeping a miracle occurred and when you woke up in the morning all your problems were gone. What would be different?" "What would you be doing, thinking, feeling to let you know that your goal was reached?" (Corey, 2012). For younger counselees, another version of the miracle question could be, "Suppose I had a magic wand and when I wave it all your problems will be gone. How would you know that the magic worked?"

During subsequent sessions, homework is provided to reinforce behaviors that result in positive change for the counselee. For instance, students may be encouraged to do more of the exceptions that were identified as times when the problem was not occurring. Scaling techniques are used to help counselees recognize progress. For example, counselees are asked to rate the problem on a scale of 1–10, with 10 meaning the problem is completely solved and 1 meaning the problem is the worst it can be. The student may rate the problem as a 5. The counselor then asks the counselee to identify steps that could be taken to move the problem to a 6, and from the responses these steps are assigned as homework.

Solution-focused brief counseling techniques are applicable with students of all ages and may be applied in individual as well as group counseling settings. Furthermore, SFBC has been used successfully with cultural groups due to the emphasis on personal strengths and the establishment of goals that are personally meaningful. Due to the emphasis some Asian cultures put on pragmatically resolving situations, this form of counseling may be preferred to other theoretic approaches, yet the egalitarian relationship that is assumed in this model could be disconcerting to those who prefer a hierarchal structure.

Student Activity 3.4   Redefining My Life

The following questions may be asked in individual or group counseling to facilitate problem resolution.

1. What do you usually do in a situation that creates a problem? Think in terms of feelings, behavior, thoughts.

_____

2. When does the problem not occur? Who are you with? What are you doing? What are you thinking? What are you feeling?

_____

3. Imagine a time in the future when you are not having the problem. What are you doing? Thinking? Feeling?

_____

4. How will you know when the problem is no longer a dilemma for you? What will be the signs? What does this say about your ability to handle problematic situations?

_____

Conceptual Application Activity 3.4

With a partner, conduct a role-play of a school counselor and a counselee using the solution-focused brief counseling approach. Use one or more of the following scenarios to assist you with this process.

•   A second grader is upset because one of her friends will not play with her or be her learning partner in class.
•   A sophomore did not get a scholarship to attend an academic camp and believes that she will never get into a good college because of this rejection.
•   A parent is concerned about her 17-year-old daughter who seems belligerent and will not listen to anything she has to say.

a. Discuss what it was like to role-play the counselor and some of the challenges in using this approach. What aspects of this theory seemed to facilitate the counseling relationship?
b. Discuss what it was like to role-play the counselees. What were some of the aspects of this counseling approach that assisted the counseling process? What aspects detracted from the counseling process?

_____

_____

Narrative Therapy

Michael White and David Epston are considered the primary contributors to narrative therapy (Archer & McCarthy, 2007). People tell stories about themselves that are reflective of how they perceive themselves and others. Narrative therapy involves a collaborative counselor–counselee relationship in which counselees are empowered to take an active role in changing their life stories. An individual's reality is constructed through the expectations and messages provided by society and influential individuals (e.g., teacher, parent, mentor) and personal beliefs about self. As a result, people live according to their life stories, which are based on past experiences and their perceptions of these life events (Seligman & Reichenberg, 2014), or *dominant plot*. A dominant plot refers to the counselee's interpretation of events and potential future possibilities (Archer & McCarthy, 2007).

Narrative therapy involves the counselor and counselee working collaboratively to: (a) co-construct the counselee's story; (b) deconstruct "impoverishing" life stories by externalizing problems as separate and apart from the individual; (c) identify unique outcomes or times when the counselee was able to separate him/herself from the influence of the problem; and (d) reconstruct a preferred, alternative story, thus enhancing coping and problem-solving skills, initiating goal setting, and improving self-image (White, 1993, 1995).

The counselor listens carefully to the stories to identify themes, the influence the stories have had on different aspects of the counselee's life, and *sparkling moments*, or the times in which the problem does not occur. A primary principle of narrative counseling is to communicate the idea that the *problem* is the problem; the *person* is not the problem. To promote this belief, the concept of *externalization*, or naming the problem, gives the student an opportunity to perceive the problem as something outside of him/herself. The counselor and counselee co-construct a 'counterplot' that challenges the existing dominant plot, while re-authoring new stories (Seligman & Reichenberg, 2014). Several techniques are used for re-authoring the story:

- Externalization: Process of separating people from their problems by emphasizing that the problem influences the person rather than the person being the problem.
- Relative Influence Question: Questions are used to "map" the influence of the problem on the student. Questions are asked about how the problem has influenced school, peers, family, and so on.
- Unique Outcomes: Also known as sparkling moments, these are used to emphasize exceptional conclusions, focus on the new life story without the problem, and ask how the unique outcomes can occur outside of the counseling office.

Narrative therapy may be implemented during individual or group counseling in school as well as clinical settings. Researchers have integrated the approach with creative counseling strategies such as play and art therapy, resulting in positive therapeutic gains (Carlson, 1997; Shovlin, 1999). Narrative therapy may also be applied in career counseling settings to address developmental tasks such as understanding self-identity, building autonomy, decision making, and goal setting (Thomas & Gibbons, 2009).

From a multicultural perspective, counselors are able to listen to students' stories through their cultural lens. Since the goal of narrative therapy is to bring awareness regarding the domineering cultural stereotypes, students may feel empowered to question these stories that were taken for granted.

Student Activity 3.5   A New Story of Me

Ask the student to tell you a story in which he/she has a problem in the area of school, friends, or family. While the story is being relayed, listen for "sparkling moments" that occur, successes or strengths that the student describes, and themes. Ask the student to describe the story in as much detail as possible. The following questions may facilitate preferred stories, or narratives that describe how the student would like life to be.

1. How is this a problem for you? (Is it evident in relationships, behaviors, feelings, or in other ways?)
2. How is it influencing your life? (Evaluate how it is influencing school, friends, work, activities, family, etc.)
3. When do you have control over the problem?
4. When is the problem easier to handle?
5. What strengths or skills do you have that can be used to solve the problem?
6. Describe how you can use these skills to conquer the problem.

Collaboratively, the counselor and student discuss meanings of the story and ways to deconstruct the stories to a new narrative that is problem free.

Conceptual Application Activity 3.5

With a partner, conduct a role-play of a counselor and counselee using a narrative approach. The following scenario may be used to assist with this activity:

JoAnna is very unhappy. No matter what she tries, nothing seems to turn out the way she would like. For instance, just this morning, she took a quiz in her algebra class, and even though she spent hours studying for it, she only got a C. Furthermore, her boyfriend recently broke up with her because she tended to "drag him down," according to JoAnna. She comes to see you because she doesn't feel as if she has many friends and is lonely.

Discuss what it was like to role-play the counselor and some of the challenges in using this approach. What aspects of this theory seemed to facilitate the counseling relationship?

Discuss what it was like to role-play JoAnna. What were some of the aspects of this counseling approach that assisted the counseling process? What aspects detracted from the counseling process?

CREATIVE COUNSELING APPROACHES

Creative counseling approaches, also known as expressive therapies, are therapeutic interventions in which the counselee uses creative energies to enhance self-awareness or self-expression. Three creative counseling approaches frequently employed in school counseling settings are art therapy, play therapy, and music therapy, which are used to enhance self-esteem, build self-concept, improve social interaction, and encourage multicultural awareness and acceptance among children from a variety of cultural backgrounds (D'Andrea & Daniels, 1995). Table 3.3 lists various types of creative counseling media.

Table 3.3 Media for Expressive Arts in Counseling

Art	Song	Images	Movement	Theater
Drawing	Songs with lyrics	Print	Bounce, skip sway	Family sculpting
Sketching	Music without lyrics	Digital	Drum circle	Role-playing
Painting	Beats	Video	Shadow movement	Puppet creation
Sculpting	Rhythms	Documentary	Body sculpting	Marionettes
Collages	Song creation	Real or created	Mind maps	Drama

Art in Counseling

For many years art has been used as an interpretative tool to better understand thoughts, memories, and feelings of individuals who may be unable or unwilling to express themselves verbally. Art is also used as a means of expressive communication with individuals who present emotional or behavioral difficulties. In this chapter, art therapy will be defined as a form of expressive communication in which the counselee expresses thoughts and feelings through the creation of art products using one or more media. Student-created art products have the potential of generating a less threatening mode of communication within the counselor–counselee relationship. Ethically, school counselors who do not have the education to use art therapy as a projective personality assessment are to refrain from interpreting materials without the appropriate supervision and training. However, art can be incorporated into counseling as a means to create a comfortable relationship, as a form of self-expression, and as a source of information.

Figure 3.1 Art in counseling provides a creative means for expressing oneself.

Source: Steve Martin Photography

Art therapy is easily integrated into the typical school counseling office through such media as multicolored paper, pencils, crayons, markers, paints, glue, magazine cutouts for a collage, modeling clay, pipe cleaners, and papier-mâché. If the school counselor is fortunate enough to have a private office and responsibilities in a single building, materials may be stored in cabinets or file drawers until ready for use. However, many school counselors are placed in more than one school, share an office with another educational professional, or travel from classroom to classroom. In these cases, a tote bag loaded with art supplies may be one solution, or requisitioning a cart with wheels to transport the materials may also be an answer.

Figure 3.2 Angry monster. Drawn by a third-grade boy who was discussing his anger issues with his school counselor.

During the initial stage of counseling, it is important to create an atmosphere of acceptance through nonthreatening, encouraging statements and to provide a choice of art activity. Art therapy, as a medium for self-expression and communication, is easily integrated into person-centered, cognitive behavioral, and solution-focused theoretical models.

Art therapy is suitable for counselees of all ages and areas of need, including developmental, academic, social, and emotional. The approach is considered suitable for children as well as resistant adolescents, who may be less cooperative with traditional "talk therapy" approaches. Art provides avenues for self-expression through the lowering of defenses by projecting images in drawings, paintings, and sculptures (Landreth, 2002) and enhances coping in times of stress and separation anxiety precipitated by illness or injury (Raghurman, 1999). In addition, the approach may be an effective treatment technique for homebound students upon their return to school following medical interventions that, at times, necessitate lengthy hospital stays, surgeries, and prolonged periods of discomfort. Finally, art therapy is also recommended as an intervention for children with special needs, such as autism, to enhance expressive communication (Emery, 2004).

Box 3.2   Questions to Ask About Artwork

When working with students regarding their artwork, the following questions can guide the discussion:

* What do you see (not what does it mean)?
* What is missing from the drawing?
* If you could go anywhere in that picture, where would you go?
* What title would you put on the picture?
* What feelings does this picture have?
* Can you relate this drawing to anything in your life?
* If you could change something about you, how would this picture be different?

Student Activity 3.6   Draw Your Feelings

Ask your student to explore a troubling time by expressing it through drawing. After the student has completed the drawing, explore the picture for deeper meaning and/or associations with other problematic areas in his/her life. Next, have the student draw a picture of what life would be like without the problem.

Conceptual Application Activity 3.6

Take a blank sheet of paper and colored markers. Think about your practicum or internship experience and draw your feelings that represent this experience. Let your mind wander while you think in terms of how you would like to represent your feelings and thoughts about this clinical experience. Do not evaluate your work and do not worry if you are unable to represent these feelings and thoughts accurately. After you are finished, put this picture away and then do this same activity at the end of your program. Compare the two pictures to see how your feelings and thoughts may have changed based on your artwork. Identify one way you might use a similar art activity with one of the students in your school.

Play in Counseling

Child-centered, nondirective play therapy is a popular treatment for children and adolescents in both school and clinical settings and is based on the claim that play is a child's primary method of communication and cognitive processing. The child processes experiences and communicates his/her perceptions of reality through the natural means of play. Play may be used to enhance the counselor–counselee relationship, foster a sense of security on the part of the student, and provide a comfortable method of expression without the stress of trying to communicate verbally (Landreth, 2002).

Box 3.3

The use of play therapy is congruent with the American School Counselor Association (ASCA) National Model. School counselors meet the needs of all students through responsive interventions and developmental programming. Expressive arts can be integrated with various theoretical models and infused across the delivery component (Trice-Black, Bailey, & Riechel, 2013).

Child-centered play therapy, based on person-centered principles, involves a complete and total acceptance of the child. The therapist does not overtly direct the play session by instructing the child as to what or how to play, but instead allows the child to lead the play process. The counselor uses verbal communication to reflect content and emotion following the child's actions or spoken words. A warm, permissive relationship is established between the counselor and counselee in order for the child to communicate what he or she may have been unable to communicate through spoken language. Play therapy incorporates a number of modalities, including representational play through the use of play objects, parallel play, interactive play between counselor and counselee (or among several children for social development), and expressive play through art making.

There are several counselor qualities and personality traits that may serve to enhance one's ability to successfully implement child-centered play therapy, which include: (a) unconditionally accepting the child counselee; (b) respecting the child as a person; (c) demonstrating sensitivity to the child's communication from both verbal and nonverbal perspectives; (d) being fully present and focused exclusively on the relationship with the child counselee at the time and moment of the therapy session; and (e) tolerating ambiguity (Landreth, 2002). In child-centered play therapy, the counselor is encouraged to allow the child counselee the option to change or not, which may create a potential challenge for many professionals, since one goal of counseling is to bring about a change. Providing the child the opportunity to decide whether to change his/her behavior builds a sense of personal accountability and decision making that may ultimately lead to change (Landreth, 2002).

Play therapy materials should include only toys or objects conducive to self-expression, as the child's expressive communication during play may be inhibited by automated toys or toys reflecting well-known figures or superheroes. A wide variety of materials facilitate personal expression, including toys for aggressive or violent expression such as punching bags, plastic knives, plastic hammers or mallets, blocks that may be thrown, and toy guns. Most authors agree that guns do not promote violence in the real life of the child counselee (Landreth, 2002; Trotter, Eshelman, & Landreth, 2001). However, when using aggressive types of toys, be sure to communicate the value of these toys with administrators who enforce zero-tolerance policies. A list of toys that may be included in initiating play in counseling is in Table 3.4.

The use of play is effective in individual as well as group counseling interventions among school-aged children. In addition, play may serve to bridge cultural differences that exist between counselor and counselee, enhance communication with culturally diverse students, relieve stress among students as they transition to new academic settings, and improve self-esteem, thus allowing students from backgrounds different than those dominantly reflected in the school environment to achieve academic gains (Baggerly & Parker, 2005).

Table 3.4 Toys for Play in Counseling

Nurturing	Expressive	Cultural considerations	Representations of nature	Toys that represent aggression
Stuffed animals	Pipe cleaners	Dolls with various skin tones	Shells	Representations of scary reptiles or animals
Dolls	Crayons	Utensils from other cultural groups	Rocks or stones	Toy guns
Families	Paints	Jewelry from other cultures	Leaves	Rubber knife
Furniture	Play-Doh	Artifacts from cultural groups	Sand	Aggressive hand puppets
Play dishes and utensils	Magazine pictures	Dolls representing ethnic groups	Twigs	Burglar mask
Nursing bottle, bib, diaper	Scissors and glue	Cultural toys	Flowers	Handcuffs

Student Activity 3.7   Expressing Self Through Games

Using Legos, blocks, or the *Jengo* game, the counselor and student take turns to make a tower. As each person places a block on the tower, a feeling statement is made. For instance, "I was upset when I got a D on my Language Arts quiz." Or, "I was frustrated when I wasn't able to understand the teacher's instructions." The game continues until the tower falls over.

Conceptual Application Activity 3.7

Observe a child playing. Make note of this child's developmental and chronological age. Note some of the actions exhibited by this child. Compare your observations with a partner's observations and notes. Discuss how you might use play in a counseling session with one of your students.

_____

_____

Music in a Counseling Setting

Music has been referred to as "truly the universal language" (Vines, 2004, p. 12) and is capable of producing a wide range of mental, emotional, physical, and/or spiritual responses (Gladding, 2010). Children are naturally active, and music provides an outlet for expressing themselves intuitively. However, outside of recess or physical education classes, the educational setting does not always welcome this means as a learning strategy.

Although school counselors do not conduct music therapy without obtaining proper certification or licensure, the use of music in large group classroom and small group counseling programs facilitates personal awareness, self-expression, and social interaction. Music provides a means for listening and sharing feelings and thoughts about the music, in the form of writing lyrics, playing an instrument, or singing. Music and song may be incorporated into elementary school counseling activities to enhance attentiveness, strengthen the social bond between the counselor and a group of children, and serve as a teaching aid to enhance coping during difficult life transitions such as parental divorce and relocation (Haigh, 2005). At the middle and high school levels, music may

Figure 3.3 Some states credential school counselors to work with pre-K students. A variety of creative strategies are used to engage these young children.

also be employed during classroom and group counseling programs to build rapport between the school counselor and student counselees.

Classroom lessons and group sessions centered on popular, classroom-appropriate song lyrics may stimulate self-expression among adolescent students and lead to class discussions on pertinent issues such as academic achievement, respect for diversity, and career opportunities (Veach & Gladding, 2007; Vines, 2005). Music has also been effective in treating conditions such as attention-deficit hyperactivity disorder (ADHD), depression, low self-esteem, posttraumatic stress disorder (PTSD), and mentally or physically disabling conditions (Emery, 2004; Jackson, 2003; Kennedy, 2008).

Figure 3.4 Music in counseling may be utilized to create music, sing, move, and listen. It is also a therapeutic means for facilitating communication without the use of words.

Source: Steve Martin Photography

Student Activity 3.8   Expressing Myself Through Music

Have students bring in a piece of music that "speaks to them." Play the music in a counseling group or in a group lesson. Ask students to listen to excerpts of the music and discuss the meaning behind the lyrics. If the music is instrumental with no lyrics, ask students what the music represents to them.

Conceptual Application Activity 3.8

Bring in music that has special meaning for you. Play the music in class and talk about the reason that the music you brought to class is meaningful to you. Describe how this music or song selection relates to your school counselor-in-training experience. How might you use a similar activity with students in your school?

_____

_____

Box 3.4   Additional Expressive Arts Techniques

Additional examples of using expressive arts in counseling include:

Drama—Create the family with handmade puppets and then act out a scene or issue that the student is uneasy with.
Words—Take a meaningful quote and rewrite it or write a short story and its personal meaning in the student's life.
Photography—Over a week's time, ask the student to take digital snapshots of his/her environment, items of importance to the student. Bring into session to discuss.
Movement—Ask your student to show you how he/she feels with movement instead of words.

CONCLUSION

School counselors, faced with overwhelming responsibilities and demands, rarely have the luxury of 50-minute sessions considered routine by professionals in community and private settings. In addition, student counselees are often resistant to counseling because they are generally referred by parents or teachers rather than through self-referrals. In view of such conditions, the need arises for counseling methods that are both time effective and effectual with school-aged youth. This chapter includes a brief overview of several counseling theories frequently employed in school settings which are generally time limited, collaborative, empowering, and lead to enhanced academic achievement and improved learning outcomes. Furthermore, creative, expressive counseling techniques such as art, play, and music are discussed in this chapter, and incorporated with students of all ages. School counselors are encouraged to develop an in-depth knowledge base of different counseling approaches and to select ideologies that appeal to themselves as practitioners within the schools and address the developmental and emotional needs of their counselees.

WEBSITES

Person-Centered Counseling

- This link will take you to a short explanation of person-centered counseling described by Carl Rogers: www.youtube.com/watch?v=ZBkUqcqRChg

Reality Therapy

- A brief description of reality therapy is provided at this website: http://reality.therapyhub.com/

- This link will take you to a YouTube depiction of reality therapy with an angry parent: www.youtube.com/watch?v=0_3oeqyrmoE

Cognitive Behavioral Approaches

- This link will connect you to the REBT network: http://wglasser.com/the-glasser-approach/reality-therapy
- This link will connect you to a YouTube description of REBT by Dr. Albert Ellis: www.youtube.com/watch?v=odnoF8V3g6g

Solution-Focused Brief Therapy

- This link will take you to the Institute for Solution-Focused Therapy: www.solutionfocused.net/solutionfocusedtherapy.html
- This link will take you to a video titled *A Brief History of the Solution-Focused Approach* and the individuals who shaped this approach: www.youtube.com/watch?v=J0hcpLKVp7o&%20feature=related

Narrative Therapy

- This link will take you to a site with resources on narrative therapy: www.goodtherapy.org/Narrative_Therapy.html
- The following is a YouTube interview on using narrative therapy with children: www.youtube.com/watch?v=XMst5HoOS6c

Using Art in Counseling

- This link will take you to art therapy activities that you can adapt with the school-aged youth that you are counseling: www.arttherapyblog.com/c/art-therapy-activities/#.U3UptS-F2vl
- This link will take you to a page that explains art therapy and provides numerous activities that you can use in individual or group counseling: www.vickyb.demon.co.uk/

Play Therapy

- This link will take you to the homepage of the Association for Play Therapy. An overview of play therapy, a shot media presentation describing play therapy, and links to play therapy organizations are found on this site: www.a4pt.org/ps.playtherapy.cfm
- This link will take you to a journal article that describes 15 effective play therapy techniques that you could adapt and implement with students in your setting: http://pegasus.cc.ucf.edu/~drbryce/Play%20Therapy%20Techniques.pdf

Music Therapy

- This website from the American Music Therapy Association provides answers to frequently asked questions about music therapy: www.musictherapy.org/faq/

REFERENCES

Archer, J., & McCarthy, C. J. (2007). *Theories of counseling and psychotherapy: Contemporary applications.* Upper Saddle River, NJ: Pearson.

Baggerly, J., & Parker, M. (2005). Child-centered group play therapy with African American boys at the elementary school level. *Journal of Counseling and Development, 83,* 387–396.

Carlson, T. D. (1997). Using art in narrative therapy: Enhancing therapeutic possibilities. *American Journal of Family Therapy, 25,* 271–283.

Carlson, L. A., & Kees, N. L. (2013). Mental health services in public schools: A preliminary study of school counselor perceptions. *Professional School Counseling, 16,* 211–221. doi: 10.5330/PSC.n.2013–16.221

Corey, G. (2009). *Theory and practice of counseling and psychotherapy* (8th ed.). Belmont, CA: Thomson Higher Education.

Corey, G. (2012). *Theory and practice of group counseling* (8th ed.). Belmont, CA: Thomson Higher Education.

Corsini, R. J., & Wedding, D. (2005). *Current psychotherapies* (7th ed.). Belmont, CA: Brooks/Cole.

D'Andrea, M., & Daniels, J. (1995). Helping students learn to get along: Assessing the effectiveness of a multicultural developmental guidance project. *Elementary School Guidance and Counseling, 30,* 144–153.

deShazer, S. (1985). *Keys to solutions in brief therapy.* New York: Norton.

Ellis, A. (2004a). *Rational emotive behavior therapy: It works for me—It can work for you.* Amherst, NY: Prometheus.

Ellis, A. (2004b). *The road to tolerance: The philosophy of rational emotive behavior therapy.* Amherst, NY: Prometheus.

Emery, M. J. (2004). Art therapy as an intervention for autism. *Art Therapy: Journal of the American Art Therapy Association, 21,* 143–147.

Frey, A. J., Cloud, R. N., Lee, J., Small, J. W., Seeley, J. R., Feil, E. G., Walker, H. M., & Golly, A. (2011). The promise of motivational interviewing in school mental health. *School Mental Health, 3,* 1–12. doi 10.1007/s12310–010–9048

Gladding, S. (2010). *The creative arts in counseling* (4th ed.). Alexandria, VA: American Counseling Association.

Guterman, J. T. (2013). *Mastering the art of solution-focused counseling* (2nd ed.). Alexandria, VA: American Counseling Association.

Hackney, H. L., & Cormier, S. (2009). *The professional counselor.* Upper Saddle River, NJ: Pearson Education.

Haigh, G. (2005, April). Finding a voice. *The Times Educational Supplement,* 15–18.

Jackson, N. A. (2003). A survey of music therapy methods and their role in the treatment of early elementary school children with ADHD. *Journal of Music Therapy, 40,* 302–323.

Kennedy, A. (2008). Creating connection, crafting wellness. *Counseling Today, 5,* 34–38.

Landreth, G. (2002). *Play therapy: The art of the relationship.* New York: Brunner-Routledge.

Raghurman, R. S. (1999). Battling separation anxiety. *American Journal of Art Therapy, 37,* 120–129.

Seligman, L., & Reichenberg, L. W. (2014). *Theories of counseling and psychotherapy* (4th ed.). Upper Saddle River, NJ: Pearson

Shahid, A. (2011, May). *'Don't say gay' bill passes Tennessee senate, would ban teachers from discussing homosexuality.* Retrieved from www.nydailynews.com/news/national/don-gay-bill-passes-tennessee-senate-ban-teachers-discussing-homosexuality-article-1.145355

Sharf, R. (2008). *Theories of psychotherapy and counseling: Concepts and cases* (4th ed.). Belmont, CA: Thomson Higher Education.

Sheldon, L. A. (2010, Fall). Using motivational interviewing to help your students. *Thought & Action,* 153–158.

Shovlin, K. J. (1999). Discovering a narrative voice through play and art therapy: A case study. *Guidance and Counseling, 14,* 7–12.

Thomas, D. A., & Gibbons, M. M. (2009). Narrative theory: A career counseling approach for adolescents of divorce. *Professional School Counseling, 12,* 223–229.

Trice-Black, S., Bailey, C. L., & Riechel, M. E. K. (2013). Play therapy in school counseling. *Professional School Counseling, 16,* 303–312. doi: 10.5330/PSC.n.2013–16.303

Trotter, K., Eshelman, D., & Landreth, G. (2001). A place for Bobo in play therapy. *International Journal of Play Therapy, 12,* 117–139.

Veach, L. J., & Gladding, S. (2007). Using creative group techniques in high schools. *Journal for Specialists in Group Work, 32,* 71–81.

Vines, G. (2004). Turn on the music. *ASCA School Counselor, 41,* 10–13.

Vines, G. (2005). Middle school counseling: Touching the souls of adolescents. *Professional School Counseling, 9,* 175–176.

White, M. (1993). Deconstruction and therapy. In S. Gilligan & R. Price (Eds.), *Therapeutic conversations* (pp. 23–51). New York: Norton.

White, M. (1995). *Re-authoring lives: Interviews and essays.* Adelaide, South Australia: Dulwich Center.

Wubbolding, R. E. (2004). Professional school counselors and reality therapy. In B. Erford (Ed.), *Professional school counseling: A handbook of theories, programs, and practices* (pp. 211–218). Austin, TX: CAPS Press.

4 An Overview of Supervisory Practices for School Counselors-in-Training

Jeannine R. Studer

CACREP Standards

Common Core

Professional Orientation and Ethical Practice

e. Counseling supervision models, practices, and processes.

The purpose of this chapter is to:

- assess personal readiness for supervision,
- assist in setting supervision goals,
- provide strategies for personal wellness,
- discuss technology in counseling and supervision.

INTRODUCTION

Supervision is considered a vital key to successful practicum and internship experiences and provides an opportunity for the school counselor-in-training to connect counseling skills learned in the classroom to authentically address K–12 student needs (Swank & Tyson, 2012). Furthermore, school counselors-in-training state that their clinical experiences are the most influential and beneficial aspect of their academic training. Therefore, practicum and internship supervision conducted by a professional school counselor who has had training in supervision and experience as a school counselor is critically important. As mentioned in Chapter 1, you may have the opportunity to choose your own supervisor, or the program placement coordinator may select a site supervisor for you. This placement will be based on the coordinator's knowledge of the school site counseling program, the supervisor's ability to supervise, philosophy of school counseling, and willingness to meet with you on a regular basis. In either case, you need to discuss your personal and professional goals with your placement coordinator to address any needs you may have. For example, I have had several students who had transportation difficulties, and finding a quality school site in which this trainee was able to obtain public transportation to a school helped address her needs. Once a supervisor is identified, meeting with this individual and learning about the school is an essential first step. The information and activities in this chapter are designed to assist you in thinking about the process of supervision under the watchful eyes of an experienced professional. Making an initial contact with your supervisor, appropriate dress, understanding school policies and procedures, and methods for introducing yourself to the individuals with whom you will work are included in this chapter.

Making the Initial Contact

Remember that you are a guest in the school. Once you have been assigned to a supervisor, making a contact is an essential first step. This contact can be conducted through a phone call or email with the supervisor, and because it makes a lasting impression, you want it to be a good one. If you make a phone call, be certain that you speak slowly and clearly. There is nothing more frustrating than receiving contact information that is given so quickly that the message needs to be replayed several times before accurate information can be understood. Keep in mind that many school counselors are difficult to reach due to their varied schedule and the number of schools to which many are assigned. Therefore, sending a clear, well-crafted, and error-free email may be a better option (refer to Figure 4.1). When you have scheduled an appointment time, be sure to dress professionally and arrive on time. Be aware that with school safety policies in place, many schools have only one entrance, which is often locked. Entry is often gained after ringing a bell and speaking into an intercom to announce the purpose of your visit. Once you gain entry, reporting to the main office, signing in, and receiving a name badge are common procedures. In addition, stopping by the main office once you have completed your visit to sign out is also common procedure.

Dress

The school is a professional setting and the attire you are accustomed to wearing in the classroom as a graduate student may not be acceptable in a pre-K–12 school environment. If you are unsure how to dress, it is better to dress up rather than face embarrassment if you are sent home to change clothes due to your inappropriate attire. Unfortunately, I am aware of incidents when my supervisees who were inappropriately dressed in revealing clothing were sent home by the school principal to change into more modest and professional attire. A nonprofessional look may include such things as visible tattoos and body piercings, open-toed sandals, flip-flops, shorts, jeans, revealing blouses, T-shirts, shirts with slogans, and short skirts. In fact, one principal told a trainee that he was expected to cover up all of his tattoos if he wanted to work in the school. Workplace dress and hygiene policies have been established to promote a productive work environment and enhance the institutional image (Brannen, 2014). (You are an adult role model to pre-K–12 students, and your appearance and behavior influence the lives of school-aged youth more than you may realize.)

Subject: Practicum/Internship Meeting:

Dear (Ms./Mrs./Mr./Dr. Last Name of Supervisor):

I am writing to schedule an appointment with you to discuss and plan my practicum (or internship) experience with you this coming semester at (name of school). I am a master's degree school counseling student enrolled at (name of school/institution). My faculty supervisor's contact information is

Name
Title
Telephone numbers
Email

I am available to meet you at your school, in your office at the following dates and times: (Provide at least three different dates and times).

I will bring my resume, proof of liability insurance, my professional disclosure statement, and the program practicum/internship handbook for your records. Please contact me if there is anything else I should bring to our initial meeting. I look forward to meeting you and conducting my practicum (or internship) under your direct supervision.

Sincerely,

(Your full name)
(Phone number and email)

Figure 4.1 Sample initial letter to site supervisor.

Each practicum and internship school is unique, and the dress code reflects the mission of each school. Some schools have a uniform policy and educational personnel are required to dress according to this procedure. Discuss the dress requirements with your site supervisor during your initial meeting.

Absences, Tardiness, and Attendance

Even though you are not being paid during your practicum and internship, you still need to act as if you were an employee of the school. When you leave the confines of the academic institution and enter the school setting, you are in direct contact with your future colleagues and potential employers. In fact, you may desire a job in the school in which you conduct your practicum or internship experience.

Ask your supervisor the procedures for reporting absences or tardiness. Anytime you suspect that you may be tardy or absent, immediately contact your site supervisor and inform him or her of your circumstances (this is especially easy if you have entered your supervisor's telephone number on your cell phone). However, occasionally mishaps occur. When you communicate with your site supervisor, do not make excuses. Briefly inform him or her of the facts, own your responsibility in causing the tardiness or absenteeism, state that it will not happen again, and move on.

Attendance is another professional responsibility. Keep in mind that the school calendar is often different than the academic calendar where you are enrolled as a school counseling student. For liability reasons many programs are reluctant to allow their students to start or end their clinical experiences in a K–12 school building when their own training institution is not in session. Other programs recognize the importance of being in the school when the school year begins or ends, and as a result allow supervisees to observe in their assigned school and accumulate indirect hours until their university/college program begins. Check with your faculty supervisor as to when you are able to begin this experience.

School Policies and Procedures

Before beginning your practicum or internship, familiarize yourself with the school policies and procedures. Ask for a faculty handbook that outlines such things as the dress code, schedule, the policy for excusing students from class, the academic calendar, grading policy, and a listing of the resources and personnel in the school. In addition, some schools also require personnel to wear identification in the form of a lanyard. Check with your site supervisor to see whether this is something that you will need and how to obtain one. In addition, most school systems are requiring individuals to have a background check and drug screen tests before they are able to enter the schools. Verify whether you will need to have these tests. Furthermore, with increased pressure for students to demonstrate academic achievement, and educators held accountable for their growth, teachers are often reluctant to dismiss students from their classes to meet with you. To create and maintain a positive working relationship with each teacher, be sure to confirm the best times to release students, the procedures for excusing them, and the policy for returning students to class. Also, communicate to the teacher and students that missing classroom time to meet with you does not excuse the student from missed work or information.

Introducing Yourself to the Students, Staff, and Parents

The various stakeholders with whom you will be working are often hesitant to release a child or adolescent to someone who is unknown to them. Arrange for a time to meet and introduce yourself to each of these constituents. Faculty meetings provide an opportune time to meet with the faculty and staff and provide your credentials and information about yourself and how you may be reached. In addition, Parent Teacher Association (PTA) meetings are an excellent opportunity to introduce yourself to parents/guardians. Bringing a professional disclosure statement to be distributed to faculty and parents/guardians is one strategy for them to know you better. This document includes such things as a description of the clinical course in which you are enrolled, education, experiences related to counseling, names of supervisors (both site and program), professional membership, nature of counseling or philosophy, and a statement regarding confidentiality. An example is in Figure 4.2.

Erin Keller
1234 Therapy Avenue
City, State Zip
Telephone Numbers
E-mail Address

Education
The University of the Career Opportunities
M.A. in school counseling—anticipated graduation 2016
The University of Apollo
B.A. Psychology 2012

Clinical Experiences
Transformational Elementary School—Practicum
Supervisor—Mrs. Ellen Salganger (contact information)
Motivational Middle School—Internship
Supervisor—Mr. Bradley Opinder (contact information)

Work Experience
Camp Counselor at Camp Shisewana, KY Summer 2009–2012
Waitress Kasorius Restaurant 2008–2010

Philosophy of Counseling
I use a solution-focused approach to counseling that is strength based, in which I believe that all individuals have assets and have the ability to set goals and reach them. In addition, I believe that school counselors support academic learning, and I work within the school system to enhance academic, career, and social/emotional issues.

Professional Memberships
Member of the American School Counselor Association (ASCA)
Member of the state school counseling association
Member of the state division counseling association

Professional Code of Ethics
I abide by the American School Counselor Association and the American Counseling Association Code of Ethics.

Confidentiality is a cornerstone of the school counseling profession. The information students share with me will be held in confidence except for the following reasons: my supervisor needs to be aware of the nature of the issue to provide the best care to the student; the student requests, in writing, that I share the information with a specified person; the student shares information that implies s/he could harm her/himself, or someone else putting someone in imminent danger. In these situations a caregiver has a legal right to this information.

Contact Information
I will be available to conduct my internship on the school campus on Mondays, Wednesdays, and Fridays from 8:00 a.m. to 3:30 p.m. throughout the semester.

Signature_____   Date_____

Figure 4.2 Critical components of a professional disclosure statement.

Conceptual Application Activity 4.1

Develop your professional disclosure statement by following the sample below:

1. Name and contact information _____

2. Education and training _____

3. Work experiences _____

4. Names of supervisors _____

5. Nature of counseling/philosophy _____

6. Professional memberships _____

7. Professional code of ethics _____

8. Hours and days available _____

You will also need a plan for meeting with students to introduce yourself, your role in the school, and how you can be contacted. When students know who you are, they are more willing to work with you. Your site supervisors can help make arrangements for you to meet students, which may include arranging a time with the teachers to enter the classroom to introduce yourself. The introduction needs to be based on the age of the students and their level of understanding. For younger students, simple terminology and creativity helps to keep their attention and assists in helping them remember you and your role. For example, one of my internship students with the last name of Womack taught her elementary school students to picture a horse by the name of Mac and to visualize saying, "Whoa, Mac" as they pantomimed pulling on the reins of the horse. Several other strategies include:

1. Stand in the hallways when students are changing classes and introduce yourself as they pass by in the halls. Shake their hands and tell them who you are and how they can contact you.
2. Post a brightly colored paper with your photograph explaining who you are, days and times you are available, where you are located, and how you can be contacted.
3. Make up business cards so that older students or adults can put them in their wallets or purses. Include your name, contact information, and where you can be reached. The website www.youprint.com/allows you to create your own customized business cards.
4. Attend extracurricular activities. Students appreciate your attendance and you will have an opportunity to understand different aspects of the school environment.
5. Eat lunch in the cafeteria and sit with groups of students to learn names and interests and to provide an opportunity for the students to get to know you.
6. Post your information on the school website.
7. For younger students, design a crossword puzzle that includes keywords such as your name, what you do, where you can be reached, and so forth. There are several online resources available for quickly and easily creating crossword puzzles. You simply need to identify key words and then a clue for each word. Computer programs can automatically create a crossword puzzle from these key words and clues. A few websites that help create crossword puzzles include:
    www.crosswordpuzzlegames.com/create.html www.armoredpenguin.com/crossword/
    www.eclipsecrossword.com/

Conceptual Application Activity 4.2

With your peers, brainstorm other ways that you could introduce yourself to parents, students, and teachers.

_____

_____

Self-reflection of Readiness for Supervision

The purpose of practicum and internship is to build your school counseling knowledge, skills, and values through application of theory in a real work setting. Too often, school counselors-in-training look at these experiences as "something that has to be done to fulfill the degree requirements." If this last statement reflects your thinking, you may need to reconsider your decision to enter the school counseling profession, because this profession requires passion with the potential to positively impact the lives of numerous children. Clinical experiences are designed to help you become an excellent school counselor, and it is up to you to use these opportunities to help yourself grow personally and professionally.

Research indicates factors such as the counselor's age, gender, education, and personality influence the counseling process (Reupert, 2006). Although these elements are important, it is the relationship between the counselor and counselee that is considered the most essential factor (Reupert, 2006) impacting counselee growth. This leads to the question, "What are other factors that promote an effective counseling session?" And, "What are the qualities that are essential to be an effective counselor?" As stated by Jeffrey Kottler, "The process is far too mysterious and complex to ever get a handle on all the nuances of [counseling]" (Shallcross, 2012). Several expert counselors provide their view of effective counselors and counseling, with responses including:

Understanding	Genuineness	Trustworthiness
Committed	Risk-taking	Tolerance
Flexibility	Unbiased	Congruence
Empathy	Authentic	Unconditional regard
Advocacy	Courage	Authenticity
Ability to listen	Compassion	Interpersonal skills
Patience	Creativity	Humility
Self-awareness	Sense of humor	Trust
Empathy	Willingness to learn	Compassion
Rapport	Insight	Respectful
Nonverbal skills	Trust	Collaborative
Nonverbal	Competence	Commitment
Encouragement	Appropriate	Self-confidence
Self-honesty	Motivated	Consistent
Forgiveness	Perception	

Conceptual Application Activity 4.3

Are there additional personal qualities an effective counselor should have other than those above? Write your responses below.

_____   _____   _____

_____   _____   _____

_____   _____   _____

Now, compare your list with those of your peers. What are some of the similarities? Differences?

_____

_____

Conceptual Application Activity 4.4

Counseling experts identified qualities that they believe are essential for effective counselors. These characteristics are listed below. Circle those you believe define who you are. When you are finished, give this list to someone who knows you well and ask that person to circle those qualities that they believe apply to you.

Understanding	Genuineness	Tolerance
Committed	Risk-taking	Congruence
Flexibility	Unbiased	Unconditional regard
Empathy	Authentic	Authenticity
Advocacy	Courage	Interpersonal skills
Ability to listen	Compassion	Humility
Patience	Creativity	Trust
Self-awareness	Sense of humor	Compassion
Empathy	Willingness to learn	Respectful
Rapport	Insight	Collaborative
Nonverbal skills	Trust	Commitment
Nonverbal	Competence	Self-confidence
Encouragement	Appropriate	Motivated
Self-honesty	Perception	Consistent
Forgiveness	Trustworthiness	

Now, compare your list with the list provided by your significant other person and discuss the similarities and differences between the two lists. If there are discrepancies between your view of self and the perceptions of that other person, discuss the different perceptions. Recognizing your strengths and areas in which you need to improve gives you an opportunity to identify personal goals for your practicum and internship experiences. Include these goals on your practicum and/ or internship contract and strategies to reach these objectives.

Goal Setting

When you have a good understanding of the practicum and internship experiences, you are less likely to be disappointed. Likewise, the supervisor also needs a thorough understanding of the clinical experience and his or her role in supervision. Not everyone enters the clinical experiences with the same training or education. For instance, those with a background in education usually have a better knowledge of such things as the school structure, policies, educational terminology, and classroom management. Those who have a human services background may have a better understanding of the counseling process and application of theories and techniques.

After you have thought about your strengths and areas in which you need more experience, gather ideas from the counselors at your school site to determine specific projects you could accomplish to meet your goals as well as those that would address curricular school needs. Some

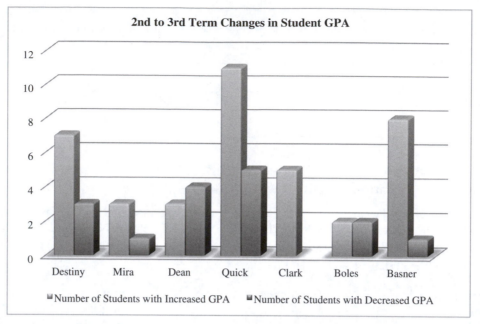

Figure 4.3 An example of a chart that represents student growth as a result of a group intervention based on classrooms of students.

examples include updating and formalizing the school critical incident management plan, creating a resource appendix for college scholarships, collecting community agency information for referral purposes, and implementing a group for students from divorced parental homes. A contract that outlines the expectations for the supervisory relationship and the activities you are to perform is essential. The contract, then, serves as a type of "job description" that outlines what you are going to do.

The American School Counselor Association (ASCA) promotes a comprehensive, developmental school counseling (CDSC) program. The ASCA Student Standards (renamed the Mindsets and Behaviors for Student Success) outline the knowledge and skills that pre-K–12 students are to know and do in the academic, career, and personal/social domains (renamed social/emotional). The standards serve as a foundation for the ASCA National Model that was developed as a prototype for school counselors to use when developing their own program (ASCA, 2012). However, many school counseling programs have not yet made the transformation to a comprehensive and developmental program. Even if you are assigned to a school with a traditional school counseling program, many activities that the counselor/supervisor performs are still reflective of those in the ASCA National Model. It is up to you to identify the activities that support a CDSC program during your clinical experiences to be prepared to take a leadership role in developing such a program when you transition into a position as a school counselor.

The following story illustrates one example of how a school counseling intern contributed to the school through a public relations activity that is a component of the management element of the ASCA National Model.

Elsa was in her internship experience at an inner-city middle school in which approximately 58% of the students were on free and reduced lunch. There was a strong need to assist students with academics, and Elsa decided that she would conduct a weekly study skills group for seventh and eighth graders for the semester that she was in her school site. Figure 4.3 illustrates the gains several of the students made in their GPA from the beginning of the semester until the completion of the group. Elsa's concrete documentation revealed to teachers that she was a contributing member of the school, and they asked her site supervisor to have future interns continue this project.

An example of personal and professional goals that are included on an internship contract based on the ASCA model is in Figure 4.4.

The school counseling faculty promotes a developmental, comprehensive school counseling program, and requests that the activities provided to the school counselor intern correspond with this model. The ASCA Student Standards (renamed Mindsets and Behaviors for Student Success) were developed for pre-K–12 students, and school counselors perform activities that meet those standards that correspond with the standards identified within the school curriculum. The intern is expected to perform identified activities to learn about his/her role in a comprehensive school counseling program, which are to be included in his/her contract. Examples are below.

Sample Goals

Professional Goal	Performance Activities	Evaluation	ASCA Program Component/Theme
The intern will develop, distribute, and analyze a needs assessment	1. Design a needs assessment for 7th-grade students 2. Administer the needs assessment 3. Analyze and graph results	Feedback from site supervisor	Management

Professional Goal	Performance Activities	Evaluation	ASCA Program Component/Theme
The intern will self-reflect on multicultural competencies	1. Read *Multicultural Issues in Counseling** 2. *Use AMCD Multicultural Counseling Competencies* as a self-analysis	Feedback from supervisor Use competencies as a checklist of areas to strengthen	Advocacy

* Lee, C. C. (2013). *Multicultural issues in counseling: New approaches to diversity* (4th ed.). Alexandria, VA: ACA.

Figure 4.4 Sample internship contract.

Conceptual Application Activity 4.5

Review the ASCA National Model in Chapter 6, Figure 6.1. In consultation with the program supervisor and your on-site school counseling supervisor, identify professional and personal goals that you wish to accomplish during your practicum and internship experiences. When you think about the activities to include on your contract, be sure they are supported in a CDSC program.

   Supervisory Contract (to be completed by intern with assistance from supervisors)

Professional Goal	Performance Activities	Evaluation	ASCA Program Component/Theme

Personal Goal	Performance Activities	Evaluation	ASCA Program Component/Theme

The ASCA National Model Components and Themes include:

Themes	**Management**	**Foundation**
Systemic change	Assessments	Program focus
Collaboration	Tools	Student competencies
Advocacy		Professional competencies
Leadership		

Accountability	**Delivery**
Data analysis	Direct student services
Program results	Indirect student services
Evaluation and improvement	

Box 4.1

Practicing school counselor supervisors were surveyed to investigate the factors that exemplify effective supervision. Seven themes emerged from their responses. Good school counseling supervision (1) facilitates the intern's professional growth and development; (2) enables a collaborative relationship between the supervisor, intern, and stakeholders; (3) establishes a learning environment that is flexible and well defined; (4) provides opportunities based on the intern's developmental level; (5) is based on the supervisor serving as a consultant, teacher, and counselor; (6) is provided by a self-aware, reflective supervisor; and (7) provides opportunities to gain a school counselor identity (Ladbury, 2012).

A personal safety plan is another preparation strategy. You may be placed in a school setting that is located in what is regarded as a high-crime area, but regardless of where your school site is located, a personal safety plan is an important consideration. Ask your supervisor to share the school crisis plan with you, and ask him/her to assist you in creating your own plan.

Personal Safety Plan

No one enters the school counseling profession thinking in terms of school violence, but the reality is that violence is very real in schools today. Some school-aged youth could pose a threat to your safety as well as others'. I once had a graduate student in our school counseling program who grew up in a small, upper-middle-class suburban area of Ohio that was characterized as fairly homogeneous and "safe." He attended a small liberal arts college with a student body similar to that of his high school. When he found out he was placed in an urban high school for his practicum, he was concerned about his safety and immediately sought out the program placement coordinator to request a different setting. He was instructed to talk with his site supervisor about the school safety plan and to ask for assistance in making up his own personal safety plan. Reluctantly, he agreed to do this. After only one week, he began to speak enthusiastically about his practicum school and relayed how much he was learning from this unique experience. Eventually, he actually thanked his placement coordinator for not transferring him to a different site, and after graduation he secured a position as a school counselor in an urban middle school. No school is exempt from school violence, and personal well-being is of utmost importance.

Most schools have adopted a policy that specifies procedures for alerting teachers and faculty when an emergency occurs. This plan outlines the action each person is to take, including the school counselor's crisis management responsibilities. Every person who works in the school should know how to implement the plan, and you are no exception. In fact, it is possible that you will be a key player in crisis intervention if a crisis plan needs to be activated. Consider the following:

- When you are working with a student who is angry, keep the office door open and ask your supervisor to sit in on the session.
- If your supervisor is not available, it may be best to speak with an angry student in the hall or waiting area if there is one available.
- Look for signs of mounting tension, irritability, and so forth. When potential violence is evident, ask the student to discuss his or her feelings because verbalizations are better than violently acting out emotions.
- Speak in a calm, quiet voice to calm the student.
- Park in a well-lighted area in the parking lot.
- Leave the school building with another person.
- Leave expensive jewelry and clothing at home.

Conceptual Application Activity 4.6

Read the school safety plan at your clinical site and compare this plan with those of your peers. Develop your own safety plan.

Wellness as an Integral Component of the Profession

Wellness is a foundation of the counseling profession. Helping students become healthy entails an integration of mind, body, and spirit (Meyers, 2014), yet it also requires us to be take care of ourselves if we are going to be effective as helpers. A study by Lawson and Myers (2011) examined levels of wellness among counselors who were members of ACA who reported activities that helped them sustain personal wellness. Wellness activities included:

- Spending time with partner/family
- Maintaining a sense of humor
- Maintaining a balance between professional and personal lives
- Maintaining self-awareness
- Reflecting on positive experiences
- Engaging in quiet leisure activities.

Conceptual Application Activity 4.7

List five stressful situations you have encountered in the past year. Now list specific ways you attempted to manage each stressful situation.

Situation

_____

_____

_____

_____

Stress Management Strategies

_____

_____

_____

_____

Put a plus (+) in front of the strategies that are positive or healthy and bring about constructive results. Put a minus (−) next to those strategies that are negative or bring about unhelpful consequences. How successful are the strategies you use? If you note a number of unhelpful strategies, it is time to try some new ways of managing your stress. Be sure to share your list with your peers and listen carefully as they share their strategies that help them handle difficult situations.

Self-care

Listening to students' stories of pain from deleterious life experiences can eventually negatively impair the ability of school counselors to provide effective care to others and to themselves (Ray, Wong, White, & Heaslip (2013). Consequently, counselors need to be "resilient and thus more well" (Lawson & Myers, 2011). Compassion fatigue (CF) may result when a caregiver is preoccupied with distressed students and experiences stress and tension (Ray et al., 2013) due to a connection with the counselee's trauma. Although CF is similar to burnout, CF is related to the student's trauma, whereas burnout, considered as a risk factor for developing CF, is related to the work environment. CF leads to a sense of helplessness, isolation from others who could serve as measures of support, and an inability to empathize with others (Injeyan et al., 2011). School counselors report not enough time to see students, a large amount of paperwork, professional job overload, job responsibilities unrelated to their training, an unmanageable case load, role ambiguity, and counseling a child in which there is a suspicion of abuse or suicide. In addition, when administrators have difficulty making crucial decisions that contribute to poor relationships with teachers and administrators, burnout may result (Wilkerson & Bellini, 2006).

In a study of secondary school counselors, participants reported difficulty in separating personal from professional life, difficulty sleeping, recurring dreams about work, headaches, weight gain, and fatigue—all indicators of burnout (Wall, 2004). Increased levels of stress impact physical, emotional, and intellectual difficulties that may result in poor performance and negative feelings among school personnel (Wilkerson & Bellini, 2006). Some of the warning signs of CF or burnout include:

- Isolating self from family and friends
- Difficulty in being emotionally engaged in relationships
- Increased absenteeism
- Decreased empathy and social skills
- Increased self-obsession
- Rejecting professional responsibilities to others (Williams, 2007)

In your internship you will be performing many school counselor activities and, as in starting a new job, this requires learning and experiencing various responsibilities in short periods of time. On top of these stressors, many supervisees continue to take additional classes while in their clinical courses and some even choose to be employed. This makes for a full and demanding schedule. Furthermore, there is the added responsibility of forming new relationships with those at the school, and with parents and community members. Taking care of yourself is vital, and time to ensure physical, emotional, and psychological health is important or your performance could be negatively impaired. The following suggestions are provided to assist in alleviating burnout and compassion fatigue (Paine, 2009):

- Know what you are able to handle.
- Recognize triggers to stress.
- Recognize your own experiences with trauma and how it could interfere with your effectiveness.
- Recognize your physiological symptoms of stress.

- Connect with supportive family and friends.
- Eat healthy foods.
- Try to get restful sleep without the use of sleep aids.
- Maintain your regular routine as much as possible.
- Ask for assistance from others.
- Practice the following:
  - o Meditation
  - o Mindfulness techniques
  - o Exercise
  - o Massage
  - o Biofeedback
  - o Listening to music
  - o Engaging in enjoyable activities
  - o Journaling
  - o Yoga

Box 4.2

School counselors have unique roles in the school which enable them to promote wellness. Yet, school counselors experience emotional exhaustion due to feelings of detachment from other educational personnel, lack of positive feedback from administrators, and few opportunities for professional development. This dissatisfaction results in reduced productivity.

Source: Mathews, 2013

The Use of Technology in Counseling and Supervision

Practicing school counselors depend on computers to be more effective on the job, and awareness of the different types of technology used by school counselors will be beneficial to you as you enter your clinical experiences. However, it is wise to balance any temptation to become technology dependent. For example, Carlson, Portman, and Bartlett (2006) warn counselors who rely on email communication that they may miss opportunities for instrumental face-to-face communication that are necessary for developing trust and rapport in counseling relationships.

On the positive side, computer-literate counselors are able to contribute to education reform, and knowledge of available technology can assist in time management (Casey, 1995, as cited in Sabella & Booker, 2003). Counselors use technology for such tasks as (1) creating and storing student information, (2) tracking courses, (3) developing schedules, (4) disseminating career information, (5) providing greater visibility of the school counseling program, (6) creating websites and sending/receiving email, and (7), administering tests. Internet convenience is also helpful when counselors want to assist teachers and parents to develop an awareness of cyberbullying (also known as harassment, intimidation, or threats) or sexting by providing links to credible Internet resources.

Computers can also assist in finding accessible professional development opportunities. By joining an electronic mailing list (or listserv) such as SCENE provided by the ASCA, discussion board questions can be posted to which numerous school counseling professionals can respond. This format is also useful for identifying professional concerns from archived questions and responses. However, even an electronic mailing list poses challenges. Almost anyone can join an electronic mailing list, so empirically based and accurate responses are not always provided. You are professionally responsible to take reasonable steps to ensure that the information you receive and disseminate is sound and valid.

Counselors also use computers to accommodate students with disabilities. For instance, for a student with impaired vision, software can translate written words to spoken text. For a student with a hearing loss, verbal instructions can be converted to text. And for a student with a fine motor physical disability, a touch screen may be a helpful accommodation.

School counselors were surveyed to determine the technology competencies considered most important to their job (Sabella, Poynton, & Isaacs, 2010). Ethical and legal knowledge of technology was considered most important, with data management skills considered as the second most important item. With the need to prove effectiveness, it is not surprising that the use of technology to track data was ranked as important, since data monitoring student progress, making decisions, and advocating for students and the program are essential school counselor tasks.

A study was conducted to examine the content of school counseling program website information, and based on this analysis school counselors were not making good use of the website as a means of transmitting information. Furthermore, the researchers discovered that a majority of the school counselors who did have website availability still referred to themselves as "guidance counselors" rather than professional school counselors (Milsom & Bryant, 2006).

As a school counselor-in-training, you may have better technology skills than your supervisor, including the ability to build a website. Your technology skills may provide an opportunity for you to contribute to your school site by introducing current software or teaching your supervisor basic technology skills to make cumbersome tasks more manageable. For example, you could educate your supervisor about technology such as EZ Analyze, a free tool designed to analyze data and create graphs, or the Time Tracker www.ezanalyze.com/, a tool that school counselors use to show where time is spent and to generate reports.

You could find that technology is also being used in supervision. Program supervisors may have difficulty making on-site visits to schools in rural communities or in areas located a considerable distance from the school counseling training program. Instead, synchronous supervision and consultation

Figure 4.5 When working with students on web searches, school counselors are aware of website evaluative criteria that answer the questions, Who? (is the author or sponsor), What? (is the purpose of this site and the qualifications of the author or publisher), When? (was the website published or revised), Where? (can you find the author or publisher), Why? (was the website published), and How? (accurate or current is the information or citations).

Source: Shutterstock

with the site supervisor may need to occur through a video call on Skype or Facetime. This type of supervision challenges contemporary thought about how supervision can be conducted, particularly in regard to issues of confidentiality and the possibility of misinterpreting messages (McAdams & Wyatt, 2010).

Conceptual Application Activity 4.8

List six different forms of technology you use every day. Now identify one possible method for which this technology could be used in a school counseling program. Compare your list with your peers' lists.

Form of Technology	Skills	Use in School
_____	_____	_____
_____	_____	_____
_____	_____	_____
_____	_____	_____

Although there are many advantages to technology, these are accompanied by safety and ethical concerns, such as awareness of antivirus software to prevent malicious computer viruses from infecting and damaging data files. Additionally, installing and updating security software to keep others from accessing computer-stored confidential records is a must.

CONCLUSION

This chapter provides essential information to consider as you are preparing for your clinical experiences. Advance preparation assists in making these new opportunities less stressful. Identifying and starting activities such as contacting your site supervisor and learning about the school policies and procedures, attendance policy, crisis plan, and personal safety plans will provide you with an orientation to help you get a better understanding of expectations. In addition, once you have a better understanding of the school needs, you can develop a contract that is aligned with the ASCA National Model for a better understanding of how a school counselor assumes a leadership role in a CDSC program.

With wellness as a basic construct of the counseling profession, you have a responsibility to practice and model healthful living for the students and stakeholders with whom you work. Supervision is an ideal time to learn about your role as a professional school counselor and leader of a CDSC program. Observe, learn, practice, and self-reflect on your fit within the profession and how your skills can make a difference in the lives of others.

WEBSITES

ASCA SCENE: https://schoolcounselor.groupsite.com/main/summary

This is a professional networking site in which you are able to pose questions, provide answers to questions asked by other professionals, and become part of a discussion group. In addition, you can receive forms, lesson plans, and other professional materials. You must be a member of ASCA to receive this information.

REFERENCES

American School Counselor Association. (ASCA). (2012). *ASCA National Model: A framework for school counseling programs* (3rd ed.). Alexandria, VA: Author.

Brannen, A. D. (2014, February 14). *United states: A few guidelines for appearance policies.* Retrieved from www.mondaq.com/unitedstates/x/293060/employee+rights+labour+relations/A+Few+Guidelines+For+Appearance+Policies

Carlson, L. A., Portman, T. A. A., & Bartlett, J. R. (2006). Professional school counselors' approaches to technology. *Professional School Counseling, 9,* 252–256.

Injeyan, M. C., Shuman, C., Shugar, A., Chitayat, D., Atenafu, E. G., & Kaiser, A. (2011). Personality traits associated with genetic counselor compassion fatigue: The roles of dispositional optimism and locus of control. *Journal of Genetic Counseling, 20,* 526–540. doi:10.1007/s10897–011–9379–4

Ladbury, J. L. S. (2012). *School counseling supervision: A qualitative summary from the perspective of school counseling site-supervisors.* (Doctoral dissertation). Retrieved from ProQuest (UMI 3523989.)

Lawson, G., & Myers, J. E. (2011). Wellness, professional quality of life, and career-sustaining behaviors: What keeps us well? *Journal of Counseling & Development, 89,* 163–171.

Lee, C. C. (2013). *Multicultural issues in counseling: New approaches to diversity* (4th ed.). Alexandria, VA: American Counseling Association.

McAdams, C. R., & Wyatt, K. L. (2010). The regulation of technology-assisted distance counseling and supervision in the United States: An analysis of current extent, trends, and implications. *Counselor Education & Supervision, 49,* 179–189.

Mathews, T. F. (2013). *The school counselors' description of their experiences of emotional exhaustion: A phenomenological study.* (Doctoral dissertation). Available from ProQuest Dissertations and Theses data base. (AAI3553926).

Meyers, L. (2014, March). In search of wellness. *Counseling Today, 56,* 34–59.

Milsom, A., & Bryant, J. (2006). School counseling departmental Web sites: What message do we send? *Professional School Counseling, 10,* 210–216.

Paine, C. K. (2009). School crisis aftermath: Care for the caregivers. *Principal Leadership, 10,* 12–16.

Ray, S. L., Wong, C., White, D., & Heaslip, K. (2013). Compassion satisfaction, compassion fatigue, work life conditions, and burnout among frontline mental health care professionals. *Traumatology, 19,* 255–267. doi: 10.1177/1534765612471144

Reupert, A. (2006). The counsellor's self in therapy: An inevitable presence. *International Journal for the Advancement of Counselling, 28,* 95–105.

Sabella, R., & Booker, B. L. (2003). Using technology to promote your guidance and counseling program among stakeholders. *Professional School Counseling, 6,* 206–213.

Sabella, R., Poynton, T. A., & Isaacs, M. L. (2010). School counselors perceived importance of counseling technologies. *Computers in Human Behavior, 26,* 609–617. doi: 10.1016/j.chb.2009.12.014

Shallcross, L. (2012, December). A recipe for truly great counseling. *Counseling Today.* Retrieved from http://ct.counseling.org/2012/12/the-recipe-for-truly-great-counseling/

Swank, J. M., & Tyson, L. (2012). School counseling site supervisor training: A web-based approach. *Professional School Counseling, 16,* 40–48. doi: 10.5330/PSC.n.2012–16.40

Wall, J. E. (2004). *Enhancing assessment through technology.* Alexandria, VA: ASCA School Counselor.

Wilkerson, K., & Bellini, J. (2006). Intrapersonal and organizational factors associated with burnout among school counselors. *Journal of Counseling & Development, 84,* 440–450.

Williams, R. (2007, March/April). Superhero or super stressed? *ASCA School Counselor,* 10–12.

5 Supervision as a Developmental Passage

Kristi A. Gibbs and Virginia A. Magnus

CACREP Standards

Common Core

Professional Orientation and Ethical Practice

e. Counseling supervision models, practices, and processes.

The purpose of this chapter is to:

- provide an overview of supervision models
- highlight challenges in supervision.

INTRODUCTION

School counselor education programs do not typically include formal training in supervision for master's-level practitioners (Dollarhide & Miller, 2006). Rather, courses in clinical supervision are typically found in doctoral programs (CACREP, 2009). However, the clinical supervision of counselors is most often provided by master's-level practitioners, many of whom have not received adequate training in supervision (Dollarhide & Miller, 2006; McMahon & Simons, 2004). This lack of training is troublesome, especially given the legal and ethical ramifications of counseling and supervision (Herlihy, Gray, & McCollum, 2002).

Magnuson, Norem, and Bradley (2001) stated that when "counselors without adequate preparation assume responsibility for supervising trainees, they may inadvertently portray supervision as a superficial requirement and miss the opportunity to adequately prepare individual members of the next generation of counselors" (p. 214). Furthermore, the Association for Counselor Education and Supervision (2011) adopted Best Practices in Clinical Supervision in which they advocate that supervisors should receive specific training in clinical supervision that includes both didactic and experiential learning. Researchers (Dollarhide & Miller, 2006; Herlihy et al., 2002) have cited lack of training in supervision as one reason that school counselors-in-training may receive inadequate supervision. Accordingly, the intent of this chapter is to provide you with a basic overview of several models of supervision along with challenges you might encounter in supervision, thereby providing a basic framework for engaging in clinical supervision.

Right about now you may be saying, "I'm a student. Do I really need to read about supervision models and challenges? Who cares if I have a basic framework for supervision?" The answer is yes, you are a student, and no, you are probably not going to be supervising anyone this semester. However, you need to know what to expect from supervision so that you will be better prepared for this experience. Furthermore, you may find yourself in a position to supervise another school counselor-in-training in as little as 2 to 3 years, at which point you will reflect back on this chapter and say, "Wow, I actually know what a supervisor is supposed to do because I read about it in my school counseling book." Also, having this knowledge may provide you with tools to be a better consumer of supervision yourself, as you are undoubtedly receiving supervision right now. So, let's get started talking a little more about supervision.

Supervision Roles

The professional literature (Bernard & Goodyear, 2009; Studer, 2006) broadly identifies three categories of supervision models: (1) developmental models, (2) integrated or social role models, and (3) models grounded in a specific counseling theory. The first two categories include models developed specifically for supervision, whereas the last category contains models that may more accurately be identified as extensions of a specific counseling theoretical orientation. Due to practicality and limitations of space, we will discuss only the first two categories in this chapter.

Developmental Models

Developmental models of supervision focus primarily on how you will grow and change over time through training and supervision (Bernard & Goodyear, 2009). Basic assumptions of developmental models of supervision include the belief that supervisees move through stages that are qualitatively different from one another. These stages require interventions and interactions from the supervisor, which differ across developmental levels (Bernard & Goodyear, 2009). Stated simply, developmental models suggest that in the first weeks of your practicum you will be at a specific developmental stage that is qualitatively different from your stage of counseling development in the last month of internship. Accordingly, you may benefit from a different supervisory environment, inquiries, and interventions in the beginning of the supervised experience compared with later stages in the internship. Furthermore, you will grow in both confidence and skill over time, calling for awareness and flexibility from your supervisor.

In this section, we will provide an overview of what Bernard and Goodyear (2009) have described as the most widely used developmental model of supervision, the integrated developmental model (IDM). This model was originally developed by Stoltenberg (1981) and expanded upon with Delworth in 1987. These authors (Stoltenberg & Delworth, 1987) describe counselor development as occurring through four levels: (1) the beginning of the journey, (2) trial and tribulation, (3) challenge and growth, and (4) integrated. Additionally, the supervisee (that's you!) is described as "progressing in terms of three basic structures—self- and other-awareness, motivation, and autonomy" (Stoltenberg & Delworth, 1987, p. 35). Interactions among these three structures and the four levels of development are described.

Level One: The Beginning of the Journey

In the first stage of counselor development, you enter the supervisory relationship with limited training and experience (Bernard & Goodyear, 2009). At this stage you are dependent on the supervisor, seeking to imitate skills and techniques rather than embracing your own style (Stoltenberg, 1981). It is our hope that as counselors and as future supervisors you will always remember the feelings associated with the beginning of this journey. Recalling memories of the early stages in your own development can help you gain confidence in your growth as a counselor. It may also help you to more effectively supervise school counselors-in-training in the future. For additional information, let us turn our focus to the aforementioned structures as they relate to level one supervisees described by Stoltenberg and Delworth (1987).

Self- and Other-Awareness. Awareness of both others and self is typically low at this stage of development. You may be extra-sensitive about any sort of evaluation. You may benefit from activities of reflection that help you understand yourself and others in the school context.

Box 5.1

"I pursued the school counseling profession because I want to help people succeed. . . . Counseling is powerful enough that the students I meet with will always carry what they gained from our therapeutic relationship within themselves."

Counseling Today (2014, July). p. 58

Source: Clair Nowajchik, Winner of the Ross Trust Graduate Student Essay for Future School Counselors.

Motivation. High levels of motivation and anxiety are evident at level one. At this stage you may find yourself very attentive and focused, and you probably want to know the "right" answer as it pertains to interventions with counselees. Because you are new to the school, you may also be concerned with learning and retaining a plethora of new information coupled with a desire to perform adequately. Naturally, these competing pressures cause some anxiety.

Autonomy. The supervisee at this level is highly dependent on the supervisor, typically expecting the supervisor to provide structure in supervision. If you are at this stage you may need more positive feedback. You may not yet be ready to work by yourself and as a result may benefit from regular input and encouragement.

Conceptual Application Activity 5.1

Spend 10 minutes with one or two peers. Reflect back to when you first began your practicum or internship experience and share with each other your thoughts and feelings regarding your self- and other-awareness, motivation, and autonomy level at that time. Consider your supervision expectations, too.

Motivation

_____

_____

Autonomy

_____

_____

Self- and Other-Awareness

_____

_____

Expectations of Supervisor

_____

_____

Level Two: Trial and Tribulation

Level two supervisees are in conflict, seeking some autonomy while continuing to be somewhat dependent on the supervisor (Stoltenberg & Delworth, 1987). According to Stoltenberg (1981), counselors at this stage are increasing self-awareness while also striving for independence. Supervisors might expect supervisees in the second or third semester of training to be at this stage of development. If you are at this stage, you may begin to find yourself more independent, but this can result in a tumultuous time for the supervision process. To help with understanding what may contribute to supervisory tension, turn your attention to the structures proposed by Stoltenberg and Delworth (1987).

Self- and Other-Awareness. The supervisee is better able to focus increasingly on the counselee. You may begin to distinguish your own values and issues from those of the counselee; however, improved consciousness also includes self-recognition of less productive thoughts, habits, and values. This increased awareness may cause frustration for you as countertransference develops.

Box 5.2

Teaching interns new ways of seeing is an important task of supervision. Using the metaphor of a rock climber as a means of recognizing the progression of steps toward becoming a competent counselor may assist you in understanding the stages of development (Sommer, Ward, & Scofield, 2010).

Motivation. Motivation and confidence are fluctuating at this stage. This may be partially due to the more advanced school counselor-in-training taking on counselees who are more difficult. You may feel confident one moment and confused or unsure the next. This confusion can impact motivation, so that you appear motivated at times for specific tasks and lack motivation at other times for different tasks, akin to an approach–avoidance response.

Autonomy. Supervisees are more assertive, choosing to implement new interventions of their own choosing. At this stage, you may no longer be imitative of your supervisor. However, dependency on the supervisor may still occasionally be present. Supervisor input may be more desired when you encounter a new counseling situation, an ambiguous ethical dilemma, or responsibility for a unique school activity.

Level Three: Challenge and Growth

At the next stage of development, supervisees should be coming into their own style; supervisees are able to understand their role in counseling. Stoltenberg and Delworth (1987) call this stage the "calm after the storm" (p. 93).

Self- and Other-Awareness. The supervisee is aware of self, including both strengths and weaknesses. Conquering areas of weaknesses could help you develop a sense of professional confidence. Empathy allows you to be fully in the moment with the counselee but also to pull back when appropriate.

Motivation. The level three supervisee is relatively stable in terms of motivation and commitment to the profession. At this stage, you may still have doubts about the profession, but these doubts should not be immobilizing. You might begin to recognize that doubts and concerns may occasionally be a natural part of the developmental process.

Autonomy. Primarily autonomous, the supervisee seeks assistance from the supervisor for specific things. However, most decisions are made independently. Supervision tends to be more collegial in nature.

Level Four: Integrated

We all start out as beginning counselors in the initial stages of development. With perseverance and supervision, many of us are privileged to practice as counselors and eventually attain this ultimate stage in counseling development. Stoltenberg and Delworth (1987) called this stage *integrated* to signify the integration of the supervisee across all three domains: motivation, autonomy, and self-/ other-awareness. These authors also assert a belief that most counselors require at least 5 or 6 years of professional experience to reach this level. So be patient and do not expect to be immediately and completely competent in all areas.

Self- and Other-Awareness. The supervisee is aware of self, including specific strengths and weaknesses. He or she has developed professional confidence and readily seeks input from others for self-improvement. Empathy allows the counselor to fluidly adjust from being fully in the "here and now."

Motivation. The level three supervisee is motivated and committed to the counseling profession. When you reach this stage, you should have few doubts about the profession and realize that occasional doubts and concerns are a natural part of the developmental process.

Autonomy. At this stage you should be very self-sufficient. Most decisions should be made independently with occasional assistance from your supervisor for specific things. Supervision is collegial in nature.

Conceptual Application Activity 5.2

Identify a counselor you think personifies level three, integrated characteristics. Write down ways this counselor demonstrates integration.

Motivation

_____

_____

Autonomy

_____

_____

Self- and Other-Awareness

_____

_____

In the preceding pages, we provided an overview of Stoltenberg and Delworth's (1987) developmental model of supervision. Our focus with the developmental model was on stages of supervisee development across time. In the pages that follow, we shift our focus to the supervisor and specific roles that might be utilized in the supervision relationship. However, before we move on, we would like to encourage you to take a few minutes to reflect and think about where you are, developmentally, in your journey toward becoming a professional school counselor. Keep in mind the four levels offered by Stoltenberg and Delworth (1987): (1) the beginning of the journey, (2) trial and tribulation, (3) challenge and growth, (4) integrated, and be mindful of your own levels of awareness, motivation, and autonomy.

Social Role Models

Social role models as described by Bernard and Goodyear (2009) delineate different roles that the supervisor might employ during the course of supervision. Three roles specifically identified in the literature are teacher, counselor, and consultant (Bernard, 1979; Bernard & Goodyear, 2009). However, it is important to note that although supervision has similarities to the aforementioned roles, it is a qualitatively different skill. Douce (as cited in Bernard & Goodyear, 2009, p. 101) stated that "supervision is a separate skill similar to teaching—but different; similar to counseling—but different; and similar to consulting—but different." As we discuss one social role model of supervision, Bernard's (1979) discrimination model, gives special attention to the nuances of each of the roles: supervisor, teacher, counselor, and consultant.

Three supervisor roles and three areas of focus for supervision are identified in the discrimination model that Bernard (1979) identifies. The focus areas are *intervention skills* (overt behaviors of the supervisee), *conceptualization skills* (covert behaviors, including how the supervisee understands what the counselee is saying and recognizes themes), and *personalization skills* (ability of the supervisee to hear feedback from both counselee and supervisor, and ability to recognize and be comfortable with the counselor's own feelings, values, and attitudes).

According to the discrimination model (Bernard, 1979) the supervisor must first determine the area of focus and then choose a role from which to respond. As previously indicated, the roles include teacher, counselor, and consultant. Bernard cautions the supervisor to remember that there are nine choices for the supervisor to consider and that each circumstance should be approached as a unique situation. As shown in Table 5.1, each of the supervisor roles is identified with a particular focus for supervision.

Figure 5.1 Supervisor giving feedback to her school counselor-in-training.

Source: Shutterstock

Table 5.1 Examples of the Discrimination Model

Focus of Supervision	Teacher	Counselor	Consultant
Process skills or intervention	Counselor would like to learn a specific skill. Supervisor teaches the skill.	Counselor rarely addresses feelings during sessions. Supervisor attempts to help counselor determine how discussing feelings impacts him or her and how this might be limiting his or her ability to focus on feelings in session.	Counselor wants to use a sand tray technique in session. Supervisor works with counselor to identify resources that provide information about the technique.
Conceptualization skills	Counselor is unable to identify themes between counseling sessions. Supervisor points out connections between sessions, helping counselor identify overarching themes.	Counselor is unable to identify appropriate goals for counselee. Supervisor helps counselor identify personal triggers that may be blocking ability to identify goals in session.	Counselor would like to conceptualize counselee from a different theoretical orientation. Supervisor discusses beliefs of that particular theory and how conceptualization might look.
Personalization skills	Counselor is unaware that his or her tendency to maintain direct eye contact makes counselee uncomfortable. Supervisor talks about multicultural diversity and the fact that making eye contact is considered disrespectful in some cultures.	Counselor becomes defensive when counselee indicates preference for a different counselor. Supervisor discusses why being liked is so important to the counselor.	Counselor would like to feel more comfortable and competent working with gay or lesbian counselees. Supervisor helps counselor to identify several things that might help to increase both his or her comfort and competence with counselees who are gay or lesbian.

Conceptual Application Activity 5.3

Consider and answer the questions to the following scenario and compare your responses with those of your peers.

Amy is a practicum student in an elementary school. Juanita, a third-grade student, comes to see Amy because she is concerned about her brother, Miguel, who is being deployed with the Army. Amy has difficulty working with Juanita because it brings up her own feelings for her father, who is also being deployed to a foreign country.

What role should the supervisor assume in the focus areas of process, conceptualization, and personalization skills?

_____

_____

Thus far we have discussed two models of supervision: the integrated developmental model (Stoltenberg & Delworth, 1987) and the discrimination model (Bernard, 1979). Although both were developed for the explicit purpose of supervising counselors, some (Luke & Bernard, 2006; Wood & Rayle, 2006) have wondered whether traditional models of counselor supervision are meeting the supervision needs of school counselors-in-training given the tasks they are expected to perform as part of their comprehensive, developmental school counseling (CDSC) programs. To address that gap, we will provide an overview of an expanded version of the discrimination model that was developed specifically for school counselors (Luke & Bernard, 2006).

School Counseling Supervision Models

School counseling supervision must attend to functions of the school counselor-in-training, which are not necessarily limited to individual and group counseling (Luke & Bernard, 2006). Accordingly, Luke and Bernard (2006) identified four domains of CDSC programs that should be addressed in supervision with school counselors-in-training: (1) large-group guidance, (2) responsive counseling and consultation, (3) individual advisement, and (4) programmatic planning, coordination, and evaluation.

The school counselor supervision model (SCSM) (Luke & Bernard, 2006) is an extension of the discrimination model, which includes the four above-mentioned domains. Accordingly, the SCSM is conceptualized as a 3 × 3 × 4 model addressing three supervisor roles, three foci of supervision, and four points of entry.

Supervisor role: teacher, counselor, consultant

Focus of supervision: intervention, conceptualization, personalization

Point of entry: large-group intervention; counseling and consultation; individual and group advisement; planning, coordination, and evaluation

Group Advisement: Planning, Coordination, and Evaluation

School counselors engage in many tasks on any given day, but most duties will fall into one of the four categories designated as a point of entry. Therefore, the first step for a supervisor utilizing the SCSM is to identify which domain (point of entry) is being addressed in supervision (Luke & Bernard, 2006).

Once the domain is determined, the supervisor should be more readily able to identify the focus of supervision and finally the supervisory role. However, when conceptualizing the SCSM model as an extension of the discrimination model, it is important to remember that "the supervisor uses the same template . . . but broadens the focus of supervision to include the interventions, conceptualization, and personalization that are involved in successfully implementing all aspects of a CSCP [comprehensive school counseling program]" (Luke & Bernard, 2006, p. 286).

Conceptual Application Activity 5.4

Spend 10 minutes with one or two peers. Reflect back to your last supervision session. Can you identify a supervision intervention your supervisor used that addressed one of the points of entry issues identified in the SCSM model? Once you have identified a point of entry, try to determine the role in which your supervisor responded, and finally which focus area was addressed.

Point of entry
Large group intervention; counseling and consultation; individual and group advisement; planning, coordination, and evaluation

_____

_____

Supervisor role
Teacher, counselor, consultant

_____

_____

Focus area
Intervention, conceptualization, personalization

_____

_____

It is vital that supervisors be grounded in some theory from which to conceptualize supervision. However, it is also important to attend to the supervisory relationship and the inherent challenges presented within that dyad. Therefore, we will transition our focus to an overview of the supervisory relationship and your role in this process.

SUPERVISORY RELATIONSHIP AND SUPERVISION CHALLENGES

Although it is essential to understand supervision models and their function in the supervision process, it is equally important for you to understand the supervisor–supervisee relationship now as well as in the future when you may become a supervisor. Bernard and Goodyear (2009) describe the supervisory relationship as the feelings and perceptions individuals have in relation to one another. Some believe that the supervisor–supervisee relationship may be at the heart of a successful practicum and internship. Although there is still much to be learned about this unique and multifaceted relationship, it is a vital element of supervision (Borders & Brown, 2005; Ladany, Walker, & Melincoff, 2001). It is important to note that the relationship that emerges is integral to your growth, education, and progress and is an essential component of the supervisory process (Holloway, 1999; Watkins, 1997). The working alliance, individual differences, and evaluation are also integral components of the supervisory relationship and are discussed next.

Working Alliance

The development of a working alliance is perceived to be as important as the supervisory relationship (Bordin, 1983; White & Queen, 2003). Bordin's concept of the supervisory working alliance has been utilized in the supervision process and defined as "a collaboration for change . . . involving three aspects: (1) mutual agreements and understandings regarding the goals sought in the change process; (2) the tasks of each of the partners; and (3) the bonds between the partners" (1983, p. 35). White and Queen (2003) maintain that the working alliance is central to understanding the supervisory relationship, given that it can influence the counseling relationship between the school counselor-in-training and his or her counselees. Furthermore, establishing safety, a trusting atmosphere, and reciprocal regard between supervisor and school counselor-in-training enhances supervisee willingness to receive suggestions and training and to modify behavior (Borders & Brown, 2005).

Individual Differences

Individual differences add to the complexity of the relationship. According to Borders and Brown (2005), "each supervisee and supervisor brings unique personalities, life experiences, interpersonal histories, professional motivations and goals to the supervisory context" (p. 68). For example, not all supervisors and supervisees interact with others in a similar manner or react to the same situation in the same way. Each is influenced by his or her respective distinctiveness.

Evaluation

Another distinguishing feature and significant part of supervision is evaluation. Indeed, evaluation is a necessary component of supervision and is inherent to the supervisory process. Baird (2002) defined evaluation as "the process of giving and receiving feedback about the quality of one's performance" (p. 78). According to Campbell (2000), the purpose of evaluation is to identify goals for subsequent knowledge instead of a reexamination of previous work. Haynes, Corey, and Moulton (2003) assert that evaluation is necessary for the accomplishment of the four goals of supervision: fostering development, ensuring counselee welfare, acting as gatekeepers for the profession, and developing autonomous professionals.

Given that the evaluation process has the potential to cause you, as a counselor-in-training, discomfort, stress, and anxiety, it is important for the supervisor to discuss evaluation openly at the outset of supervision (Baird, 2002; Borders & Brown, 2005; Haynes et al., 2003). Evaluation is a delicate balancing act: You need honest and helpful feedback in order to learn and grow, yet the supervisor must strive to maintain the bonds established in the relationship.

The evaluative component of supervision further complicates the supervisory relationship for several reasons, including, but not limited to, the following: it may be the first time you have experienced supervision, you may fear supervisor disapproval, and you may be anxious about having your performance and skills examined (Kiser, 2008). Evaluation can cause difficulties, because there is an inherent power differential ever-present in the process. This unequal distribution of power can produce stress and conflicts in the relationship because "supervisees are asked to be vulnerable and self-disclose their professional inadequacies and their personal biases to the same person who will grade them, write letters of recommendation, or complete reference forms for licensure" (Borders & Brown, 2005, p. 67). Borders and Brown (2005) further state that power differences should be acknowledged in view of the fact that evaluation is an integral part of the supervisory process.

In sum, the supervisor–supervisee relationship is an essential component of supervision. The interactions between participating individuals can enhance or impede your training and, therefore, must be carefully considered.

Conceptual Application Activity 5.5

Spend 10 minutes with one or two peers. Reflect back to your last supervision session. Can you identify a supervision intervention your supervisor used that addressed one of the points of entry issues identified in the SCSM model? Once you have identified a point of entry, try to determine which role your supervisor responded in and, finally, which focus area was addressed.

Think of a time when you received evaluative feedback from your supervisor. Was the feedback helpful? If so, why? If not, why not?

1. How might your supervisor give you feedback that would be more helpful?

    _____

    _____

2. Did you implement the feedback you received? If so, how?

    _____

    _____

OTHER CHALLENGES

Several other challenges underlie the basic principles of the supervisory relationship. For example, multicultural influences, supervisee anxiety and resistance, the parallel process, and dual roles/relationships warrant discussion and are included in the next sections.

Multicultural Influences

The environment and community in which we develop and mature influence each of us. Additionally, we are oriented to family norms, attitudes, and family culture. These same norms and values can be expected to influence the counselee–counselor relationship as well as your relationship with your supervisors. To work successfully with individuals from diverse backgrounds, it is vital to be aware of your personal history, other individuals' personal histories, and the impact of both on the counseling and supervision relationship (Baird, 2002; Borders & Brown, 2005). As maintained by Borders and Brown (2005), some supervisees may not be able to identify problems or issues stemming from multicultural concerns; thus, "it is the supervisor's responsibility to introduce multicultural issues early in the supervision relationship, check in about them often, and invite the supervisee to discuss them at any time" (p. 70). You are likely to encounter multicultural issues you may not know how to manage. In such situations, it will be important for you to discuss them with your supervisor during group supervision. At the same time, it is an opportunity for self-discovery, self-evaluation, and for expanding your knowledge and awareness of multicultural issues.

Multicultural issues, different worldviews, and unique values will likewise be present within the supervisor–supervisee relationship. In addition to dealing with these issues related to your counselees, it is important for you and your supervisor to discuss your own diverse life experiences, thoughts, and perspectives. This open discussion, mutual respect, and willingness to learn from one another models a healthy counselor–counselee relationship. Diversity as it relates to differences in schools is discussed in greater detail in Chapter 13.

Anxiety

Anxiety is an expected facet of practicum and internship. In fact, Borders and Brown (2005) suggest that it is a known aspect of supervision. Furthermore, Bernard and Goodyear (2009) contend that supervisees feel apprehension not only when working with counselees, but also during supervision. Certainly, observation and evaluation are customary components of both practicum and internship, and can be very intimidating, particularly if you have never experienced supervision. Supervisees often feel incompetent, vulnerable, and unskilled as they begin to put knowledge and skills into practice. Nonetheless, anxiety in and of itself can be beneficial because it encourages you to be prepared for supervision. Conversely, too much anxiety may interfere with your effectiveness and the ability to recall needed skills during sessions.

As previously mentioned, the evaluative nature and power differential in supervision can influence supervisee anxiety. Even if you have successfully completed the academic part of the program, you must also successfully complete the practical experience under the watchful eyes of supervisors and peers. Feelings of anxiety may also stem from fears associated with performance. During the practicum and internship, you will present cases and video and audiotape recordings and experience site observation that can cause feelings of anxiety (Bernard & Goodyear, 2009; Borders & Brown, 2005; Haynes et al., 2003).

Performance anxiety can threaten your sense of competence and ability; it is not unusual for you to have an unrealistic view of the counseling process and set high expectations for yourself even though you lack experience. Your anxiety will decrease over time, however, as you understand that feelings of anxiety, concerns about counseling skills, receiving feedback, and having to self-disclose are normal and expected elements of supervision. Also, keep in mind that feelings of anxiety decrease with experience and change in any given situation. Once you recognize that dealing with the anxiety in supervision is normal and helpful, you will be able to learn from it and in turn grow from it (Haynes et al., 2003).

Resistance

A consequence of anxiety is resistance, and it is a common aspect of the supervisory process that you may experience as a counselor-in-training. Borders and Brown (2005) state that "supervisees necessarily must find ways to handle their anxiety, and sometimes their attempts are not productive. . . .

[R]esistance may reflect the supervisees' attempt to reduce anxiety to a manageable and productive level" (p. 72). Some of the underlying factors related to supervisee resistance include rigidly holding to a specific theory, giving advice or problem solving before the counselee has identified the problem, being confrontational surrounding taping, and expressing vulnerability associated with the evaluation process (Borders & Brown, 2005; Haynes et al., 2003; Watkins, 1997).

Resistant activities, as with anxiety, can impede the learning process; therefore, recognizing the basis for the resistance and finding ways to diminish the supposed threat will increase your ability to deal with resistance in a positive manner. Open and honest discussion of resistance in supervision can increase awareness of resistant behaviors and in the process enhance your development.

Parallel Process

Parallel process is similar to transference and countertransference, traditional concepts in psychoanalytic theory. Searles (1955) was the first to make use of the concept of parallel process, which he referred to as "the reflective process." He defined parallel process as "the process at work currently in the *relationship between* patient [in schools, this would be the student] and therapist . . . often reflected in the *relationship between* therapist and supervisor" (p. 135). Furthermore, Friedlander, Siegel, and Brenock (1989) explain parallel process by stating, "supervisees unconsciously present themselves to their supervisors as their counselees have presented to them. The process reverses when the supervisee adopts attitudes and behaviors of the supervisor in relating to the counselee" (p. 149). In summary, exploration and reflection of the parallel process in supervision can be constructive when it enhances your ability to gain insight into the way you interact with counselees (Bernard & Goodyear, 2009; Borders & Brown, 2005; Haynes et al., 2003).

Dual Roles

Kiser (2008) defines dual roles or relationships as follows: "Dual relationships occur when a helping professional assumes a second role with a counselee or colleague in addition to the professional role" (p. 253). The American School Counselor Association (2010) Code of Ethics states in section A.4.a., "Dual Relationships," that the professional school counselor should, "[a]void dual relationships that might impair his/her objectivity and increase the risk of harm to the student." This same ethical code applies to you as well. According to Studer (2006), school counselors-in-training may need help in clarifying actions or behaviors that interfere with the ability to be objective in a counseling or supervisory relationship and consequently cause harm. Supervisors are responsible for helping you avoid, identify and correct, and learn from dual relationships.

Haynes et al. (2003) indicate that dual role or relationship issues oftentimes come up during fieldwork and clinical experiences, and supervisees must learn to work through and come to terms with boundary issues. Borders and Brown (2005) suggest two possible types of dual roles: social and sexual. Social role boundaries may be less difficult for the school counselor to maintain with students, given that their counselees are usually younger than they are. However, the possibility of social relationships increases when working with parents similar in age and interests and with whom you may develop a personal relationship. Maintaining constructive and professional boundaries may be more challenging with students' adult parents or caregivers. Be mindful that your professional obligations and responsibilities to your students supersede social relationships, and remember that you should avoid any social interaction that might cause loss of objectivity (Borders & Brown, 2005; Haynes et al., 2003).

Conceptual Application Activity 5.6

Read and respond to the following case study. Compare your answers with those of your peers.

Caroline is in her fourth year working as an elementary school counselor when one of her former professors asks if she would be willing to take a school counselor intern. Not sure initially,

Caroline hesitates. With encouragement from her former professor, she cautiously agrees. The following semester, James, a timid intern, shows up at Caroline's school ready to begin his internship. As expected, James is thrown right in. With Caroline's assistance, he begins leading classroom lessons, starts two groups with first- and third-grade girls, and even sees two students for individual counseling. When the university instructor goes to the school for a site visit, both James and Caroline report that everything is great.

Seven weeks into the semester, James is watching the evening news, shocked at the tragedy unfolding on the television. An automobile accident involving multiple cars has traffic backed up on the interstate as helicopters are airlifting victims to nearby hospitals. James thinks back about 10 years to a time when he first heard that his 16-year-old sister had died after a truck ran a stoplight, hitting the car she was driving. As James goes to sleep that evening, he is saddened by the possibility of fatalities connected with the car accident he had witnessed earlier in the evening. It is not until early the following morning that James begins to realize the full extent to which this event is going to affect his life. Two of the victims from the accident were an 8-year-old boy and his father. The child attended the school where James is interning and the boy's 6-year-old sister was in one of James's groups. He had no idea where to begin as he attempted to focus on helping the students while grappling with his own reactions to the tragedy. Fortunately, James has a supervision session scheduled for the following day. Conceptualizing supervision from the school counseling supervision model, how would you proceed with James?

1.   Where do you think the supervising counselor should begin in working with James?

2.   What focus area would you want your supervisor to take if you had a situation similar to James? Process skills? Conceptualization? Personalization?

3.   What role would you want your supervisor to assume? Teacher? Counselor? Consultant? Why?

_____

_____

Sexual involvement with a counselee is prohibited by virtually all ethical codes. Even given the legal and professional liability and consequences, sexual relationships between students and school professionals continue to be in the news media; it is clear that these sexual relationships do occur from time to time. What happens to well-intentioned school professionals that leads to misconduct and poor professional judgment? Counseling, by its very nature, can be isolated and intimate. As part of the therapeutic process, counselees share private information, in confidence, with the school counselor or with you, as the school counselor-in-training. These interactions are often conducted in a private or semiprivate setting. Counseling session interactions may occur on a sporadic or regular basis over a long period of time. All of these factors are similar to more personal and intimate relationships outside of counseling and can be confusing to the counselee and to you. Role confusion occurs and builds when the school counselor or you, as a school counselor-in-training, fail to regularly review and maintain the primary reason or goal of the relationship, which is helping the counselee to change or adapt to environmental conditions or relationships outside the counseling setting or relationship. It is paramount that you establish, review, and maintain this therapeutic focus with your counselees. It is equally important that your supervisor do this with you.

Role confusion and dual roles are issues for you to discuss and clarify during supervision. Undoubtedly, sexual relationships confound and impede the counseling and supervision relationship and cause injury to the counselee or supervisee. Therefore, it is imperative that sexual relationships are avoided at all costs and any potential issues be brought up in supervision.

Finally, Borders and Brown (2005) suggest that the closeness of the supervisory relationship and the power differential make it difficult to avoid dual role problems. As a means of prevention, Haynes et al. (2003) suggest that supervisors clarify their role at the beginning of supervision; supervisors who set up appropriate professional boundaries are good role models and teach you how to develop appropriate boundaries.

CONCLUSION

School counseling students graduating from a school counseling program accredited by the Council for Accreditation of Counseling and Related Educational Programs (CACREP) typically receive an average of approximately 100-plus hours of supervision (combined site and university) over the course of a 700-hour field experience. The considerable amount of time devoted to supervision provides perspective about the importance of the supervisory relationship. Given this significance, it is our sincere hope that reading this chapter has provided you with the necessary information to approach supervision in an intentional manner, informed with theory about models of supervision and challenges of the supervisory relationship.

WEBSITES

- This link provides information on supervising school counselors. Although school counselor supervisors are the intended audience, school counselors-in-training can learn more about supervision: www3.canisius.edu/~farrugia/Supervision91611/SupSCIntrnsRes.pdf
- This article provides practical steps for supervising school counselors-in-training: http://school-counselor.org/magazine/blogs/september-october-2012/six-steps-to-intern-supervisionhttp://schoolcounselor.org/magazine/blogs/september-october-2012/six-steps-to-intern-supervision

REFERENCES

American School Counselor Association. (2010). *Ethical standards for school counselors.* Alexandria, VA: Author.
Association for Counselor Education and Supervision. (2011). Best practices in clinical supervision. Retrieved from www.acesonline.net/wp-content/uploads/2011/10/ACES-Best-Practices-in-clinical-supervision-document-FINAL.pdf
Baird, B. N. (2002). *The internship, practicum, and field placement handbook: A guide for the helping professions* (3rd ed.). Upper Saddle River, NJ: Prentice Hall.
Bernard, J. M. (1979). Supervisor training: A discrimination model. *Counselor Education and Supervision, 19,* 60–68.
Bernard, J. M., & Goodyear, R. K. (2009). *Fundamentals of clinical supervision* (4th ed.). Boston: Allyn & Bacon.
Borders, L. D., & Brown, L. L. (2005). *The new handbook of counseling supervision.* Mahwah, NJ: Lahaska Press.
Bordin, E. S. (1983). A working alliance based model of supervision. *The Counseling Psychologist, 11*(1), 35–42.
CACREP. (2009). *2009 standards.* Retrieved from www.cacrep.org/2009standards.pdf
Campbell, J. M. (2000). *Becoming an effective supervisor: A workbook for counselors and psychotherapists.* Philadelphia: Accelerated Development.
Dollarhide, C. T., & Miller, G. M. (2006). Supervision for preparation and practice of school counselors: Pathways to excellence. *Counselor Education and Supervision, 45,* 242–252.
Friedlander, M. L., Siegel, S. M., & Brenock, K. (1989). Parallel process in counseling and supervision: A case study. *Journal of Counseling Psychology, 36*(2), 149–157.
Haynes, R., Corey, G., & Moulton, P. (2003). *Clinical supervision in the helping professions: A practical guide.* Pacific Grove, CA: Brooks/Cole.
Herlihy, B., Gray, N., & McCollum, V. (2002). Legal and ethical issues in school counselor supervision. *Professional School Counseling, 6,* 55–60.
Holloway, E. (1999). A framework for supervision training. In E. Holloway & M. Carroll (Eds.), *Training counseling supervisors: Strategies, methods, and techniques* (pp. 8–36). London: Sage Publications.
Kiser, P. M. (2008). *The human services internship: Getting the most from your experience* (2nd ed.). Belmont, CA: Thompson Brooks/Cole.

Ladany, N., Walker, J.A., & Melincoff, D.S. (2001). Supervisory style: Its relationship to the supervisory working-alliance and supervisor self-disclosure. *Counselor Education and Supervision, 40*(4), 263–275.

Luke, M., & Bernard, J.M. (2006). The school counseling supervision model: An extension of the discrimination model. *Counselor Education and Supervision, 45*, 282–295.

Magnuson, S., Norem, K., & Bradley, L.J. (2001). Supervising school counselors. In L.J. Bradley & N. Ladany (Eds.), *Counselor supervision: Principles, process, & practice* (3rd ed., pp. 207–221). Philadelphia: Brunner-Routledge.

McMahon, M., & Simons, R. (2004). Supervision training for professional counselors: An exploratory study. *Counselor Education and Supervision, 43*, 301–309.

Searles, H.F. (1955). The informational value of the supervisor's emotional experiences. *Psychiatry, 18*, 135–146.

Sommer, C.A., Ward, J.E., & Scofield, T. (2010). Metaphoric stories in supervision of internship: A qualitative study. *Journal of Counseling & Development, 88*, 500–507.

Stoltenberg, C.D. (1981). Approaching supervision from a developmental perspective: The counselor complexity model. *Journal of Counseling Psychology, 28*, 59–65.

Stoltenberg, C.D., & Delworth, U. (1987). *Supervising counselors and therapists.* San Francisco: Jossey-Bass.

Studer, J.R. (2006). *Supervising the school counselor trainee: Guidelines for practice.* Alexandria, VA: American Counseling Association.

Watkins, C.E., Jr. (1997). *Handbook of psychotherapy supervision.* New York: Wiley.

White, V.E., & Queen, J. (2003). Supervisor and supervisee attachments and social provisions related to the supervisory working alliance. *Counselor Education and Supervision, 43*(3), 203–218.

Wood, C., & Rayle, A.D. (2006). A model of school counseling supervision: The goals, functions, roles, and systems model. *Counselor Education and Supervision, 45*, 253–266.

Section II

The American School Counselor Association (ASCA) National Model as a Structure for Understanding the Role of the Professional School Counselor

6 The ASCA National Model as a Supervisory Guide

Jeannine R. Studer

CACREP Standard

Counseling, Prevention, and Intervention

C. Knowledge

2. Knows how to design, implement, manage, and evaluate programs to enhance the academic, career, and personal/social (now renamed social/emotional) development of students.

Foundations

A. Knowledge

Understands current models of school counseling programs (e.g., American School Counselor Association [ASCA] National Model) and their integral relationship to the total educational program.

The purpose of this chapter is to:

- review the ASCA National Model
- introduce the ASCA National Model as a template for supervision
- discuss time percentage recommendations as a tool to guide supervisory activities.

INTRODUCTION

In recent years, the school reform movement has served as a catalyst for all school personnel to demonstrate how their programs contribute to the growth of all their students; school counselors are no exception. Although some people believe that educational accountability is a recent focus, demonstrating effectiveness has historically been an issue. Since "guidance workers," now known as professional school counselors, first entered schools in the early part of the 20th century, people were curious as to how these professionals made a difference in the lives of students (Gysbers, 2004). As a profession we have been remiss in demonstrating contributions to student success despite the urging of our predecessors to prove how we are significant contributors to student growth. By now you have probably been introduced to a traditional approach to school counseling and how comprehensive, developmental school counseling (CDSC) programs have replaced this service-oriented approach with one that is proactive and preventive. In this chapter my intention is to assist you in understanding school counselor activities that mirror programming advocated by the ASCA.

A SUMMARY OF THE DEVELOPMENT OF THE ASCA NATIONAL STANDARDS (NOW ASCA MINDSETS AND BEHAVIORS FOR STUDENT SUCCESS)

The profession of school counseling has a relatively brief history. Yet, despite societal changes and historical efforts of leaders of the American School Counselor Association (ASCA) to standardize our profession, counselors continued to perform numerous but different tasks. These tasks varied from school to school, grade to grade, and even among counselors within the same school setting.

The initial impetus behind our profession was the Industrial Revolution, in which there was a need to train school-aged youth for the emerging occupations that resulted from this event. Teachers were given this task with no training and no relief from their classroom responsibilities. Later, the push to compete with Russia's "Sputnik" in the race for space drove the first "guidance counselors" to direct or guide students into the fields of math and science. Making a difference was measured by increased student enrollment in math and science majors in colleges and universities. In the 1960s and 1970s, the proliferating free spirit movement brought about greater recognition of concerns such as civil rights, women's issues, and students with special needs. School personnel, including "guidance counselors," were confronted with increasing student diversity and legislative mandates and requirements that supplemented their already existing responsibilities. As a result, school counselors responded to these cumulative issues from a reactive stance rather than proactively engaging in prevention activities. Slowly, there was a shift in evaluating essential tasks, and with this awareness there was a change in the vocational title from "guidance counselor" to *professional school counselor*. (Unfortunately, I am aware that even today, not all school counselors embrace this title and continue to refer to themselves as guidance counselors.)

The ASCA responded to the demand for educational reform by standardizing the school counselor role and developed the ASCA National Standards (revised in 2012 to ASCA Student Standards, and recently renamed the Mindsets and Behaviors for Student Success). Initially implemented in 1997, these standards identify student competencies and indicators in the academic, career, and personal/social (renamed social/emotional) domains. In 2003 these standards were incorporated into the first edition of the ASCA National Model, which serves as a prototype of a comprehensive, developmental school counseling (CDSC) program (ASCA, 2012). The model contributes to legitimizing the school counseling profession and assists school counselors as they reorganize and reconstruct their traditional approach to working with students and other constituents. The National Model was revised in 2012 to reflect the trends of the profession (ASCA, 2012).

A Review of a CDSC Program

The fundamental philosophy underlying ASCA supported programs is to create "unity and focus toward improving student achievement" (ASCA, 2012, p. xii). In addition, the ASCA National Model (2012):

- ensures that all students have equal access to a rigorous curriculum that is delivered systematically,
- identifies the knowledge and skills all students are to acquire upon graduation from high school,
- emphasizes data collection and analysis to make informed decisions.

The foundation, delivery, accountability, and management components are the organizational structures of the ASCA National Model and provide guidelines for school counselors in leading a CDSC program (American School Counselor Association, 2012). Core themes of leadership, advocacy, collaboration and teaming, and systemic change are repeated throughout the components to emphasize the vital services school counselors perform within these areas (Education Trust, 2009). The ASCA National Model is shown in Figure 6.1.

Historically, the school counselor's role and identity changed as economic, political, and social variables influenced educational initiatives, and the ASCA continually advocated for school counselors and their contributions to the educational mission of the institute. Yet, there continues to be debate as to the primary role of professional school counselors. Today, with the growing numbers of students

Figure 6.1 ASCA National Model. Reprinted with permission from the American School Counselor Association (2012). *The ASCA National Model: A Framework for School Counseling Programs*, third edition.

who display risky behaviors, there is a growing need for school counselors to engage in prevention and risk management (Joe & Bryant, 2007). In a study by Harris and Jeffery (2010), school counselors reported working with students in such high-risk behaviors as suicide attempts, self-mutilation, bullying, and eating disorders. Yet some participants in this study believed that despite their interactions with students' high-risk behaviors, this was not their role (Harris & Jeffery, 2010). Others (Brown & Trusty, 2005) believe that school counselors can show their contributions to student growth by "establishing the efficacy of interventions that increase academic achievement" (p. 14). Comparatively, in a study by Amatea and Clark (2005), administrators believed that the school counselor's role was to serve as a collaborator with other teachers, parents, administrators, etc., to improve student growth. To add even more confusion, the ASCA position statement on the role of the professional school counselor states, "professional school counselors are certified/licensed *educators* . . . making them uniquely qualified to address all students' academic, career and personal/social development needs" (ASCA, n.d.). Therefore, a fundamental professional identity question remains, "is the school counselor a mental health expert who works in an educational setting, an educator who works with social/emotional and career concerns to increase academic growth, or a collaborator with others?"

Conceptual Application Activity 6.1

Discuss these issues with your site supervisor and learn about his/her perceptions on school counseling. In class, share what you learned from your site supervisor with your peers and discuss your perception of the school counselor's role in the school.

_____

_____

Regardless of how you see yourself within the school setting, the ASCA National Model is a template for you to utilize during your clinical experiences and when you transition into a role as a professional school counselor. The Foundation component serves as the *what* of the program (ASCA, 2012) or a supporting program base. The Delivery component describes direct and indirect student services. The Accountability component is designed for program analysis and decision making, and the Management component stipulates tools and assessments for addressing program needs (ASCA, 2012).

Box 6.1

School counselor interns at the high school level are more likely to receive experience in individual planning than are middle and elementary school interns, whereas elementary and middle school trainees are more likely to engage in accountability procedures than are high school counselors-in-training (Studer & Oberman, 2006).

The four themes of leadership, advocacy, collaboration and teaming, and systemic change are assimilated into the model framework. Leadership includes assisting student success through the delivery of a CDSC program and performing tasks that support school counseling training and education (ASCA, 2012). Leadership is a concept that is not always attributed to school counselors but is often viewed as an administrator role. Yet, school counselors do serve as leaders of CDSC programs and assume positions of authority and decision making by building a respectful school culture to construct collaborative relationships (Wingfield, Reese, & West-Olatunji, 2010). As an advocate, counselors assist all students and serve as support for students who have not had the same opportunities afforded to more advantaged students. As a collaborator, the school counselor works cooperatively with others to ensure that student needs are "recognized and the staff knows how to access additional help or resources when needed" (ASCA, 2012, p. 17). Finally, as a systems change agent, the school counselor works on behalf of students and with students at the micro and macro levels. Each of the ASCA National Model components and your role as a trainee in each of these areas will be discussed in more detail in the following chapters.

As you discover the advantages of working within a CDSC program, it will be stimulating and educational to put these concepts into practice during your clinical experiences. However, it may be discouraging to you when you recognize that not all school counselors have implemented a program that reflects the philosophy of the ASCA. Some programs still have a traditional focus. If this is the situation in your clinical setting, recognize that school counselors are still performing many of the tasks that reflect a CDSC program. This is an opportune time to recognize and identify those tasks that reflect this philosophy and to include them in your clinical contract. If your supervisor is unfamiliar with the ASCA National Model or uncertain as to where to begin this type of programming, this is an opportune time for you to be the teacher and share your knowledge with him/her. Tracking activities has several benefits. First, this procedure will help you gain a better understanding of how school counselors operate in a traditional type of a program. Second, you can share the list of corresponding activities with your school counselor supervisors to inform them of the specific ways they already embrace the contemporary philosophy and National Model. Third, you can distribute the ASCA National Model guidelines to compare the corresponding components and themes with those that are not yet conducted on a routine basis. Sharing this tracked data may provide new insight and encourage system change.

It seems clear that there is much to gain from implementing a complete and effective school counseling program following the ASCA National Model, and when you are able to provide substantial research to reveal how CDSC programming enhances the growth of students, you are advocating for the profession and for the students with whom you are working. Evidence as to how this programming is critical to the growth and achievement of school-aged youth is summarized below.

Figure 6.2 Elementary students in a classroom activity.

Source: Shutterstock

STUDIES SUPPORTING THE BENEFITS OF A COMPREHENSIVE, DEVELOPMENTAL SCHOOL COUNSELING PROGRAM

The Utah State Department of Education in 2000 (as cited in Sink, Akos, Turnbull, & Mvududu, 2008) conducted a statewide study of Utah secondary schools which revealed that students in schools with a more fully implemented CDSC program enrolled in more math and science courses and scored higher on the ACT than did students from traditional programs. Furthermore, students in a CDSC program were better prepared for career preparation.

A statewide study of middle schools in the state of Washington concluded no significant differences between CDSC middle schools compared with non-CDSC middle schools. Although this was a disappointing finding, upon further analysis it was found that sixth- and seventh-grade students in schools in which a CDSC program had been implemented for 5 or more years scored significantly better in identified academics (Sink et al., 2008). Therefore, counselors who are in the process of implementing a comprehensive school counseling program are to be aware of the time it takes to implement a program, to celebrate the successful steps that are taken toward full implementation, and to embrace the positive results that are attained after a period of time. Other research has been conducted that focused on the domains inherent to the ASCA National Model; the results of these studies may be used as a foundation for possible projects that you could implement as a trainee in your clinical experiences.

Academic Domain

School counselors work collaboratively with teachers to improve the achievement of underperforming students. Students who do not achieve academically are at risk for dropping out of school or not being successful in postsecondary education or in a career (Berger, 2013). An 8-week group intervention was provided to 13 high school students from three different high schools in South Florida with the intention of increasing student achievement as defined by the GPA and decreasing absences and discipline referrals. The researcher used a version of the Achievement Orientation Model

(AOM) that was designed to increase the motivation level of underachieving youth. In addition, the School Motivation and Learning Strategies Inventory (SMALSI) was used to measure motivation before and after the group intervention. Although two participants revealed significant changes in GPA, overall there were no significant differences between the pre- and post- test results. However, students reported that not only did the group help them learn something new about themselves in relation to goals and motivation, they also learned effective skills to enhance academic achievement. Furthermore, one of the school administrators requested that the school counselors continue the curriculum for future students (Berger, 2013). It is possible that more robust results may have occurred if this program had been in effect and measured over a period of time.

In another study, by Brigman, Webb, and Campbell (2007), the Student Success Skills (SSS) program designed to teach academic, social, and self-management skills was used with students in grades 5–9 in group classes and small group interventions. The final results of this intervention revealed significant gains in academic achievement and improved behavioral performance.

Career Domain

The Social Cognitive Career Theory (SCCT) was developed to explain the contextual factors and cognitive variables on career development. Through the use of this theory as a guiding model, Tang, Pan, and Newmeyer (2008) conducted a study with high school students from a Midwest high school to determine the effectiveness of this theory, how learning experiences influence career choices, and in what way gender and career choices intersect. Females expressed higher self-efficacy in careers that involve working with people and ideas, and communicated more interest in careers that led to self-satisfaction. Boys were more interested in careers that involved data and things. A significant implication for school counselors is the awareness of how self-efficacy and learning experiences shape career interests.

One hundred and fifty-two inner-city eighth- and ninth-grade students participated in a study to ascertain whether or not there were significant gender and ethnicity differences in vocational personality (Turner et al., 2008). The Self-Directed Search (SDS) was used to measure participants' interests in activities as well as their perceptions of ability and self-competence (Turner et al., 2008). Although this study did not reveal any differences in personality type among ethnic groups, there were gender differences. Boys expressed interest in realistic and investigative careers, whereas girls expressed greater interest in artistic careers. The results of this study indicate that school counselors need to assist students with careers based on personal interests as opposed to gender-based careers.

Social/Emotional Domain

The Social/Emotional Domain was formerly known as the Personal/Social Domain. Children who have experienced the death of a parent feel emotions such as shock, guilt, and anger and often have an impaired support system due to the grief experienced by surviving family and friends (Eppler, 2008). In many cases, it is the school counselor who has the training and available resources to facilitate the child's recovery from this devastating event. Eppler (2008) studied the resiliency factors that serve as defenses against greater traumatization and promote successful growth among children aged 9–12 who mourned the death of a parent. In order for the researcher to better understand each child's unique experiences and to serve as a guide for the child to remember the circumstances surrounding his/her parent's death, participants were given a series of questions, such as "What are some of your early family memories?" and "Who do you talk to when you are sad/happy/scared?" Each child was then asked to write a biblio-narrative to express his/her grief, which was then analyzed to identify resiliency factors. Bereaved children expressed sadness as the primary emotion, yet they also revealed the ability to thrive in the midst of challenging times. School counselors are able to use the components of the ASCA National Model to conduct support groups with these children. Furthermore, school counselors are able to integrate strength-based activities into the school setting by providing information and resources to teachers and parents to better understand the bereavement process and methods for assisting the grieving child (Eppler, 2008).

THE PROFESSIONAL SCHOOL COUNSELOR STANDARDS: SCHOOL COUNSELOR COMPETENCIES

You are entering the profession at a time of significant transition. As mentioned earlier, school counselor supervisors may lack familiarity with the new model, which may create an understandable tension coupled with anxiety. Direct service to students, as acknowledged in the Delivery component, has traditionally been one of the most challenging counseling components for school counselors. Administrators and teachers experience enormous amounts of pressure to perform and complete ever-growing responsibilities. Teachers are trained for their unique and specific classroom responsibilities, and principals are often experienced teachers who returned to school for administrative training. Therefore, most administrators understand the role of the teacher and their role as administrator. However, few teachers and administrators were informed as to the roles and responsibilities of the school counselor. This could be problematic when principals assign tasks to school counselors based on their personal experiences in a pre-K–12 school, to school counselors with whom they have worked as professionals in the schools, or based on the perceptions of others.

School counselor responses to task requests by administrators must be measured carefully. Helping others often creates a natural tension for the school counselor, as he/she is a trained helper and wants to assist whenever and however he/she is able. Yet, there could be legal/ethical implications when performing tasks for which we are not trained, and there is the additional risk that these tasks would define our role.

School Counselor Professional Competencies are identified within the 2012 ASCA National Model document to define activities of school counselors as they assume leadership within their school counseling program. You can use these competencies to self-evaluate your knowledge, abilities, skills, and attitudes that are essential to your success as a competent, effective professional. Activity 6.2 is designed as a checklist for you to use in evaluating your competencies. Some school counselor supervisors may also be interested in assessing their competencies. Furthermore, those areas in which you believe more experience is needed can be used for developing your own contract objectives and goals during the clinical experiences.

Conceptual Application Activity 6.2

Implementing the ASCA National Model in Clinical Experiences

Read through the list of competencies below and discuss with your site supervisor the types of activities that he/she ordinarily performs. This list of competencies can also be used to assist you in determining the competencies that you have already accomplished, those that can be incorporated into your clinical contract, and those that can be conducted once you enter the profession of school counseling. Indicate those activities that you would like to accomplish during the clinical experience.

SCHOOL COUNSELING PROGRAMS		
I-A. Knowledge *School counselors should articulate and demonstrate an understanding of:*	**My knowledge**	**My supervisor's knowledge**
I-A-1. The organizational structure and governance of the American educational system as well as cultural, political, and social influences on current educational practice		
I-A-2. The organizational structure and qualities of an effective school counseling program that aligns with the ASCA National Model		
I-A-3. Impediments to student learning and use of advocacy and data-driven school counseling practices to act effectively in closing the achievement/opportunity gap		

SCHOOL COUNSELING PROGRAMS		
I-A-4. Leadership principles and theories		
I-A-5. Individual counseling, group counseling, and classroom guidance programs ensuring equitable access to resources that promote academic achievement; personal, social, and emotional development; and career development including the identification of appropriate postsecondary education for every student		
I-A-6. Collaborations with stakeholders such as parents and guardians, teachers, administrators, and community leaders to create learning environments that promote educational equity and success for every student		
I-A-7. Legal, ethical, and professional issues in pre-K–12 schools		
I-A-8. Developmental theory, learning theories, social justice theory, multiculturalism, counseling theories, and career counseling theories		
I-A-9. The continuum of mental health services		
I-B. Abilities and Skills *An effective school counselor is able to accomplish measurable objectives demonstrating the following abilities and skills:*	**My abilities and skills**	**My supervisor's abilities and skills**
I-B-1. Plans, organizes, delivers, and evaluates the comprehensive school counseling program that aligns with the ASCA National Model		
I-B-1a. Creates a vision statement examining the professional and personal competencies and qualities a school counselor should possess		
I-B-1b. Describes the rationale for a comprehensive school counseling program		
I-B-1c. Articulates the school counseling themes of advocacy, leadership, collaboration, and system change		
I-B-1d. Describes, defines, and identifies the qualities of an effective school counseling program that benefits a comprehensive school counseling program for all stakeholders		
I-B-1e. Describes the benefits of a CDSC program to stakeholders		
I-B-1f. Describes the history of school counseling to create a context for the state of the profession		
I-B-1g. Uses technology effectively and efficiently to plan, organize, deliver, and evaluate the CDSC program		
I-B-1h. Demonstrates multicultural, ethical, and professional competences		
I-B-2. Serves as a leader in the school and community		
I-B-2a. Understands and defines leadership and its role in a CDSC program		
I-B-2b. Identifies and applies a model of leadership to a CDSC program		
I-B-2c. Identifies and demonstrates professional and personal qualities and skills of effective leaders		
I-B-2d. Identifies and applies components of the ASCA National Model requiring leadership (e.g., advisory council, management system, and accountability)		
I-B-2e. Creates a plan to challenge non-counseling tasks		
I-B-3. Advocates for student success		
I-B-3a. Understands and defines advocacy and its role in a CDSC program		
I-B-3b. Identifies and demonstrates benefits of advocacy with stakeholders		
I-B-3c. Describes school counselor advocacy competencies, including dispositions, knowledge, and skills		

SCHOOL COUNSELING PROGRAMS		
I-B-3d. Reviews advocacy models and develops a personal advocacy plan		
I-B-3e. Understand the process for development of policy and procedures at all levels		
I-B-4. Collaborates with stakeholders to promote and support student success		
I-B-4a. Defines collaboration and its role in CDSC programs		
I-B-4b. Identifies and applies models of collaboration and differences between consultation, collaboration, and counseling and coordination strategies		
I-B-4c. Creates statements or other documents that outline various roles of student service providers		
I-B-4d. Understands and knows how to apply a consensus-building process		
I-B-4e. Understands how to facilitate group meetings		
I-B-5. Acts as a systems change agent to create student success		
I-B-5a. Defines and understands system change and its role in a CDSC program		
I-B-5b. Develops a plan to deal with personal and institutional resistance to change		
I-B-5c. Understands the impact of policies, procedures, and practices that support and/or impede student success		
I-C. Attitudes and Beliefs *School counselors believe:*	**My attitudes and beliefs**	**My supervisor's attitudes and beliefs**
I-C-1. Every student can learn, and every student can succeed		
I-C-2. Every student should have access and opportunity to a quality education		
I-C-3. Every student should graduate from high school and be prepared for career or education		
I-C-4. Every student should have access to a CDSC program		
I-C-5. Effective school counseling is a collaborative process involving all stakeholders		
I-C-6. School counselors can and should be leaders in the school and district		
I-C-7. The effectiveness of school counseling programs should be measured using perception, process, and results data		
II: FOUNDATIONS		
II-A. Knowledge *School counselors should articulate and demonstrate an understanding of:*	**My knowledge**	**My supervisor's knowledge**
II-A-1. Beliefs and philosophy of the school counseling program that align with current school improvement and student success initiatives at the school, district, and state levels		
II-A-2. Educational systems, philosophies and theories, and current trends in education, including federal and state legislation		
II-A-3. Learning theories		
II-A-4. History and purpose of school counseling, including role transformations		
II-A-5. Human development theories and developmental issues affecting student success		
II-A-6. District, state, and national student standards and competencies		
II-A-7. Legal and ethical standards and principals of the school counseling profession and district and building policies		
II-A-8. Three domains of academic achievement, career planning, and personal/social development (now social/emotional)		

SCHOOL COUNSELING PROGRAMS		
II-B. Abilities and Skills *An effective school counselor is able to accomplish measurable objectives demonstrating the following abilities and skills.*	**My abilities and skills**	**My supervisor's abilities and skills**
II-B-1. Develops the beliefs and philosophy of the school counseling program that align with current school improvement and student success initiatives at the school, district, and state beliefs		
II-B-1a. Examines personal, district, and state beliefs, assumptions, and philosophies about student success, specifically what students should know and be able to do		
II-B-1b. Demonstrate knowledge of a school's particular educational philosophy and mission		
II-B-1c. Conceptualizes and writes a personal philosophy about stakeholders and a CDSC program that is consistent with the educational system		
II-B-2. Develops a school counseling mission statement aligning with the school, district, and state mission		
II-B-2a. Critiques a school district mission statement and identifies or writes a mission statement that aligns with beliefs		
II-B-2b. Writes a sample mission statement that is specific, concise, clear, and comprehensive, describing a school counseling program's purpose and a vision for how the program benefits every student		
II-B-2c. Communicates the philosophy and mission of the school counseling program to all appropriate stakeholders		
II-B-3. Uses student standards to drive the implementation of a CDSC program		
II-B-4. Applies the ethical standards and principles of the school counseling profession and adheres to the legal aspects of the role of the school counselor		
II-B-4a. Practices ethical principles of the school counseling profession in accordance with the ASCA Ethical Standards for School Counselors		
II-B-4b. Understands the legal and ethical nature of working in a pluralistic, multicultural, and technological society		
II-B-4c. Understands and practices in accordance with school district policy and local, state, and federal statutory requirements		
II-B-4d. Understands the unique legal and ethical nature of working with minor students in a school setting		
II-B-4e. Advocates responsibly for school board policy and local, state, and federal statutory requirements that are in the best interests of students		
II-B4f. Resolves ethical dilemmas by employing an ethical decision-making model appropriate to work in schools		
II-B-4g. Models ethical behavior		
II-B-4h. Continuously engages in professional development and uses resources to inform and guide ethical and legal work		
II.-B-4i. Practices within the ethical and statutory limits of confidentiality		
II-B-4j. Continually seeks consultation and supervision to guide legal and ethical decision making and to recognize and resolve ethical dilemmas		
II-B-4k. Understands and applies an ethical and legal obligation not only to students but to parents, administration, and teachers		
II-C. Attitudes and Beliefs *School counselors believe:*	**My attitudes and beliefs**	**My supervisor's attitudes and beliefs**
II-C-1. School counseling is an organized program for every student and not a series of services provided only to students in need		

SCHOOL COUNSELING PROGRAMS		
II-C-2. School counseling programs should be an integral component of student success and the overall mission of schools and school districts		
II-C-3. School counseling programs promote and support academic achievement, personal and social development, and career planning for every student		
II-C-4. School counselors operate within a framework of school and district policies, state laws and regulations, and professional ethics standards		
III. DELIVERY		
III-A: Knowledge *School counselors should articulate and demonstrate an understanding of:*	**My knowledge**	**My supervisor's knowledge**
III-A-1. The concept of a guidance curriculum		
III-A-2. Counseling theories and techniques that work in school		
III-B-3. Counseling theories and techniques in different settings, such as individual planning, group counseling, and classroom guidance		
III-B-4. Classroom management		
III-B-5. Principles of career planning and college admissions, including financial aid and athletic eligibility		
III-B-6. Principles of working with various student populations based on ethnicity, etc.		
III-B-7. Responsive services		
III-B-8. Crisis counseling, including grief and bereavement		
III-B. Abilities and Skills *An effective school counselor is able to accomplish measurable objectives demonstrating the following abilities and skills.*	**My abilities and skills**	**My supervisor's abilities and skills**
III-B-1. Implements the school counseling core curriculum		
III-B-1a. Cross-references ASCA Student Standards with the guidance curriculum		
III-B-1b. Develops and implements a developmental guidance curriculum addressing all students' needs		
III-B-1c. Demonstrates classroom management and instructional skills		
III-B-1d. Develops materials and instructional strategies to meet student needs and school goals		
III-B-1e. Encourages staff involvement to ensure the effective implementation of the school guidance curriculum		
III-B-1f. Knows, understands, and uses a variety of technology to deliver the school counseling curriculum		
III-B-1g. Understands multicultural trends in choosing a school counseling core curriculum		
III-B-1h. Understands the resources available for students with special needs		
III-B-2. Facilitates student planning		
III-B-2a. Understands student planning as a component of a CDSC program		
III-B-2b. Develops strategies to implement individual student planning		
III-B-2c. Helps students establish goals		
III-B-2d. Understands the current labor market trends and career opportunities		
III-B-2e. Helps students learn the importance of college and other postsecondary education and navigate the college admission process		

SCHOOL COUNSELING PROGRAMS		
III-B-2f. Understands the relationship of academic performance to the world of work, family, and community		
III-B-2g. Understands methods for helping students monitor and direct their own learning and personal/social/career development		
III-B-3. Provides responsive services		
III-B-3a. Understands how to make referrals to appropriate professionals when necessary		
III-B-3c. Compiles resources to utilize with students, staff, and families to effectively address issues through responsive service		
III-B-3d. Understands appropriate individual and small-group counseling theories and techniques		
III-B-3e. Demonstrates an ability to provide counseling for students during times of transition, separation, heightened stress and critical change		
III-B-3f. Understands what defines a crisis, the appropriate response, and a variety of intervention strategies to meet the needs of the individual, group, or school community before, during, and after crisis response		
III-B-3g. Provides team leadership to the school and community in a crisis		
III-B-3h. Involves appropriate school and community professionals as well as the family in a crisis situation		
II-B-3i. Develops a database of community agencies and service providers for student referrals		
III-B-3j. Applies appropriate counseling approaches to promoting change among consultees within a consultation approach		
III-B-3k. Understands and is able to build effective and high-quality peer helper programs		
II-B-3l. Understands the nature of academic, career, and personal/social counseling in schools and the similarities and differences among school counseling and other types of counseling		
II-B-3m. Understands the role of the school counselor and the school counseling program in the school crisis plan		
III-B-4. Implements system support activities for the comprehensive school counseling program		
III-B-4a. Creates a system support planning document addressing school counselor's responsibilities for professional development, consultation and collaboration, and program management		
II-B-4b. Coordinates activities that establish, maintain, and enhance the school counseling program as well as other educational programs		
III-B-4c. Conducts in-service training for other stakeholders to share school counseling expertise		
III-B-4d. Understands and knows how to provide supervision for school counseling interns consistent with the principles of the ASCA National Model		
III-C. Attitudes and Beliefs *School counselors believe*	**My attitudes and beliefs**	**My supervisor's attitudes and beliefs**
III-C-1. School counseling is one component in the continuum of care available to students		
III-C-2. School counselors coordinate and facilitate counseling and other services to ensure that all students receive the care they need, even though school counselors may not personally provide the care themselves		
III-C-3. School counselors engage in developmental counseling and short-term responsive counseling		
III-C-4. School counselors should refer students to district or community resources to meet more extensive needs		

SCHOOL COUNSELING PROGRAMS		
IV: MANAGEMENT		
IV-A-1. Knowledge *School counselors should articulate and demonstrate an understanding of:*	My knowledge	My supervisor's knowledge
IV-A-1. Leadership principles, including sources of power and authority and formal and informal leadership		
IV-A-2. Organization theory to facilitate advocacy, collaboration, and systemic change		
IV-A-3. Presentation skills for programs such as teacher in-services and results reports to school boards		
IV-A-4. Time management, including long- and short-term management using tools such as schedules and calendars		
IV-A-5. Data-driven decision making		
IV-A-6. Current and emerging technologies such as use of the Internet, web-based resources, and management information system		
IV-B. Abilities and Skills *An effective school counselor is able to accomplish measurable objectives demonstrating the following abilities and skills.*	My abilities and skills	My supervisor's abilities and skills
IV-B-1. Negotiates with the administrator to define the management system for the comprehensive school counseling program		
IV-B-1a. Discusses and develops the components of the school counselor management system with the other members of the counseling staff		
IV-B-1b. Presents the school counseling management system to principal and finalizes an annual management agreement		
IV-B-1c. Discusses the anticipated program results when implementing the action plans for the school year		
IV-B-1d. Participates in professional organizations		
IV-B-1e. Develops a yearly professional development plan to demonstrate how the counselor advances relevant knowledge, skills, and dispositions		
IV-B-1f. Communicates effective goals and benchmarks for meeting and exceeding expectations		
IV-B-1g. Uses personal reflection, consultation, and supervision to promote professional growth and development		
IV-B-2. Establishes and convenes an advisory council for the comprehensive school counseling program		
IV-B-2a. Uses leadership skills to facilitate vision and positive change for the comprehensive school counseling program		
IV-B-2b. Identifies appropriate education stakeholders for advisory council		
IV-B-2c. Develops meeting agenda		
IV-B-2d. Analyzes school data and school counseling program goals with the council		
IV-B-2e. Records meeting notes and distributes them as appropriate		
IV-B-2f. Analyzes and incorporates feedback from advisory council related to school counseling program goals as appropriate		
IV-B-3. Collects, analyzes, and interprets relevant data to monitor and advantage student behavior and achievement		
IV-B-3a. Analyzes, synthesizes, and disaggregates data to examine student outcomes and to identify and intervene as needed		
IV-B-3b. Uses data to identify policies, practices, and procedures that lead to systemic barriers, successes, and areas of weakness		
IV-B-3c. Uses student data to demonstrate a need for systemic change in such areas as course enrollment patterns; equity and access; and the achievement, opportunity, and information gap		

SCHOOL COUNSELING PROGRAMS

IV-B-3d. Uses data to establish goals and activities to close the achievement, opportunity, and information gap		
IV-B-3e. Knows how to use and analyze data to evaluate the school counseling program and research activity outcomes and identify gaps between and among different groups of students		
IV-B-3f. Uses school data to identify and assist individual students who do not perform at grade level and do not have opportunities and resources to be successful in school		
IV-B-3g. Knows and understands theoretical and historical bases for assessment techniques		
IV-B-4. Organizes and manages time to implement an effective school counseling program		
IV-B-4a. Identifies appropriate distribution of school counselor's time based on delivery system and school's data		
IV-B-4b. Creates a rationale for school counselor's time to focus on the goals of the comprehensive school counseling program		
IV-B-4c. Identifies and evaluates "fair share" responsibilities, which articulate appropriate and inappropriate counseling and non-school counseling-related activities		
IV-B-4d. Creates a rationale for the school counselor's total time spent in each component of the National Model		
IV-B-5. Develops calendars to ensure the effective implementation of the school counseling program		
IV-B-5a. Creates annual, monthly, and weekly calendars to plan activities to reflect school goals		
IV-B-5b. Demonstrates time management skills that include scheduling, publicizing, and prioritizing time and task		
IV-B-6. Designs and implements data-driven action plans that align with school and school counseling program goals		
IV-B-6a. Uses appropriate academic and behavioral data to develop guidance curriculum, close the gap between action plans, and determine appropriate students for the target group or intervention		
IV-B-6b. Identifies ASCA domains, standards and competencies being addressed by the plan		
IV-B-6c. Determines the intended impact on academics and behavior		
IV-B-6d. Identifies appropriate activities to accomplish objectives		
IV-B-6e. Identifies appropriate resources needed		
IV-B-6f. Identifies data-appropriate strategies to gather process, perception, and results data		
IV-B-6g. Shares results of action plans with staff, parents, and community		
IV-C. Attitudes and Beliefs *School counselors believe*	**My attitudes and beliefs**	**My supervisor's attitudes and beliefs**
IV-C-1. A school counseling program and guidance department must be managed like other programs and departments in a school		
IV-C-2. One of the critical responsibilities of a school counselor is to plan, organize, implement, and evaluate a school counseling program		
IV-C-3. Management of a school counseling program must be done in collaboration with administrators		
V. ACCOUNTABILITY		
V-A. Knowledge *School counselors should articulate and demonstrate an understanding of:*	**My knowledge**	**My supervisor's knowledge**
V-A-1. Basic concept of results-based school counseling and accountability issues		

SCHOOL COUNSELING PROGRAMS		
V-A-2. Basic research and statistical concepts to read and conduct research		
V-A-3. Use of data to evaluate program effectiveness and to determine program needs		
V-A-4. Program audits and results reports		
V-B: Abilities and Skills *School counselors are able to demonstrate the following abilities and skills.*	**My abilities and skills**	**My supervisor's abilities and skills**
V-B-1. Uses data from results reports to evaluate program effectiveness and to determine program needs		
V-B-1a. Uses formal and informal methods of program evaluation to design and modify comprehensive school counseling programs		
V-B-1b. Uses student data to support decision making in designing effective school counseling programs and interventions		
V-B-1c. Measures results attained from school guidance curriculum and closing-the-gap activities		
V-B-1d. Works with members of the school counseling team and with the administration to decide how school counseling programs are evaluated and how results are shared		
V-B-1e. Collects process, perception, and results data		
V-B-1f. Uses technology in conducting research and program evaluation		
V-B-1g. Reports program results to professional school counseling community		
V-B-1h. Uses data to demonstrate the value the school counseling program adds to student achievement		
V-B-1i. Uses results obtained for program improvement		
V-B-2. Understands and advocates for appropriate school counselor performance appraisal process		
V-B-2a. Conducts self-appraisal related to school counseling skills and performance		
V-B-2b. Identifies how school counseling activities fit within categories of performance appraisal instrument		
V-B-2c. Encourages administrators to use performance appraisal instrument that reflects appropriate responsibilities for school counselors		
V-B-3. Conducts a program audit		
V-B-3a. Completes a program audit to compare current school counseling program implementation with the ASCA National Model		
V-B-3b. Shares the results of the program audit with administrators, the advisory council, and other appropriate stakeholders		
V-B-3c. Identifies areas for improvement for the school counseling program		
V-C. Attitudes *School counselors believe:*	**My attitudes and beliefs**	**My supervisor's attitudes and beliefs**
V-C-1. School counseling programs should achieve demonstrable results		
V-C-2. School counselors should be accountable for the results of the school counseling program		
V-C-3. School counselors should use quantitative and qualitative data to evaluate their school counseling program and to demonstrate program results		
V-C-4. The results of the school counseling program should be analyzed and presented in the context of the overall school and district performance		

> **Box 6.2**
>
> School counselors-in-training reported that individual counseling and group counseling were the tasks most frequently conducted during their internship, whereas meeting with an advisory board, program planning, and tasks associated with the management system were performed less frequently during this clinical experience (Oberman & Studer 2014). Although the time spent on group and individual counseling activities is not surprising due to these being significant program expectations, supervisees also need experience in tasks that are more commonly performed by more experienced members of the profession.

RECOMMENDED PERCENTAGE OF TIME PERFORMING SCHOOL COUNSELING ACTIVITIES

From the school counselor competencies listed above, it is obvious that the school counselor performs a myriad of activities and has a responsibility for gaining the knowledge, skills, and behaviors needed to perform the job effectively. Yet, too often the school counselor's time is disproportionately spent in some areas and not others.

The ASCA National Model recommends that 80% of time be spent in direct and indirect student services, and 20% be spent in program planning and school support (ASCA, 2012). These percentages vary according to the school level and the developmental ages of the students, so it is possible that you or your supervisor will not necessarily meet these criteria exactly. However, keeping track of your time and analyzing where time is spent can provide information that you can share with stakeholders. As a counselor-in-training, you will probably receive requests to assist with activities that do not meet the philosophy and intent of a CDSC program. In a few cases I have had some school counseling students who openly refused to participate in an activity that they felt were beyond the scope of their supervisory contract. This is not an appropriate time to decline, and may even create ill will. Instead, go ahead and participate in the experience so that you can take what you learned to advocate for yourself when you are hired as a professional school counselor.

Table 6.1 Recommended Percentage of Time Spent in the Delivery Components

Delivery System Direct Services	Elementary School Counselor Time Spent	Middle School Counselor Time Spent	High School Counselor Time Spent
*Guidance Curriculum	35–45%	25–35%	15–25%
*Individual Student	5–10%	15–25%	25–35%
*Planning	30–40%	30–40%	25–35%
*Responsive Services	10–15%	10–15%	15–20%

Indirect Services
*Referrals
*Consultation
*Collaboration

Source: ASCA National Model: A Framework for School Counseling Programs. Alexandria, VA: ASCA

> **Conceptual Application Activity 6.3**   Tracking Time and Activities
>
> Chapter 9 contains a data tracking sheet that can be used to monitor where time is spent. Use this form or one that you have designed and observe your school counselor supervisor for one week. Note how much time he/she spends in each of the elements within the Delivery components.

Each week, compute the time spent by delivery area and compare your results with the recommended percentages above. In addition, as you perform the tasks identified in your practicum or internship contract, track how your time is spent in these areas. After accumulating one week of data for your supervisor and one week of data for yourself, compare the time you spent on tasks with those of your supervisor. Keep in mind that time differences may be due to your program responsibilities and/or tasks that need to be performed by an experienced professional with more advanced skills. You may also want to identify strategies for learning some of the tasks that are reserved for more experienced counselors.

- How are your Delivery System component activities similar or different?
- How do your Delivery System activities and time spent on these activities compare with those recommended by school level, according to the ASCA recommended time analysis?

Supervisor Time—Direct Activities

Time Engaged in Delivery System Component Activity (measure in .25 hour increments)	School Counseling Curriculum	Individual Planning	Responsive Services

Supervisor Time—Indirect Activities

Time Engaged in Indirect Activities (measure in .25 increments)	Referrals	Consultation	Collaboration

School Counselor-in-Training Time—Direct Activities

Time Engaged in Delivery System Component Activity (measure in .25 hour increments)	School Counseling Curriculum	Individual Planning	Responsive Services

School Counselor-in-Training Time—Indirect Activities

Time Engaged in Indirect Activities (measure in .25 increments)	Referrals	Consultation	Collaboration

What strengths and limitations did you identify in the school counselor's time analysis?

_____

_____

In what areas did you gain experience? Where would you like to receive additional training?

_____

_____

How could you gain experience in the areas in which you feel you need additional training?

_____

_____

CONCLUSION

The ASCA National Model was designed as a template for school counselors to use when developing a CDSC program. Within this chapter the various components and elements are summarized along with practical strategies for you to consider as you delve into the school counselor's role during your clinical experiences. A brief overview of the development of the ASCA National Model and the research that documents how students grow in the academic, career, and social/emotional domains as a result of participation in this type of programming is discussed. As you engage in activities during your clinical experiences, note how your supervisor spends time within the ASCA National Model, and where you spend your time. Even though your clinical experiences may not be in a school setting that has transformed its school counseling program to one that reflects the philosophy and goals of a CDSC program, note the myriad activities performed by the school counselor that easily fit within this model. Through observation and participation you will have opportunities to understand how this type of empirically based programming reveals its benefits to students, parents, teachers, and the community.

WEBSITES

- An executive summary of the ASCA National Model and a brief description of the components and elements is found on this link: http://ascamodel.timberlakepublishing.com/Files/Executive%20Summary%203.0.pdf
- This link provides information on how to obtain the ASA National Model: *A Framework for School Counseling Programs* (3rd ed.): http://ascanationalmodel.org/

REFERENCES

Amatea, E.S., & Clark, M.A. (2005). Changing schools, changing counselors: A qualitative study of school administrators' conceptions of the school counselor role. *Professional School Counseling, 9,* 16–27.

ASCA [American School Counselor Association]. (n.d.). *The role of the professional school counselor.* Retrieved from www.schoolcounselor.org/asca/media/asca/home/RoleStatement.pdf

ASCA. (2012). *The ASCA national model: A framework for school counseling programs* (3rd ed.). Alexandria, VA: Author.

Berger, C. (2013). Bring out the brilliance: A counseling intervention for underachieving students. *Professional School Counseling, 17,* 86–96. doi: 10.5330/PSC.n.2013–17.80

Brigman, G. A., Webb, L. D., & Campbell, C. (2007). Building skills for school success: Improving the academic and social competence of students. *Professional School Counseling, 10,* 279–288.

Brown, D., & Trusty, J. (2005). The ASCA national model, accountability, and establishing causal links between school counselors' activities and student outcomes: A reply to Sink. *Professional School Counseling, 9,* 13–15.

Education Trust. (2009). *Professional development.* Retrieved from www.edtrust.org/dc/tsc

Eppler, C. (2008). Exploring themes of resiliency in children after the death of a parent. *Professional School Counseling, 11,* 189–196.

Gysbers, N. C. (2004). Comprehensive guidance and counseling programs: The evolution of accountability. *Professional School Counseling, 8,* 1–14.

Harris, G. E., & Jeffery, G. (2010). School counsellors' perceptions on working with student high-risk behavior. *Canadian Journal of Counselling, 44,* 150–190.

Joe, S., & Bryant, H. (2007). Evidence-based suicide prevention screening in schools. *Children & Schools, 29,* 219–227.

Oberman, A. H., & Studer, J. R. (2014). *An exploratory study of the tasks school counselor trainees perform in internship.* Manuscript submitted for publication.

Sink, C. A., Akos, P., Turnbull, R. J., & Mvududu, N. (2008). An investigation of comprehensive school counseling and academic achievement in Washington state middle schools. *Professional School Counseling, 1,* 43–53.

Studer, J. R., & Oberman, A. H. (2006). The use of the ASA National Model in supervision. *Professional School Counseling, 10,* 82–87.

Tang, M., Pan, W., & Newmeyer, M. (2008). Factors influencing high school students' career aspirations. *Professional School Counseling, 11,* 285–295. doi: 10.55330/PSC.n.2010–11.285

Turner, S. L., Conkel, J. L., Starkey, M., Landgraf, R., Lapan, R. T., Siewert, J. J., … Huang, J. (2008). Gender differences in vocational personality types: Implications for school counselors. *Professional School Counseling, 10,* 317–326. doi: 10.5330/PSC.n.2010–11: 317

Wingfield, R. J., Reese, R. F., & West-Olatunji, C. A. (2010). Counselors as leaders in schools. *Florida Journal of Educational Administration & Policy, 4,* 114–128.

7 The ASCA National Model Themes and the Clinical Experiences

Jeannine R. Studer

CACREP Standards

Foundations

B. Skills and Practices

2. Demonstrates the ability to articulate, model, and advocate for an appropriate school counselor identity and program.

Collaboration and Consultation

M. Knowledge

1. Understands the ways in which student development, well-being, and learning are enhanced by family-school-community collaboration.
2. Knows strategies and methods for working with parents, guardians, families, and communities to empower them to act on behalf of their children.

Leadership

O. Knowledge

1. Knows the qualities, principles, skills, and styles of effective leadership.
2. Knows strategies of leadership designed to enhance the learning environment of schools.
4. Understands the important role of the school counselor as a systems change agent.

The purpose of this chapter is to:

- introduce the themes of systemic change, collaboration, leadership, and advocacy
- describe implementation strategies within the ASCA themes
- identify leadership characteristics.

INTRODUCTION

Diverse social structures have had a profound impact on our society, and schools are no exception (Gysbers, 2001). With recent attention placed on educational reform, the public eye has scrutinized school counseling programs to determine how these programs are essential to the achievement of youth. Unfortunately, up until recently there was little evidence that school counselors contributed to student growth, which resulted in the eventual elimination of many school counselor positions.

During the decade of the 1990s there was renewed alarm concerning the lack of a relationship between school counselor training and pre-K–12 student outcome. To better understand this issue,

Table 7.1 A New Vision for School Counselors

Leadership	Advocacy	Team and Collaboration	Counseling and Coordination	Assessment and Use of Data
Develop and implement prevention programs; career and college readiness activities; individual planning activities; problem-solving strategies	Provide data to assist stakeholders in viewing student outcomes	Work with teams of others to ensure responsiveness to equality and cultural variety in academic, vocational, and personal/social areas	Counsel with individuals or groups of individuals	Assess and interpret student needs with attention to cultural diversity
Offer data on student outcomes that reveal achievement gaps and give leadership for stakeholders to view data with equity as a core value	Employ data to bring about change through the use of community and school resources	Collaborate with helping professionals in and outside of the educational setting	Coordinate community resources to enhance student achievement	Determine and evaluate counseling strategies to measure student outcomes
Organize mentoring to enhance academic achievement	Advocate for students to enlarge their career awareness	Collaborate with school and community groups to concentrate on incentives for student growth	Act as a link between stakeholders and assist in initiating plans/supports for achieving goals	Assess barriers to learning
Participate in a leadership position to define counseling functions	Advocate for rigorous academic preparation for all students	Partner with others to establish staff training on academic, career, and social/emotional needs	Coordinate faculty and staff training initiatives for the benefit of all students	Interpret student data for systemic change

Adapted from *NCTSC The New Vision for School Counselors: Scope of the Work*. Retrieved from www.edtrust.org/

the DeWitt Wallace–Reader's Digest Fund provided monies to the Education Trust to develop a plan to transform school counseling. This initiative led to a "new vision" of school counseling with an emphasis on school counselor roles to include leadership, advocacy, teaming and collaboration, counseling and coordination, and assessment and use of data (Education Trust, n.d.; Goodnough & Pérusse, 2001). To advance these essential areas, the National Center for Transforming School Counseling (NCTSC) was established to train school counselors for the purpose of closing the achievement gap and creating opportunities for all students (Education Trust, n.d.). Table 7.1 illustrates these roles.

The ASCA adopted the four themes of leadership, advocacy, collaboration, and systemic change that were identified by the Education Trust and integrated them throughout the four components of the ASCA National Model. A discussion of each of these themes and in what manner school counselors are able to undertake activities to support these themes is below.

SYSTEMIC CHANGE

Change can occur either piecemeal, in which small adjustments are made to an already existing educational structure, or through a systemic process in which an entirely new structure is developed (Joseph & Reigeluth, 2010). Professional identity is associated with systemic change in that the roles and tasks performed by the school counselor define his/her attitudes, beliefs, and views of how school counselors function in the school. Identifying with a profession is a process that begins in the training program and continues throughout the career.

The interpersonal aspects of identity development are acquired as trainees learn what is expected and how to interact, and appropriate attitudes and strategies for problem solving are attained. Professional development takes time in that trainees move from mirroring expert opinions, relying on direction, and repeating skills and qualities to a personal integration of counseling, responsibility for professional growth, and an identity that is integrated with the academic community (Gibson, Dollarhide, & Moss, 2010). As competencies and personal philosophy are developed, the self is integrated into the professional community and the foundation for bringing about systemic change occurs.

Systemic change includes attention to working on educational policies and relationships and policymakers who influence school programming. It also means working within all the district schools to effect the change the profession supports. Comprehensive, developmental programming is only possible when standards are articulated within a curriculum that is appropriate to the needs of all students from pre-K–12 grades. Furthermore, it means collaborating with individuals who are impacted by the changes that create and improve student growth.

Six areas necessary for systemic change to occur include: (1) stakeholder ownership, (2) organizational understanding, (3) knowledge of systemic change process, (4) evolving perspective of education, (5) systemic view of education, and (6) systems design (Joseph & Reigeluth, 2010).

Stakeholder Ownership

Change occurs when stakeholders subscribe to the process. Educating and mobilizing others to support student growth and achievement are essential ingredients to begin the change process. In addition, recognizing emotional reactions to change and addressing these responses will ease the transformation process. This is particularly important when school personnel believe changes that involve additional activities are thrust upon them with little input (Seo et al., 2012).

Organizational Understanding

The school culture comprises characteristics such as personalities, policies, activities, and rules. Systemic change occurs when stakeholders are given an opportunity to challenge existing program structures and norms through a democratic format. When ideas, views, and contributions are expressed, participation is promoted and welcomed.

Knowledge of Systemic Change Process

Change is possible when stakeholders are able to envision and design a system that actively involves all individuals. When a positive vision is portrayed as to how the school counselor is able to contribute to school-wide goals, the school counselor's leadership will more likely be recognized (Wingfield, Reese, & West-Olatunji, 2010). This momentum is facilitated when documentation is provided that reflects where time is spent on tasks, and data are collected that inform how student growth has been improved.

Box 7.1

Functioning at the systems level requires that school counselors be knowledgeable of the factors that influence the educational system. These factors include effective teaching, positive classroom environments, and consultation with stakeholders regarding systemic transformation. School counselors without a background in education may benefit from understanding knowledge borrowed from teacher education such as differentiated instruction, self-regulated learning, and educational leadership (Galassi & Akos, 2012).

Evolving Perspective of Education

Stakeholders often base their perceptions of the school counseling program and the school counselor's role on personal experiences in K–12 with a school counselor, classes, or workshops based on the school counselor's role, or professional experiences within a school setting. These experiences serve as a foundation for how others believe a school counselor is to function. Dissatisfaction could result when the school counselor performs roles that contradict these individuals' expectations. The school counselor has a responsibility to educate others about the benefits of a CDSC program, the school counselor's role in leading the program, and appropriate and inappropriate activities.

Systemic View of Education

Frustration is evident when multiple attempts are made to solve a problem without success. These unsuccessful results could be due to being "stuck" because of a distorted view of the problem, or perhaps as a result of treating the student as a label such as "learning disabled" without an awareness of how the student can reach success. Or, it is also possible that they are too close to the issue (Hylander, 2012). Change may occur when a problem is viewed from a different lens, and this new perspective may be facilitated when the counselor works with others and assumes various positional stances (Hylander, 2012) that range from approach to neutral to moving away.

When the counselor uses an approach mode, the use of basic counseling skills such as active listening, paraphrasing, and reflecting offers an opportunity for others to feel heard and able to share his/her affective, cognitive, and behavioral perceptions of an issue. The counselor assumes a neutral stance by confirming what is heard, both positively and negatively. This stance is assisted by asking questions such as "How long has the problem been going on?" and "How have others been affected by this problem?" From here, the counselor is able to move from a neutral position to one that challenges the view by offering an alternative explanation. This confrontation may create discomfort, particularly if not enough time was given to discuss the issue. Questions such as "What would you have done if a different student had done this?" could facilitate a perception shift and a new view of the problem.

Systems Design

As school counselors gather data to show how they contribute to student success and stakeholders engage in a process to envision a changed structure, possibilities for a new and transformed system emerge. The change process takes approximately 5–6 years to complete, and effective change occurs as new strategies, newly acquired roles, and novel successful strategies are implemented (Gysbers & Henderson, 2012).

Conceptual Application Activity 7.1

Think about a time in your life when a new program, system, or policy was implemented. What was your reaction to this new way of doing things? What helped you adapt to this new structure? What could have been done to make the process go smoother? Discuss your answers with your peers. How will you do things to promote change as a change agent or as a recipient of these new methods?

LEADERSHIP

Although leadership has different definitions, for the purposes of this chapter the term 'leadership' was defined by Northouse in 2004 as "a process whereby an individual influences a group of individuals to achieve a common goal" (as cited in Mason & McMahon, 2009).

Conceptual Application Activity 7.2

Think in terms of people you view as leaders. What are some of the characteristics that make them effective in this role? Compare your answers with those of your peers and with the list of leadership characteristics in Table 7.2. Are there any traits that you believe are missing? Are there any traits that surprised you?

_____

_____

Table 7.2 Leadership Skills and Activities

Clarifier	Informer	Evaluator
Planner	Monitor	Creator
Organizer	Supporter	Empowering
Motivator	Managing conflict	Team builder
Problem solver	Consultant	Networker
Delegator	Gives recognition	Keeps confidences
Risk taker	Making decisions as a team	Shares vision
Integrity	Compassionate	Engaging
Humility	Collaborative	Communicator
Genuine	Self-aware	Confident
Listener	Respectful	Ethical
Well-educated	Open-minded	Interested in feedback
Evaluative	Consistent	Initiator

Shared Leadership

Leadership practices in the school have historically been perceived as skills belonging to the school administration (Mason & McMahon, 2009), who are able to either facilitate or prevent the efforts of other school personnel. For instance, school administrators are instrumental in determining how school counselors will spend their time. A common myth is that leadership exists only at the highest levels of an organization, yet when administrators with legitimate power provide support for other individuals who share similar principles or values to inspire others through positive behaviors, collaborative goals can be achieved. As Dollarhide, Smith, and Lemberger (2007) note, leadership is not a separate, individual activity but rather one in which all colleagues are considered equal and every viewpoint is heard with respect.

School counselors are leaders of a CDSC program and engage in strategies that promote equity and diversity by building school/family/community partnerships (Wingfield et al., 2010). School counselors are able to assume a leadership role through creative collaborative relationships and instruction with stakeholders about the benefits of the ASCA National Model and its contribution to academic achievement for ALL students. In particular, when school counselors provided organized services, classroom instruction for all students, and effective referral and follow-up procedures, a more collaborative relationship among stakeholders was revealed (Mason, 2010). Until the Transforming School Counseling Initiative and ASCA National Model for School Counseling programs were implemented, counselor training programs had historically not given much attention to the skills associated with effective leadership (Mason & McMahon, 2009).

Despite an apparent lack of attention to concepts related to leadership, more management practices are found among experienced school counselors than among their less experienced peers

Figure 7.1 School counselor discussing a transformed school counseling program.

Source: Shutterstock

(Shillingford & Lambie, 2010). Furthermore, more robust comprehensive programming occurs when school counselors assume more leadership roles (Mason & McMahon, 2009). In a study of school principals' perspectives of the school counselor position, participants revealed that exemplary school counselors fell into three basic themes. The first theme incorporated systemic interactions including the subthemes of leadership and the ability to see the "big picture." The second theme was the demonstration of professional behaviors and style that included the subthemes of interpersonal ability and approachability, counselor trustworthiness, and problem solver. The third theme was value to stakeholders, which comprises the ability to mediate issues between home and school, be a confidential resource and support, and bring value to the school community (Dollarhide et al., 2007). When school counselors are able to demonstrate these essential tasks, principals revealed that they are more likely to share leadership positions.

Transformational Leaders

The core of a counseling bond is the formation of a relationship, and it is this connection that is also closely aligned with transformational leadership. A transformational leader is a change agent who is able to create a clear vision while focusing on the success and growth of every member (Mason & McMahon, 2009). The four "I"s of transformational leaders include: Idealized Influence, Inspirational Motivation, Individualized Consideration, and Intellectual Stimulation (see Table 7.3).

When leaders display the characteristics associated with transformational leadership, a trusting, effective environment that builds confidence and self-empowerment is an end result (Avey, Avolio, & Luthans, 2011). School counselors are able to cultivate these characteristics to influence the principal's view of their role, and when they establish positive relationships with their administrator, a greater understanding of how the school counselor positively impacts the growth of school-aged youth is a likely outcome. Leadership can be demonstrated as school counselors navigate their role throughout the components of the ASCA National Model.

Table 7.3 Four "I"s of Transformational Leadership

Idealized Influence (II)	The leader is a role model whom members trust and respect. Transformational leaders follow through on what they state they will do.
Inspirational Motivation (IM)	The leader's personality encourages and motivates others, and the leader is able to articulate a clear vision to inspire others to fulfill agreed-upon goals.
Individualized Consideration (IC)	The transformational leader displays genuine concern for others' needs and feelings. Lines of communication are open so that every member of the team has an opportunity to share in a trustful environment.
Intellectual Stimulation (IS)	The leader challenges members to "think outside of the box" to inspire innovation and creativity. The status quo is challenged.

Conceptual Application Activity 7.3

Look at the components, elements, and themes of the ASCA National Model and identify leadership tasks that school counselors could undertake to address each of these areas. Several examples are provided to help you with this task.

Components	*Leadership tasks*
Foundation	
Program focus	Look at the mission of the school and create a school counselor vision and mission statement that mirror these objectives if one has not already been created. If one has been created, analyze the statements and share with your peers.
*Vision statement	
*Mission statement	
*Program goals	
Student competencies	
*Mindsets and Behaviors for Student Success	
*Other student standards	
Professional competencies	
*School counselor competencies	
*Ethical standards	
Management	
Assessments	During the week, track where your time is spent. Determine whether or not this time is congruent with the 80/20 formula for direct and indirect activities. Discuss this use of time with your supervisor.
*School counselor assessment	
*Program assessment	
*Use of time	
Tools	
*Annual agreement	
*Advisory council	
*Use of data	
*School data profile	
*Program results	
Data	
*Curriculum plans	
*Lesson plan	
*Calendar	

Delivery	
Direct student services *Core curriculum *Individual student *Planning *Responsive services Indirect student services *Referrals *Consultation *Collaboration	Create a strategy that can be used at your school site to assist students with their individual plans. For instance, at the high school level you may wish to develop a 4-year plan. At the middle school level individual students could be assisted with their career goals using the SMART acronym. At the elementary level, you could design a transition plan for students to move to the next grade or building level.
Accountability	
Data analysis *School data analysis *Use-of-time analysis Program results *Curriculum analysis *Small group analysis *Closing-the-gap analysis Evaluation and improvement *School counselor competencies *Program assessment *School counselor performance	Examine the school report card and identify areas that need to be addressed. Disaggregate these data and develop a plan to address them.

Counselors serve a vital role as leaders with essential skills that promote advocacy for individual students, marginalized groups, and the counseling profession itself (Myers & Sweeney, 2004, as cited in Cashwell & Minton, 2012).

ADVOCACY

Counselors have the skills to challenge institutional barriers that impede the academic, vocational, and personal/social (now renamed social/emotional) growth of students. Advocacy can be viewed as a skill that is used to deliberately challenge power structures, make connections, educate others about self-advocacy skills, and use data to share how the school counselor is able to meet the needs of all students (Locke & Bailey, 2014). Or, advocacy can be viewed as speaking or acting on behalf of another person or group to facilitate desired change (Kress & Paylor, 2012). For the purposes of this chapter, advocacy is described as a compass to intentionally navigate power structures, create bonds, teach self-advocacy skills, and use data to educate others as to how the school counselor works to close the achievement gap (Locke & Bailey, 2014). The TRAINER acronym serves as a seven-step model for advocacy (Chang, 2012; Eriksen, 1997; Hof, Dinsmore, Barber, Sur, & Scofield 2009; Milsom, 2009, as cited in Sweeney, 2012) with steps that include:

1. *T*argeting and concretely identifying a problem. This step requires determining an area to pursue and garnering support from others. At times we do not look at a problem from a broad perspective; and when we are able to bring clarity to an issue, other individuals may be encouraged to move toward problem resolution.

2. **R**esponding to a target area of concern. This includes looking at multiple levels such as the school institution, the community, and unjust policies both internally and externally. Internal supports could include time, money, personnel, expertise, and motivation, whereas external resources could include people outside of the counseling profession, such as those in the community, school, or agencies.

3. **A**rticulating involves planning and coherently communicating strategies to address an identified issue. Counselors use their basic counseling skills such as answering questions, listening, responding, and providing options that lead to problem resolution.

4. **I**mplementing a plan of action often requires ensuring that all individuals involved are aware of their responsibilities and attending to an ongoing assessment of the process. Strategic planning includes examining both long- and short-term goals that can be addressed by answering the questions:

   What is the main concern?
   Who is the target audience?
   What information does this group need to know?
   What is the time frame?
   What is the best method for introducing the concerns?

5. **N**etworking results in partnership initiatives to address an issue. Not only are members aware of personal responsibilities, they also take time to acknowledge success, including the efforts and progress of all individuals involved.

6. **E**valuating the strategy includes looking at evaluative results or other data that signal strategy effectiveness. Formative assessment occurs during the process to revise steps that are not working as well as anticipated, and summative assessment is conducted at the conclusion of the strategy to determine the entire effectiveness of the plan.

7. **R**etargeting by reviewing the evaluation data assists in future plan development as well as determining how data are to be presented while targeting future goals.

Conceptual Application Activity 7.4

Using the TRAINER model described above, identify a marginalized or underserved group of individuals in your internship school. Using the seven steps included in the model, design an action plan and present it to the class.

_____

_____

Despite a greater awareness of students who are disenfranchised, our societal institutions, including schools, continue to focus on some students while disregarding others due to constructs such as sexual orientation, socioeconomic level, disabilities, and so on (Lock & Bailey, 2014). Utilizing advocacy skills for the benefit of others and teaching self-advocacy skills are able to close the gap between students who are assisted and those who are not.

Advocacy Skills

Putting advocacy into action is often more difficult than it may appear. School counselors have a responsibility to work with all students, but at times school policies or rules that are designed to provide a safe school environment sometimes negatively impact certain individuals. School administrators often base decisions on what is in the best interests of the students and the school as a whole, whereas school counselors advocate for individual students, particularly when they are adversely affected by these policies. For instance, a student who lives in a rural area is often picked up late by his school bus due to the difficulty of traveling ill-kept or snow-covered roads. At times this route makes him tardy for his first-period class. Although this young student explained the situation to his teacher, the teacher replied that she had to follow school policy and give him a demerit for his tardiness. After several days of receiving demerits, the student went to his school counselor to express his frustration about how these marks affected his school record. The school counselor met with both the teacher and the principal on the student's behalf, and after explaining the situation, they agreed that demerits should not be given over circumstances beyond the student's control. In this instance, the school counselor advocated for the student to modify school policy.

Challenging rules and policies may have the potential to create conflict among professions, but positive outcomes are more likely when using strategies such as:

1. Understanding differences between and among groups of people.
2. Developing strong partnerships in the community and creating a list of the institutions, agencies, individuals, and resources that have the capacity to provide services to students and their families.
3. Communicating your education and training and your role in the school to stakeholders, including limits of confidentiality.
4. Encouraging students to collaborate with their peers who are experiencing similar situations and join in efforts to influence decision makers to address these concerns (Green & McCollum, 2004).
5. Working with administrators to discuss policies that may negatively impact students.

Through advocacy efforts on behalf of or with students, others can learn these skills so that they can self-advocate (Lee, 2012). School counselors have opportunities to teach these skills through classroom lessons, small counseling groups, or individual counseling.

Self-advocacy Skills

Self-advocacy strategies enable students to systematically gain control over their own learning and development to acknowledge and apply personal strengths, recognize areas to improve, and make decisions that impact their growth. In a study by Mishna, Muskat, Farni, and Wiener (2011), sixth- and seventh-grade students who were diagnosed with a learning disability were taught self-advocacy skills through a group intervention. During the group process, these students were taught to identify personal strengths, strategies for completing school work, techniques for dealing with bullies, how to ask for help with school work, relaxation strategies, and problem-solving skills. Group members revealed a significant improvement in self-advocacy skills. Student Activity 7.1 can be adapted for students in various grades to teach self-advocacy skills.

Student Activity 7.1   Catching My Dreams

Begin a discussion with students regarding their vision about their future. Prompt the discussion with questions such as: Where do you want to live? What type of job do you want? Do you want to go to college? Do you want to get married? have children? Ask if they have already begun to take the steps that are needed to reach these goals. Next, have students make a collage that illustrates these dreams. The board is to be divided into three sections. One section is to represent future dreams, the second section depicts a history that symbolizes what has been accomplished so far, and the final part of the board displays the steps that need to be taken to reach the future dreams. The collage can be made through drawings, pictures cut from magazines, or art materials such as pipe cleaners, cotton balls, or crepe paper.

COLLABORATION

Collaboration is a type of interaction in which two or more individuals work in partnership toward a shared goal (Friend & Cook, 2009, as cited in Murawski & Spencer, 2011). Historically, schools had little connection with the outside community due to the perception that education was the purview of school personnel (Hobbs & Collison, 1995). Yet, collaborative relationships occur both within and outside of the school setting with the potential to improve student well-being. With multiple influences pressuring our school-aged youth, no single individual can address the issues presented by any student, and school personnel are increasingly looking for supplementary resources to support their educational goals. School counselors have the essential leadership and interpersonal skills to work with educational team members to address students' academic, vocational, and personal/social (renamed social/emotional) growth. The Partnership Process Model for School Counseling is a seven-stage model to assist school counselors in creating school–family–community partnerships (Bryan & Henry, 2012). The steps in this model include: (a) preparing to partner, (b) assessing needs and strengths, (c) coming together, (d) creating a shared vision and plan, (e) taking action, (f) evaluating and celebrating progress, and (g) maintaining momentum.

Preparing to Partner

Too often negative attitudes toward families impede productive working relationships, particularly when these beliefs are focused on those from traditionally marginalized groups. When individuals within the school setting view families as valuable, then capable and successful educational partners (Amatea, Mixon, & McCarthy, 2013) will be a likely result. In addition, when assessment of data demonstrates how partnerships create a collaborative vision for how students and their families can be better served, an opportunity is created to work toward a common goal. Questions to consider at this stage include:

- What are your beliefs, attitudes, and values about families?
- What is the vision for a partnership?
- What is the vision of the school?
- How can administrative support be garnered for this partnership? (Bryan & Henry, 2012)

Box 7.2

Culture influences the collaboration process. For instance, some cultures may communicate frequently and may result in the view that a parent is constantly questioning the school personnel. Persons from another culture may feel uncomfortable asking questions or making requests. A family with strong religious beliefs may bring these beliefs into the meeting and may leave participants feeling uncomfortable. Or, parents/guardians with a child with a disability may be embarrassed, in denial regarding the disability, or defensive (Murawski & Spencer, 2011). A productive consultation results when cultural differences are acknowledged.

Assessing Needs and Strengths

A needs assessment and data collected from all stakeholders provide direction for areas that need to be addressed. These data are more effective when there is a focus on strengths that identify the resources, personnel, and strategies that are already successful, rather than viewing areas from a deficit perspective. Cultural brokers, or community liaisons who understand traditionally disenfranchised community members, are instrumental resources who are able to assist in recognizing the community assets, as well as identifying potential, collaborative team members who can work together on identifying resources and solving problems. Questions to ask at this stage include:

- What are the needs and strengths of the educational personnel, including bus drivers, custodians, and so on?
- What are the needs and strengths of parents and guardians?
- What are the needs and strengths of community members and organizations?
- What partnerships are already in existence? (Bryan & Henry, 2012)

Coming Together

Partnering includes attention to diverse members and ideas. An effective partnership is created when administrative support is provided for time, space, and assistance to create a collaborative community. This process is enhanced through trusting, reliable two-way communication and a clear understanding of roles among professionals. When individuals are able to interact and rely on each other in both formal and informal arenas, individual opinions and talents are respected, which facilitates task identification and implementation (Bronstein, 2002).

Questions to consider at this stage include:

- Who are the potential team members?
- Who are the cultural brokers who can identify potential members?
- What roles will members play?

Creating a Shared Vision and Plan

The school counselor's interpersonal communication skills and awareness of group facilitation assist in building a collective image of the future. Goal attainment is achieved through a strength-based approach in which enthusiasm and hope are vital ingredients. Brainstorming creates a greater range of fundamentally different ideas and more innovative solutions than an individual professional member is able to generate. In addition, team commitment to goal development and assumption of personal responsibility for goal failure or success creates a greater sense of shared success. Questions to consider at this stage are:

- What strategies can facilitate a shared vision and plan?
- What existing partnerships are currently addressing identified needs?
- How can the new partnership assist in meeting the identified needs?
- What are the goals and expectant outcomes?

Box 7.3 Considerations for hosting a successful parent/guardian event

a. Create a flyer and send it home with every student. In addition, post the information on the school webpage advertising the special event.

b. Solicit community businesses for donations for door prizes.

c. Offer child care services while parents are attending the informational event. Students from the school clubs could provide the services and may consider showing a movie and providing refreshments (keep in mind allergies).

d. Provide parents/guardians with refreshments (local businesses may be willing to provide snacks).

e. Have evaluation forms ready to obtain feedback from parents/guardians.

Source: Adapted from Serres & Simpson, 2013

Taking Action

Territoriality is often an outcome when professionals believe that their knowledge and skills are superior to those of other professionals. This belief often leads to strained relationships, particularly when other professionals are engaged in similar roles or tasks. In addition, some could be concerned about job elimination or additional tasks added to an already full workload when others are involved in a project. Yet, when roles, strategies, and ideas are shared, new and more fulfilling outcomes lead to greater satisfaction.

Questions to consider include:

- What strategies is the team able to implement?
- What is the time line?
- How will barriers and challenges be addressed?
- How can the media be involved in promoting this process?

Evaluating and Celebrating Progress

Taking time to review team meetings, evaluating each individual meeting, and assessing the outcome provides a greater understanding of the process and builds stronger relationships. Mellin, Anderson-Butcher, and Bronstein (2011) stated that reserving the last 5 minutes of each meeting for gathering thoughts on how well the meeting went and creating ideas to strengthen the process or collecting interview and/or reaction statements offers an opportunity for formative evaluation. At this stage, contributions of all partners are acknowledged and celebrated through public expressions of appreciation, thank-you cards, and/or recognition ceremonies. Questions to consider include (Bryan & Henry, 2012):

- How will individual and partnership contributions be acknowledged?
- How did the partnership make a difference?
- What is the best method to celebrate the collaboration?

Maintaining Momentum

Success builds upon success, with a goal to continue partnership achievements to maintain the momentum for future goal direction. The collaborative team should discuss strategies that were successful, those that need to be revised, and the barriers that stood in the way of progress. Consider maintaining current members and recruiting future members so that partnerships may continue to support future endeavors. Questions to deliberate include:

- What strategies will facilitate improvement or development of future partnerships?
- How will the partnership be maintained?
- How can new members be recruited while maintaining current ones?

Confidentiality Considerations

School counselors always need to address confidentiality when working collaboratively. Oftentimes, it is the school counselor who is the only team member who has an ethical professional responsibility to maintain confidentiality. Unless the school counselor shares the ASCA Ethical Code that highlights confidentiality with the team members, there may be the erroneous belief that the school counselor is withholding valuable information. With this ethical obligation, the school counselor needs to determine how much information to share and whether or not to tell the student that information will be shared with others. Providing specific information may assist others in understanding the student's behavior but also poses a potential ethical dilemma for the counselor in deciding how much information is too much to share. Counselors often ask themselves the question "How will sharing this information help the student?" Answers to this question assist in protecting the student's privacy while revealing necessary information.

Conceptual Application Activity 7.5

Discuss with your supervisor some of the collaborative activities in which he/she has been involved. Ask about the strengths and weaknesses of this process. Did any of the steps from The Partnership Process Model for School Counseling occur? Share your results with your peers.

_____

_____

CONCLUSION

The Transforming School Counseling Initiative (TSCI) was developed as a result of the concern that school counselors were not adequately meeting the needs of all students. The National Center for Transforming School Counselors was created with several themes to close the achievement gap among students. The ASCA adopted the themes of systemic change, leadership, advocacy, and collaboration as integral to the components of the ASCA National Model. Systemic change includes such concepts as stakeholder ownership, organizational understanding, knowledge of the change process, an evolving and systemic perspective of education, and systemic design. Leadership is a process in which an individual influences others to achieve a common goal. Transformational leaders include an Idealized Influence, Inspirational Motivation, Individualized Considerations, and Intellectual Stimulation.

Advocacy includes challenging power structures, teaching self-advocacy skills, and using data to show how school counselors meet the needs of all students. The TRAINER acronym is used as an advocacy model. Finally, collaboration can be addressed through the Partnership Process Model for School Counseling.

WEBSITES

- This link will take you to an article from the ASCA School Counselor magazine on school counselor leadership issues: www.ascaschoolcounselor.org/article_content.asp?article=889
- This link will take you to information on community asset mapping as a collaborative strategy www.thefreelibrary.com/School+counselors+and+collaboration%3a+finding+resources+through . . .-a0229067304

REFERENCES

Amatea, E. S., Mixon, K., & McCarthy, S. (2013). Preparing future teachers to collaborate with families contributions of family systems counselors to a teacher preparation program. *The Family Journal, 21,* 136–145. doi: 10.1177/1066480712466539

Avey, J., Avolio, B. J., & Luthans, F. (2011). Experimentally analyzing the impact of leader positivity on follower positivity and performance. *Leadership Quarterly, 22,* 282–294.

Bronstein, L. R. (2002). Index of interdisciplinary collaboration. *Social Work Research, 26,* 113–126.

Bryan, J., & Henry, L. (2012). A model for building school-family-community partnerships: Principles and process. *Journal of Counseling & Development, 90,* 408–420.

Cashwell, C. S., & Minton, C. B. (2012). Leadership and advocacy in counselor education programs: Administration and culture. In C. Chang, C. Minton, A. Dixon, J. Myers, & T. Sweeney (Eds.), *Professional counseling excellence through leadership and advocacy* (pp. 165–184). New York: Routledge.

Chang, C. Y. (2012). Professional advocacy: A professional responsibility. In C. Chang, C. Minton, A. Dixon, J. Myers, & T. Sweeney (Eds.), *Professional counseling excellence through leadership and advocacy* (pp. 95–108). New York: Routledge.

Dollarhide, C. T., Smith, A. T., & Lemberger, M. E. (2007). Critical incidents in the development of supportive principals: Facilitating school counselor-principal relationships. *Professional School Counseling, 10,* 360–369.

Education Trust. (n.d.). *History of TSCI.* Retrieved from www.edtrust.org/node/139

Education Trust. (n.d.). *The new vision for school counselors: Scope of the work.* Retrieved from www.edtrust.org/sites/edtrust.org/files/Scope%20of%20the%20Work_1.pdf

Eriksen, K. (1997). *Making an impact: A handbook on counselor advocacy.* Washington, DC: Accelerated Development.

Galassi, J. P., & Akos, P. (2012). Preparing school counselors to promote academic development. *Counselor Education and Supervision, 51,* 50–63. doi: 10.1002/j.1556–6978.2012.00004.x

Gibson, D. M., Dollarhide, C. T., & Moss, J. M. (2010). Professional identity development: A grounded theory of transformational tasks of new counselors. *Counselor Education & Supervision, 50,* 21–38.

Goodnough, G. E., & Pérusse, R. (2001). A comparison of existing school counselor program content with the education trust initiatives. *Counselor Education and Supervision, 41,* 100–110.

Green, E. J., & McCollum, V. J. (2004, Sept.-Oct.). Empowerment through compassion. *ASCA School Counselor.* Alexandria, VA: American School Counselor Association.

Gysbers, N. C. (2001). School guidance and counseling in the 21st century: Remember the past and into the future. *Professional School Counseling, 5,* 96–105.

Gysbers, N., & Henderson, P. (2012). *Developing & managing your school guidance and counseling program* (5th ed.). Alexandria, VA: American Counseling Association.

Hobbs, B. B., & Collison, B. B. (1995). School-community agency collaboration: Implications for the school counselor. *School Counselor, 43,* 58–65.

Hof, D. D., Dinsmore, J. A., Barber, S., Suhr, R., & Scofield, T. R. (2009). Advocacy: The T.R.A.I.N.E.R. model. *Journal for Social Action in Counseling and Psychology, 2,* 15–28.

Hylander, I. (2012). Conceptual change through consultee-centered consultation: A theoretical model. *Consulting Psychology Journal: Practice and Research, 64,* 29–45.

Joseph, R., & Reigeluth, C. M. (2010). The systemic change process in education: A conceptual framework. *Contemporary Educational Technology, 1,* 97–117. Retrieved from www.cedtech.net/articles/12/121.pdf

Kress, V., & Paylor, M. J. (2012). Theoretical foundations of client advocacy. In C. Chang, C. Minton, A. Dixon, J. Myers, & T. Sweeney (Eds.), *Professional counseling excellence through leadership and advocacy* (pp. 121–135). New York: Routledge.

Lee, C. (2012). Social justice as the fifth force in counseling. In C. Chang, C. Minton, A. Dixon, J. Myers, & T. Sweeney (Eds.), *Professional counseling excellence through leadership and advocacy* (pp. 109–120). New York: Routledge.

Locke, D. C., & Bailey, D. F. (2014). *Increasing multicultural understanding* (3rd ed.). Los Angeles: Sage.

Mason, E. (2010). Leadership practices of school counselors and counseling program implementation. *NASSP Bulletin, 94,* 274–285.

Mason, E. C. M., & McMahon, H. G. (2009). Leadership practices of school counselors. *Professional School Counseling, 13,* 107–115.

Mellin, E. A., Anderson-Butcher, D., & Bronstein, L. (2011). Strengthening interprofessional team collaboration: Potential roles for school mental health professionals. *Advances in School Mental Health Promotion, 4,* 51–61. doi.org/10.1080/1754730X.2011.9715629

Mishna, F., Muskat, B., Farnia, F., & Wiener, J. (2011). The effects of a school-based program on the reported self-advocacy knowledge of students with learning disabilities. *Alberta Journal of Educational Research, 57,* 185–203.

Murawski, W. W., & Spencer, S. (2011). *Collaborate, communicate, & differentiate: How to increase student learning in today's diverse schools.* Thousand Oaks, CA: Sage.

Seo, M. G., Yaylor, M. S., Hill, N. S., Zhang, X., Tesluk, P. E., & Lorinkova, N. M. (2012). The role of affect and leadership during organizational change. *Personnel Psychology, 65,* 121–165.

Serres, S. A., & Simpson, C. (2013). Serving educational pie: A multidisciplinary approach to collaborating with families. *Children & Schools, 35,* 189–191. doi: 10.1093/cs/cdt012

Shillingford, M. A., & Lambie, G. W. (2010). Contribution of professional school counselors' values and leadership practices to their programmatic service delivery. *Professional School Counseling, 13,* 208–217.

Sweeney, T. (2012). Professional advocacy: Being allowed to do good. In C. Chang, C. Minton, A. Dixon, J. Myers, & T. Sweeney (Eds.), *Professional counseling excellence through leadership and advocacy* (pp. 81–93). New York: Routledge.

Wingfield, R. J., Reese, R. F., & West-Olatunji, C. A. (2010). Counselors as leaders in schools. *Florida Journal of Educational Administration & Policy, 4,* 114–128.

8 Understanding the Foundation Component of the ASCA National Model as a School Counselor-in-Training

Caroline A. Baker and Sibyl Cato West

CACREP Standards

Foundations

B. Skills and Practices

2. Demonstrates the ability to articulate, model, and advocate for an appropriate school counselor identity and program.

The purpose of this chapter is to:

- apply the Foundation element of the American School Counselor Association (ASCA) National Model to clinical experiences, including
  - using data and information to develop SMART goals related to program focus,
  - reviewing Professional Competencies and Student Standards,
  - examining your personal and professional values in relation to the school community,
  - reviewing Professional Competencies and Student Standards (renamed ASCA Mindsets and Behaviors for Student Success),
  - exploring ethical standards and legal considerations at the foundational level.

INTRODUCTION

Think about the school in which you are working as an intern or practicum student. It is probably durable, serving hundreds if not thousands of students and staff every day, having done so for many years. How did the building come to exist? What had to take place in order for the structure to be sound and stable? It is reasonable to assume that a team of people collaborated to design the building and thought about its function, the needs of the population to be served, and the longevity of the building materials. In other words, the project of designing and building a school rested on a solid foundation of ideas, resources, beliefs, and building materials. Likewise, the Foundation component of the American School Counselor Association (ASCA, 2012) serves as the structure from which the Management and Delivery System components assemble, and it is integral to the Accountability component. Comprehensive, developmental school counseling (CDSC) programs rely upon a sturdy, team-oriented, clear foundation. What will be the program focus? What kinds of goals will the CDSC program identify and meet? How do school counselor personal and professional values inform the program focus and functioning? And how do ethical standards influence programs?

This chapter will help you understand the answers to the questions above, as well as the implementation and application of the Foundation component of the National Model. The Foundation component includes: (1) a program focus including beliefs, vision and mission statements, and program goals; (2) student competencies, including ASCA Student Standards (renamed Mindsets and Behaviors for Student Success) and other standards; (3) professional competencies such as the school counselor competencies; and (4) the ASCA Ethical Standards for School Counselors. The ultimate goal of a CDSC program requires a solid foundation to ensure that all students receive the necessary services to help them succeed, and you are instrumental in contributing to this aim.

PROGRAM FOCUS

Although you may have already taken a class on the ASCA National Model and developed vision and mission statements as an assignment in this class, keep in mind that as you gain more experience in understanding the school counselor's role, your beliefs surrounding the school counseling program and school counselor's role will probably change. You will develop new insights and knowledge with each person you encounter, and in turn these opportunities will impact your thoughts about yourself and the profession. Therefore, your values are ever-evolving, and what you think is essential to the profession at this time may not be a priority in the future. As you read this chapter, the conceptual application activities are designed to help you either rethink these initial efforts or to help you begin the process of developing these fundamental declarations if you have not had an opportunity before this time.

Creating the focus of your school counseling program is one of the most important aspects of your role as a professional school counselor. The program focus articulates your beliefs, vision and mission statements, and targeted goals that the school counseling program hopes to achieve regarding the academic, career, and personal/social (renamed social/emotional) development of students. Without a defined program focus, school counselors have a greater chance of being assigned non–school counseling duties that detract from student needs being met.

Beliefs

A belief is defined as "an opinion or conviction, or . . . confidence in the truth or existence of something not immediately susceptible to rigorous proof" (Dictionary.com, 2008). Think about the experiences you have had with your pre-K–12 school counselors. Did you have good experiences and fond memories of your interactions with these individuals? Or, did you have disagreeable involvements? Did these situations serve as catalysts for entering the school counseling profession? Building a belief system about school counselors and the program they lead requires you to think about your beliefs regarding education, students, and other stakeholders. As you shape your beliefs, you may find that they will be transformed through conversations with school counselors and other professions. And it is likely that the experiences you have in the school will inform how you think about school counseling. It is likely that your beliefs will change as you continue to gain experience in the schools. Conceptual Application Activity 8.1 is designed to assist with this process.

Conceptual Application Activity 8.1

The following questions are designed to help you think about your beliefs surrounding school counseling.

1. What is the role of the school counselor? _____

    _____

2. How is the school counselor an integral professional in the school setting? _____

    _____

3. How are students different as a result of participating in a school counseling program?

    _____

4. How do school counselors work with stakeholders? _____

_____

5. How do school counselors demonstrate their effectiveness? _____

_____

6. Share your beliefs statements with your peers, and as a group write a short paragraph that is a consensus of your beliefs. _____

_____

Vision and Mission

Professional school counselors who believe in and follow the principles behind the ASCA National Model and who effectively meet the needs of their school serve as excellent resources for describing and modeling a school counseling identity. These professionals have integrated their training, values, and beliefs with the existing school and district mission statements to form a collaborative alliance that functions as a framework to facilitate student success. If you are provided with the opportunity to create or revise a vision or mission statement for your school building or school counseling program, be aware that the task will not be simple. The task is to look ahead to the future and to incorporate personal, professional, and collective values about student success and what success will look like in 5 or more years. Keep in mind, however, that the reason you are creating a vision is to pave the way toward greater student and school success. The ASCA National Model (ASCA, 2012) provides excellent examples of vision statements for you to consider while you undertake this task.

Mission statements provide a direction for reaching the school counseling program vision. According to the ASCA National Model (ASCA, 2012), an effective mission statement incorporates the mission of the school district and state regarding education and addresses the success of every student. This means that the collective belief must be that all students can succeed and must be given access to equitable resources to do so. In addition, the focus of the mission statement should have each student in the forefront, with an indication of the long-range objectives for all students. Creating a mission statement from scratch is not an easy task, especially if the school counselor is new to the role or to the school building. Including key stakeholders, such as teachers, parents, and administrators, is essential for forming a vision and associated mission statement for the CDSC program.

Conceptual Application Activity 8.2   Vision and Mission

Using your notes from the activities above, develop your own vision and mission statement for your site's school counseling program. Carefully craft your statements using data and your beliefs about students. Once you feel comfortable with your statements, compare them with the vision and mission statements endorsed by your site. How do they compare? Was there anything you left out or included that was significantly different from your site's statements? What will you take away from this activity? Discuss this with your site supervisor.

_____

_____

Program Goals

The SMART acronym may be used to assist in the creation of school counseling program goals based on school data which help you to execute and achieve the vision and mission statement of your school counseling program. SMART goals are "*s*pecific, *m*easurable, *a*ttainable, *r*esults-oriented, and *t*ime bound" (ASCA, 2012, p. 25). Several steps assist in establishing a SMART goal.

1. Examine school, district, and state report card data to identify problem areas within the school, such as academic achievement gaps between groups of students, discipline rates, attendance issues, inequitable access to resources, etc. Other types of data include needs assessments, interviews with stakeholders, classroom observations, and pre- and post-tests. Collect data from a variety of sources to clearly identify a problem area that will be targeted using the SMART goal format.
2. After the data have been examined and a problem is identified, the next step is to outline current interventions being provided to target the problem, if any. In other words, what are the academic, career, and personal/social (renamed social/emotional) developmental activities occurring now which correspond to this gap? Creating a comprehensive list is a concrete method for school counselors to identify what is being done, and, conversely, what is not being done to address this gap.
3. At this stage, you will have formed a tentative and vague goal to start shaping into a refined SMART goal. However, this is an opportune time to review the school improvement plan and to discuss school goals with administrators. Aligning the goals, activities, and interventions of the school counseling program with the school's instructional accountability goals is an integral step to garner the support of stakeholders.
4. Finally, format your SMART goals by indicating exactly how each one is:
    1. Specific: What exact problem do you want to address and how does your goal state precisely what it will do?
    2. Measurable: Is your goal something that can be measured or evaluated in formative or summative ways?
    3. Attainable: Is your goal realistic or possible, considering current resources and funding? What might you need to achieve your goal?
    4. Results-oriented: Does your goal promote results, based on attainability and measurability? Do you know what you want the end results of the goal to be?
    5. Time-bound: Is there a finite time period in which to achieve this goal, or will this goal permit people involved to work indefinitely? Having a finite time period increases the likelihood of successful achievement of SMART goals.

Keep in mind that SMART goals are flexible with room for evaluation and revision after your intervention is complete. This will help to refine your goals in the future.

Box 8.1

"I don't care how much power, brilliance, or energy you have. If you don't harness it and focus it on a specific target and hold it there, you're never going to accomplish as much as your ability warrants."

Source: Zig Ziglar

Conceptual Application Activity 8.3   Developing SMART Goals

At your site, investigate the school's report card, discipline reports, and attendance records and interview stakeholders such as your site supervisor and administrators. Review the ASCA Student

Standards (renamed Mindsets and Behaviors for Student Success). Once you gather enough information to understand the school climate, develop three SMART goals that the counseling office could target. Discuss with your site supervisor the possibilities of successful completion of your SMART goals. How might you revise them? What are your first steps in achieving your goals?

ASCA MINDSETS AND BEHAVIORS FOR STUDENT SUCCESS: K–12 COLLEGE- AND CAREER-READINESS STANDARDS FOR EVERY STUDENT

The ASCA National Standards were first developed as a smorgasbord of competencies from which school counselors were able to choose for the purpose of addressing the knowledge, skills, and attitudes that students need to attain academic, career, and social/emotional success. These standards were later retitled the ASCA Student Standards to assess student growth and development (ASCA, 2012). To align with current research and trends, these standards are now renamed the ASCA Mindsets and Behaviors for Student Success: K–12 College- and Career-Readiness Standards for Every Student. These Mindsets and Behaviors are found in a database in which key terms are entered and specific standards are identified (ASCA, 2014).

The ASCA Mindsets and Behaviors align with grade-level competencies and Common Core state standards to facilitate school counselors' ability to support student growth through collaboration, group and individual counseling, and team teaching.

Like the ASCA Student Standards, the ASCA Mindsets and Behaviors are organized according to the academic, career, and social/emotional domains (formerly personal/social); however, unlike the ASCA Student Standards, the Mindsets and Behaviors are applicable to any of these three domains. General categories and subcategories classified according to factors that contribute to academic achievement subsume these standards. These standards are found in Table 8.1 below (ASCA, 2014).

Table 8.1 General Categories and Subcategories of ASCA Mindsets and Behaviors

Category 1: Mindset Standards
Personal psycho-social attitudes and individual beliefs about his/her academic ability

School counselors encourage the following mindsets for all students:

1. Self-confidence in ability to succeed
2. Belief in development of whole self, including integration of academics with activities at school, home, and the community that enhance learning and life experiences
3. Understanding that postsecondary education and lifelong learning are necessary for long-term career success
4. Belief in using abilities to their fullest to achieve high-quality results and outcomes
5. Positive attitude toward work and learning

Category 2: Behavior Standards
Students will demonstrate learning strategies, self-management skills, and social skills

The Behavior Category is subgrouped into:

a. *Learning Strategies:* Strategies used to aid in thinking, remembering, or learning
b. *Self-management:* Ability to focus on a goal, avoid distractions, and prioritize
c. *Social Skills:* Appropriate behaviors that enhance social interactions between others

These ASCA Student Standards, renamed Mindsets and Behaviors for Student Success, supplement the Common Core standards and state-developed student competency standards. By cross-walking these standards with the state's standards to identify overlap and to establish program goals, more credibility is provided for their application. Furthermore, the cross-walk may serve as a checklist to show what the school counselor is doing and what activities need to be done to eliminate disparities in the CDSC program foundation.

SCHOOL COUNSELOR PROFESSIONAL COMPETENCIES

Not only do students have identified knowledge, skills, and behaviors to achieve as a result of participating in a school counseling program, school counselors also have a responsibility to reach identified competencies to serve as effectual leaders of a CDSC program. The School Counselor Professional Competencies are outlined in the *ASCA National Model: A Framework for School Counseling Programs*, third edition (ASCA, 2012). School counselors are able to assess their competence and areas for growth on an annual basis. Furthermore, you can use this checklist to evaluate your competencies as you begin your clinical experiences and to ascertain personal goals as you progress through the profession. Combining knowledge of personal values, professional ethics, federal and state laws, student standards, and professional competencies yields a vast body of information that aids in forming a CDSC program focus.

Conceptual Application Activity 8.4   Professional Competencies and Goals

Review ASCA's School Counselor Professional Competencies to determine your areas of strength and areas for growth. Ask your site supervisor to complete it with you. Once you have discussed the results with your site supervisor, develop three goals for your own professional and personal development. Are the goals specific, measurable, attainable, results-oriented, and time-bound?

_____

_____

As you begin to understand the elements that support the foundation component, you are also applying a code of conduct that guides our profession. The ASCA Ethical Standards for School Counselors (ASCA, 2010) support the mission of the profession and the principles that define ethical behavior and practices. Although Chapter 12 provides you with more detailed considerations regarding these practices, the following section presents a glimpse of how our values shape the professional decisions we make.

VALUES, ETHICAL STANDARDS, AND LAWS

A solid CDSC program foundation requires knowledge of personal and professional values, familiarity with professional ethical standards, and awareness of laws and policy. Perhaps the starting place for developing a strong CDSC program foundation is to identify personal and professional values about education and students and to compare those values with the ASCA Ethical Standards for School Counselors (ASCA, 2010) and state and local laws. How do you define a value? Although there are numerous definitions, a definition provided by the American Psychological Association (2007) states that a value is "a moral, social, or aesthetic principle accepted by an individual or society as a guide to what is good, desirable, or important" (p. 975). Your idea of "good, desirable, or important" might mean such things as collaborating through teamwork, working hard to achieve goals, helping all students succeed, and balancing work with self-care. But what do these values actually look like in practice? How do they compare with your ethical code or established law?

Box 8.2

"Cheshire Cat, asked Alice. Would you tell me, please, which way I ought to go from here? That depends a good deal on where you want to go, said the Cat. I don't much care where, said Alice. Then it doesn't matter which way you go, said the Cat."

Source: Charles "Lewis Carroll" Dodgson, *Alice's Adventures in Wonderland*

The ASCA Ethical Standards for School Counselors (ASCA, 2010) outline best practice for navigating often ambiguous situations to ensure that student and parent rights are upheld. When school counselors face sensitive or tricky situations, ethical standards provide guidance as to the collectively agreed upon standards of practice. The ethical code also outlines a decision-making model to employ in situations with which you may be confronted. Further, consultation with professional peers, while maintaining confidentiality, is considered ethical practice.

Sometimes our values align with the ethical code. Sometimes they do not. An example might be regarding cultural competence and working with diverse populations. The ASCA Ethical Standards state: "Professional school counselors affirm the multiple cultural and linguistic identities of every student and all stakeholders" (ASCA, 2010, p. 5). Are you able to do this for all students, regardless of their identity? How might your values impact your work with students and other stakeholders?

Conceptual Application Activity 8.5   What Do You Believe?

Read the following case outline and respond to the questions.

A student with wrinkled, dirty clothes and unkempt hair comes to you and reports that a teacher constantly harasses her and makes rude comments about her friends. You have seen the student in the halls and at lunch, always with a group of friends. After looking up the student's file, you find that the student has been to the counseling office for several concerns throughout her high school career.

a.   How did you immediately picture the student? In your mind, how did you picture the student's race, gender, age, ability level, socioeconomic status, sexual orientation, and personality? What about the teacher?

b.   How do you define yourself regarding the aspects of identity listed above? Are your characteristics the same or different from the student's?

c.   Reflect on how your reaction to the student might differ depending on her demographic identity. For example, if the student were of a different race or gender than you, would that result in a different assessment of the presenting concern?

d.   How might your beliefs affect your work with students and the foundation and focus of your comprehensive counseling program?

Figure 8.1 School counselors have an ethical responsibility to maintain confidentiality unless the student indicates harm to self or others.

Source: Shutterstock

Further, how do the state and federal laws intersect with your ethical code and your values? The ASCA Ethical Standards require that confidentiality be upheld to ensure that students feel safe in the counseling relationship; confidentiality must be broken, however, to "prevent serious and foreseeable harm to the student" (p. 2). You might be a parent or teacher, so your values might tell you that information would be helpful to share with anyone invested in the student. Law may tell you that your information is legally required or subpoenaed in a civil or criminal case involving your students. Although it is usually the student who has privilege, the counselor has the responsibility of maintaining this right (Wheeler & Bertram, 2012). Check to see whether or not "privileged communication," a legal term, exists between the student and school counselor in your state.

When you get into your practicum and internship sites, pay close attention to how your site supervisor handles sensitive situations and ask questions to gain an understanding of the reasons events were handled in a certain manner. Do you feel comfortable with the way in which he or she talks to other school professionals about certain students and certain confidential situations? If not, how would you handle it? Similarly, school personnel may seek a counseling relationship with you; you will need to identify how to maintain appropriate professional and role boundaries.

Conceptual Application Activity 8.6   Ethical Case Processing

Ask your site supervisor to tell you about a recent ethical decision he/she had to make. Find out what ethical codes applied to the case, the decision-making model that was used, whether your site supervisor consulted with another professional to determine the decision, and what the outcome was. On your own, reflect on this discussion and determine your own ideas about working through the ethical case.

_____

_____

CONCLUSION

School counselors play vital roles in the success of all students and are essential in integrating the school counseling program with the mission of the school. In order to do this, a stable, informed, thoughtful foundation for the CDSC program is crucial. How do school counselors do this? They identify personal beliefs and values about education and the people participating in the process. They assess professional competencies in practicing as a school counselor. They review and become familiar with professional ethics and local and federal laws. They work toward student competency in areas outlined by states and the school counseling profession. They pull together data to inform their work and to develop SMART goals that support the counseling program mission and vision. Once these tasks are initiated and maintained, the CDSC program foundation paves the way for a program delivery and management system, which will ultimately lead to a school counseling program run on a solid basis and influenced by data-driven accountability.

WEBSITES

The Education Trust can be found at this link: www.edtrust.org. It is committed to closing the achievement gap for students so that all can reach high academic achievement. The National Center for Transforming School Counseling helps school counselors advocate for marginalized students.

This link will take you to a website on how school counselors-in-training implement the ASCA National Model: http://counselingoutfitters.com/vistas/vistas12/Article_98.pdf

REFERENCES

American Psychological Association. (2007). *Dictionary of psychology.* Washington, DC: Author.

ASCA [American School Counselor Association]. (2010). *Ethical standards for school counselors.* Retrieved from www.schoolcounselor.org/asca/media/asca/home/EthicalStandards2010.pdf

ASCA. (2012). *The ASCA National Model: A framework for school counseling programs.* Alexandria, VA: Author.

ASCA. (2014). *Draft of the mindsets and behaviors for student success: K-12 college- and career-readiness standards for every student.* Retrieved from www.schoolcounselor.org/asca/media/asca/home/MindsetsBehaviors.pdf

Dictionary.com. (2008). *Belief.* Retrieved from http://dictionary.reference.com/browse/belief?db=dictionary

Wheeler, A. M., & Bertram, B. (2012). *The counselor and the law: A guide to legal and ethical practice.* Alexandria, VA: American Counseling Association.

9 Understanding the Management Component of the ASCA National Model as a School Counselor-in-Training

Jeannine R. Studer

CACREP Standards

Academic Development

K. Knowledge

2. Understands the concepts, principles, strategies, programs, and practices designed to close the achievement gap, promote student academic success, and prevent students from dropping out of school.

   The purpose of this chapter is to:

- present an overview of the management system in a comprehensive, developmental school counseling (CDSC) program,
- discuss school climate and office environment,
- examine school counselor, program, and use-of-time assessment,
- share information regarding organizational tools to manage CDSC programs.

INTRODUCTION

A program cannot exist without people who are responsible for certain duties, a plan for when activities will occur, and administrative support for the system structure. Not only is it important for you to be aware of all the individuals with whom you will be interacting, it is also essential for you to be aware of the hierarchy of supervision and communication patterns that exist. When you first enter the school, policies and procedures will already be in place, and it is up to you to determine how your academic training requirements can be fulfilled within the parameters of the school mission and goals.

The Management System, like all the components in the American School Counselor Association (ASCA) National Model, does not stand by itself. This component can be compared to a general contractor building a house, who is responsible for balancing multiple roles that are scheduled on a master calendar. The general contractor must have oversight control and agreements among the subcontractors, all of whom need to be aware of the scheduled completion dates and how each person will work with other individuals involved with the project. Finally, consideration needs to be given to how stakeholders will view the final results (e.g., the home buyer's satisfaction with the completed home). Much like the layout of a home, the school structure will partially dictate when and where you will conduct activities and is influenced by the physical floor plan of the school (e.g., the location of offices, classrooms, cafeteria, gymnasium, theater). Within this component, assessments and tools are created to manage the organizational structure of the school counseling program, yet space, school culture, and climate influence decisions and the school counselor's role.

136

The School Counselor's Office

The location of the school counselor's office and office space arrangement may determine how often people come to see you and contribute to making people feel comfortable when they come to your office. At times, school counselors-in-training complain that other educational resource personnel (e.g., school psychologist, speech therapist) share the space they were given for counseling purposes. Obviously, these shared space arrangements make scheduling individual counseling sessions challenging. In one case, a student counselor-in-training was frustrated when no office space was available, and only after her site supervisor helped her reframe her predicament was this situation viewed as an opportunity to be creative. She adapted by conducting counseling sessions while walking around the school track with some of her counselees. In another instance she went to an empty gym and shot hoops with her counselee—with a twist. They would take turns shooting the basketball and with each shot each person would make a statement about him/herself. The school counselor-in-training shared information about herself, and in turn the counselee revealed a fact about himself without the pressure of making eye contact or being compelled to talk in an office setting.

Conceptual Application Activity 9.1

Tour the school building to which you are assigned and pay attention to space arrangements such as the administrator's office location in relation to the school counselors' offices. Consider the following questions: Where are the school counseling offices located? Are they labeled School Counseling or something else (e.g., guidance counselor)? Is there enough room to conduct individual and group counseling? Is the office decor and furniture arrangement inviting? Is the office in a private place for counseling to occur? Do the walls and space allow for voices to be overheard? Is there an appropriate place for students and others to wait outside the office? Will students be greeted by someone at a front desk or a sign directing them to the location of a school counselor? Is there clerical assistance available and accessible to the school counselors? Are there adequate spaces for books and other materials? Is there ample storage for materials and electronic equipment? Is there computer space available that can be accessed privately? Is there a printer/fax located in an area where the printed material can remain confidential? Does the equipment need to be shared with other personnel? Is there a common area with bulletin board space available for advertising counseling events or college or career information? What suggestions for improvements would you make?

_____

_____

Sometimes the school counselor's office is located in close proximity to the administrator's office, causing students to associate visiting the school counselor with discipline. Even though your role is to assist students to accept personal responsibility associated with their behaviors, you are not the school disciplinarian. As stated by the ASCA position statement *The Professional School Counselor and Discipline,* "The professional school counselor has specialized training and skills in preventing disruptive student behavior. The professional school counselor is not a disciplinarian but should be a resource for school personnel as they develop individual and school-wide discipline procedures" (ASCA, 2013, para. 1). School counseling offices located in a thoroughfare area open to visitors, administration, staff, and students may be easily accessible but may not provide the privacy that counseling students requires. In other schools, the school counselors' offices are located in remote settings that are difficult to find and could significantly diminish the number and frequency of students who seek school counselor assistance.

Conceptual Application Activity 9.2

Observe the location of the school counselor offices. Are they in a suite, or are they located in different parts of the building? Look specifically at the arrangement of your site supervisor's office. Is the counselor's desk situated in a position that serves as a barrier between the counselor and counselee? Is there open space between the counselor and those seeing the counselor that creates an inviting impression for those who visit? Are papers stacked up on the desk and on shelves?

Other considerations for an inviting office may include decor placed on walls, the furniture style, desk decorations, paint color, and so forth. For instance, if the counselor has religious/spiritual artifacts in the office, these could make students uncomfortable or comfortable depending on if they think their beliefs would or would not be accepted. Your first impressions may be similar to others' first impressions. Share your impressions with those of your peers.

Conceptual Application Activity 9.3

In the space next to each of the items listed, place an *I* next to the items that would make the counseling office inviting, and place a *U* next to the items that would make the counseling office uninviting for students and other visitors. Add items of your own to the list and compare with lists by your peers.

_____ Family pictures	_____ Posters of athletics
_____ Confederate flag	_____ College/university diploma
_____ Rainbow symbol	_____ Candy jar
_____ Symbolic jewelry	_____ National Rifle Association Certificate
_____ Bible	_____ Candles or scents
_____ College diplomas	_____ School mascot memorabilia
_____ Counselor wearing jeans	_____ Kleenex
_____ "Right to Life" poster	_____ Pictures of pets
_____ College posters	_____ Motivational quotes
_____ Professional licenses	_____ Family planning poster
_____ Aquarium	_____ Music playing

The school counselor may be able to advocate for the profession by educating others about the tasks for which he/she is trained. Documentation of where time is spent and graphs that reveal effectiveness of various activities are concrete examples that can be shown to school decision makers to illustrate the importance of the school counselor's role. In addition, assessments reveal counselor and program successes and areas that need to be addressed or improved, and tools are utilized to guide these assessments.

ASSESSMENTS

As discussed in Chapter 8, the School Counselor Professional Competencies identify the knowledge, skills, and attitudes that effective school counselors possess to lead a CDSC program. The foundation component of the ASCA also offers the School Counseling Program Assessment for annual evaluations of the program and how well all students are assisted within this plan.

Within the Management Component, the Use-of-Time Assessment is an enumerative instrument that is used to track where time is spent. The ASCA recommends that school counselors spend 80% of their time in direct student services, such as face-to-face student interactions. The remaining 20% of time is to be spent in indirect services that occur with others on behalf of students (see Figure 9.1).

Conceptual Application Activity 9.4

In the chart below, track the time you spend in direct and indirect activities. Although many of the activities you will be performing are based on your practicum and internship contract, this will give you an opportunity to not only gauge where your time is spent, but also to determine where additional experiences are needed.

| Direct Services—80% | | | | Indirect Services—20% | | | |
	Responsive Services	Individual	Group		Consultation	Collaboration	Referrals	Management & Foundation
7:00				7:00				
7:30				7:30				
8:00				8:00				
8:30				8:30				
9:00				9:00				
9:30				9:30				
10:00				10:00				
10:30				10:30				
11:00				11:00				
11:30				11:30				
12:00				12:00				
12:30				12:30				
1:00				1:00				
1:30				1:30				
2:00				2:00				
2:30				2:30				
3:00				3:00				
3:30				3:30				
4:00				4:00				
				7:00				

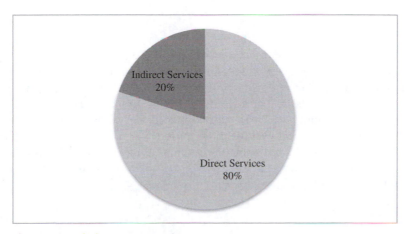

Figure 9.1 Chart of recommended percentage of time.

TOOLS

Management Agreements

All individuals who are essential to the school counseling program are included in the management plan so that all individuals are aware of who is responsible for each activity, when and where it will occur, the evaluation means, and the supplies or equipment that are needed. As stated previously, the school counseling program does not stand alone; it is an integral component of the school mission. For example, the standards chosen from the Mindsets and Behaviors for Student Success (formerly the ASCA Student Standards) can be addressed in a classroom in partnership with the school counselor and teacher. Or, the school social worker or community human service workers may be invited into the school to discuss pertinent issues. In some cases, a written contract that identifies monetary arrangements will be needed for outside individuals who assist with programming. Before making these types of arrangements, the building administrator, your supervisor, and/or individuals outside of the school system who are facilitating program activities are to be informed of all contractual agreements.

Furthermore, to prevent any misunderstanding as to the expectations surrounding the school counselor's role, a job description or annual agreement clarifies the school counselor's duties. Too often, when the responsibilities of the school counselor are not clearly defined, other stakeholders will express their opinions as to what the school counselor should be doing. These impressions are often based on perceptions from interactions rather than actual knowledge of the school counselor's training. The job description that is mutually agreed upon not only serves as a contract specifying duties, but can also be used to identify personal and professional goals that fulfill the mission and vision of the school counseling program.

Box 9.1

With the wide variety of skills school counselors implement, the use of a particular skill depends on the anticipated outcome. For instance, *informing* involves one-way communication that flows from counselor to student. *Teaching* involves two-way communication in which information is provided and students participate to apply the knowledge. *Advising* is counselor/student centered and helps students with decision making. *Counseling* is student focused, and students are able to resolve personal issues with the assistance of the counselor.

Source: Gysbers & Henderson, 2012

Advisory Council

An advisory council serves as a support system for the CDSC program and is composed of key stakeholder representatives. To provide credibility to these members, appointments should be supported by the administration and endorsed by the school board. It is not unusual for the school to have an advisory council to assist in providing feedback and concerns and to be liaisons to the school community, and although the school counseling advisory board serves in the same capacity, the focus is on the maintenance and evaluation of the CDSC program. The advisory board is usually composed of no more than 12 individuals who characterize varying viewpoints. Meetings with the advisory council generally occur at the beginning of the school year and again at the end of the school year to review, evaluate, and plan for the following year.

Figure 9.2 Selecting a diverse advisory board helps to ensure that the needs of all students are addressed.

Source: Shutterstock

Conceptual Application Activity 9.5   Advisory Council

Attend a meeting of the school counseling program advisory committee. Note the representatives who are part of this board. Discuss the advisory member composition with your peers. Are there similarities? Are there individuals who you believe should be on the board that are not represented? Discuss your reasons for selecting such individuals.

_____

_____

Use of Data

Data help us to understand school needs, students who are not receiving vital services, program and intervention effectiveness, and counselor efficacy. Data touch the myriad of National Model components and elements, and within the Management component the school profile is reviewed and evaluated and decisions are made based on disaggregating data to determine whether certain groups of students are not reached. Program data are categorized as process, perception, and results.

Process Data

These types of data are also known as enumerative data and indicate where time is spent, with whom, and when activities occur. Your clinical log is an example of process data. Counselors often complain about the difficulty of tracking the myriad of tasks they perform each day. EZAnalyze (www.ezanalyze. com) and the Time Elapsed Analysis and Reporting System (TEARS; www.schoolcounselor.com/tears)

are software programs that calculate activities and time spent in these tasks and offer a summary to share with stakeholders. Although these data are important, they are not enough. More robust perception and outcome forms of data are needed to show the effectiveness of counseling interventions.

Conceptual Application Activity 9.6

Use the table in Conceptual Application Activity 9.4, a chart you have created, or the technological applications mentioned above to track the time you spend each day in the various components of the ASCA National Model. In which areas do you spend the majority of your time? How does your time compare with those of your peers? Use the information to compare how your time is spent.

Perception Data

These type of data are used to understand changes in attitudes, behavior, or knowledge and are collected through such means as pre- and post-tests, needs assessments, program or activity assessments, surveys, or questions. A needs assessment is a type of instrument that collects perception data and provides comprehensive data regarding multiple stakeholder opinions.

Needs Assessments. These types of assessments may be compared with other school data, such as those on the school profile, and assist in determining program goals, competencies, and indicators for student success in the academic, career, and personal/social (renamed social/emotional) domains. Figure 9.3 is an example of the results of a needs assessment that was given to teachers by a school counseling intern. Additional examples of needs assessments that can be adapted for your particular school are found on the ASCA website (www.schoolcounselor.org).

In the example below, elementary school teachers were asked to indicate the areas they believed were most needed by the students in their school, and the intern categorized the top needs and responses by topics, which she presented in the chart. If you are unfamiliar with creating computer-generated graphs, a helpful, simplistic website that can assist you in converting data into graph form is available from the National Center for Education Statistics at the "Kids' Zone" graph link at http://nces.ed.gov/nceskids/createagraph/default.aspx.

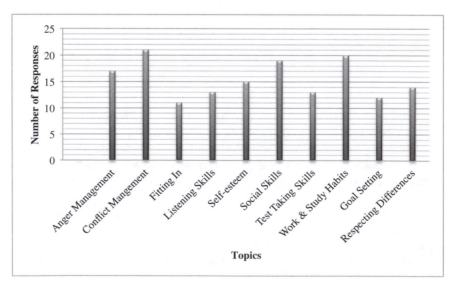

Figure 9.3 Example of a needs assessment.

Conceptual Application Activity 9.7

After analyzing the school profile and disaggregating data, look at the needs assessment examples available from the ASCA website (www.schoolcounselor.org). Design your own needs assessment that you can use with the stakeholders in the school in which you are interning. Show this assessment to your supervisor and administrator to review and see if you can gain permission to distribute and analyze the results of the needs assessment. Share your results with your classmates.

_____

_____

Outcome Data

Outcome data reveal how interventions and activities are effective in reaching goals. Outcome results include short-term data that assess change within a few weeks or months; intermediate data measure program effectiveness for an academic year time frame; and long-term data analyze changes year after year over multiple years. Attendance reports, discipline referrals, progress reports, and unit/semester exams provide short-term data that you can use to monitor the impact of school counseling intervention programs on student behaviors and/or knowledge. Outcome evaluations compare pre-program data with post-program data as presented in school report cards, student data management systems, and other measures of student performance. These data can be beneficial to your site supervisor in determining areas to address with the school counseling curriculum, and your efforts in collecting this information may create a legacy in the school for others to continue.

Action Plans

Action plans may be in the form of the school counseling curriculum, small groups, and closing-the-gap activities. These plans are similar in that information regarding the goals, student standards, type of activity, timeline, individuals responsible for the activities, and evaluation are developed and shared. In the contract you have developed for practicum or internship, you and your supervisors have identified various activities in which you will be involved; these tasks can be written as an action plan. As you are developing plans for your contract, or as you begin a new counseling position, you will be called upon to perform tasks that may require a lot of preparation time. It is not unusual for you to experience anxiety as you anticipate your role in implementing this task, and it is also not uncommon for you to use this as an opportunity to enhance your knowledge and skill. For instance, as stated by a former intern:

> When completing my school counseling internship, my supervisor placed me in charge of a financial aid night presentation. Fear mixed with great consternation immediately overcame me! However, this forced me to learn as much about financial aid as possible in preparation for the presentation. Not only did I learn about a subject to which I previously had little knowledge, a secondary benefit was the invaluable relationships (business and personal) that I developed with various financial aid directors at postsecondary institutions.

Conceptual Application Activity 9.8

Using the information in your contract, complete the following chart, or with the help of your supervisor, design one that more accurately reflects the templates adapted by the school board.

ASCA/State Domain, Standard	Grade Level	Description of Activity	Materials	Process Data	Perception Data	Outcome Data

Lesson Plans

Lesson plans are created from the domains, competencies, and indicators identified from the Mindsets and Behaviors for Student Success or other student standards. Good instruction requires advance planning, identification of the knowledge and skills you want students to acquire, the sequence in which you will teach these outcomes, and activities that you will use to maximize learning and are intended to keep students motivated and on task (Ormrod, 2011). A *lesson plan* is a written guide of how you will carry out a class lesson. A typical lesson plan includes the following:

- Goal(s) and objective(s) of the lesson
- Instructional materials and equipment that will be used
- Instructional strategies and the sequence in which they will be presented
- Assessment method(s) to be used for student learning.

In writing lesson plans, *goals* refers to the long-term outcome of instruction, and *objectives* refers to the specific desired outcome of a unit or lesson. One way to look at an instructional goal is to think of it as a standard as outlined in the ASCA Student Standards (renamed Mindsets and Behavior for Student Success). Three standards are in each of the academic, career, and personal/social (renamed social/emotional) domains, and competencies and indicators are found within each of the standards that more specifically define appropriate skills, knowledge, or behavior to be acquired (ASCA, 2012). For example, using the academic domain, a sample lesson plan is in Figure 9.4. In association with this competency there are several indicators that more specifically identify the attitudes, behavior, or knowledge the student is to demonstrate. The competencies and indicators are written as objectives that can be evaluated.

Well-written lessons include four key components, sometimes referred to as the ABCDs of learning (Erford, 2010). First is the audience (A) for whom the objective is being directed; in most cases the students. The second is a statement of the expected behavioral (B) outcome(s) that will result from the lesson. Thirdly, is the condition(s) (C) under which the learning will occur, and finally, lesson objectives need to include the degree (D) of the expected performance, or the frequency with which students will demonstrate the competency (Goodnough, Pérusse, & Erford, 2011).

ASCA Student Standard— Students will complete school with the academic preparation essential to choose from a wide range of substantial postsecondary options, including college.
  ASCA Student Competency— A:B2 Plan to Achieve Goals
  ASCA Student Indicator:

- A:B2.7 Identify postsecondary options consistent with interests, achievement, aptitude, and abilities
- A:C1.6 Understand how school success and academic achievement enhance future career and vocational opportunities

---

Figure 9.4 Understanding college admissions lesson plan (standards are from the ASCA Student Standards).

Materials Needed

- Student profile sheets
- Activity directions
- 8 student volunteers

Directions

- 8 student volunteers will come to the front of the classroom and each student will be given a "student profile" sheet. On one side of the sheet is a GPA and on the other side there are a series of statements.
- Students line up in order of GPA printed on their student profile (from highest to lowest). They should hold up the profile with the GPA side facing the audience.
- The school counselor will read the activity directions and students will rearrange themselves according to the information on each profile sheet.

Follow-up Activities

This activity is most effective when used at the beginning of a classroom lesson surrounding college admissions procedures or postsecondary options. When used at the ninth-grade level, it can stimulate discussion on how students can become more involved in school and community activities in order to boost their chances of admission to a selective college. When used with older high school students, it can be a reminder that the college admissions process is not always straightforward and that a high GPA does not guarantee admission to some institutions.

Evaluation

Students will participate in a discussion following the activity. Some questions could include:

- Were you surprised at the outcome of the activity? Why or why not?
- Did this activity help you better understand some of the factors involved in the college admissions process?
- Now that you have this information, identify changes you plan to make in either your academic schedule or your extracurricular activities.

Student Profile Sheet

Put the GPA in large letters on the front side of the paper, and the student profile on the back.

4.1 GPA	• You took a strong academic program. • You forgot to change the name of the college when word-processing the essay that was sent to several schools.
4.0	• You attended an enriching summer program between your junior and senior years. • You decided not to take AP classes (even though your school offered them) because you wanted to protect your GPA.
3.7 GPA	• The topic of your essay was sports (as a metaphor for life). • You are an Eagle Scout. • You are all-region in basketball.
3.5 GPA	• Your intended major is Greek. • You participated in NO extracurricular activities. • You attended an enriching summer program between your junior and senior years.
3.3 GPA	• You applied early decision to your first-choice college. • Your intended major is psychology. • You plagiarized an American History paper and got caught.

Figure 9.4 (Continued)

3.1 GPA	• Your intended major is psychology or pre-med.
	• You wrote an essay that everyone passed around the office because it was so good.
	• You are the first in your family to attend college.
	• You are a varsity athlete.
	• You made a "D" junior year, but wrote the college to explain extenuating circumstances.
	• You've taken a strong academic program.
2.9 GPA	• You direct the gospel choir at church.
	• You are quiet and don't know your teachers well enough to ask for a recommendation.
	• You've participated in community service.
	• You've taken a strong academic program.
	• You're from a single-parent household and must work to help with expenses.
2.8 GPA	• You are a legacy at the college to which you are applying.
	• You did not write the optional essay for your college application.
	• You've participated in some community service.
	• Your last name is Kennedy and the college library is named after your grandfather.

Activity Directions

Give each student volunteer a student profile and line up in order of GPA from highest to lowest. Students are to hold the profile with the GPA facing the audience and follow the instructions on their profile. The school counselor reads the following directions.

1. If you have taken an exceptionally strong academic program, move up two spaces.
2. If you direct the gospel choir at your church, move up one space.
3. If you clearly stated that this college is your first choice by making an early decision application and commitment, move up two spaces.
4. If your intended major is psychology or pre-med, move down one space.
5. If your intended major is Greek, move up one space.
6. If you do not know any of your teachers well enough to feel comfortable asking for a recommendation, move down two spaces.
7. If, when you were word-processing your college essay, you forgot to change the name of the college you were applying to, move down three spaces.
8. If you are a legacy, move up two spaces.
9. If you did not write the optional college essay, move down one space.
10. If the topic of your college essay was "sports as a metaphor for life," move down one space.
11. If you wrote the "essay of the year," the one that everyone passed around the office, move up two spaces.
12. If you plagiarized an American History paper and got caught, sit down, you're out of the competition.
13. If you will be the first in your family to attend college, move up two spaces.
14. If you attended an enriching summer program between your junior and senior years, move up two spaces.
15. If you have participated in no extracurricular activities, move down three spaces.
16. If you have participated in a significant community service project, move up one space.
17. If you are an Eagle Scout, move up two spaces.
18. If you are a varsity athlete, move up one space. If you're all-region in a sport, move up another space.
19. If you got a "D" in an academic course at the end of your junior year, move down three spaces.
20. If you wrote a letter to the college admissions office and explained the extenuating circumstances surrounding a grade of "D," move up one space.
21. If you decided to protect your GPA by not taking AP classes offered at your school, move down two spaces.

Figure 9.4 (Continued)

22. If you come from a single-parent household and must work part-time to help with expenses, move up two spaces.
23. If your last name is Kennedy, and the name of the college library is Kennedy, and it's not a coincidence, move all the way to the front of the line and stay there.

Figure 9.4 (Continued)

It is important to remember that a lesson plan is merely a guide and not a strict "recipe" in which there has to be rigid adherence to achieve a desired outcome (Ormrod, 2011). As you progress through a lesson, you may find that students are not as knowledgeable of the topic as you originally thought, or you might have to review a concept that you expected students to have already mastered. You may also find that the students will show particular interest or curiosity about a particular topic that could mean spending more time than you originally intended in teaching that topic. The thing to remember in conducting a classroom lesson is to be flexible. The ultimate goal is to reach a desired outcome; how you and the students get there is a journey. You want the journey to be engaging, challenging, and rewarding for both you and the students.

Conceptual Application Activity 9.9

Ask your site supervisor to share copies of his/her lesson plans. Note the various categories that are used to organize the information. Is this lesson plan one that is written according to district policy? What materials are cross-walked with the Mindsets and Behaviors for Student Success? Are lesson plans required to be filed with the central office? Share the information you found with your classmates and discuss the similarities and differences.

_____

_____

Calendars

Having a yearly calendar of what you will be doing throughout the academic year provides an opportunity for all interested personnel to be cognizant of when events will occur and their responsibilities in meeting program standards. Activities are identified on a master calendar to indicate the activity, person(s) responsible, date, location, audience or recipients, and additional comments. Table 9.1 is an example of a calendar of events.

Keeping track of all the activities that a counselor performs each day is difficult, and school counselors have learned to organize themselves according to a system that works best for them. For instance, taking time to identify dates of standardized tests such as the PSAT ahead of time and marking dates on the calendar as a reminder to order the materials prevents last minute, stressful requisition of materials. Or, if you are planning a career day at some date in the future, indicating this event on the calendar in advance will also keep you organized and aware of tasks that need to be conducted prior to this date. *Timetable* is a free application designed for students, but is also used by educators to keep track of upcoming assignments, dates, meetings, and other activities that need to be scheduled. This application can be accessed at www.techsupportalert.com/content/simplify-your-life-student-timetable.htm.

Table 9.1 Example of Events on a Calendar for Planning Purposes, Informing Stakeholders of Upcoming Events, and Documenting Process Data

August	September
Schedule new students	Individual student meetings with seniors
Orientation for incoming students	Order test materials
Information session for new teachers and substitutes about the school counseling program	Visit classrooms to introduce members of school counseling program
Analyze data from school report card	Design group for study skills

October	November
Parent conferences scheduled	Student Study Team meetings
Data collection	Parent/guardian workshop
Conduct divorce group	College night
PSAT testing	Advisory board meeting
Senior classroom programming	Analyze data

Calendars can be in the form of a personal, daily hard copy agenda or a weekly file divided into compartments for each day of the week with the appropriate information filled in in each section. Finding available dates on our calendar to schedule appointments or meetings can be problematic. However, to make scheduling easier, *Doodle* is a free, electronic solution for scheduling events, in which invited individuals are able to indicate available times and dates. This tool is found at http://doodle.com/en/.

Several managerial strategies that you can utilize while conducting your activities in the clinical setting include:

- Divide projects by those that take precedence and categorizing these tasks into priorities such as A = important and urgent; B = important but not urgent; C = urgent but not important; D = delegate to more appropriate personnel. From my experience, it seems that most counselors are good at managing A-level priorities but are not as adept at handling B-, C-, and D-level activities.
- Other helpful time-saving organizational tools are electronic or notebook calendars, master lists, file folders, large accordion folders, and computerized systems.
- Before leaving the office at the end of the day, review all your unfinished tasks and calendar to identify upcoming activities. Prioritize tasks that need to be addressed the next day.

Conceptual Application Activity 9.10

Ask your supervisor to show you his or her personal calendar of events. Ask him or her how it is organized and what managerial strategies have been most helpful. For instance, some elementary counselors use a different color marker for each grade level. When that color appears on the calendar it serves as a reminder that an activity is to occur for that particular grade. Other counselors have a different personal calendar for each grade level. In a few sentences, describe the management system used by your supervisor. Share your supervisor's technique with your peers.

CONCLUSION

The Management component includes assessments and tools to effectively plan, apply, and assess a CDSC program. School counselors are able to access the School Counselor Competencies Checklist developed by the ASCA to evaluate knowledge, abilities, and attitudes to determine areas that they have mastered and those areas in which improvement is needed. Furthermore, school counselors annually evaluate their school counseling program to determine areas in which attention is needed and to establish goals for the following academic year. Tools are used to support the school counseling program in the form of annual agreements, advisory councils, data, action and lesson plans, and calendars. Finally, the ASCA recommends that school counselors spend 80% of their time on direct student services, with the additional 20% spent on indirect student services. Annual appraisal of where time is spent assists in allocating time that is more in line with this endorsement.

Tools such as annual agreements, the use of an advisory council, and the use of data to determine effectiveness of interventions provide concrete documentation of the essential role of the school counselor in meeting the needs of all students. Action and lesson plans are used to inform all stakeholders when activities will occur throughout the year and the standards that will be addressed. Finally, annual calendars provide a means for organization and advance notification of the various school counseling activities that will occur.

WEBSITES

- Post-it Notes + Evernote (www.post-it.com)

Using this auto-tag application gives users the opportunity to stamp the time, date, and person responsible for an activity. Access to your electronic calendar automatically adds the description of the activity.

- Jump-Start Assessment Tools (www.jumpstart.com/parents/resources/assessment-tool)

This site provides a number of resources, activities, worksheets, and assessments to use with school-aged youth in grades K–12.

- *LessonPlanet* (www.lessonplanet.com/search?keywords=School+Counselor&type_ids[ ]=357918& type_ids[ ]=357917&gclid=CODr2YWHpb4CFU8Q7AodbyAApA)

This site provides a number of lesson plans, activities, projects, and videos for school counselors who work with students in all grades.

REFERENCES

ASCA [American School Counselor Association]. (2012). *The ASCA National Model: A framework for school counseling programs*. Alexandria, VA: Author.

ASCA. (2013). *The professional school counselor and discipline*. Retrieved from www.schoolcounselor.org/asca/media/asca/home/position%20statements/PS_Discipline-%281%29.pdf

Erford, B.T. (2010). How to write learning objectives. In B.T. Erford (Ed.), *Professional school counseling: A handbook of theories, programs and practices* (2nd ed., pp. 279–286). Austin, TX: Pro-ED.

Goodnough, G.E., Pérusse, R., & Erford, B.T. (2011). Developmental classroom guidance. In B.T. Erford (Ed.), *Transforming the school counseling profession* (3rd ed., pp. 154–177). Upper Saddle River, NJ: Pearson Education.

Gysbers, N.C., & Henderson, P. (2012). *Developing & managing your school guidance & counseling program* (5th ed.). Alexandria, VA: American School Counselor Association.

Ormrod, J.E. (2011). *Educational psychology: Developing learners* (7th ed.). Boston, MA: Allyn & Bacon.

10 Understanding the Delivery System Component of the ASCA National Model as a School Counselor-in-Training

Jeannine R. Studer

CACREP Standards

Foundations

A. Knowledge

7. Understands the operation of the school emergency management plan and the roles and responsibilities of the school counselor during crises, disasters, and other trauma-causing events.

Academic Development

K. Knowledge

3. Understands curriculum design, lesson plan development, classroom management strategies, and differentiated instructional strategies for teaching counseling-and guidance-related material.

Collaboration and Consultation

M. Knowledge

2. Knows strategies to promote, develop, and enhance effective teamwork within the school and the larger community.
6. Understands the various peer programming interventions (e.g., peer mediation, peer mentoring, peer tutoring) and how to coordinate them.

The purpose of this chapter is to:

- provide information on how school counselors-in-training are able to gain experience in the Delivery Component during their clinical experiences,
- introduce strategies and interventions within each of the elements in the Delivery System component,
- identify direct and indirect student service activities.

INTRODUCTION

The delivery component is composed of direct and indirect student services, and answers the question "*What* activities and strategies will be used to address student needs?" According to the ASCA, 80% of the school counselor's time is to be spent on direct student services, and the remaining 20% of the school counselor's time is to be spent on indirect services. An overview of these areas is presented below.

DIRECT STUDENT SERVICES

Direct student services include face-to-face interactions between the school counselor and students. These services include the school counseling curriculum, individual student planning, and responsive services.

School Counseling Core Curriculum

Through the school counseling curriculum the school counselor, in partnership with teachers, is able to provide classroom instruction by introducing activities that relate to academic, career, and personal/social (now social/emotional) concerns. The curriculum includes creating a lesson plan with appropriate standards and activities, and delivering the lesson with knowledge of classroom management.

When "guidance workers" first entered schools, most states required teaching credentials for individuals who entered the school counseling profession. Over the years most states eventually dropped this requirement, and today only a few states still mandate an education background for those entering the school counseling profession. Some states have replaced this requisite with a mandate that preservice school counselors participate in designated activities in a school environment with opportunities to understand the school environment, policies, and procedures. Furthermore, there are many administrators who continue to adhere to the belief that a background in teaching is necessary and will only consider hiring school counselors with teaching credentials.

All school counselors will spend some time in the classroom, regardless of the level in which they are assigned. However, most elementary school counselors spend more of their time teaching class-room lessons than do middle and high school counselors who visit classrooms periodically. Therefore, effective classroom management is an essential part of the job.

Being a former teacher may be helpful for school counselors. For example, experience in teaching lessons in front of a large group may assist in establishing credibility with teachers (Bender, 2005), particularly when consulting with teachers on classroom management strategies that worked for you as a teacher. However, for those of you who do not have a teaching background, counseling skills such as reflective listening, paraphrasing, and summarizing may come more naturally, and you will not need to "unlearn" more directive, authoritarian teaching language or behavior. Take advantage of your role as a supervisee to learn under an experienced counselor, visit highly effective teachers in your building to gain ideas, and if possible, get experience by teaching a variety of ages in different types of settings such as in suburban, rural, and urban schools.

You have already read about lesson plans in Chapter 9, and to help you acquire more confidence in being prepared for classroom presentations, strategies for effective classroom management are presented below. In addition, information on study skills that you can adapt to assist in classroom achievement is described.

Classroom Instruction and Management

Classroom management is one area that creates the most difficulty for school counselors-in-training largely due to a lack of training and experience in leading large groups or a classroom of students (Geltner & Clark, 2005). There is a difference between discipline and classroom management. Discipline plans have rules that temporarily stop unwanted behavior, whereas classroom manage-ment plans have procedures that teach students responsible skills that can be adapted through-out lifetime situations (Wong & Wong, 2009). For novices, it is easy to lose control of a large group or classroom, and once this occurs it is equally easy to become retaliatory in an attempt to regain group control. If you react adversely due to your inability to control a group of stu-dents, the result is a loss of student interest and a lack of respect for you as the educator. Puni-tive measures typically leads to a lack of constructive relationships rather than promoting positive contacts.

Knowledge and practice of effective strategies will assist you in becoming a successful large group or classroom facilitator. The following ideas and strategies are provided to help you begin to think about managing a large group or classroom:

- Demonstrate respect to students and other group members. Be prepared, address others using respectful language and tone, expect students/group members to contribute to the learning process, and provide opportunities for them to contribute.
- Give students important and active roles in the group. Meaningful roles keep students involved and engaged in the process. Students can be recorders/secretaries, summarizers, critical thinkers, timekeepers, co-facilitators, demonstrators, observers/monitors, evaluators, and so forth. Clearly explain each role and the corresponding responsibilities.
- Involve students in making rules and norms. Establish rules and consequences and follow them consistently and predictably. Most teachers post classroom rules and involve students in making the rules; as counselors-in-training, follow their example. Post the rules and consequences and review them from time to time as you remind students that they were instrumentally involved in establishing the rules and consequences. Be willing to revise rules and consequences when circumstances deem it appropriate.
- When possible, arrange seating in a U-shape, circle, or other configuration so that you can see all students and students can see one another. When students sit in rows, discipline problems often occur in the back. Sitting in front helps everyone feel equally engaged and accountable.
- Explain, rehearse, and reinforce procedures. Give clear, concise, step-by-step instructions before involving students in an activity and then rehearse these procedures. Just as coaches have their players rehearse skills, effective classroom instructors introduce concepts, teach, model, and rehearse procedures. Reinforce students when correct procedures are demonstrated, and reteach the desired skill if necessary (Wong & Wong, 2009).
- When you are teaching or facilitating, physically move around the room. If students are acting in a distracting manner, use physical closeness and approach them silently. You can do this even if you are listening or talking to other students across the room. Oftentimes, your presence and the students' awareness that you are attending to them are enough of a prompt for them to change behavior.
- Develop transition rituals with time warnings that help students move from active to quieter learning activities. For example, you can flick the lights and verbally state, "We'll be shifting to from large to small group activity in 5 minutes," or "Small group sharing time starts in 3 minutes so please rearrange your chairs for small group."
- State what action or behavior you desire rather than the behavior you do not want. For instance, instead of saying, "Don't talk when someone else is talking" say, "Raise your hand and wait until you are called on before you talk." Strategies adapted from solution-focused brief therapy accentuate what you want so that students develop a picture of acceptable behavior.
- Address the situation rather than the student (e.g., rather than, "You were rude when I asked you to be quiet" say, "This is a time to pay attention"). Remain focused on behavior and the situation. This objectivity helps to depersonalize the message, making it less threatening, belittling, or insulting to the student.
- Point out choices and consequences. For example, "you can either take the time to work on this assignment in class, or you will have to work on it at home."
- Use the Premack principle or "Grandma's rule." You have probably heard the statement, "If you eat all of your dinner, then you can have dessert." By providing an incentive as a result of performing something that may not be viewed favorably, the student is more likely to follow through on what is expected. For example, "Choosing to work on this assignment in class will likely provide more free time when you are home."
- Use pre-established gestures to get the attention of the class. For instance, you could raise your hand as a prompt for other students to raise their hands as an alert for activity transition, or information you want to give students. A common mistake is to raise your voice over the combined talking and noise generated within a group or classroom, which typically creates more noise indistinguishable from the already existing sounds.

- Find or create humor in situations and use this humor to connect with students. By incorporating humor, the activity can be more enjoyable and motivating. Laugh with your students. Poking fun at yourself, admitting mistakes, and laughing at your errors shows students that you are human.
- Use your basic counseling skills such as attentive listening, summarizing, and open-ended questions.

Facilitating large groups are professional activities conducted by school counselors and school counselors-in-training at all settings. Although managing groups of students can be challenging, implementing positive and consistent group strategies can make classroom instruction fun and productive. A list of classroom management resources that you may find helpful is included at the end of this chapter.

Conceptual Application Activity 10.1

Read the following scenarios and decide on the classroom management strategy you would use in response to the situation.

You are conducting a classroom lesson on social skills in a fourth-grade classroom and you notice that Christina seems disengaged and uninterested despite the other students being actively involved in the lesson. When you quietly walk to her desk to prompt her to stay focused on the activity, she immediately starts to sob loudly and uncontrollably.

What would you do?

_____

_____

Roberto is a ninth grader with whom you have developed rapport during the short period of time you have been interning in the high school. You are scheduled to talk about career planning in his social studies class, and as you are providing directions to the class, you notice Roberto talking to one of his peers. When you politely remind the class to pay attention to the instructions, Roberto yells, "I think this is a stupid lesson and you don't know what you are even talking about." After this outburst the class starts snickering at his comments.

How do you handle this?

_____

_____

Study Skills Strategies

School counselors, like other members of the school community, are under pressure to provide evidence of their contributions to the educational objectives of the schools (Sink & Stroh, 2006). In fact, Carey, Harrity, and Dimmitt (2005) state that through data collection and documentation strategies we are showing our contributions to the school mission that assist in increasing academic performance, and as a result could possibly eliminate unrelated school functions. One way this can be accomplished is to employ a study skills curriculum. You are able to teach these skills through the school counseling curriculum or through small groups focused on academic outcomes. Consequently, teachers may have a greater appreciation for the school counselor as student performance is improved, and as an outcome teachers may be more amenable to releasing students from class. Note taking, memory aids, and performance anxiety are discussed for you to consider in facilitating academic achievement during your clinical experiences.

Note Taking. The Cornell method of note taking is often called the "T-note system" because it involves sectioning a piece of notebook paper into an upside-down T. Notes are taken in the largest section using the R-Q-R³ method; next to these notes is a 2 1/2-inch cue section, and the final section is a 2-inch border at the bottom in which review notes are summarized. Although many students take notes using computers, a PDF converter can be downloaded to create a T-note system on the computer. See http://pdf-format.com/uc/join/join.aspx

Memory Aids. Mnemonic devices are memory aids that assist in memorizing information that does not necessarily need to be understood (Carter, Bishop, & Kravits, 2006). For example, a picture-association technique helps students learn vocabulary by associating unknown words with something that is known. For instance, if students are learning the Spanish word for flower, or *flor*, you may ask students to connect this word to something that they can identify. For instance, students may visualize a floor (to represent *flor*) with a rose on it. To strengthen the memory, have students imagine a color on the rose such as red, then have them to close their eyes, think of the red rose, and repeat the Spanish word *flor* for flower. Repeat this exercise until students create a strong connection (Wyman, 2001).

Creating an acronym or acrostic are also useful memory techniques. Acronyms involve looking at a list of words that the student is trying to commit to memory and taking the first letter of each word to form a new word or list of letters. With the proliferation of texting and e-mailing, a common acronym is BTW, or "by the way." An acrostic is similar to an acronym, but instead of making a new word the letters are used to make a sentence. One more recent acrostic for remembering the order of the planets Mercury, Venus, Earth, Mars, Jupiter, Saturn, Uranus, and Neptune (since Pluto lost its planet status) is, "**M**y **v**ery **e**nergetic **m**other **j**ust **s**erved **u**s **n**ectar."

You can incorporate these strategies in your clinical experiences by working with individual students or through instruction in classes. You may also want to consider developing a peer-tutoring group in which a group of students are trained to teach these strategies to their peers.

Student Activity 10.1   Are You Listening?

Some students have difficulty following directions, which leads to poorer academic growth. Teaching listening skills and how to focus on information that is provided is one strategy that you can teach to students.

   Materials needed: Plain white paper and pencil or other writing utensil

1.   Have students find a partner. Decide who will be partner A and who will be partner B.
2.   Ask students to sit back to back
3.   Partner A will read the following instructions while partner B draws a picture according to the instructions. Partner B may not ask questions.

   Directions to be given by Partner A:

a.   Draw a small circle in the center of the paper.
b.   Draw a line straight down from the circle.
c.   Halfway down the line make a long oval shape to the left side of the line that touches the line.
d.   Draw half circles around the small circle in the center of the paper.
   When finished, show the picture that has been drawn, and as a group discuss the following questions:
   What was difficult about this exercise?
   What would have made this exercise easier?
   What does this activity teach you about listening?

Performance Anxiety. Students are under more pressure today than ever before, and some individuals believe an epidemic of stress is evident among our school-aged children (Conner, Pope, & Galloway, 2009/2010). Daily stressors are associated with behavioral problems, depression, and poorer academic achievement (Kraag, Van Breukelen, Kok, & Hosman, 2009). Furthermore, students with excessive worry or physical arousal are often unable to concentrate on academics (Thompson, Robertson, Curtis, & Frick, 2013). In a longitudinal study by Kraag, et al. (2009), 70% of high school students reported feeling anxious about schoolwork, and over 50% stated that they often or constantly worried about grades, tests, and college acceptance. In this same study, students on average reported that they spent approximately 3.07 hours on homework, with another 2 hours spent on extra curricular activities each weekday. Stress that impacts mental and academic well-being is also reported among younger students.

To help students identify stressors, develop coping skills, and problem-solving behaviors, fifth and sixth graders participated in the "LearnYoung, LearnFair" curriculum. These lessons consisted of 8 weekly, one-hour sessions, and 5 weekly, one-hour booster sessions followed these regular curricular instructions. The results of this study indicated reduced stress and a greater ability to utilize problem-solving strategies (Kraag et al., 2009).

As a school-counselor-in-training you could contribute to increased achievement by teaching study skills, and you may consider implementing additional strategies that reduce stress such as deep breathing, yoga, relaxation, and mindfulness.

Individual Student Planning

Individual student planning is intended to facilitate personal and/or career goal setting (ASCA, 2012) through appraisal and advisement strategies. Although high school counselors spend more time in this area compared with middle and elementary school (Gysbers & Henderson, 2012), goal setting is also essential at the lower grade levels.

Appraisal

Generally, appraisal refers to the selection of a test or assessment instrument, orientation to the instrument's purpose, administration procedures, monitoring/proctoring practices, and interpretation of the test or instrument results. Based on test outcomes, and in conjunction with additional information from various sources, students can begin to more accurately assess their abilities and interests, and determine areas in which improvement is needed (Cobia & Henderson, 2003).

Students will be more apt to understand and take a test instrument more seriously when they are told the purpose of the test or inventory in advance, and how the results will assist them. When students are involved in assessment processes, they are better able to make effective decisions specific to their needs (Stiggins, 2005). Furthermore, conducting a meeting to explain test results to parents and guardians also provides an informational forum to answer questions about career and educational planning (Cobia & Henderson, 2003). As stated by the ASCA position statement on high-stakes testing, "Professional school counselors advocate for the use of multiple criteria when educational decisions are made about student performance and oppose the use of a single test to make important educational decisions. . . . (2014, para. 1).

Box 10.1

Academic programs are becoming more and more rigorous. And yet, educators are wondering how this trend impacts students. An elementary school in New York cancelled its annual kindergarten end of the year program. Administrators stated that this decision was made because the emphasis of the school is to assist the kids in being college and career ready, and programs such as this would detract from time on learning (Career-focused Kindergartners, 2014). School counselors have a responsibility to help students find balance in their lives by setting personal as well as academic goals.

As a school counselor-in-training, you also need to be aware of students with disabilities who struggle with traditional testing formats who may require unique testing accommodations. The Individuals with Disabilities Education Act (IDEA) and Individuals with Disabilities Education Improvement Act (IDEIA) mandate that reasonable adaptations and accommodations are available for optimal test-taking conditions. Additional information on working with students with disabilities is found in Chapter 13.

Conceptual Application Activity 10.2

Observe your site supervisor as he or she orients students to a particular test, monitors/proctors the test, and interprets test results. What are some of the strategies that you feel are most useful in explaining test scores? Were there some areas that you think could have been explained differently?

_____

_____

Conceptual Application Activity 10.3

Take an opportunity to orient, administer, or interpret test results to one of your counselees. What were some of the particular challenges in performing this activity? Is there anything that you feel may have assisted you in this task?

_____

_____

Advisement

School counselors and school counselors-in-training often find themselves providing information to students, parents/guardians, teachers, and so forth, to assist with academic, career, or social/emotional decision making. Helping students and parents/guardians plan for the future while facilitating career readiness, finding postsecondary schools well matched to the student's interests and skills, and applying to college or vocational programs are all common advising activities for school counselors, especially those at the high school level. Advisement activities can be conducted individually or in small groups, and it is wise to include school personnel and parents/guardians in the process.

When Hope High School located in Providence, Rhode Island was being reconstituted due to poor performance, the school counseling program instituted Individual Learning Plans (ILP), an evidence-based program that assisted students with academic, career, and personal/social goals (now social/emotional) (West & Sutherland, 2007). Integral to this plan were the components of the Academic Learning Plan (ALP) and the Individual, Physical, Academic, Social Success Plan (I-PASS). The ALP consisted of a curriculum worksheet in which coursework, grades, and credits were collaboratively monitored by teacher advisors. The I-PASS was designed for students to establish personal goals in the physical (health and nutrition), academic (attendance, educational, career/college), and social and emotional/civic (community extracurricular activities, family and friends) arenas. Quarterly reviews provided an opportunity for students to meet with their advisors to determine progress. The outcome of this program was more student accountability through the provision of opportunities to review, assess, and evaluate achievement on a quarterly basis with their advisor and school counselor (West & Sutherland, 2007). Not only did this program provide an opportunity for collaboration among stakeholders, students were able to consistently assess their progress, evaluate goals that were met, and identify obstructions to goal attainment.

Conceptual Application Activity 10.4

Read and respond to the following scenario and discuss your answers with your peers.

Mario is a struggling 18-year-old who has not earned the appropriate credits to be considered an 11th grader. He has only earned enough credits equivalent to those of a 9th grader and he comes to you for career information. You discuss his high school curriculum and ask him about his future career/academic goals. He indicates that he would like to attend college to become a social studies teacher, but his parents do not support this goal and are urging Mario to drop-out of school to assist with the family trucking business. As Mario's father states, "After all, I don't have a high school diploma and own a successful business. You don't need a fancy college degree—you can do just fine without it."

_____

_____

As students shift to higher-education settings or careers, counselors who have worked with them in assessment and advisement often continue to assist them as they transition to other settings (Cobia & Henderson, 2003). Follow-up studies of graduates are conducted to gather information on how well the various school programs assisted in making these transitions, and whether programs or the curriculum need revision to meet the needs of graduates who enter the workforce or higher educational settings.

Conceptual Application Activity 10.5

Ask your supervisor to share a follow-up study that has been conducted of past graduates and his or her reactions to the study outcomes. How was the follow-up study conducted? What trends do you notice? Were there any changes that were made as a result of the results? Share and discuss what you found with your peers.

_____

_____

Responsive Services

Helping students overcome concerns, life circumstances, or problems that stand in the way of personal development growth is the primary purpose of responsive services (Gysbers & Henderson, 2012). A continuum of services such as small group and individual counseling, and crisis response are fundamental to this element (ASCA, 2012).

Box 10.2

The ASCA (2014) conducted a study to identify the concerns students struggle with the most as they enter the school. Twenty-eight percent of elementary school-aged students were most concerned about being away from parents, among middle school students peer issues were the top concern (20%), and homework was the chief concern among high school students (20%). School counselors are instrumental in assisting students with transition concerns that could occur from grade-to-grade or school-to-school.

Small Group and Individual Counseling

Approximately 1 out of 4 students suffer from some form of mental illness that negatively influences their well-being, yet nearly 75% of these students do not receive the counseling services that are so badly needed (DeKruyf, Auger, & Trice-Black, 2013). Furthermore, although school counselors have the skill to provide mental health counseling for students, they frequently do not have the time or support to provide this service (Brown, Dahlbeck, & Sparkman-Barnes 2006).

School counselors have an advantage for providing group and individual counseling not only because they have a thorough understanding of the school and culture, but they have also cultivated their relationships with teachers and students, and their proximity in the school provides easy access to students. Furthermore, students and their families feel more comfortable going to a known place with familiar personnel.

Small group counseling is a time-effective method in reaching more students who may be experiencing similar concerns. Arranging for small groups (and individual counseling, for that matter) in the schools can be problematic since some teachers are reluctant to release students from classes due to the pressure to reveal academic achievement in subject areas.

Crisis Counseling

School shootings such as that which occurred at Sandy Hook, New Jersey, the death of a student or staff member, a national terrorist attack, or a natural disaster such as a flood or tornado are some of the disasters that impact our school-aged youth. And, the school counselor is often the only individual in the school with the training to provide counseling for students with immediate concerns. Yet, Allen et al., (2002) revealed that only one-third of experienced school counselors received training in crisis counseling. The goal of crisis counseling is to restore the individual to a higher, or at least the same level of functioning that existed before the crisis. In addition to providing the type of counseling that is necessary, the school counselor conducts lessons to prepare students for critical incidents that may create long-term distress and could lead to post-traumatic stress disorder (PTSD).

Although it is nearly impossible to predict what tragedy will impact a school, prevention is key to intervening and debriefing. School counselors are able to teach preventive strategies so that students will be better prepared to cope when tragedy does strike. As you work with a student who is in crisis one question to ask yourself is, "How do I work with this student?" And, "What is my role when a crisis impacts the school?" Unfortunately, many students who display reactions to stress are inadvertently and incorrectly placed in special education classes as a result of cognitive impairment that is associated with stress responses. Common stress responses are found in Table 10.1.

Suicide

A student who is contemplating suicide is one of the most difficult situations any counselor confronts. Suicide is the third leading cause of death for individuals between the ages of 15–24 (Suicide. org, n.d.), and is preventable. Talking about suicide has shown to decrease the risk. In fact, 80% of

Figure 10.1 School counselor comforting a grieving student.

Source: Shutterstock

Table 10.1 Common Student Responses to Stress

Physical

- Agitation
- Hyper-alertness
- Erratic heartbeat
- Difficulty breathing
- Gastrointestinal distress
- Sleep difficulties (excessive or inability to sleep)
- Tension in the form of aches and pains

Cognitive

- Negative outlook
- Difficulty solving problems
- Disorganization with concentration troubles
- Sluggish or hyperactive thoughts
- Inability to see an alternative perspective
- Egocentrism

Emotional

- Generalized distress
- Anger or hostility
- Depression
- Anxiety, fear, or panic
- Powerlessness
- Guilt
- Shame

Social/Behavioral

- Substance abuse
- Eating disorders
- Lack of interest in activities
- Inability to perform daily activities
- Restricted social contacts
- Questioning spiritual faith
- Rigid adherence to or rejection of values

individuals who have contemplated or completed suicide actually told someone about their intent (Shallcross, 2010). Box 10.3 contains the S-L-A-P acronym that can be used to assess present risk of suicide, and the D-I-R-T acronym (Box 10.4) is used to assess previous suicide attempts. However, remember that parents/guardians need to be contacted and this communication needs to be documented if you are working with a student who expresses suicidal ideation. In addition, be aware of the school policies regarding the protocol in reporting suicidal ideation, and be sure to contact your site supervisor and program supervisor.

Box 10.3   The S-L-A-P Suicide Assessment

Specifics of the plan. Ask the student about the suicidal plan. The more specific the plan, the higher the suicide risk.

Lethality of the plan. The more lethal the suicidal plan, the higher the risk. Guns or jumping from high places are more fatal methods of committing suicide.

Availability. Determine the availability of the indicated method of suicide. If guns are available in the house and the student indicates this is the means in which he/she will attempt suicide, the higher the risk.

Proximity of Helping Resources. Identify the significant supportive individuals in the student's life and reconnect him/her with these trusting, helpful resources.

Box 10.4   The D-I-R-T Assessment of Previous Suicide Attempt

Dangerous. Ask about previous attempts and evaluate the dangerousness of this assessment.

Impression of Dangerousness. Ask the student regarding his/her impression of the lethality of the means that was used.

Rescue. Did the student make a suicide attempt and leave room for being discovered?

Timing. When did the attempt occur? The more recent the attempt, the higher the risk.

Box 10.5   National Suicide Prevention Lifeline

A 24-hour hotline is available at 1–800–273–8255, or a live chat can be accessed at www.suicidepreventionlifeline.org

---

Conceptual Application Activity 10.6

With a classmate, one person will take the role of a counselor and the other the role of a student. Practice using the S-L-A-P and D-I-R-T acronym and assess for suicide. Using the following scenario.

Roberto is an 8th grader who was referred to you by his health teacher. According to the teacher Roberto's grades have been dropping and he recently wrote a paper in which he discussed wanting to take his mother's blood pressure medicine to allow him to "slide into a deep sleep and never wake up." After the role play, discuss the aspects that were most difficult, and brainstorm solutions for these complications.

Conceptual Application Activity 10.7

Discuss with your supervisor the various types of crises that have occurred in the school and how these situations were handled. What was his or her role in these crises? Ask to see a copy of the crisis intervention plan.

_____

_____

Peer Facilitation Programs

Peer facilitation programs are another preventive strategy that school counselors develop to improve students' academic achievement, teach problem resolution, and enhance the school culture. Although these programs vary among schools, the programs generally consist of peer helpers, peer mentors, peer mediators, and peer tutors.

Peer helpers commonly assist classroom teachers such as helping students with disabilities or engaging in tasks for teachers. *Peer mentors* usually assist with school transitions in which an upper level student will work with a younger student as he/she moves to the next grade or school. *Peer tutors* provide instruction with same-age peers who are struggling with academic issues, or with younger students who need additional assistance with a subject. Finally, *peer mediators* are trained in conflict management and meet with students who are having minor conflicts to resolve the issue without it becoming more serious. Students are effective at learning and following prescribed courses of action or mediation. Typical steps for peer mediation include (adapted from Kittrell, Comiskey, & Carroll, 2006):

1. Getting acquainted and comfortable, and establishing the rules.
2. Identifying the issues from all perspectives and the people directly involved.
3. Brainstorming all possible solution ideas without eliminating any options.
4. Discussing all ideas, finding commonality among ideas, and eliminating implausible or ineffective options.
5. Democratically choosing the best option or options.
6. Making an agreement or written contract among all parties to include a follow-up schedule.
7. Carrying out the agreement.
8. Following up with all involved parties and celebrating success or beginning the process again.

School counselors often implement, train, monitor, and evaluate peer facilitation programs as preventative responses to academic, career, and/or personal/social (now social/emotional) issues. Training peers as facilitators may include such things as basic helping skills, communication skills, problem solving, role-plays, identifying feelings, and active listening. Appropriate peer selection, training, and supervision are necessary for the program to be successful. When students are trained to work proactively with their peers, a healthier school culture may develop.

Conceptual Application Activity 10.8

To practice mediation skills, get in groups of three to role-play the following scenario using the steps above. Identify one person as the mediator, one person as Alysia, and one person as Marcus.

Two students, Alysia, an eighth-grade girl, and Marcus, a seventh-grade boy, are involved in a physical altercation in the middle school cafeteria during lunch period. You come into the cafeteria and observe Alysia hitting Marcus repeatedly over the head with her lunch tray. Marcus is swinging, kicking, and swearing at Alysia while she repeatedly strikes him. A moderately sized group of bystanders are gathered around the pair and are chanting, "Hit him again, harder, harder!" You quickly intervene by stepping through the crowd and between Alysia and Marcus. Once Alysia and Marcus see you step between them, they stop physically fighting. Marcus continues to sling verbal assaults, which Alysia returns as they glare at each other. You summon a nearby female faculty member and instruct her to escort Alysia to the main office and stay with her until you arrive. You escort Marcus to your school counseling office where you find another school counselor, inform her of the incident, and request she monitor Marcus while he sits in your office on one side of your desk to cool down. You retrieve Alysia and escort her to your office, have her sit in a chair on the opposite side of your desk from Marcus, and position yourself between the two students. You leave your door open and request that the other school counselor remain nearby in case you need her assistance.

How did the process work? Were there any instances where you were stuck? What would have helped make this process easier?

_____

_____

INDIRECT STUDENT SERVICES

Indirect student services refer to the work of school counselors with other stakeholders on behalf of students through such means as referrals, consultation, and collaboration.

Referrals

The school counselor/student ratio in most schools far exceeds the 1:250 ratio recommended by the ASCA, with a national average of 1:450, and California having the highest ratio of 1:1,016 (U.S. Department of Education, 2011). With these extreme numbers, it may be more appropriate to make a referral. When making a referral, consider the following questions:

- Am I competent to deal with this concern?
- Do I have enough time and energy to work with this concern?
- Is reasonable progress being made related to my counseling?

Be sure to seek advice from your supervisor as to the protocol in making referrals. For instance, in some school districts educational personnel are not allowed to make referrals for fear that the school district would be responsible for covering the cost of these outside agencies.

At times a referral is needed when students have issues in which the school counselor does not have the training or the time to work effectively with them. Referral sources may include community mental health agencies, employment and training centers, juvenile services, and/or social service personnel. Having a list of community resources is a helpful aid for expediting this process. Providing a minimum of three resources allows the parent/guardian to choose the service that will best meet the needs of the student and protects you from consequences if the referral did not work out as expected. Be sure to have a signed parental/guardian consent form to give you permission to discuss the student with outside individuals.

Consultation

Consultation is an interpersonal relationship in which school counselors help stakeholders attend to the academic, career, and personal/social (now social/emotional) needs of students (Gysbers & Henderson, 2012). Consultation is often viewed as a problem-solving approach in which school counselors interact with adults and professionals related to the student such as parents, custodial caregivers, guardians, coaches, teachers, administration, community professionals, and so forth. With the emphasis on academic growth that is evident in our educational system today, social and emotional development is often overlooked, and school counselors often have difficulty underscoring the importance of social/emotional development (Velsor, 2009). School counselors are one of the few educational personnel with a focus on assisting students with skills that facilitate students' ability to: 1) understand and interact with others effectively, 2) appropriately express personal feelings, 3) adapt to change, and 4) self-motivate (Velsor, 2009). School counselors are able to consult with others to reveal the association between social/emotional skills, academic learning, and career development. School counselors who are able to embrace a consultation approach with a focus on prevention for all students are able to integrate social/emotional growth into the school culture.

When serving as a consultant a relationship is built wherein goals are mutually shared and understood. Several steps are followed during consultation which are not discrete, but rather fluid and may require a return an initial step (Dinkmeyer & Carlson, 2006).

1. Establishing the relationship
2. Gathering data and identifying the problem
3. Setting mutual goals
4. Using strategies to address the goals
5. Evaluating the final response.

When serving as a consultant, keep in mind confidentiality, equality, intersection of roles, communication, and cultural differences. As a consultant it is sometimes difficult for teachers to understand that counselors abide by a code of ethics that includes confidentiality; be sure to communicate the importance of this ethical responsibility to all parties. Knowing how much information to share is often tricky. One question that you could ask yourself when faced with this dilemma is, "What information should be shared that will help this student at this time?"

As a consultant, be sure to strive for a relationship build on equality. You are on an equal level with the consultee, (the person with whom you will be consulting), and a strong relationship is created when you recognize individual strengths and encourage new ideas for resolving an issue. When proposing an intervention that could create potential resistance you may state something like, "You've probably already thought of this. . . . " Or, "this might be difficult to try, but. . . . "

At times it is difficult to be a consultant without changing into a counselor role. Keep in mind that the focus of most consultations is for the benefit of the student, not the consultee. Although counselors are trained in effective communication skills such as active listening, paraphrasing, questioning, reflecting, and summarizing which enhance an effective consultation, communication techniques that lead to individual counseling are to be avoided. Finally, successful consultants possess an awareness of cultural differences including an understanding of how his/her communication style and views could influence the consultation process.

Conceptual Application Activity 10.9

Talk with your supervisor about some of the consultation concerns in which he/she has served as a consultant. What are some of the most common issues that lead to a need for consultation? What were some of the strategies that were most effective? Discuss your responses with those of your classmates.

Collaboration

An effective collaborative process includes components such as shared leadership responsibilities, a well-defined purpose, accountability strategies, time for interaction, time to celebrate successes, effective process monitoring, clear rules, reasonable goals, and evaluation (Johnson & Johnson, 2000, as cited in DeVoss & Andrews, 2006). School counselors are able to provide a leadership role in the school within the school counseling program and in other educational initiatives. Additional information on collaboration is found in Chapter 7.

CONCLUSION

The Delivery System component answers the question "What strategies and activities will be used to address student needs?" This component consists of direct activities that are face-to-face interactions with students, and indirect activities that include interactions with others on behalf of the student. Direct activities include the school counseling core curriculum that involves delivery of the school counseling goals and objectives, and management of students in the classroom. Individual student planning including appraisal and advisement, with small group and individual counseling, and crisis counseling as additional direct services. Indirect student services include referrals, consultation with other stakeholders, and collaboration.

WEBSITES

- The Teachers' Guide provides many useful links to techniques that can be used for better classroom discipline and commonly used techniques that are not helpful for teachers: http://theteachers guide.com/classroommanagement.htm
- TeacherVision.com is a Web site offering organized topics that can be used in lesson planning and activities, and many are in a printable format: http://theteachersguide.com/classroom management.htm
- Responsive Classroom is a website in which resources are provides for educators as well as helpful hints in the classroom: www.responsiveclassroom.org/resources-educators

REFERENCES

Allen, M., Burt, K., Bryan, E., Carter, D., Orsi, R., & Durkan, L. (2002). School counselors' preparation for and participation in crisis intervention. *Professional School Counseling, 6,* 96–102.

American School Counselor Association (2012). *The ASA National model: A framework for school counseling programs (3rd ed.).* Alexandria, VA: Author.

American School Counselor Association (2014). The professional school counselor and high-stakes testing. Retrieved from www.schoolcounselor.org/asca/media/asca/PositionStatements/PS_High-StakesTesting.pdf

American School Counselor Association (2014, June). *ASCA School Counselor, 51,* 40.

Bender, J. M. (2005). *Ready . . . set . . . go!* Chapin, SC: Youthlight, Inc.

Brown, C., Dahlbeck, D. T., & Sparkman-Barnes, L. (2006). Collaborative relationships: School counselors and non-school mental health professionals working together to improve the mental health needs of students. *Professional School Counseling, 9,* 332–335.

Career-focused kindergartners (2014, May 9). *The Week,* p.p. 32.

Carey, M., Harrity, J., & Dimmitt, C. (2005). The development of a self-assessment instrument to measure a school district's readiness to implement the ASCA national model. *Professional School Counseling, 8,* 305–312.

Carter, C., Bishop, J., & Kravits, S. L. (2006). *Keys to success: Building successful intelligence for college, career, and life* (5th ed.). Upper Saddle River, NJ: Pearson.

Cobia, D. C., & Henderson, D. A. (2003). *Handbook of school counseling.* Upper Saddle River, NJ: Pearson.

Conner, J., Pope, D., & Galloway, M. (2009/2010). Success with less stress. Educational Leadership, 67, 54–58. Retrieved from www.challengesuccess.org/Portals/0/Docs/Educational-Leadership-Article-2009–12.pdf

DeKruyf, L., Auger, R.W., & Trice-Black, S. (2013). The role of school counselors in meeting students' mental health needs: Examining issues of professional identity. *Professional School counseling, 16,* 271–282. doi: 10.5330/PSC.n.2013–16.271

DeVoss, J.A., & Andrews, M.F. (2006). *School counselors as educational leaders.* Boston: Lakasha Press.

Dinkmeyer, D., & Carlson, J. (2006). *Consultation: Creating school-based interventions (3rd ed.).* New York, NY: Routledge.

Geltner, J.A., & Clark, M.A. (2005). Engaging students in classroom guidance: Management strategies for middle school counselors. *Professional School Counseling, 9,* 164–166.

Gysbers, N.C., & Henderson, P. (2012). *Developing and managing your school guidance program* (5th ed.). Alexandria, VA: American Counseling Association.

Kraag, G., VanBreukelen, G.J.P., Kok, G., & Hosman, C. (2009). 'Learn young, learn fair', a stress management program for fifth and sixth graders: Longitudinal results from an experimental study. *Journal of Child Psychology and Psychiatry, 50,* 1185–1195. doi: 10.111/j.1469–7610.2009.02088.x

Kittrell, J., Comiskey, J., & Carroll, L. (2006, February). *Establishing peer mediation in middle and high schools.* Presentation at the University of Tennessee, Knoxville.

Shallcross, L. (2010, July). Confronting the threat of suicide. *Counseling Today.* Alexandria, VA: American Counselor Association.

Sink, C.A., & Stroh, H.R. (2006). Practical significance: The use of effect sizes in school counseling research. *Professional School Counseling, 9,* 401–411.

Stiggins, R.J. (2005). *Student-involved assessment FOR learning* (4th ed.). Upper Saddle River, NJ: Pearson.

Suicide.org (n.d.). *Suicide statistics.* Retrieved from www.suicide.org/suicide-statistics.html

Thompson, E.H., Robertson, P, Curtis, R., & Frick, M.H. (2013). Students with anxiety: Implications for professional school counselors. *Professional School Counseling, 16,* 222–234. doi: 10.5330/PSC.n.2013–16.222

U.S. Department of Education (2011, January). *United states student-to-counselor ratios for elementary and secondary schools.* Retrieved from www.counseling.org/PublicPolicy/ACA_Ratio_Chart_2011_Overall.pdf

Velsor, P.V. (2009). School counselors as social-emotional learning consultants: Where do we begin? *Professional School Counseling, 13,* ??

West, D.S., & Sutherland, S.R. (2007, July). At the heart of high school reform. ASCA School Counselor. Retrieved from www.ascaschoolcounselor.org/article_content.asp?article=933

Wong, H., & Wong, R. (2009, June). *Successful teaching for teachers who want to be effective.* Paper presented at the American School Counselor Association Conference, Dallas, TX.

Wyman, P. (2001). *Learning vs testing: Strategies that bridge the gap.* Tucson, AZ: Zephyr Press.

11 Understanding the Accountability Component of the ASCA National Model as a School Counselor-in-Training

Aaron H. Oberman

CACREP Standards

Assessment

G. Knowledge

3. Identifies various forms of needs assessments for academic, career, and personal/social (now named social/emotional) development.

Research and Evaluation

I. Knowledge

1. Understands how to critically evaluate research relevant to the practice of school counseling.
2. Knows models of program evaluation for school counseling programs.
3. Knows basic strategies for evaluating counseling outcomes in school counseling (e.g., behavioral observation, program evaluation).
4. Understands the outcome research data and best practices identified in the school counseling research literature.

J. Skills and Practices

2. Develops measurable outcomes for school counseling programs, activities, interventions, and experiences.
3. Analyzes and uses data to enhance school counseling programs.

The purpose of this chapter is to:

- introduce the importance of program and professional
- present different strategies for collecting program effectiveness data
- describe data analysis techniques.

INTRODUCTION

In this age of educational reform, all members of the school community have a responsibility to show how their efforts have made a difference in the lives of school-aged youth. School counselors are no exception. Accountability practices are especially critical in a time when a struggling economy and resulting budget cuts may cause programs to be negatively impacted. Programs that lack proof of progress or effectiveness are more likely to be seen as lacking value and therefore more vulnerable to public scrutiny and possible elimination. School counseling programs may be considered as one of the areas targeted for reduction, resource reallocation, or elimination when education finances are tight (Gibson & Mitchell, 2007). Despite these potential threats to school counseling programs, some school counselors still resist the need to be accountable to those they serve (Stone & Dahir, 2011). Further evidence of this lack of commitment to the accountability component was found in a study that investigated where school counselors spend their time. School counselors at all levels concentrated their time on components of the ASCA National Model with little time spent on the accountability arena (Barnett, 2011).

Your reasons for entering the school counseling profession probably did not include a vision of operationally defining goals and objectives, tracking progress and "crunching the numbers," or analyzing data as part of your job description. Did any of your reasons for entering the school counseling profession include any aspect of school counselor accountability? If so, accountability may be an easier task for you. If not, accountability may be more challenging for you as a school counselor-in-training, and later as a professional school counselor. Regardless of your level of affinity toward accountability and regardless of your educational experience, you are still professionally responsible for revealing how you make a difference in the growth of students. Data analysis, program results, and evaluation and improvement are three key areas within the accountability component of the ASCA National Model.

DATA ANALYSIS

School counselors use the school data profile analysis and use-of-time analysis to improve the school counseling program. Each of these elements is analyzed yearly, and based on this annual appraisal, program goals are established (ASCA, 2012).

School Data Profile Analysis

It may be important for you as a school counselor-in-training to peruse the school report card for the school in which you are placed. This analysis includes such information as the school's attendance, behavior, and achievement data to understand the school culture (ASCA, 2012). Investigating these data at the start of each school year serves as a basis for establishing a baseline for determining continuous program and school improvements. As a counselor-in-training you have an opportunity to see strengths and weaknesses in the school counseling program, and you can be instrumental in collecting and analyzing data. Learning how to make decisions based on these data will provide opportunities for you to contribute to student growth in your school setting now and will give you the skills to continue to collect this information when you transition to being a full member of the school counseling profession. Addressing school concerns will also leave a lasting legacy at the school, and one in which your efforts will be appreciated. Look at Conceptual Application Activity 11.1 with a partner and identify an area of concern and intervention strategies for addressing this issue.

High School Profile
Enrollment—1600
Grades 9–12

Conceptual Application Activity 11.1

	2013–2014	2012–2013	State Average
Graduation rate	67%	65%	83%
College readiness	25%	23%	53%
Race/ethnicity			
Black/African American	60%	58%	

Asian	0%	1%	
American Indian	0%	0%	
Pacific Islander	0%	0%	
White	22%	25%	
Hispanic/Latino	13%	14%	
Two or more races	4%	2%	
Students with disabilities	20%	20%	14%
Low income	3%	77%	50%
Homeless	1%	2%	2%
English learners	0%	1%	10%
Student mobility	14%	22%	13%
Chronic truancy rate	25%	17%	10%
Student attendance	87%	91%	94%

What areas of concern have you located? Brainstorm strategies for addressing this concern.

Box 11.1

The Support Personnel Accountability Report Card (SPARC) documents program commitment and interventions. The report includes an identification and intervention of critical data elements, partners involved with the intervention, principal's comments, results of the intervention, and changes that resulted. For more information, go to http://sparc.schoolcounselorcentral.com/

Use-of-Time Analysis

School counselors track where time is spent, and although this strategy may be time-consuming, it is a necessary part of our job. As indicated in previous chapters, the ASCA National Model (ASCA, 2012) recommends at least 80% of the counselor's time be spent on direct services such as school lessons curriculum, individual student planning, and responsive services. The other 20% or less is spent on indirect tasks that include program management and accountability efforts. Enumerative data (or process data) reveal where the school counselor or counselor-in-training is devoting time and are essential for targeting areas of program improvement and apprising administrators and other stakeholders about the best ways for the counselor to meet student needs. Although your training program will most likely provide a form to document where you spend your time, Chapter 9 provides a form that can be adapted to track time spent on various tasks. Although tracking your activities does reveal where time is spent, it does not inform you as to how successful or effective you are in performing these tasks.

PROGRAM RESULTS

Accountability encompasses analyzing data that are created based on curriculum results, small-group results, and closing-the-gap measures to address the changes that occur as a result of your efforts within the school counseling program. School counselors benefit, as does the school, when documentation reveals how you achieved the goals you have established (Brown & Trusty, 2005; Myrick, 2003). Graduation from your school counseling training program does not make you an expert school counselor, but instead demonstrates that you have met the minimum standards to begin your career as a professional school counselor. Being able to provide outcome evidence to your stakeholders that you are positively impacting the student body displays your value to the educational community.

There are various methods by which you are able to record your activities and the impact of these activities on student achievement. These data can be in the form of qualitative or quantitative results.

Quantitative data are expressed using numbers. Examples are to rank order 10 items from least desired (ranked 10) to most desired (ranked 1), to choose a point on a Likert scale from 1 to 6, or to assign a categorized number (e.g., 1–3, weak; 4–6, moderate; 7–10, strong). Relatively simple quantitative analyses such as means, medians, and modes are popular ways to summarize data that are easily understood by the school's stakeholders.

Qualitative data are expressed through words. An open-ended written summary of a student expressing how individual counseling helped her improve her schoolwork, a third-party observer's feedback critiquing your guidance lesson, or a parent's handwritten note thanking you for your input in developing her son's Individualized Education Plan (IEP) are a few examples of qualitative data.

Process, perception, and outcome data are types of documents for examining how students have grown as a result of program and classroom guidance interventions, or analyzing small counseling groups that were implemented by the school counselor to address student learning needs.

Types of Data

Process

As discussed previously, process data show stakeholders what counseling or guidance lesson actually occurred. Some examples include the number of parent conferences, students who participated in a group or guidance lesson, or consultations that occurred with teachers.

Perception

Perception data are gathered to determine what students learned as a result of the intervention. These data are usually collected in a self-report format to see what students think or believe they know, value, or can accomplish (ASCA, 2012). Some examples of perception data include surveys or pre/post-test assessments.

Outcome

These data show stakeholders the effect the school counseling activities are having on areas such as attendance, student achievement, and behavior (ASCA, 2012). Some examples of these data include changes in promotions to the next grade level, number of discipline referrals, and graduation rates.

There are numerous methods for collecting information regarding the effectiveness of your program strategies and interventions. An experimental design for determining program outcomes is one method of quantitatively revealing the impact of an intervention. Action research is an organized method for addressing an immediate issue and to inform practice. The MEASURE acronym is a system for conducting action research.

Experimental Action Research

An experimental action research approach can be used to measure the effectiveness of an intervention on similar groups of students. As an example, one group would be considered as a treatment/experimental group and the other as a control group. The treatment/experimental group would receive the treatment or intervention, while the control group does not receive the treatment/

intervention (or is delayed in receiving the treatment/intervention). For this approach to be most effective, students should be randomly assigned to each group (each student should have an equal chance of being selected into either group).

For instance, suppose you want to determine if the study skills lesson you are teaching students is improving their test-taking abilities. Using an experimental approach, you could collect data from teachers of two fifth-grade classes. (These would be convenience groupings, but not randomly assigned groups.) Ideally, you would collect pre-intervention data on both groups to establish a baseline average test score for each group. Following the pre-test, one class would receive a series of classroom lessons on study skills, while the other class would receive no lessons during this time. The group receiving the study skills lesson is considered the treatment/experimental group, while the class not receiving instruction is the control group. After the sessions are completed, you would assess the post-treatment/intervention test scores of both groups and compare these scores to their pre-test scores to see if there was any improvement or differences between the two groups' test scores. If the change between pre-test and post-test scores for the treatment/intervention group improved significantly more than did those for the control group, you have an indicator that your study skills lessons may have had a positive impact on test score improvement (note that you would need to conduct a statistical analysis such as a t-test to determine whether or not the change between the two groups is considered to be significant). When evidence suggests that a strategy was effective, you have an ethical responsibility to provide this treatment to all students. In this case, the fifth graders who did not receive the study skills intervention would now have the opportunity to receive the same lessons on study skills.

At times, school counselors are hesitant to engage in research due to: (1) the results not turning out as expected, (2) lack of confidence in research or statistical abilities, and (3) fear that positive outcomes will generate additional responsibilities. However, even if the results did not turn out as anticipated, it may simply mean that the activities, goals, or procedures need to be altered. Furthermore, counselor educators are often looking for practitioners with whom they can partner to conduct research. Connect with a professor at a nearby college or university to assist you in research methodologies.

Conceptual Application Activity 11.2

Ask your supervisor to assist you in developing an experimental action–based assessment in which you can collect data to compare groups. Discuss your assessment and intervention with your peers and discuss the pros and cons of developing this type of intervention and assessment.

_____

_____

Now that you are apprised as to how data can indicate program and curricular areas of strength and areas that need attention using an experimental design, you may also consider using action research to address these areas. The MEASURE program is a systematic approach for identifying and addressing a problematic area.

MEASURE

Stone and Dahir (2011) developed the MEASURE action research protocol. The MEASURE acronym stands for mission, elements, analyze, stakeholders-unite, reanalyze, and educate.

Stone and Dahir (2011) purport that school counselors should first align their role in the school with the school's *m*ission. Second, school counselors need to determine what *e*lements they are trying to impact or change. Next, school counselors are to examine and *a*nalyze the data to establish goals for the counseling program. After analyzing the data, counselors collaborate with the school's stakeholders and *u*nite them to create an action plan that will address the needs of the school. Fifth, counselors *r*eanalyze the data to see whether any changes have taken place and make modification as needed. Finally, school counselors use a report card that reveals program effectiveness and those areas that need attention. This report *e*ducates stakeholders as to how the school counselor promotes students, is integral to the academic mission, and provides direction for future goals.

*M*ission—The school counseling program is connected to the school mission.	The school counseling mission statement addresses the three Ps (purpose, practice, and principles). What are the student needs? How do school counselors address these needs? What beliefs guide this work ?
*E*lements—Identify elements that impede student growth	Critical analysis of information attained through data assists in identifying an issue to address.
*A*nalysis—What are the data that indicate an issue to address?	Disaggregating data may provide a more comprehensive picture of factors that are impeding student growth.
*S*takeholders—*U*nite	Identification of individuals who are able to address the issue. This could mean community members, teachers, school board members, etc.
*R*eanalyze, *R*eflect, and *R*evise	Data are addressed while an intervention occurs to make necessary changes (formative assessment), and again at the end of the intervention to determine how well the strategy met the identified goal (summative).
*E*ducate	Documenting and sharing results of the intervention educates stakeholders as to how the school counselor is essential to the school environment.

Conceptual Application Activity 11.3

Use the MEASURE accountability system to target an identified area for improvement in the school in which you are an intern. With the assistance of your supervisor, determine strategies for improving this target area. Compare your system with those of your peers.

At times an assessment instrument is necessary to show evidence of program or intervention effectiveness. Since there are very few ready-made instruments that will meet all of your programmatic needs, it is likely that you will need to design the instrument. Similar to the awareness of the demand to be accountable to your stakeholders, creating an assessment instrument can seem like a daunting task for school counselors.

Assessment Instruments to Measure Effectiveness

As a school counselor-in-training, you do not receive extensive training in data collection and analysis; therefore, you may feel like you do not have the training required to conduct sophisticated assessments or research (Gladding, 2012). To develop an effective assessment instrument, you first need to determine what is being assessed and how the results will be used. It is also important to consider where and when the assessment will happen. Certain times during the academic year may be better than others to conduct various lessons and to collect evaluative information pertinent to your counseling program (Studer, Oberman, & Womack, 2006). Moreover, it is important to constantly revise the instrument to make sure the data being collected are in line with your school counseling program's established goals. A pilot group of individuals who are similar to the target population you will be assessing can take the instrument you have designed and provide feedback on it. Revisions can then be made based on their feedback.

1. Why is the assessment being done?

2. Who is being surveyed?

3. What is the best method for data collection?

4. When is the best time to conduct this assessment?

5. Where will the assessment take place?

6. How will you share the information in an easy-to-understand format?

Figure 11.1 Sample checklist to create an assessment tool.

Some of the questions to consider when designing your instrument include the type of data to collect, how to collect the data, the types of questions or items that will yield accurate and meaningful results, analysis methods, and the manner in which to share the information with stakeholders. Observational forms, pre- and post-test instruments, surveys, and retrospective assessments are examples of assessment tools. Refer to Figure 11.1 for a sample assessment instrument checklist.

Observations

Observations are used when you want to document behavioral patterns without interfering with the behavior you wish to observe. This assessment includes selecting the behavior to be observed, developing a system for documentation, and then deciding if an intervention is needed. For instance, suppose a teacher is concerned about anger outbursts from a fifth-grade student. You would observe in the classroom or other designated place to determine baseline data on the number of times this identified behavior occurs in a determined time frame. Based on this observation, an intervention can be created, and a follow-up observation of the behavior in the same environment will be tallied to assess how well the intervention worked. See Figure 11.2 for an example of an observation form.

Location_____   Name_____   Date_____

Definition of Behavior to be Observed _____

_____

_____

Time   Tally   Description of Behaviors

____   ____   _____

____   ____   _____

____   ____   _____

Summary_____

Signature of Observer_____

Figure 11.2 Observation form.

Figure 11.3 School counselor observing student behavior during a classroom activity.

Source: Shutterstock

Conceptual Application Activity 11.4

Ask a teacher if you can sit in the classroom to observe student behavior. Select a student you would like to observe and make note of the behaviors this individual exhibits in a certain amount of time. Choose one of the behaviors and use the observation form above to note numbers of times this behavior occurs.

Pre- and Post-Test

One method for collecting information about a strategy is to conduct a pre-test assessment prior to completing an activity and a similar post-test assessment after a task or intervention has been completed. The information gathered from this type of assessment would be compared to determine if the activity was successful. For example, suppose you wanted to conduct a six-session counseling group focused on helping middle school students build social skills and friendships. To gather data you could give a pre-test to the group participants at the beginning of the first session to determine knowledge, skills, or attitudes toward social skills and friendship. After conducting the six sessions, you could give the same assessment as a post-test during the last group session. Pre- and post-test data would be compared to determine if the information and activities resulted in an increase in the students' knowledge, skills, or attitudes related to social skills and building friendships with peers at school. See Figure 11.4 for an example of a pre-test/post-test.

Scale: 1 = never, 2 = rarely, 3 = sometimes, 4 = most of the time, 5 = always

1. I know how to be a friend.
    1   2   3   4   5

2. I know what qualities to look for in a friend.
    1   2   3   4   5

3. I only talk to classmates I know.
    1   2   3   4   5

4. I feel comfortable introducing myself to new people.
    1   2   3   4   5

5. I know how to react if someone doesn't want to be my friend.
    1   2   3   4   5

6. I would like to make friends with people who are different than me.
    1   2   3   4   5

7. I know what is appropriate to share with others about my friendships.
    1   2   3   4   5

8. I must have a best friend.
    1   2   3   4   5

9. I can tell my family about my friendships.
    1   2   3   4   5

Figure 11.4 Friendship group.

Conceptual Application Activity 11.5

Talk with your site supervisor about implementing an upcoming school counseling activity that is based on an identified school counseling program competency. Design a pre- and post-test that allows you to assess a change in student knowledge, attitudes, or behavior. Compare your activity and assessment with those developed by your peers. Discuss the successes and challenges in performing this activity assessment.

_____

_____

Surveys

Another method of gathering data is through the use of surveys that could be given to students, teachers, parents, and administrators. These instruments can be oral or written and may be distributed by surface mail, email, online, or in person. As an example, suppose that you wanted to learn what your stakeholders believe are the most critical concerns impacting students. Survey items could include open- and closed-ended questions, multiple-choice, rank order, and short-answer items. Open-ended items allow for more comments from your stakeholders, while closed-ended or multiple-choice questions could be used to target feedback on a specific issue. See Figure 11.5 for examples of each type of question.

Open Questions

1. This year I would like to learn more about ...
2. The school counselor should focus his/her time on ...

Closed Questions

1. Do students need more help with study skills? Yes or No
2. Does the school counselor meet your needs? Yes or No

Multiple-Choice Items

1. Which of the following groups would you be most likely to participate in?
   a. Anger management
   b. Friendship
   c. Bullying
   d. Divorce
   e. Study skills
2. Which of the following topics are most needed in your class?
   a. Time management
   b. Stress
   c. Career development
   d. Anger management
   e. Other _____

Figure 11.5 Sample survey questions.

Conceptual Application Activity 11.6

Ask your site supervisor about surveys he or she has designed, adapted, borrowed, or purchased. Bring this survey to class to compare with those of your peers, and talk about the advantages and disadvantages of each of the formats.

_____

_____

Retrospective Assessments

A retrospective assessment strategy is similar to the pre-test/post-test methodology; however, the counselor asks the student to refer or reflect back to a previous time for comparative purposes. For example, a teacher refers a student who originally seemed engaged and interested in class but is now very quiet and does not like to participate. Using a retrospective assessment method, you would ask the student to think back to how he or she felt, thought, or behaved in this class at the beginning of the school year. You could instruct this student to place an *X* on a scale from 1 to 5 indicating his or her recollections of specified feelings, thoughts, or behaviors in the class. Then, you could prompt the student to rate how he or she is currently feeling, thinking, or behaving according to the same identifiers, and to place an *O* on the same scale. These two notations are then evaluated to see if positive, negative, or no change has taken place. Any discrepancy between the two scales would then serve as a place to begin counseling. Refer to Figure 11.6 for an example.

Feelings at First Counseling Session

Frustrated		X			
Stressful			X		
Angry				X	
Nervous			X		
Happy			X		
Worried			X		
	1	2	3	4	5

Feelings at Fifth Counseling Session

Frustrated		O			
Stressful				O	
Angry			O		
Nervous			O		
Happy			O		
Worried		O			
	1	2	3	4	5

1 = I never have this feeling.
2 = I rarely have this feeling.
3 = I sometimes have this feeling.
4 = I usually have this feeling.
5 = I almost always have this feeling.

Trends

Frustrated—no change
Stressful—negative change
Angry—positive change
Nervous—no change
Happy—no change
Worried—positive change

Figure 11.6 Example of retrospective assessment.

Conceptual Application Activity 11.7

Work with your site supervisor to design a retrospective assessment that can be used in your counseling duties. Share your assessment with your peers and discuss the challenges and successes you had in designing this assessment.

_____

_____

EVALUATION AND IMPROVEMENT

School counselor competencies assessment, school counselor performance appraisal, school counselor program assessment, and program goals are additional evaluation and improvement elements integral to the Accountability component. The evaluative criteria that will be used to assess your skills as a supervisee are outlined prior to beginning your clinical experiences and are a topic of conversation between you and your supervisors so that everyone is aware of the criteria that will be used for this evaluation. Receiving and applying feedback is crucial to your training, as the supervisors have your best interests in mind and want you to succeed as a school counselor. Rather than being upset if the feedback you receive is not as favorable as you would like it to be, instead recognize that utilizing this advice will facilitate your transition into the profession. Therefore, embrace this experience and use this feedback as an opportunity for growth.

Box 11.2

Marilee was an intelligent, motivated school counselor-in-training. However, she had no real work experience as she spent her summers in academic camps throughout her high school years and took summer classes while she was in her bachelor's program at a major university. Furthermore, her parents, although well-meaning, bought her a condominium and car and gave her an allowance to cover all her living expenses so that she would have more time to study. The result was a student who had difficulty relating to her classmates and problems understanding different life styles and issues related to diversity.

Marilee's challenging dispositions were apparent during her clinical experiences when she would observe her supervisor conduct classroom lessons and automatically wrote down what the supervisor said and did, word for word. The result was Marilee mimicking her supervisor with little effort to create her own lessons, with a reluctance to engage in group and individual counseling for fear that she wasn't "doing it right." During the middle of the semester, the supervisor decided that Marilee just wasn't reaching the appropriate developmental markers that previous supervisees had attained at this point in their internship. Although the supervisor had discussed her concerns with Marilee throughout the weeks, little improvement had been noted, and a meeting among the faculty supervisor, Marilee, and the site supervisor was scheduled.

When Marilee listened to the concerns her supervisors presented, she immediately became defensive, cried uncontrollably, and raced out of the room, saying, "None of these statements are true—I have done everything everyone has asked." The next day she contacted an attorney who threatened legal action if the supervisors continued to be uncooperative. Unfortunately, the end result of this situation was a poorly trained supervisee and supervisors who refused to provide a recommendation for her.

In the example above, the school counselor-in-training was unable to graciously listen to feedback and make appropriate changes to positively alter the concerns that were presented. Instead, she chose to blame the school, supervisors, and program rather than reflectively looking inward. Take advantage of the assessments your supervisors provide. They are in a position to guide you to facilitate your transition into being an effective school counselor. As you gain more experience, hopefully you will continue to reflect on your values, motives, and knowledge so that you can learn from your mistakes and successes and enhance the lives of the students with whom you interact.

School Counselor Competencies Assessment

Use the school counselor competencies assessment to self-evaluate your knowledge, abilities, skills, and attitudes at this stage of your career. If you use this assessment on a regular basis, you are able to monitor your professional growth and annually evaluate your abilities, as well as use it as a basis for personal goal setting.

Conceptual Application Activity 11.8

Talk with your supervisor about the evaluation instrument that is used to evaluate his/her performance and whether or not this assessment is a favorable indication of the work your supervisor performs. What suggestions does your supervisor have for improvement?

_____

_____

School Counselor Performance Appraisal

The school counselor performance appraisal is based on the ASCA National Model and includes such areas as development and management, delivery of a comprehensive, developmental school counseling (CDSC) program, and accountability. Although this is a useful instrument that is compatible with the role and function of a 21st century counselor, there are other evaluative forms that may be used as a counselor-in-training or as a professional school counselor. The following section describes peer, student, self, and portfolio assessment strategies.

Peer Assessment

Peer assessment is one strategy for determining your performance as a supervisee and could be an evaluative method that will be valuable to you when you become a professional school counselor. As a counselor-in-training, your site and faculty supervisor will evaluate you, and in some instances your school counseling peers may also provide you with personal feedback. More likely than not, while you are a student training for the counseling profession, this will be the last time that you will be provided feedback on your clinical skills. As a professional school counselor, it is most likely that a school administrator will evaluate you, and in many cases this individual will not have a background in counseling. Yet, group and individual counseling are significant parts of your job, and receiving feedback on your skills facilitates your development. Seeking someone who is considered an expert to observe and evaluate your clinical skills such as the district school counselor director, school counselors within the district, or local counselor educators is a step toward enhancing these skills. Having an open dialogue with your evaluator as to your training and education and how your counseling skills can be utilized to improve student growth is an advocacy skill that promotes professional understanding.

Student Assessment

A student assessment is another useful form of evaluation. Not only are you able to receive qualitative feedback regarding your counseling interventions, you can also receive quantitative data from the students to determine change in their knowledge, skills, or attitudes due to their participation in school counseling interventions. These results can be documented in the Analysis of Curriculum Results Report and Analysis of Small-Group Results Report for program improvement information (ASCA, 2012).

A more straightforward method for requesting student feedback is through a rating scale. Incorporating a basic rating scale from 1 (poor) to 5 (excellent) is a simple technique for tracking how the students experienced the counseling or group school counseling session. Although this method can give you a basic understanding of how students felt about the sessions, other methods could be implemented to determine the extent to which thoughts, feelings, or behavior changed. For instance, subjective case notes provide a means for school counselors and school counselors-in-training to refresh their memory on what occurred in counseling so that future counseling sessions may continue seamlessly. You may want to familiarize yourself with the SOAP (subjective, objective, analysis, plan) method of writing case notes to assist in remembering the

Confidential

Student Counselor-in-Training _____

Student Counselee (first name or initials) _____

Date of Session _____

Session # _____ Type of Session _____

Start Time _____ End Time _____

Subjective Impressions

How did the counselee present self (e.g., affect, behavior, nervousness)

What were your subjective reactions to the counselee?

Objective Impressions

What are the facts that were discussed during counseling?

What did you say?

What did the counselee say?

What was the presenting issue?

Analysis

How did the session address the goals of counseling?

Plan

What are your goals for the next session?

What do you need to prepare to address these goals?

What aspect of the problem needs continued focus?

Figure 11.7 The SOAP method of writing case notes.

specific concerns each counselee brings to counseling (Cameron & Turtle-song, 2002). Figure 11.7 provides an outline of the SOAP acronym that can be adapted for your personal case note needs. S = subjective impressions; O = objective impressions; A = analysis; P = plan.

Although confidentiality is a cornerstone of the profession, confidentiality in counseling sessions for a supervisee cannot be guaranteed, because it is generally a program requirement to audio- or video-record sessions and to keep case notes on counselees for supervision purposes. However, once a person has become a professional school counselor, there is debate as to the wisdom of keeping case notes. Two cautionary suggestions in keeping these records are: (a) any information that is shared is no longer private and becomes part of the student records, and (b) the school counselor's personal notes (and yours, as a supervisee) can be subpoenaed. Although your school counseling training program has probably provided you with forms to use in conjunction with this requirement, a sample form is provided in Figure 11.8. EZAnalyze is an electronic Excel-based tool in which you can track your activities, create graphs, and analyze your data. You can download this tool for free at www.ezanalyze.com/.

Box 11.3

"I use Google.docs to create templates for spreadsheets and graphs. Although making templates takes a little practice, after you get the hang of it, it is easy to use. When I first started as a school counselor, I felt so lonely trying to collect data by myself, but eventually I learned to collaborate with faculty, parents, and even my students. I learned to start small, and it was fun seeing the results that were generated with the help of others."

Source: Elementary school counselor

Counselor-in-Training _____

Date _____

Counselee Initials and Grade Level: _____

Counselee's Presenting Problem:

Session Goals:

What were your feelings regarding the counselee?

What detracted from working most effectively with the student?

What was your theoretical model in working with this student?

What techniques did you implement in the session? Why?

What strategies did you use to evaluate the session?

What were your strengths in the session?

What areas would you like to improve?

Plans for next session:

Rate yourself on the session from 1 (needs improvement) to 5 (excellent). Explain your rating.

Figure 11.8 Counselor-in-training tape review form.

Self-assessment

Identifying and setting professional and personal goals at the beginning of the school year and self-evaluating at the end of the year is another method of determining your effectiveness in the educational system. As mentioned earlier, one helpful strategy to self-evaluate is to utilize the ASCA School Counselor Competencies Assessment as a checklist (ASCA, 2012). Although personal goals are helpful for improving your role and function within the school, they are often not objective, and therefore do not have the same evaluative weight as assessments conducted by a third-party stakeholder.

In addition, your clinical training program may require you to journal your weekly thoughts, feelings, and behaviors to track and assess your progress from the beginning of the clinical experience until you have completed the program requirements. Self-reflection of your work with students as well as the overall program is helpful for both school counselors and counselors-in-training in order to process the identified goals and objectives set forth for the program. Figure 11.9 provides an example of prompts that may assist you with this process.

Name _____ Date _____

Total number of hours for week _____ Direct _____ Indirect _____

Summarize the activities in which you were involved this week:

On a scale of 1 to 10, with 1 indicating a stressful, anxiety-filled week and 10 indicating a productive, successful week, what number best indicates your weekly experience? _____ Explain.

What were some of the most difficult challenges you faced this week, and discuss what made these events difficult.

What were some of your accomplishments and successes? Explain.

What do you need from supervision this week?

What are your professional goals for next week?

What are your personal goals for next week?

Any questions or concerns?

Student's Signature: _____

Figure 11.9 Practicum and internship weekly journal reflections.

Portfolio

As a school counselor-in-training, you may be required to submit a portfolio that will be reviewed by your faculty members before graduation. A portfolio is a working document that typically includes an accumulation of documents or artifacts that demonstrate your acquired competencies during your graduate school counselor training. A portfolio is considered a capstone assignment and could be in the form of a large binder filled with information or in an electronic format that summarizes your training experience. Artifacts you might include in your portfolio include your philosophy of school counseling, current résumé, samples of lessons or group plans, an outline of a CDSC program you developed as a class assignment, media displaying your skills, and other types of data that document your progress as a school counselor-in-training. If you are interviewing for a position, you can bring this document to the interviewer's office or provide the interviewer a link in advance to access your electronic portfolio before the interview.

Program Goal Analysis

The professional school counselor thoughtfully analyzes the data that have been collected throughout the school year, carefully scrutinizes the results of the interventions, and intentionally facilitates goal development for the following school year. As discussed in Chapter 8, the ASCA uses the SMART acronym as a tool for goal setting. S = specific; M = measurable; A = attainable; R = realistic; T = time-bound. In other words, the goal needs to be specific and worded in such a way that it is easy to evaluate. An attainable, realistic goal is one that can be reached by the students for whom the goal is established, and a description of the time frame sets a specific time for when the intervention or program is to occur.

CONCLUSION

As a professional school counselor in the 21st century, it is imperative to demonstrate how your program impacts the student body and other stakeholders. Analyzing the school report card is one method by which school counselors are able to determine areas that need to be improved, and in doing so data collection reveals the number of participants that were involved in an intervention, and what these individuals know, believe, or can perform describes process and perception data. In addition, outcome data show the success of the intervention. Action research through the use of the MEASURE acronym describes a method in which you are able to systematically engage in accountability procedures. Observational forms, pre- and post-test instruments, surveys, and retrospective assessments are examples of assessment tools. It is possible that you may need to design your own assessment instruments if a standardized instrument is not available.

School counselor assessment can occur through a standardized form that is adapted by the school district, or through the ASCA School Counselor Competencies Assessment and Performance Appraisal. Peer, student, self, and portfolio assessment strategies are additional evaluative tools to measure school counselor performance.

WEBSITES

• This link will take you to the school counselor performance appraisal form that is based on the ASCA National Model. This form can be adapted to integrate with your job description: www. vsca. org/PSC Manual/School Counselor Performance AppraisalForm.doc
• This link will take you to an article that describes accountability practices of school counselors throughout the decades: www.counselingoutfitters.com/vistas/ACAPCD/ACAPCD-01.pdf

REFERENCES

ASCA [American School Counselor Association]. (2012). *The ASCA National Model: A framework for school counseling programs* (3rd ed.). Alexandria, VA: Author.

Barnett, A. (2011). *Exceptions of school counselors toward their professional roles* (Doctoral dissertation). Retrieved from ProQuest Information & Learning (AAI3408692).

Brown, D., & Trusty, J. (2005). The ASCA national model, accountability, and establishing causal links between school counselors' activities and student outcomes: A reply to Sink. *Professional School Counseling, 9,* 13–27.

Cameron, S., & Turtle-song, I. (2002). Learning to write case notes using the SOAP format. *Journal of Counseling and Development, 80,* 286–292.

Gibson, R.I., & Mitchell, M.H. (2007). *Introduction to counseling and guidance* (7th ed.). Upper Saddle River, NJ: Merrill Prentice-Hall.

Gladding, S.T. (2012). *Counseling: A comprehensive profession* (7th ed.). Upper Saddle River, NJ: Merrill Prentice-Hall.

Myrick, R.D. (2003). Accountability: Counselors count. *Professional School Counseling, 6,* 174–189.

Stone, C.B., & Dahir, C.A. (2011). *School counselor accountability: A MEASURE of student success* (3rd ed.). Upper Saddle River, NJ: Merrill Prentice-Hall.

Studer, J.R., Oberman, A.H., & Womack, R.H. (2006). Producing evidence to show counseling effectiveness in the schools. *Professional School Counseling, 9,* 385–391.

12 Applying the American School Counselor Association (ASCA) Ethical Standards to Clinical Experiences

Melinda M. Gibbons and Shawn L. Spurgeon

CACREP Standards

Foundations

A. Knowledge

2. Understands ethical and legal considerations specifically related to the practice of school counseling.

B. Skills and Practices

1. Demonstrates the ability to apply and adhere to ethical and legal standards in school counseling.

The purpose of this chapter is to:

- describe the ethical principles used in counseling
- review an ethical decision-making model
- demonstrate the application of the ethical decision-making model to school counseling issues
- illustrate the American School Counselor Association (ASCA) Ethical Standards
- apply the ASCA Ethical Standards to various case examples.

INTRODUCTION

Professional counselors and counselors-in-training, regardless of their work setting, are required to abide by the ethical code of their profession. As individuals training for the school counseling profession, you are constantly faced with ethical dilemmas and often have to make clinical decisions that require knowledge of ethical codes and a strong ethical decision-making model. Although you have probably already taken a class in ethical/legal standards, this chapter reviews the principles on which ethical codes are based and outlines common ethical decision-making models used by professional counselors. The current ethical decision-making model adopted by the American Counseling Association (ACA) will be discussed. Following this model, a summary of the ASCA Ethical Standards (2010) will be provided along with case examples and activities for you to consider. Finally, general discussion questions on ethics in school counseling are included. The complete *Ethical Standards for School Counselors* is found in Appendix A for your reference during your clinical experiences.

Ethical Principles

School counselors-in-training need strong ethical decision-making skills for the dilemmas they will face in the education setting. Ethical guidelines do not provide a definitive answer for every dilemma a school counselor will face, but instead serve as a guide to meet the challenges these situations may create. The cornerstone of ethical guidelines is Kitchener's (1984) moral principles of autonomy, justice, beneficence, nonmaleficence, fidelity, and veracity which serve as a foundation to help clarify difficult dilemmas.

Autonomy is the principle that allows clients the freedom to choose their own paths without criticism of their choices. Kitchener (1984) stated that the essence of this principle is that counselors encourage counselees to act on their values in making sound, appropriate decisions related to their well-being. The key considerations for counselors are the counselee's ability to make rational, sound decisions, and the counselor's need to help the counselee understand the consequences related to those decisions. Counselees should not be allowed to make decisions that will cause harm to themselves or that may harm others.

Kitchener (1984) defined *justice* as "treating equals equally and treating unequals unequally but in proportion to their relative differences" (p. 49). Justice takes into consideration the unique nature of problems individuals face, and counselors who demonstrate this principle must consider the individual and the unique nature of his or her problem. To this end, you need to be able to provide a sound rationale for treating the individual differently and need to be able to articulate this difference to the individual. The treatment must be both appropriate and necessary.

Beneficence requires that counselors strive to "do good" when working with counselees. Often considered the foundation of ethical principles, counselors should consider the welfare of their counselees in all situations. Counselors and supervisees maintain a proactive stance when considering treatment options for their counselees and advocate for them when it is in their best interest to do so. An important aspect of this principle is that counselors need to be willing to prevent counselees from harming themselves and from harmful situations when necessary.

Nonmaleficence is a medical concept that requires counselors to not cause harm to others. Though all the principles are valued and important, researchers consider this principle to be one of the most important (Forester-Miller & Rubenstein, 1992; Remley & Herlihy, 2007; Stadler, 1986). Kitchener (1984) simplified this principle as the "above-all-do-no-harm" principle. Counselors are expected to avoid things that inflict harm on their counselees and to not engage in actions that risk harming others.

Fidelity highlights the idea that counselees need to be able to trust their counselors, and counselors need to be able to help counselees see the value in the therapeutic relationship. Counselors have a responsibility to honor commitments with their counselees and maintain a sense of loyalty, transparency, and honesty. Counselors work to fulfill all obligations with counselees to the best of their abilities, without using their power to threaten the therapeutic relationship.

Veracity refers to truthfulness when working with individuals. For professional counselors, this means that you have an obligation to be honest with your counselees. This serves as a vital part of developing a strong, therapeutic relationship with your client; the more honest you are, the more likely your counselee will respect you as a professional. It includes the counselor's ability to provide honest feedback to a counselee who is not living optimally. Honesty must also be extended to other professionals with whom the counselor works.

Conceptual Application Activity 12.1

Discuss Kitchener's ethical principles with your site supervisor and how to apply them to your counseling sessions. Ask your supervisor to share with you instances in which he or she used them to make an ethical decision. Discuss your supervisor's responses with those of your peers.

Ethical Decision-Making Models

Kitchener's (1984) moral principles serve as the foundation for the ethical dilemmas you will face in training and practice. When making decisions, you are expected to relate these principles to specific situations to clarify the issues involved; at times this may create even more complex problems for the counselor. In challenging cases that require difficult decision-making, you can employ an ethical decision-making model to sift through the confusion to help resolve the dilemma. Some of the more commonly used ethical decision-making models include Forester-Miller and Rubenstein (1992), Remley and Herlihy (2001), and Tarvydas (2003). You may wish to research these models and determine that which best fits your values. Or, you may decide to use the ACA ethical decision-making model that incorporates aspects of these models or others.

The ACA has adopted an ethical decision-making model that highlights the principles espoused by Kitchener (1984) and incorporates the work of Van Hoose and Paradise (1979), Stadler (1986), Haas and Malouf (1989), Forester-Miller and Rubenstein (1992), and Sileo and Kopala (1993). The model provides a seven-step, sequential approach to addressing any ethical dilemma. The model is very practical in nature and you will find that it serves as a useful approach to resolving ethical issues. We have modified the model to include the ASCA Ethical Standards rather than the ACA Code of Ethics. The steps are as follows:

1. Identify the problem.
2. Apply the ASCA Ethical Standards for School Counselors.
3. Determine the nature and dimensions of the dilemma.
4. Generate potential courses of action.
5. Consider the potential consequences of all options and choose a course of action.
6. Evaluate the selected course of action.
7. Implement the course of action.

Identify the Problem

Try to gather as much information about the situation as possible to develop a snapshot of the dilemma. It is important to be as specific and objective as possible and to separate the facts from innuendos, assumptions, and suspicions. This fact-checking process serves as a critical step in the decision-making process. First, you need to determine if the problem is one concerning ethics, laws, the profession, a clinical situation, or a combination of two or more of these. Check with your site supervisor if you believe the situation is a legal issue and, if a legal consultation is necessary, have your supervisor accompany you to the attorney who represents the school district for consultation. Oftentimes the problem can be resolved by implementing a policy developed by the school, and you may be the instrumental person in bringing about this adaptation. Remember to examine the problem from different perspectives and avoid a simplistic solution because ethical situations can be very complex (Remley & Herlihy, 2007).

Apply the ASCA Ethical Standards

After you have clarified the problem, refer to the Ethical Standards (ASCA, 2010) to determine if the issue is addressed. Sometimes there is a standard that directly addresses the situation, or several standards that are applicable, specific, and clear. Follow the course of action indicated. This often leads to a resolution of the problem. Read the ethical codes carefully so that you can effectively apply them to the situation, but if the problem seems more complex and a resolution does not seem apparent, then you probably have a true ethical dilemma. Further steps will be needed to proceed in making an ethical decision.

Determine the Nature and Dimensions of the Dilemma

Be sure to examine the problem and the various aspects that are influenced by the issue by viewing different strategies. You may start by considering Kitchener's (1984) moral principles and deciding which principles apply to the specific situation, determine those principles that take priority, and review the relevant literature to ensure you are using the most current professional thinking in reaching a decision. Consultation is a key part of this step. You can connect with your supervisors and former or current professors to help you review the information you have gathered. Oftentimes, these professionals present a perspective you may or may not have considered or that you do not perceive objectively. You also can consult your state or national professional associations for help with the dilemma.

Generate Potential Courses of Action

After you have determined the nature and dimensions of the dilemma, you need to brainstorm as many possible courses of action as possible. Your creativity and openness to exploration are critical aspects in this process (Kitchener, 1984). Consider all options in your investigation, write down the courses of action you generate, and be sure to consult with your site and faculty supervisor. It is not uncommon for practicing school counselors to seek help from colleagues in generating options for consideration.

Consider the Potential Consequences of All Options and Determine a Course of Action

Analyze the courses of action you have generated by evaluating each option and assessing the potential consequences for everyone involved. You need to consider who will be affected by the course of action as well as the consequences for you. Options that will not produce the desired results or could produce more problematic consequences need to be eliminated. After you have rejected these options, review the remaining selections to determine those that provide the most effective resolution to the situation. The selected course of action will need to address the priorities you identified in Step 1 and the best solution for the situation.

Evaluate the Selected Course of Action

Be sure to review the selected course of action to see if it presents any new ethical considerations. If it does, then you will need to go back to the beginning and reevaluate each step of the process. It may be that you chose the wrong option or incorrectly identified the problem. Stadler (1986) stated a selected course of action can be tested for appropriateness by asking three simple questions:

- For the test of publicity, ask yourself, "Would I want my behavior reported in the press?"
- In applying the test of justice, ask yourself, "Would I treat others similarly in this situation?"
- To determine universality, ask yourself, "Would I recommend the same course of action to another counselor in the same situation?"

If you can answer each question in the affirmative and you are satisfied that you have selected an appropriate course of action, then you are ready to implement the plan.

Implement the Course of Action

The implementation stage sometimes presents a challenging dilemma for school counselors-in-training. Appropriate action can often have devastating consequences for the individual involved as well as for you. Your ego strength and the values you place on the importance of ethical and professional behavior will be critical in helping you carry out the plan you have developed (Remley & Herlihy, 2007). Once you have completed this step, you should follow-up and assess the effectiveness and consequences of your actions for future ethical dilemmas you could face.

Van Hoose and Paradise (1979) suggested that a counselor "is probably acting in an ethically responsible way concerning a client if: (1) he or she has maintained personal and professional honesty, coupled with (2) the best interests of the client, (3) without malice or personal gain, and (4) can justify his or her actions as the best judgment of what should be done based upon the current state of the profession" (p. 58). Ethical decision making requires you to apply ethical codes and to examine your own values in dealing with complex problems. Each professional will have a unique perspective when assessing an ethical dilemma; there is rarely one right answer to a complex ethical dilemma. The use of a systematic ethical decision making model will help you adhere to the ethical standards developed by the counseling profession.

THE ASCA ETHICAL STANDARDS

To reiterate, this chapter is based on the belief that you have fully explored the ACA Code of Ethics. As school counselors-in-training, however, you are also required to understand the ASCA Ethical Standards for School Counselors, heretofore referred to as the Standards (ASCA, 2010). Therefore, this section reviews each piece of the Standards and provides examples for better understanding.

ASCA views the Standards as a guide for professional school counseling practice regardless of whether the school counselor is a member of the organization or a supervisee. It is assumed that all school counselors abide by these Standards in order to maintain an acceptable standard of practice. The Standards are divided into responsibilities to the various stakeholders: students, parents/guardians, colleagues/other professionals, school and community, self, and the school counseling profession. Specific issues are detailed under each stakeholder section.

Responsibilities to Students

The Standards clearly state that school counselors have a primary obligation to their students. Counselors are reminded to focus on career, personal/social (renamed social/emotional), and academic issues with all students, to respect the beliefs of their students, and to know the laws and policies applicable to working with students. These responsibilities are as follows:

Confidentiality

School counselors are reminded that informed consent and an explanation of confidentiality are required before counseling can begin. Issues related to communicable diseases, court requests, student records, and parental/guardian rights are issues related to confidentiality. Consider the following ethical situations in the remaining activities in this chapter, and use the ethical decision-making model described earlier to determine a course of action for each situation. The section of the Standards that helps address each ethical dilemma is in parentheses.

Conceptual Application Activity 12.2

Read and respond to the following scenario.

a. A middle school supervisee discusses the limits of confidentiality during her first classroom visits each year. She further explains her role as a school counselor-in-training and encourages students to come see her if they have academic, career, or personal/social (renamed social/emotional) concerns. Her rationale for explaining confidentiality in classroom lessons is that when a student comes for counseling, she will not have to spend their limited time together discussing the issue of confidentiality. (A.2.a, A.2.b)

b. A male high school student tells you that he has syphilis. The student further mentions that he has had unprotected sex with three partners in the last 6 months. When you suggest he tell the partners about the disease, he refuses because he fears his parents will find out. You discuss this situation with your supervisor and the decision is made that you must inform the sexual partners about the potential of disease. (A.2.c)

c. A fourth-grade boy has been seeing you about feelings of sadness and anger related to his parents' recent divorce. His mother calls you and wants to know what her son has been discussing in counseling. After discussing this situation with your site supervisor you explain the concept of confidentiality and refuse to divulge any information. (A.2.g)

What are your concerns about each example? Have you acted ethically in each case? How would you respond in each situation? Review the Standards and then reconsider your response if needed.

_____

_____

Counseling Plans, Dual Relationships, Referrals

The next three sections focus on other professional responsibilities of counselors and school counselors-in-training as related to their work with students. The counselor and supervisee are ethically required to implement a comprehensive school counseling program and to advocate for students regarding their postsecondary plans. School counselors and supervisees also are required to avoid dual relationships if at all possible. Finally, referrals must be made when it is necessary.

Conceptual Application Activity 12.3

A high school supervisee suspects a student has an eating disorder. She has spoke with the student, who acknowledges losing a lot of weight in a short period of time. In consultation with the site supervisor, the supervisee contacts this student's parents and provides the parents with three possible referrals for mental health professionals who specialize in this disorder. (A.5).

Was the counselor ethically appropriate? What would you have done in this situation?

_____

_____

Group Work and Danger to Self or Others

Policies related to counseling work with counselees are discussed in the next sections of the Standards. In particular, informing students about the limits of confidentiality and the purposes of counseling are covered extensively. For example, school counselors and school counselors-in-training are ethically bound to screen group members, inform them that confidentiality cannot be guaranteed in a group setting, notify parents/guardians of group participation if appropriate, and follow-up with group members following initial meetings. In addition, you must break confidentiality when there is imminent risk to the student or others by the student.

Box 12.1

School counselors struggle with the concept of confidentiality that is a legal and an ethical mandate. Law states that parents are the guiding factors in their lives of their children due to:

1. The susceptibility of children to make choices that may be life changing.

2. The difficulty of stressed youth to competently make informed choices.

3. The unique parent/child relationship.

Source: Stone, 2013a

Conceptual Application Activity 12.4

Read and respond to the following scenario.

As a counselor-in-training, you have been asked to lead a small group on anger management with seventh-grade boys. Your site supervisor gives you the names of six boys she believes would benefit from the group (A.6).

What are your next steps? What might be some ethical considerations related to running this type of group?

_____

_____

Student Records, Evaluation and Assessment, Technology, Peer Support

School counselors and supervisees have a responsibility to create and secure written records on students, separate these records from the cumulative record, understand the legal limits of keeping written records, and destroy records after an appropriate length of time. Part of your training is to understand how to select, administer, and interpret assessments that you are qualified to use, apply caution in using these assessments, and to close educational gaps as appropriate. When using technology, school counselors and supervisees are to advocate for equal access, attempt to maintain confidentiality of student records, protect students from inappropriate online material, and generally protect students from harm. Finally, if you engage in peer support programs, you assume responsibility for all students participating in the program.

Conceptual Application Activity 12.5

Read and respond to the following scenario.

Jim is a counselor-in-training at Happy Days Elementary School, and he is fortunate to have a veteran counselor serve as his supervisor. This experienced counselor explains that it is best not to keep case notes on students because many students are from families of divorce and the records can be subpoenaed if they exist. (A.8)

What are the ethical dilemmas posed in this scenario? How can you apply the decision-making model to help determine the best course of action?

_____

_____

Responsibilities to Parents/Guardians

Two main ethical responsibilities regarding the rights of parents/guardians are covered in the Standards. First, school counselors and school counselors-in-training are responsible for recognizing and respecting parental/guardian rights. These include viewing the parent/guardian as a collaborative partner, understanding the legal rights of parents/guardians, respecting confidentiality with parents/guardians, and demonstrating sensitivity to diverse populations. Second, school counselors and supervisees are to recognize and understand parental/guardian rights related to confidential information. This includes working to inform parents/guardians about the importance of confidentiality with students, acknowledging the importance of parents/guardians in the counseling relationship, providing pertinent information to parents/guardians, and keeping parents/guardians informed regarding student progress.

Conceptual Application Activity 12.6

Read and respond to the following scenarios.

a. Josie, a fifth-grade student, is having difficulty completing her homework. You believe that Josie lacks organizational skills and that keeping a daily planner and separate homework folder will help greatly. You call Josie's mom and ask her to buy a planner for Josie and review it every day for homework assignments. Josie's mom becomes frustrated and explains that she works until 9 p.m., and when she comes home, Josie is already up in her room. You discuss this situation with your supervisor who believes that Mom is part of the reason why Josie is not doing her homework. (B.1 and B.2)

b. Sam's mother and father have recently divorced. His mom has custody and his dad has weekend visitation. Because Sam lives with his mom, his report cards and progress reports are mailed to that address. Sam's father calls and requests that copies of all academic information be sent to his home as well. (B.2.d)

Consider your reactions to each case. What would you do in each situation? What are the ethical issues involved?

_____

_____

Responsibilities to Colleagues and Professional Associates

School counselors and counselors-in-training have a responsibility to maintain professional relationships with their colleagues and other professionals. The Standards include the importance of creating professional relationships with school staff, treating all colleagues with respect and equality, and understanding referral sources. Regarding information sharing, the Standards discuss the importance of understanding and following confidentiality guidelines and providing school staff with necessary and objective information that is in the best interests of the student. Also discussed is the need for the release of information forms and knowledge of what is appropriate information to share with parents/guardians.

Conceptual Application Activity 12.7

Read and respond to the following scenario.

a. You are working with a seventh-grade girl who has been physically abused by a parent. She has been having outbursts in class and recently was sent to in-school suspension for shouting at a teacher. While you know that maintaining confidentiality is vital, you also believe that sharing information about the student's home life with her teachers would be helpful to both the teachers and the student.

What steps would you take to ensure confidentiality for the student while also respecting professional relationships with school staff? (C.1 and C.2)

_____

_____

b.   Jon is working with a 10th-grade student on academic issues when the student reports that she has begun seeing a mental health counselor for anxiety and depression. Jon decides that, since he is solely focusing on academic concerns, it is appropriate for him to continue counseling the student while she sees the outside therapist as well.

Is this the correct course of action? (C.2)

_____

_____

_____

Responsibilities to School and Community

The school personnel as a whole and local community members are other stakeholders with whom school counselors and counselors-in-training work. School counselors must examine the educational program of the school to ensure that it works in the best interests of all students. Relatedly, school counselors and supervisees are to understand the school's mission and work to support that mission by connecting their counseling program to the total school philosophy. If counselors or supervisees learn of behavior that is in opposition to the school mission, they must inform the administration while still upholding confidentiality of counseling relationships. Additionally, school counselors have a commitment to accept a position for which they meet the qualifications and work to create a developmental and comprehensive counseling program in the school. Finally, school counselors and school counselors-in-training should work to collaborate with outside agencies and organizations from the local community to enhance student services. This collaboration includes structuring programs to include community resources that add to the comprehensive nature of the program.

Box 12.2

In the case of Woodlock vs. Orange Ulster B.O.C.E.S. 2006/2008 a school counselor found herself in a disagreement with her principal when her phone calls, e-mails, and faxes to her administration went unanswered. The school counselor eventually took it upon herself to report her complaints to a different individual who was outside of the chain of command, and eventually she was terminated. This case teaches us that although it may sometimes be difficult to negotiate with administrators, school counselors do have a responsibility to follow the school guidelines and policies and to find alternative methods for working with authority personnel.

Source: Stone, 2013b

Conceptual Application Activity 12.8

Read and respond to the following scenario.

You are interviewing for a job as a school counselor for a rural K–12 school. Although you are certified as a pre-K–12 counselor, your fieldwork was with K–8 students in a suburban area serving mostly middle-income families. The principal informs you that your primary duties will include classroom lessons for the lower grades, and career and college planning for the high school students. In addition, she would like for you to coordinate a peer helper program and to develop a program designed to better connect with the many low-income families in the community.

What might you need to address to remain ethical and still have the chance of obtaining the job? (D.1)

_____

_____

Responsibilities to Self

Ethical school counselors as well as supervisees demonstrate professional competence and honor diversity as part of their job. As such, they know the limits of their abilities and work within those boundaries. In addition, school counselors and counselors-in-training avoid activities where they are unable to provide adequate services and engage in personal and professional growth activities to broaden and increase their knowledge of the counseling profession. School counselors and supervisees have an obligation to honor diversity in their constituents, and to constantly evaluate their own beliefs and actions to ensure they are doing so. In addition, the establishment of a knowledge base regarding the various diverse groups they may encounter in the schools is an essential component. For a full list of these diverse populations, consult section E.2.d of the Standards.

Conceptual Application Activity 12.9

Read and respond to the following scenario.

A 12th-grade student whose parents are illegal immigrants comes to you to discuss his plans after high school. He has average grades and wants to discuss the possibility of continuing his education.

What do you need to know to work effectively with this student? What personal values and beliefs might you need to consider? (E.2)

_____

_____

Responsibilities to Profession

This section of the Standards focuses on the school counselor and trainee as stakeholders of the profession. It stresses the importance of following the Standards, advocating for the profession, and generally recognizing that each school counselor and you, as a school counselor-in-training, are representatives of the school counseling profession. Participation in research, professional organizations, and formal and informal mentoring relationships are all mentioned as ways to support the school counseling profession.

Figure 12.1 Attending professional conferences and saying current on issues that impact students is an ethical obligation.

Source: Shutterstock

Conceptual Application Activity 12.10

Patricia is a staunch supporter of the Right to Life organization. She takes every opportunity that is available to talk about the importance of this organization and their principles. Discuss Patricia's ethical responsibilities regarding her stance (F.1.f.)

Maintenance of Standards

School counselors have a professional duty to maintain ethics at all times, which includes monitoring the actions of those within the profession. If you believe that a school counselor is not behaving in an ethical fashion, the first step is to confidentially share your concerns with another member of the profession. From here, it is considered good practice to discuss your concerns with the individual in question. If the concern is not resolved at this level, a thorough documentation of steps you have taken and abiding by the channels established by the school district and state school counselor association are the next channels. A referral can be made to the ASCA Ethics Review Board as a final recourse.

Conceptual Application Activity 12.11

Juan is a middle school counselor and has heard several rumors from numerous former students regarding the actions of a high school counselor in his district. According to students' reports, this school counselor has parties at her home on the weekends that are attended by many of the high school students. What could Juan do to address these rumors? (G.1.)

Conceptual Application Activity 12.12

Read and respond to the following discussion questions:

a. It is impossible for school counselors-in-training to anticipate all the potential ethical dilemmas they will face in their career, so how can you best prepare yourself for these potential situations?

b. As a school counselor-in-training, what can you do when you see another school counselor acting in what you consider to be an unethical manner?

c. What ethical dilemmas are you most concerned about, and why?

Discuss these questions with your peers.

CONCLUSION

Understanding the ethical codes for the profession is a vital part of being an effective school counselor. The ASCA Ethical Standards for School Counselors (2010) can be used within the framework of a comprehensive ethical decision-making model to help school counselors-in-training be prepared for and able to effectively address ethical dilemmas faced daily in their profession. Being familiar with both the Standards and the decision-making model enhance a school counselor's ability to successfully serve his or her constituents.

WEBSITES

- This Web page titled "Dual Relationships & Other Boundary Dilemmas" by Ken Pope shares information regarding decision making about crossing identified boundaries. Ethical scenarios and questions are provided: www.kspope.com/dual/dual.php
- For more information regarding confidentiality, privileged communication, and your legal muscle, read the article found at www.ascaschoolcounselor.org/article_section.asp?edition=91&section=140

REFERENCES

American School Counseling Association (ASCA). (2010). *Ethical standards for school counselors.* Alexandria, VA: Author.

Forester-Miller, H., & Rubenstein, R. L. (1992). Group counseling: Ethical and professional issues. In D. Capuzzi & D. R. Gross (Eds.), *Introduction to group counseling* (pp. 307–323). Denver, CO: Love Publishing Co.

Haas, L. J., & Malouf, J. L. (1989). *Keeping up the good work: A practitioner's guide to mental health ethics.* Sarasota, FL: Professional Resource Exchange, Inc.

Kitchener, K. S. (1984). Intuition, critical evaluation and ethical principles: The foundation for ethical decisions in counseling psychology. *Counseling Psychologist, 12,* 43–55.

Remley, T. P., & Herlihy, B. (2001). *Ethical, legal, and professional issues in counseling.* Upper Saddle River, NJ: Prentice-Hall.

Remley, T. P., & Herlihy, B. (2007). *Ethical, legal, and professional issues in counseling* (Updated 2nd ed.). Upper Saddle River, NJ: Pearson Prentice Hall.

Sileo, F., & Kopala, M. (1993). An A-B-C-D-E worksheet for promoting beneficence when considering ethical issues. *Counseling and Values, 37,* 89–95.

Stadler, H. A. (1986). Making hard choices: Clarifying controversial ethical issues. *Counseling & Human Development, 19,* 1–10.

Stone, C. (2013b, March). Political acumen: A skill for school counselor effectiveness. *ASCA School Counselor.* Retrieved from www.schoolcounselor.org/magazine/blogs/march-april-2013/political-acumen-a-skill-for-school-counselor-eff

Stone, C. (2013a, July). Serious and foreseeable harm or clear, imminent danger. *ASCA School Counselor.* Retrieved from www.schoolcounselor.org/magazine/blogs/july-august-2011/serious-and-foreseeable-harm-or-clear,-imminent-da

Tarvydas, V.M. (2003). The ethical imperative for culturally competent practice. *Rehabilitation Education,* *17*(2), 117–123.

Van Hoose, W.H., & Paradise, L.V. (1979). *Ethics in counseling and psychotherapy: Perspectives in issues and decision-making.* Cranston, RI: Carroll Press.

Appendix A
Ethical Standards for School Counselors
(Adopted 1984; revised 1992, 1998, 2004 and 2010)

PREAMBLE

The American School Counselor Association (ASCA) is a professional organization whose members are school counselors certified/licensed in school counseling with unique qualifications and skills to address all students' academic, personal/social [revised to read social/emotional, E. Sparks, personal communication, July, 17, 2014], and career development needs. Members are also school counseling program directors/supervisors and counselor educators. These ethical standards are the ethical responsibility of school counselors. School counseling program directors/supervisors should know them and provide support for practitioners to uphold them. School counselor educators should know them, teach them to their students and provide support for school counseling candidates to uphold them.

Professional school counselors are advocates, leaders, collaborators and consultants who create opportunities for equity in access and success in educational opportunities by connecting their programs to the mission of schools and subscribing to the following tenets of professional responsibility:

- Each person has the right to be respected, be treated with dignity and have access to a comprehensive school counseling program that advocates for and affirms all students from diverse populations including: ethnic/racial identity, age, economic status, abilities/disabilities, language, immigration status, sexual orientation, gender, gender identity/expression, family type, religious/spiritual identity and appearance.
- Each person has the right to receive the information and support needed to move toward self-direction and self-development and affirmation within one's group identities, with special care being given to students who have historically not received adequate educational services, e.g., students of color, students living at a low socio-economic status, students with disabilities and students from non-dominant language backgrounds.
- Each person has the right to understand the full magnitude and meaning of his/her educational choices and how those choices will affect future opportunities.
- Each person has the right to privacy and thereby the right to expect the school-counselor/student relationship to comply with all laws, policies and ethical standards pertaining to confidentiality in the school setting.
- Each person has the right to feel safe in school environments that school counselors help create, free from abuse, bullying, neglect, harassment or other forms of violence.
- *In this document, ASCA specifies the principles of ethical behavior necessary to maintain the high standards of integrity, leadership and professionalism among its members. The Ethical Standards for School Counselors were developed to clarify the nature of ethical responsibilities held in common by school counselors, supervisors/directors of school counseling programs and school counselor educators. The purposes of this document are to:
  - Serve as a guide for the ethical practices of all professional school counselors, supervisors/directors of school counseling programs and school counselor educators regardless of level, area, population served or membership in this professional association;
  - Provide self-appraisal and peer evaluations regarding school counselors' responsibilities to students, parents/guardians, colleagues and professional associates, schools, communities and the counseling profession; and

- Inform all stakeholders, including students, parents and guardians, teachers, administrators, community members and courts of justice, of best ethical practices, values and expected behaviors of the school counseling professional.

A.1. RESPONSIBILITIES TO STUDENTS

Professional school counselors:

a.   Have a primary obligation to the students, who are to be treated with dignity and respect as unique individuals.
b.   Are concerned with the educational, academic, career, personal and social needs and encourage the maximum development of every student.
c.   Respect students' values, beliefs and cultural background and do not impose the school counselor's personal values on students or their families.
d.   Are knowledgeable of laws, regulations and policies relating to students and strive to protect and inform students regarding their rights.
e.   Promote the welfare of individual students and collaborate with them to develop an action plan for success.
f.   Consider the involvement of support networks valued by the individual students.
g.   Understand that professional distance with students is appropriate, and any sexual or romantic relationship with students whether illegal in the state of practice is considered a grievous breach of ethics and is prohibited regardless of a student's age.
h.   Consider the potential for harm before entering into a relationship with former students or one of their family members.

A.2. CONFIDENTIALITY

Professional school counselors:

a.   Inform individual students of the purposes, goals, techniques and rules of procedure under which they may receive counseling. Disclosure includes the limits of confidentiality in a developmentally appropriate manner. Informed consent requires competence on the part of students to understand the limits of confidentiality and therefore, can be difficult to obtain from students of a certain developmental level. Professionals are aware that even though every attempt is made to obtain informed consent it is not always possible and when needed will make counseling decisions on students' behalf.
b.   Explain the limits of confidentiality in appropriate ways such as classroom lessons, the student handbook, school counseling brochures, school Web site, verbal notice or other methods of student, school and community communication in addition to oral notification to individual students.
c.   Recognize the complicated nature of confidentiality in schools and consider each case in context. Keep information confidential unless legal requirements demand that confidential information be revealed or a breach is required to prevent serious and foreseeable harm to the student. Serious and foreseeable harm is different for each minor in schools and is defined by students' developmental and chronological age, the setting, parental rights and the nature of the harm. School counselors consult with appropriate professionals when in doubt as to the validity of an exception.
d.   Recognize their primary obligation for confidentiality is to the students but balance that obligation with an understanding of parents'/guardians' legal and inherent rights to be the guiding voice in their children's lives, especially in value-laden issues. Understand the need to balance students' ethical rights to make choices, their capacity to give consent or assent and parental or familial legal rights and responsibilities to protect these students and make decisions on their behalf.

e. Promote the autonomy and independence of students to the extent possible and use the most appropriate and least intrusive method of breach. The developmental age and the circumstances requiring the breach are considered and as appropriate students are engaged in a discussion about the method and timing of the breach.

f. In absence of state legislation expressly forbidding disclosure, consider the ethical responsibility to provide information to an identified third party who, by his/her relationship with the student, is at a high risk of contracting a disease that is commonly known to be communicable and fatal. Disclosure requires satisfaction of all of the following conditions:

- Student identifies partner or the partner is highly identifiable.
- School counselor recommends the student notify partner and refrain from further high-risk behavior.
- Student refuses.
- School counselor informs the student of the intent to notify the partner.
- School counselor seeks legal consultation from the school district's legal representative in writing as to the legalities of informing the partner.

g. Request of the court that disclosure not be required when the release of confidential information may potentially harm a student or the counseling relationship.

h. Protect the confidentiality of students' records and release personal data in accordance with prescribed federal and state laws and school policies including the laws within the Family Education Rights and Privacy Act (FERPA). Student information stored and transmitted electronically is treated with the same care as traditional student records. Recognize the vulnerability of confidentiality in electronic communications and only transmit sensitive information electronically in a way that is untraceable to students' identity. Critical information such as a student who has a history of suicidal ideation must be conveyed to the receiving school in a personal contact such as a phone call.

A.3. ACADEMIC, CAREER/COLLEGE/POST-SECONDARY ACCESS AND PERSONAL/SOCIAL [RENAMED SOCIAL/EMOTIONAL] COUNSELING PLANS

Professional school counselors:

a. Provide students with a comprehensive school counseling program that parallels the ASCA National Model with emphasis on working jointly with all students to develop personal/social, academic and career goals.

b. Ensure equitable academic, career, post-secondary access and personal/social opportunities for all students through the use of data to help close achievement gaps and opportunity gaps.

c. Provide and advocate for individual students' career awareness, exploration and post-secondary plans supporting the students' right to choose from the wide array of options when they leave secondary education.

A.4. DUAL RELATIONSHIPS

Professional school counselors:

a. Avoid dual relationships that might impair their objectivity and increase the risk of harm to students (e.g., counseling one's family members or the children of close friends or associates). If a dual relationship is unavoidable, the school counselor is responsible for taking action to eliminate or reduce the potential for harm to the student through use of safeguards, which might include informed consent, consultation, supervision and documentation.

b. Maintain appropriate professional distance with students at all times.

c. Avoid dual relationships with students through communication mediums such as social networking sites.

   d.   Avoid dual relationships with school personnel that might infringe on the integrity of the school counselor/student relationship.

A.5. APPROPRIATE REFERRALS

Professional school counselors:

a.   Make referrals when necessary or appropriate to outside resources for student and/or family support. Appropriate referrals may necessitate informing both parents/guardians and students of applicable resources and making proper plans for transitions with minimal interruption of services. Students retain the right to discontinue the counseling relationship at any time.

b.   Help educate about and prevent personal and social concerns for all students within the school counselor's scope of education and competence and make necessary referrals when the counseling needs are beyond the individual school counselor's education and training. Every attempt is made to find appropriate specialized resources for clinical therapeutic topics that are difficult or inappropriate to address in a school setting such as eating disorders, sexual trauma, chemical dependency and other addictions needing sustained clinical duration or assistance.

c.   Request a release of information signed by the student and/or parents/guardians when attempting to develop a collaborative relationship with other service providers assigned to the student.

d.   Develop a reasonable method of termination of counseling when it becomes apparent that counseling assistance is no longer needed or a referral is necessary to better meet the student's needs.

A.6. GROUP WORK

Professional school counselors:

a.   Screen prospective group members and maintain an awareness of participants' needs, appropriate fit and personal goals in relation to the group's intention and focus. The school counselor takes reasonable precautions to protect members from physical and psychological harm resulting from interaction within the group.

b.   Recognize that best practice is to notify the parents/guardians of children participating in small groups.

c.   Establish clear expectations in the group setting, and clearly state that confidentiality in group counseling cannot be guaranteed. Given the developmental and chronological ages of minors in schools, recognize the tenuous nature of confidentiality for minors renders some topics inappropriate for group work in a school setting.

d.   Provide necessary follow up with group members, and document proceedings as appropriate.

e.   Develop professional competencies, and maintain appropriate education, training and supervision in group facilitation and any topics specific to the group.

f.   Facilitate group work that is brief and solution-focused, working with a variety of academic, career, college and personal/social issues.

A.7. DANGER TO SELF OR OTHERS

Professional school counselors:

a.   Inform parents/guardians and/or appropriate authorities when a student poses a danger to self or others. This is to be done after careful deliberation and consultation with other counseling professionals.

b.   Report risk assessments to parents when they underscore the need to act on behalf of a child at risk; never negate a risk of harm as students sometimes deceive in order to avoid further scrutiny and/or parental notification.

c.   Understand the legal and ethical liability for releasing a student who is in danger to self or others without proper and necessary support for that student.

A.8. STUDENT RECORDS

Professional school counselors:

a.   Maintain and secure records necessary for rendering professional services to the student as required by laws, regulations, institutional procedures and confidentiality guidelines.
b.   Keep sole-possession records or individual student case notes separate from students' educational records in keeping with state laws.
c.   Recognize the limits of sole-possession records and understand these records are a memory aid for the creator and in absence of privileged communication may be subpoenaed and may become educational records when they are shared or are accessible to others in either verbal or written form or when they include information other than professional opinion or personal observations.
d.   Establish a reasonable timeline for purging sole-possession records or case notes. Suggested guidelines include shredding sole possession records when the student transitions to the next level, transfers to another school or graduates. Apply careful discretion and deliberation before destroying sole-possession records that may be needed by a court of law such as notes on child abuse, suicide, sexual harassment or violence.
e.   Understand and abide by the Family Education Rights and Privacy Act (FERPA, 1974), which safeguards student's records and allows parents to have a voice in what and how information is shared with others regarding their child's educational records.

A.9. EVALUATION, ASSESSMENT AND INTERPRETATION

Professional school counselors:

a.   Adhere to all professional standards regarding selecting, administering and interpreting assessment measures and only utilize assessment measures that are within the scope of practice for school counselors and for which they are trained and competent.
b.   Consider confidentiality issues when utilizing evaluative or assessment instruments and electronically based programs.
c.   Consider the developmental age, language skills and level of competence of the student taking the assessments before assessments are given.
d.   Provide interpretation of the nature, purposes, results and potential impact of assessment/evaluation measures in language the students can understand.
e.   Monitor the use of assessment results and interpretations, and take reasonable steps to prevent others from misusing the information.
f.   Use caution when utilizing assessment techniques, making evaluations and interpreting the performance of populations not represented in the norm group on which an instrument is standardized.
g.   Assess the effectiveness of their program in having an impact on students' academic, career and personal/social development through accountability measures especially examining efforts to close achievement, opportunity and attainment gaps.

A.10. TECHNOLOGY

Professional school counselors:

a.   Promote the benefits of and clarify the limitations of various appropriate technological applications. Professional school counselors promote technological applications (1) that are appropriate for students' individual needs, (2) that students understand how to use and (3) for which follow-up counseling assistance is provided.

b. Advocate for equal access to technology for all students, especially hose historically underserved.

c. Take appropriate and reasonable measures for maintaining confidentiality of student information and educational records stored or transmitted through the use of computers, facsimile machines, telephones, voicemail, answering machines and other electronic or computer technology.

d. Understand the intent of FERPA and its impact on sharing electronic student records.

e. Consider the extent to which cyberbullying is interfering with students' educational process and base guidance curriculum and intervention programming for this pervasive and potentially dangerous problem on research-based and best practices.

A.11. STUDENT PEER SUPPORT PROGRAM

Professional school counselors:

a. Have unique responsibilities when working with peer-helper or student-assistance programs and safeguard the welfare of students participating in peer-to-peer programs under their direction.

b. Are ultimately responsible for appropriate training and supervision for students serving as peer-support individuals in their school counseling programs.

B. Responsibilities to Parents/Guardians

B.1. Parent Rights and Responsibilities
Professional school counselors:

a. Respect the rights and responsibilities of parents/guardians for their children and endeavor to establish, as appropriate, a collaborative relationship with parents/guardians to facilitate students' maximum development.

b. Adhere to laws, local guidelines and ethical standards of practice when assisting parents/guardians experiencing family difficulties interfering with the student's effectiveness and welfare.

c. Are sensitive to diversity among families and recognize that all parents/guardians, custodial and noncustodial, are vested with certain rights and responsibilities for their children's welfare by virtue of their role and according to law.

d. Inform parents of the nature of counseling services provided in the school setting.

e. Adhere to the FERPA act regarding disclosure of student information.

f. Work to establish, as appropriate, collaborative relationships with parents/guardians to best serve student.

B.2. Parents/Guardians and Confidentiality
Professional school counselors:

a. Inform parents/guardians of the school counselor's role to include the confidential nature of the counseling relationship between the counselor and student.

b. Recognize that working with minors in a school setting requires school counselors to collaborate with students' parents/guardians to the extent possible.

c. Respect the confidentiality of parents/guardians to the extent that is reasonable to protect the best interest of the student being counseled.

d. Provide parents/guardians with accurate, comprehensive and relevant information in an objective and caring manner, as is appropriate and consistent with ethical responsibilities to the student.

e. Make reasonable efforts to honor the wishes of parents/guardians concerning information regarding the student unless a court order expressly forbids the involvement of a parent(s). In cases of divorce or separation, school counselors exercise a good-faith effort to keep both parents informed, maintaining focus on the student and avoiding supporting one parent over another in divorce proceedings.

B. Responsibilities to Colleagues and Professional Associates

C.1. Professional Relationships

Professional school counselors, the school counseling program director/site supervisor and the school counselor educator:

a. Establish and maintain professional relationships with faculty, staff and administration to facilitate an optimum counseling program.
b. Treat colleagues with professional respect, courtesy and fairness.
c. Recognize that teachers, staff and administrators who are high functioning in the personal and social development skills can be powerful allies in supporting student success. School counselors work to develop relationships with all faculty and staff in order to advantage students.
d. Are aware of and utilize related professionals, organizations and other resources to whom the student may be referred.

C.2. Sharing Information with Other Professionals

Professional school counselors:

a. Promote awareness and adherence to appropriate guidelines regarding confidentiality, the distinction between public and private information and staff consultation.
b. Provide professional personnel with accurate, objective, concise and meaningful data necessary to adequately evaluate, counsel and assist the student.
c. Secure parental consent and develop clear agreements with other mental health professionals when a student is receiving services from another counselor or other mental health professional in order to avoid confusion and conflict for the student and parents/guardians.
d. Understand about the "release of information" process and parental rights in sharing information and attempt to establish a cooperative and collaborative relationship with other professionals to benefit students.
e. Recognize the powerful role of ally that faculty and administration who function high in personal/social development skills can play in supporting students in stress, and carefully filter confidential information to give these allies what they "need to know" in order to advantage the student. Consultation with other members of the school counseling profession is helpful in determining need-to-know information. The primary focus and obligation is always on the student when it comes to sharing confidential information.
f. Keep appropriate records regarding individual students, and develop a plan for transferring those records to another professional school counselor should the need occur. This documentation transfer will protect the confidentiality and benefit the needs of the student for whom the records are written.

C.3. Collaborating and Educating Around the Role of the School Counselor

The school counselor, school counseling program supervisor/director and school counselor educator:

a. Share the role of the school counseling program in ensuring data- driven academic, career/college and personal/social success competencies for every student, resulting in specific outcomes/indicators with all stakeholders.
b. Broker services internal and external to the schools to help ensure every student receives the benefits of a school counseling program and specific academic, career/college and personal/social competencies.

D. Responsibilities to School, Communities and Families

D.1. Responsibilities to the School
  Professional school counselors:

a. Support and protect students' best interest against any infringement of their educational program.
b. Inform appropriate officials, in accordance with school policy, of conditions that may be potentially disruptive or damaging to the school's mission, personnel and property while honoring the confidentiality between the student and the school counselor.
c. Are knowledgeable and supportive of their school's mission, and connect their program to the school's mission.
d. Delineate and promote the school counselor's role, and function as a student advocate in meeting the needs of those served. School counselors will notify appropriate officials of systemic conditions that may limit or curtail their effectiveness in providing programs and services.
e. Accept employment only for positions for which they are qualified by education, training, supervised experience, state and national professional credentials and appropriate professional experience.
f. Advocate that administrators hire only qualified, appropriately trained and competent individuals for professional school counseling positions.
g. Assist in developing: (1) curricular and environmental conditions appropriate for the school and community; (2) educational procedures and programs to meet students' developmental needs; (3) a systematic evaluation process for comprehensive, developmental, standards-based school counseling programs, services and personnel; and (4) a data-driven evaluation process guiding the comprehensive, developmental school counseling program and service delivery.

D.2. Responsibility to the Community
  Professional school counselors:

a. Collaborate with community agencies, organizations and individuals in students' best interest and without regard to personal reward or remuneration.
b. Extend their influence and opportunity to deliver a comprehensive school counseling program to all students by collaborating with community resources for student success.
c. Promote equity for all students through community resources.
d. Are careful not to use their professional role as a school counselor to benefit any type of private therapeutic or consultative practice in which they might be involved outside of the school setting.

E. Responsibilities to Self

E.1. Professional Competence
  Professional school counselors:

a. Function within the boundaries of individual professional competence and accept responsibility for the consequences of their actions.
b. Monitor emotional and physical health and practice wellness to ensure optimal effectiveness. Seek physical or mental health referrals when needed to ensure competence at all times.
c. Monitor personal responsibility and recognize the high standard of care a professional in this critical position of trust must maintain on and off the job and are cognizant of and refrain from activity that may lead to inadequate professional services or diminish their effectiveness with school community members. Professional and personal growth are ongoing throughout the counselor's career.

d. Strive through personal initiative to stay abreast of current research and to maintain professional competence in advocacy, teaming and collaboration, culturally competent counseling and school counseling program coordination, knowledge and use of technology, leadership, and equity assessment using data.

e. Ensure a variety of regular opportunities for participating in and facilitating professional development for self and other educators and school counselors through continuing education opportunities annually including: attendance at professional school counseling conferences; reading Professional School Counseling journal articles; facilitating workshops for education staff on issues school counselors are uniquely positioned to provide.

f. Enhance personal self-awareness, professional effectiveness and ethical practice by regularly attending presentations on ethical decision-making. Effective school counselors will seek supervision when ethical or professional questions arise in their practice.

g. Maintain current membership in professional associations to ensure ethical and best practices.

E.2. Multicultural and Social Justice Advocacy and Leadership
Professional school counselors:

a. Monitor and expand personal multicultural and social justice advocacy awareness, knowledge and skills. School counselors strive for exemplary cultural competence by ensuring personal beliefs or values are not imposed on students or other stakeholders.

b. Develop competencies in how prejudice, power and various forms of oppression, such as ableism, ageism, classism, familyism, genderism, heterosexism, immigrationism, linguicism, racism, religionism and sexism, affect self, students and all stakeholders.

c. Acquire educational, consultation and training experiences to improve awareness, knowledge, skills and effectiveness in working with diverse populations: ethnic/racial status, age, economic status, special needs, ESL or ELL, immigration status, sexual orientation, gender, gender identity/expression, family type, religious/spiritual identity and appearance.

d. Affirm the multiple cultural and linguistic identities of every student and all stakeholders. Advocate for equitable school and school counseling program policies and practices for every student and all stakeholders including use of translators and bilingual/multilingual school counseling program materials that represent all languages used by families in the school community, and advocate for appropriate accommodations and accessibility for students with disabilities.

e. Use inclusive and culturally responsible language in all forms of communication.

f. Provide regular workshops and written/digital information to families to increase understanding, collaborative two-way communication and a welcoming school climate between families and the school to promote increased student achievement.

g. Work as advocates and leaders in the school to create equity based school counseling programs that help close any achievement, opportunity and attainment gaps that deny all students the chance to pursue their educational goals.

F. Responsibilities to the Profession

F.1. Professionalism
Professional school counselors:

a. Accept the policies and procedures for handling ethical violations as a result of maintaining membership in the American School Counselor Association.

b. Conduct themselves in such a manner as to advance individual ethical practice and the profession.

c. Conduct appropriate research, and report findings in a manner consistent with acceptable educational and psychological research practices. School counselors advocate for the protection of individual students' identities when using data for research or program planning.

d. Seek institutional and parent/guardian consent before administering any research, and maintain security of research records.

e.   Adhere to ethical standards of the profession, other official policy statements, such as ASCA's position statements, role statement and the ASCA National Model and relevant statutes established by federal, state and local governments, and when these are in conflict work responsibly for change.

f.   Clearly distinguish between statements and actions made as a private individual and those made as a representative of the school counseling profession.

g.   Do not use their professional position to recruit or gain clients, consultees for their private practice or to seek and receive unjustified personal gains, unfair advantage, inappropriate relationships or unearned goods or services.

F.2. Contribution to the Profession
   Professional school counselors:

a.   Actively participate in professional associations and share results and best practices in assessing, implementing and annually evaluating the outcomes of data-driven school counseling programs with measurable academic, career/college and personal/social competencies for every student.

b.   Provide support, consultation and mentoring to novice professionals.

c.   Have a responsibility to read and abide by the ASCA Ethical Standards and adhere to the applicable laws and regulations.

F.3 Supervision of School Counselor Candidates Pursuing Practicum and Internship Experiences:
   Professional school counselors:

a.   Provide support for appropriate experiences in academic, career, college access and personal/social counseling for school counseling interns.

b.   Ensure school counselor candidates have experience in developing, implementing and evaluating a data-driven school counseling program model, such as the ASCA National Model.

c.   Ensure the school counseling practicum and internship have specific, measurable service delivery, foundation, management and accountability systems.

d.   Ensure school counselor candidates maintain appropriate liability insurance for the duration of the school counseling practicum and internship experiences.

e.   Ensure a site visit is completed by a school counselor education faculty member for each practicum or internship student, preferably when both the school counselor trainee and site supervisor are present.

F.4 Collaboration and Education about School Counselors and School Counseling Programs with other Professionals
   School counselors and school counseling program directors/supervisors collaborate with special educators, school nurses, school social workers, school psychologists, college counselors/admissions officers, physical therapists, occupational therapists and speech pathologists to advocate for optimal services for students and all other stakeholders.

G. Maintenance of Standards

Professional school counselors are expected to maintain ethical behavior at all times.
   G.1. When there exists serious doubt as to the ethical behavior of a colleague(s) the following procedure may serve as a guide:

1.   The school counselor should consult confidentially with a professional colleague to discuss the nature of a complaint to see if the professional colleague views the situation as an ethical violation.

2.   When feasible, the school counselor should directly approach the colleague whose behavior is in question to discuss the complaint and seek resolution.

3. The school counselor should keep documentation of all the steps taken.
4. If resolution is not forthcoming at the personal level, the school counselor shall utilize the channels established within the school, school district, the state school counseling association and ASCA's Ethics Committee.
5. If the matter still remains unresolved, referral for review and appropriate action should be made to the Ethics Committees in the following sequence:

- State school counselor association
- American School Counselor Association
- The ASCA Ethics Committee is responsible for:
    - Educating and consulting with the membership regarding ethical standards.
    - Periodically reviewing and recommending changes in code.
    - Receiving and processing questions to clarify the application of such standards. Questions must be submitted in writing to the ASCA Ethics Committee chair.
    - Handling complaints of alleged violations of the ASCA Ethical Standards for School Counselors. At the national level, complaints should be submitted in writing to the ASCA Ethics Committee, c/o the Executive Director, American School Counselor Association, 1101 King St., Suite 625, Alexandria, VA 22314.

G.2. When school counselors are forced to work in situations or abide by policies that do not reflect the ethics of the profession, the school counselor works responsibly through the correct channels to try and remedy the condition.

G.3. When faced with any ethical dilemma school counselors, school counseling program directors/supervisors and school counselor educators use an ethical decision-making model such as Solutions to Ethical Problems in Schools (STEPS) (Stone, 2001):

1. Define the problem emotionally and intellectually
2. Apply the ASCA Ethical Standards and the law
3. Consider the students' chronological and developmental levels
4. Consider the setting, parental rights and minors' rights
5. Apply the moral principles
6. Determine Your potential courses of action and their consequences
7. Evaluate the selected action
8. Consult
9. Implement the course of action.

From American School Counselor Association. (2010). Ethical Standards for School Counselors. Retrieved from www.schoolcounselor.org/asca/media/asca/Resource%20Center/Legal%20and%20Ethical%20Issues/Sample%20Documents/EthicalStandards2010.pdf. Reprinted with permission.

Section III

Diversity and Developmental Issues Among School-Aged Youth

Guidelines for the School Counselor-in-Training

13 Understanding Differences in the Schools

Jolie Ziomek-Daigle and Michael Jay Manalo

CACREP Standards

Foundations

A. Knowledge

6. Understands the effects of (a) atypical growth and development, (b) health and wellness, (c) language, (d) ability level, (e) multicultural issues, and (f) factors of resiliency on student learning and development.

Counseling, Prevention, and Intervention

B. Knowledge

1. Knows the theories and processes of effective counseling and wellness programs for individual students and groups of students.

D. Skills and Practices

1. Demonstrates self-awareness, sensitivity to others, and the skills needed to relate to diverse individuals, groups, and classrooms.

Diversity and Advocacy

E. Knowledge

1. Understands the cultural, ethical, economic, legal, and political issues surrounding diversity, equity, and excellence in terms of student learning.
4. Understands multicultural counseling issues, as well as the impact of ability levels, stereotyping, family, socioeconomic status, gender, and sexual identity, and their effects on student achievement.

The purpose of this chapter is to:

- assess school counselor-in-training awareness, knowledge, and skills in regard to counseling diverse student populations,
- gain experience with creating a school profile to help identify the needs of the school, students, and gaps related to achievement, attainment, and opportunities,
- expand knowledge and skills around student cultural and ethnic diversity issues, increase knowledge and skills related to gender differences between students, and develop sensitivity to the needs of students of various levels of socioeconomic status,
- increase knowledge and skills of trainees to counsel students with disabilities,

- add knowledge and skills to counsel gifted students understand the interactions among various aspects of identity for students who have multiple exceptionalities,
- gain knowledge and skills to counsel and advocate for students in regard to sexual orientation and gender expression,
- develop knowledge and skills related to students who are English Language Learners.

INTRODUCTION

In this chapter, you will assess your diversity competency (i.e., awareness, knowledge, and skills), learn how to develop a school profile to better understand your school's students, recognize multiple identities among people in your school (e.g., multicultural, students with disabilities, students with giftedness, students with various sexual orientations), and apply various scenarios and activities to practice developing your counseling competence.

Appreciating differences in the schools begins with understanding ourselves in relation to others and our student populations. The population of the United States can be described as multiethnic, multicultural, and multilingual (Holcomb-McCoy & Chen-Hayes, 2007). The diversity that is represented in the United States and most likely represented in the schools can be broadly defined to include (a) race/ethnicity, (b) gender, (c) physical or mental ability, (d) sexual orientation/gender expression, (e) socioeconomic status, and (f) other characteristics of background or group membership (Lee & Hipolito-Delgado, 2007). Moreover, it is estimated that while the non-Hispanic white population in the United States is still the largest major racial and ethnic group, the growth of this group is slowing, while the Latino, Asian American, and African American populations are growing rapidly (Lee, 2013). With the knowledge that student populations will be as diverse as ever, school counselors-in-training can begin with an assessment of their own awareness, knowledge, and skills in relation to working with diverse populations.

ASSESSMENT OF SCHOOL COUNSELOR-IN-TRAINING AWARENESS, KNOWLEDGE, AND SKILLS

In terms of assessing multicultural competence, faculty members and your supervisors will determine if you have gained awareness, knowledge, and skills to work with diverse student populations in the school setting. At this juncture in your graduate training, you most likely have gained multicultural awareness and knowledge through foundational courses. These skills will be further assessed during clinical placements. Therefore, you should graduate with an increased awareness and knowledge related to issues of diversity as well as advanced skills that are consistently in a state of refinement.

Holcomb-McCoy and Chen-Hayes (2007) suggest ways that you can increase your multicultural competence, including: (a) investigate your own cultural or ethnic heritage; (b) attend workshops and events on multicultural and diversity issues; (c) join counseling organizations focused on cultural and diversity issues, such as Counselors for Social Justice (CSJ), the Association for Multicultural Counseling and Development (AMCD), and the Association for Lesbian, Gay, Bisexual, Transgender Issues in Counseling (ALGBTIC); (d) read literature by culturally diverse authors; and (e) become immersed in multicultural and diversity-focused literature such as journals from the aforementioned associations. It is important for you to realize that professional development extends throughout the career of a school counselor and does not stop at graduation. By utilizing the ways mentioned earlier, you can further develop your diversity awareness and multicultural competence to remain lifelong, reflective practitioners.

This section is intended to advance your competence as you embark on practicum and internship experiences. Holcomb-McCoy (2004) created a multicultural checklist containing nine sections (i.e., multicultural counseling, multicultural consultation, understanding racism and student resistance, understanding racial and/or ethnic identity development, multicultural assessment, multicultural family counseling, social advocacy, developing school–family–community partnerships, and understanding cross-cultural interpersonal interactions) with 51 items in total. To provide you with a better understanding of your multicultural competence and areas you need to address, complete the School Counselor Multicultural Competence Checklist in Table 13.1.

Table 13.1 School Counselor Multicultural Competence Checklist

Competence		
I. Counselor Awareness of Own Cultural Values and Biases		
A. Attitudes and Beliefs	Met	Unmet
1. I am aware and sensitive to my own cultural heritage and to valuing and respecting differences.		
2. I am aware of my own cultural backgrounds and experiences and attitudes, values, and biases that influence psychological processes.		
3. I am able to recognize the limits of my own competencies and expertise.		
4. I am comfortable with differences that exist between myself and my students in terms of race, ethnicity, culture, and beliefs.		
B. Knowledge	Met	Unmet
1. I have specific knowledge about my own racial and cultural heritage and how it personally and professionally affects my definitions of normality-abnormality and the process of counseling.		
2. I have knowledge and understanding about how oppression, racism, discrimination, and stereotyping affect me personally and in my work.		
3. I possess knowledge about my social impact on others, including communication style differences and how this style may clash or foster the counseling process.		
C. Skills	Met	Unmet
1. I seek out educational, consultative, and training experience to improve my understanding and effectiveness in working with culturally different populations. I am able to recognize the limits of my competencies and (a) seek consultation, (b) seek further training or education, (c) make referrals to more qualified individuals or resources, or (d) engage in a combination of these.		
2. I seek to understand myself as a racial and cultural being and am actively seeking a nonracist identity.		
II. Counselor Awareness of Student's Worldview		
A. Attitudes and Beliefs	Met	Unmet
1. I am aware of my negative emotional reactions toward other racial and ethnic groups that may prove detrimental to my students in counseling. I am willing to contrast my own beliefs and attitudes with those of my culturally different students in a nonjudgmental fashion.		
2. I am aware of stereotypes and preconceived notions that I may hold toward other racial and ethnic minority groups.		
B. Knowledge	Met	Unmet
1. I possess specific knowledge and information about the particular group I am working with. I am aware of the life experiences, cultural heritage, and historical background of culturally different students.		
2. I understand how race, culture, ethnicity, and so forth may affect personality formation, vocational choices, manifestation of psychological disorders, help-seeking behavior, and the appropriateness or inappropriateness of counseling approaches.		
3. I understand and have knowledge about sociopolitical influences that impinge upon the life of racial and ethnic minorities.		
C. Skills	Met	Unmet
1. I familiarize myself with relevant research and the latest findings regarding mental health and mental disorders of various ethnic and racial groups. I actively seek out educational experiences that foster their knowledge, understanding, and cross-cultural skills.		
2. I am actively involved with minority individuals outside of the counseling setting (community events, social and political functions, etc.) so that my perspective of minorities is more than an academic or helping exercise.		
III. Culturally Appropriate Intervention Strategies		
A. Attitudes and Beliefs	Met	Unmet
1. I respect students' religious and/or spiritual beliefs and values, including attributions and taboos, because they affect worldview, psychosocial functioning, and expressions of distress.		

(Continued)

Table 13.1 (Continued)

Competence		
2. I respect indigenous helping practices and respect minority community intrinsic help-giving networks.		
3. I value bilingualism and do not view another language as an impediment to counseling.		
B. Knowledge	Met	Unmet
1. I have a clear and explicit knowledge and understanding of the generic characteristics of counseling and therapy and how they may clash with the cultural values of minority groups.		
2. I am aware of institutional barriers that present minorities from using mental health services.		
3. I have knowledge of the potential bias in assessment instruments and use procedures and interpret findings keeping in mind the cultural and linguistic characteristics of the students.		
4. I have knowledge of minority family structures, hierarchies, values, and beliefs. I am knowledgeable about the community characteristics and the resources in the community as well as the family.		
5. I am aware of relevant discriminatory practices at the social and community level that may be affecting the psychological welfare of the population being served.		
C. Skills	Met	Unmet
1. I am able to engage in a variety of *verbal* and *nonverbal* helping responses. I am able to send and receive both verbal and nonverbal messages *accurately* and *appropriately*. I am not tied to only one method or approach to helping but recognize that helping styles and approaches may be culture bound.		
2. I am able to exercise institutional intervention skills on behalf of my students. I can help students determine whether a "problem" stems from racism or bias in others so that students do not inappropriately personalize problems.		
3. I am not averse to seeking consultation with traditional healers and religious and spiritual leaders and practitioners in the treatment of culturally different students when appropriate.		
4. I take responsibility for interacting in the language requested by the student and, if not feasible, make appropriate referral. If appropriate I will (a) seek a translator with cultural knowledge and appropriate professional background and (b) refer to a knowledgeable and competent bilingual counselor.		
5. I have the training and expertise in the use of traditional assessment and testing instruments. I not only understand the technical aspects of the instruments but I am also aware of the cultural limitations.		
6. I attend to as well as work to eliminate biases, prejudices, and discriminatory practices. I am cognizant of sociopolitical contexts in conducting evaluation and providing interventions and develop sensitivity.		
7. I take responsibility in educating my students to the processes of psychological intervention, such as goals, expectations, legal rights, and the counselor's orientation.		

Source: Gysbers & Henderson (2012), printed with permission

Conceptual Application Activity 13.1

Using the Multicultural Checklist (Table 13.1), respond to the following questions and process your answers in small groups with your peers.

1.   What are my strengths and stated competencies?

_____

_____

2.   In what areas do I need to gain competence?

_____

_____

3. In using my strengths and competencies, how can I help other professionals in gaining competence?

_____

_____

4. In reviewing the areas in which I need to gain competence, how can I work with other professionals to get there?

_____

_____

ASSESSMENT OF SCHOOL SITE AND DEVELOPING A SCHOOL PROFILE

You can assess a school site to better understand not only the needs of the individual students but the student body as well. School profiles provide a backdrop of the school based on accessible, existing data. Information that is revealed from a school profile may include gaps in achievement, attainment, funding and opportunities, and certain student groups that may be isolated and not receiving the full range of services from the school. School profiles provide the data for school counselors-in-training and school counselors to take action in terms of better defining their school counseling program and the services that are offered. Baseline data are to be collected on an ongoing basis to monitor the progress of student groups and emerging needs (ASCA, 2012). Some baseline data needs to determine potential areas of discrimination could include

- Percent of students enrolled in the free or reduced lunch program
- Percent of students who have passed or failed state standardized tests
- Percent of students who scored at or above the national averages on the ACT and SAT
- Percent of students who are homeless
- Percent of students enrolled in the special education program
- Percent of students enrolled in the gifted education program
- Percent of students who are bilingual and enrolled in the English for Speakers of Other Languages (ESOL) program
- School's daily and weekly attendance rate
- School's daily and weekly suspension rate
- School's daily and weekly behavior referrals rate
- School's dropout rate
- Student pregnancy/teenage parent rate.

Conceptual Application Activity 13.2

Look at the demographic profile of the school in which you are completing your practicum or internship experience and determine the numbers of students who fit into the baseline data categories. Compare your list with those of your peers.

_____

_____

Culturally and Ethnically Diverse Students

We are different from one another. We also share similarities. In an attempt to categorize these differences and similarities, key aspects of who we are have been identified and used to help people understand one another culturally. Race, ethnicity, age, gender, sexual orientation, gender expression, disability, socioeconomic status, and disability are some aspects of culture. Culture, however, incorporates much more than these variables. Culture considerations also include, but are not limited to, views and practices related to individualism versus collectivism, masculinity and feminism, communication practices, physical proximity and closeness, religion/spirituality, language(s) spoken, structure and predictability, work ethic, political views, holidays recognized and celebrated, geographic region in which one is reared or lives, food and music preferences, value placed on education, family status, and so on. Our focus in this section will remain on increasing your awareness of cultural and diverse student populations. As discussed earlier, the development or review of an existing school profile will help you understand the backdrop and unique needs of the school and certain student groups. Understandably, a school profile may also reveal equity gaps that a multiculturally competent school counselor will need to work toward reconciling. These gaps are usually most noticeable in achievement, attainment, funding, and other opportunities (Holcomb-McCoy & Chen-Hayes, 2007).

Conceptual Application Activity 13.3

Read the following scenarios, answer the questions that appear at the end of each scenario, and then discuss your answers in small groups with your peers.

Sara is a first-year professional school counselor in an inner-city setting. The student population consists of the following: 82% African American, 12% Latino/a, and 6% biracial. Ninety-five percent of the students are enrolled in the free or reduced lunch program. Sara is white and from a middle- to upper-class background. Her dad worked while her mom stayed at home. She does not speak a second language because her parents did not "like the idea" of her taking a foreign language while she was in school. Her school did not have a free or reduced lunch program that she knew of and, generally, she socialized with people who looked and acted similarly to the way she did. While in graduate school, Sara took one course on multicultural counseling and completed her practicum and internship at a rural, white, working-class high school.

In regard to Sara's new position, how can she assess her multicultural competence?

_____

_____

Where and how can she begin this work?

_____

_____

What could be her goals in this area as a professional school counselor?

_____

_____

What could be her specific outreach strategies to students, parents, administrators, teachers, and community members?

_____

_____

Veronica is a first-year school counseling student. She is African American, grew up in a rural and poor area in a Southern state, and was raised by her aunt. Because of her aunt's influence and many determined teachers and school counselors, Veronica was committed to her schoolwork and rose to the top of her class in high school. She was enrolled in the gifted education program and knew the program would help her to reach her educational goals, but she did not like being the only student of color with others who grew up in very different circumstances. Veronica is now deciding on practicum and internship placements and has this awareness in mind. She is considering interning at a middle-/upper-class high school because she feels that she has biases against upper-class families and does not really think "those families" have problems. Veronica knows that all families do have problems and that all students struggle at some point, so she wants to push herself to experience something different than what she already knows.

How should Veronica proceed in identifying her clinical placements?

_____

_____

With whom should she consult on a consistent basis?

_____

_____

How can she become familiar with the school culture and the lives of her students and families?

_____

_____

Although universities are doing a better job in the recruitment and retention of diverse students, many school counseling graduates continue to be white, female, and middle class. Given that people of European descent have been the dominant group throughout the years of formalized education in the United States, it would behoove you to gain an understanding of oppression and privilege. An extension of Conceptual Application Activity 13.2 can be spent on further understanding the influences of power and prejudice as they relate to oppression. In addition, you can begin by interviewing your own family members to better understand their histories. Holcomb-McCoy and Chen-Hayes (2007) suggest that school counselors-in-training read Howard Zinn's *A People's History of the United States* or excerpts from the book so that they can analyze the information and messages they received in school or within the family while growing up.

Box 13.1

Underage migrants from Mexico, Honduras, El Salvador, and Guatemala are entering America in record numbers. Many leave of their own volition to escape violence and threats of death. Undocumented children and adolescents account for approximately 15% of the immigrants living in our country and are often referred to as the "1.5 generation" due to their fit somewhere between the first and second generation. Although these children were not born in this country, many have received much of their education here, but without a method for legalizing their status. This undocumented status makes it difficult for these youth to obtain higher education or enter the workforce.

Students With Disabilities

Until the 1960s and 1970s, students with disabilities such as mental illness or mental disability were commonly institutionalized and held separate from the rest of society (Hallahan & Kauffman, 2006). It was not until more recently that these students were integrated into mainstream classrooms and schools. Additionally, there have been several legislative movements such as Section 504 of the Rehabilitation Act of 1973, the Education for All Handicapped Children Act (PL 94–142) in 1975, the Individuals with Disabilities Education Act (IDEA) in 1990, the Americans with Disabilities Act (ADA) in 1990, and the reauthorized and renamed Individuals with Disabilities Education Improvement Act (IDEIA) in 2004. These directives have greatly shaped the role and function of school personnel (including school counselors and school counselors-in-training) in working with students with disabilities. Though these legislative acts have been helpful in providing accommodations to students, school counselors must also recognize where legislation for disabilities may or may not overlap. For example, a student with attention-deficit hyperactivity disorder (ADHD) may qualify for accommodations either under IDEA, under Section 504, or under neither act depending upon the nature of the student's disability and other health conditions (Lockhart, 2003).

Disabilities that are often present in school settings are listed in Table 13.2. These terms can be used as a reference as you work with various school-aged children, as it is important for you to realize that the terminology used for certain disabilities or disorders in schools may be different from the terminology used by non-school mental health professionals; for example, depression is commonly classified in schools as an emotional or behavioral disorder (EBD; Hallahan & Kauffman, 2006). Furthermore, some states use different terminology to describe the same syndrome.

Although much research to date in working with students with disabilities has focused on a deficit- or pathology-based model, other researchers have suggested that a strengths-based approach may also be in order. Dykens (2006) cites research that families with children who have intellectual disabilities may have stressors related to raising such a child but may also find the experience of having a child with disabilities in the family leads to a more fulfilling life. For example, the family of a child with a disability may find that they are better able to accept differences in other people, are more socially and politically active and aware, and are connected emotionally (Hallahan & Kauffman, 2006).

Table 13.2 Common Disabilities Present in School Settings

Common Disabilities	Standard Accommodations and Interventions
Traumatic brain injury	Recording lessons
Hard of hearing/deaf	Allow extra time for testing/amplifications devices/sign interpretation
Visual impairment	Seating near teacher and away from sources that create distractions/auditory description of content/color contrast such as overlays
Communication disorders	Tutoring
Students with ADD or ADHD	Masking templates to block off content not of immediate concern to the student/visual cues for time on task/self-monitoring systems/permit overactive
Orthopedic impairments	Large pencils or utensils for gripping/minimize or eliminate board copying
Intellectual disabilities	Tutoring/have students repeat directions
Emotional or behavioral disorders	Tutoring/communication in a supportive manner/establish clear expectations
Autism spectrum disorders	Repetition of instruction/positive reinforcement/picture schedules
Learning disabilities	Teach adaptive skills

The American School Counselor Association (ASCA, 2013) has provided a position statement on working with students with disabilities. In addition to providing direct counseling services to these students, the ASCA calls school counselors to collaborate with the school professionals in the delivery of services. The work of these teams typically results in written Individualized Education Programs (IEPs), 504 plans, transition planning, and other documentation. The statement also urges school counselors to be aware of community support resources for referrals, both while the student is in school as well as for postsecondary employment and education options. The ASCA's statement also advises school counselors to not serve in certain supervisory or administrative roles in the planning for students with disabilities that would better be served by school administrators or special education coordinators. Such inappropriate roles include the school counselor making the sole determination as to a student's placement or retention, coordinating a 504 team, and supervising the actual implementation of the student's plan.

A more recent development is a classification system known as Response to Intervention (RTI). Although RTI is viewed as a general education initiative, IDEA was the original impetus behind this mandate (Shepard, Shahidullah, & Carlson, 2013). RTI is a process in which students who may be identified to have learning-related problems or other special needs or concerns like behavior are given instructional and behavioral interventions and monitored for how they respond to such interventions. RTI requires that the interventions utilized with students be evidence based and measurable with respect to their outcomes. In addition to being utilized with students who may be identified to have disabilities, the RTI process involves more universal screenings to determine which students may be in need of more intensive services such as IEPs, 504 plans, etc., (Klotz & Canter, 2006). RTI is commonly referred to as a multi-tiered approach (usually depicted as a pyramid). Tier 1 (the base of the pyramid) consists of more universal, classroom-based instruction, screening, and large-group interventions such as consistent reinforcement, preferential seating, guided choices, and untimed tests. Tier 2 includes more specialized interventions for students who are identified to need more targeted strategies such as smaller-group or more intensive instruction in reading or math, as in an extended learning time block. Tier 3 (the highest level of the multi-tiered pyramid) consists of the most intensive set of interventions for students who do not respond to interventions provided at Tier 1 or 2. In Tier 3, students may be considered for and formally identified as needing special education services and/or provided additional assessments (National Center for Learning Disabilities, 2013).

More importantly, RTI in conjunction with IDEA provides increased flexibility in terms of serving students who may not necessarily be identified to have a severe discrepancy between intellectual ability and achievement (as has traditionally been used to identify students with learning disorders) but may also be used with students who may not meet such criteria but nevertheless have a need for specialized services. As such, it eliminates the need for a "wait to fail" approach to identifying and serving students who may have special needs (Klotz & Canter, 2006).

In serving students with special needs, school counselors should be aware of the differences among these various forms of serving students, including RTI, IEPs, Section 504 plans, and transition plans. RTI is more of a general framework or process that involves universal screenings and interventions at the lowest (Tier 1) level up to more specialized services (including formal identification for special education services) at the highest level (Tier 3). An IEP may be considered as part of the RTI process and is typically only implemented at higher levels of intervention in the RTI process or may only be mandated for students who are formally identified to qualify for IDEA services (Tilly, 2013).

Section 504 plans are similar to IEPs in that both were developed under civil rights statutes in order to help serve students with special needs; specifically, IEPs were developed under the IDEIA of 2004, and 504 plans were developed under Section 504 of the Rehabilitation Act of 1973. Zirkel (2009b, p. 68) refers to IDEA and Section 504 as "sister civil rights statutes." However, Zirkel points out that there are differences between IEPs and Section 504 plans, particularly with the implementation of the more recent Americans with Disabilities Act Amendment (ADAA) in 2009. In particular, Zirkel discusses that 504 plans generally cover a wider range of both mental and physical health issues, such as ADHD, dyslexia, food allergies, and diabetes, than would typically fall under the purview of an IEP. The passage of the ADAA provided for a broader set of criteria that would allow students to qualify for a 504 plan if their impairment affects a "major life activity to a substantial extent" (Zirkel, 2009b, p. 68). For example, not only would students qualify for a

504 plan for mental or cognitive impairments such as difficulty with concentrating, but students may also qualify for more physical health related problems that impact learning, such as irritable bowel syndrome and Crohn's disease. As Zirkel (2009b) states regarding the revised standards, "the overall effect is obviously to expand the number and range of students eligible under Section 504" (p. 69). School counselors should be aware, then, that in the past they may have been encouraged to use a Section 504 plan as a "consolation prize" (p. 69) for students who would not qualify for an IEP under IDEA and that in the past "Section 504 has taken a backseat to the IDEA in public schools" (Zirkel, 2009a, p. 211). However, at present the expanded qualifying criteria for Section 504 plans make them equally valid and robust options in terms of serving students who may have disabilities.

In addition to the overall process of RTI and specific documentation such as IEPs and 504 plans, an important piece of awareness for school counselors in working with students with disabilities is how to best support them in transitioning from the K–12 environment to postsecondary educational options such as college. The transition for students from high school to college is known to be particularly difficult for all students who make this transition but in particular for students with disabilities (Lapan, Tucker, Se-Kang Kim, & Kosciulek, 2003). From a legal standpoint, the Americans with Disabilities Act (ADA) and Section 504 both provide provisions not only for K–12 education but also for students in postsecondary settings (U.S. Department of Education, 2011b). As such, school counselors should be aware from both a legal and a professional standpoint of the need to support students with disabilities through the postsecondary transition process. IEPs often include a section related to planning for postsecondary transitions and may document current levels of functioning, but school counselors should be aware that an IEP or 504 plan by itself may not serve as sufficient documentation for a student to receive necessary disability accommodations in a college setting (although it may be helpful in partially substantiating such needs) (U.S. Department of Education, 2011b). Students transitioning to college may require more formal documentation of a disability through means such as formal psychological testing. Additionally, school counselors may be able to help students with disabilities be more successful with their postsecondary transitions by paying particular attention to conducting career development activities with high school students (Lapan et al., 2003).

Conceptual Application Activity 13.4

Read and respond to the following questions and then process the questions with your peers in small groups.

1. From your clinical placement experiences, how closely do school counselors work with the special education coordinator? How involved are the school counselors in working with the special education population in general? What are the specific practices that you have observed?

    _____

    _____

2. What unique issues would students face with comorbid disabilities or disabilities that also overlap with other identities discussed in this chapter (e.g., a student with both a learning disability [LD] and ADHD, a student with intellectual disabilities who is Hispanic, a student with a reading disorder who is a lesbian)?

    _____

    _____

3. What considerations should you, as a school counselor-in-training, think about in terms of a student with disabilities' transition to college, the workforce, or adulthood?

_____

_____

4. Do you think that all students with disabilities or other special needs require accommodations? Why or why not?

_____

_____

5. Many students with disabilities have a significant physical health component of their condition. As a school counselor-in-training, how could you make yourself more aware of the physical and medical needs of these students?

_____

_____

Students Who Are Gifted

Oftentimes, school counselors will not be required to identify gifted students but may need to help facilitate the process for parents and teachers. Consultation with the gifted education teacher or the district office in terms of how you can partner in servicing this student group would be helpful to you as a school counselor-in-training. School counselors often work with these students through such means as connecting parents to the gifted education teacher or school district office, counseling students individually or in small groups, conducting a classroom unit for the gifted, facilitating curriculum changes, and discussing postsecondary options based on student academic strengths.

According to the National Association for Gifted Children (2008), gifted children may have characteristics that include general intellectual ability, specific academic aptitude, creative thinking and production, leadership, psychomotor ability, and talent in visual and performing arts. Conversely, according to Delisle and Galbraith (2002), some misconceptions of gifted students may include that all are white and from middle- to upper-class families, are loved by teachers, excel in all subjects, enjoy school and learning, and will succeed no matter the circumstances. Further, Wood (2008) suggests that asynchronous development, affective regulation, and being from an already challenged population (e.g., a student of color, LGBTQ [lesbian, gay, bisexual, transgender, and queer], lower socioeconomic status) can present additional unique challenges for the gifted student population.

Conceptual Application Activity 13.5

Read and respond to the question at the end of the following scenario, and in small groups process your answer with your peers.

Mr. Stevens is a social studies teacher at Anytown High School. He is also the father of Greg, a 15-year-old freshman who just started at Anytown this school year. Mr. Stevens has been good friends with one of the school counselors, Mr. Sheetz, for several years since the two started working together at the high school. Mr. Stevens and Mr. Sheetz work out at the local gym together and share their love of adventure sports through their frequent rock climbing and whitewater kayaking trips. As luck would have it, Greg happens to be one of the students whom Mr. Sheetz is assigned to counsel. Mr. Sheetz was concerned about this at first, but since he feels he already knew Greg and Mr. Stevens fairly well, he did not anticipate Greg to be a frequent visitor to his office. He knew Greg to have had a few disciplinary problems in middle school and that Greg was a somewhat sensitive and emotional teenager in general, but Mr. Stevens had always said that Greg had persevered and done well in school. One afternoon while Mr. Sheetz and Mr. Stevens are on bus duty together, Mr. Stevens has a concerned look on his face. "You know, ever since Greg started high school here, he just hasn't been quite the same," Mr. Stevens tells Mr. Sheetz. "Mrs. Park in math said that Greg has been having some strange emotional outbursts in class and that his grades on his past few quizzes have been very low. Some days when we get home he just locks himself in his room and I think I hear him crying. Other times, he stays up all night working on homework and fixing his skateboard." Before Mr. Sheetz can respond, Mr. Stevens adds, "You know, I saw this TV special on kids with bipolar disorder, and I hate to say it but Greg sounds an awful lot like some of the kids on that show. Do you think he might be bipolar? I just get scared thinking of him being in that EBD classroom with all those crazy kids." Mr. Stevens' walkie-talkie buzzes and he gets called into the building. "Well, I've got to run, but I'll tell you more about it later at the gym, OK?" says Mr. Stevens. As Mr. Sheetz watches Mr. Stevens walk away, he sighs, anticipating what their conversation will be about at the gym that night.

What should Mr. Sheetz do?

_____

_____

School counselors have a responsibility to monitor the total development of gifted students in the personal/social domain (renamed social/emotional), not just in academics. An example would be the development of characteristics related to the happiness, well-being, life satisfaction, self-regulation (Peterson, 2006), and peer relations of gifted students. Additionally, school counselors need to be aware of and actively engage in updated identification and retention practices so that all students from diverse gender, racial, ethnic, socioeconomic, and disability backgrounds benefit from the services a gifted education program can offer. Gifted programs may look different from state to state but also district to district. Most likely, a school counselor will be asked to serve on the gifted placement committee to review student referrals for evaluation and reevaluation. Certain instruments are used that provide data to help committee members make a recommendation through the use of certain criteria and multiple assessments. For example, in the Clarke County (Georgia) School District (Clarke County, 2013), students are evaluated in the areas of mental ability, achievement, creativity, and motivation. Students must receive a score or a certain percentile in three of the four categories to be placed in a gifted program.

Conceptual Application Activity 13.6

Read and respond to the question at the end of each of the following scenarios and discuss your answers in small groups with your peers.

Karl is a 10th grader and enrolled in the gifted education program. He is African American and from a middle-class family. Karl did not want to enroll in the gifted program and have to make new friends in the classes, but his parents insisted, stating, "If you got it, use it." Karl is one of two students of color and has to sit by himself during lunch because all of his old friends eat lunch at a different time. He is having trouble with the accelerated pace in his new classes and does not finish all of his nightly homework. Karl's grades have slipped slightly, and he is not used to receiving B's. He volunteers after school and helps the technology teacher update the school computers and has aspirations to become a computer technician. You are providing career counseling to him during your internship, and Karl's parents called and want you to get him more motivated to succeed.

How would you proceed?

_____

_____

Delia is in ninth grade and is classified as twice exceptional. She has cerebral palsy and uses an electric wheelchair at school. Delia is also enrolled in the gifted education program, and her talents are in math and science. It has been a hard semester for her, and she has not liked the transition to high school. Delia has to leave the ninth-grade hall twice a day to rush across campus to the gifted classes. She runs into other students and has to use ramps that take time to maneuver around. She is late to all of her classes almost every day. Delia also gets self-conscious when she interrupts the class. She loves being in the gifted classes because she is learning new things, making friends, feels inspired, and knows she wants to be an civil engineer. As a counselor-in-training, you are also learning about the school culture and want to help Delia.

How can you assist her?

_____

_____

The following strategies illustrate ways of working with students who are gifted within the academic, career, and personal/social domains (renamed social/emotional) (Wood, 2008).

Academic Counseling Domain

- Facilitate gifted identification and placement, and allow for flexible plans
- Assess for decision-making, organization, and time-management skills
- Provide inventories that help students understand learning styles, learning preferences, personality characteristics, and personal/social (renamed social/emotional) domains.

Career Counseling Domain

- Explore possible careers as an extension of talents through inventories and the Internet
- Help connect students to job shadowing, apprenticeships, and internships
- Explore leisure and free-time activities
- Encourage contribution to society via service learning or volunteering.

Social/Emotional Counseling Domain (formerly Personal/Social)

- Normalize student feelings, experiences, and the unique characteristics of giftedness
- Validate feelings of loneliness, uniqueness, being different than others

- Work on regulation of emotions and negative thinking
- Consider stress-reducing activities and relaxation techniques
- Include expressive arts such as play, music, bibliotherapy, journaling, and drama.

Gender Differences Among Students

School counselors should be aware of both the similarities and differences between their male and female students whom they serve. Some available data indicate that males and females are enrolled in school in similar numbers in pre-K and kindergarten programs nationally as of 2001 (NCES, 2012). However, the same source also exposes other data suggesting educational inequities between males and females. For example, the report by the National Center for Education Statistics (NCES) also describes that females repeat grades and drop out of school at lower rates than males. Males are also believed to have more behavioral problems at school. In terms of specific subjects taught at school, the report also states that females have historically outperformed their male student counterparts in reading and writing, while in other areas such as math and science male students outperformed females (although this gap appears to be narrowing). As a result, school counselors should be aware of the differences in perception and expectations that their male and female students may experience and that these differences may play themselves out in the counseling context, particularly with respect to potential career aspirations for these students.

Legislative mandates also require school counselors and school counseling trainees to be sensitive to gender differences and to inequities in opportunities presented to their students. Title IX of the Education Amendments of 1972 prohibits discrimination on the basis of sex in programs that receive federal funding (including public schools). Some data that have been tracked in recent years in relation to Title IX compliance have shown that gaps in educational opportunities have been closing between males and females, such as the increased number of female students who successfully obtain postsecondary degrees and the increased number of female athletes in postsecondary settings (NCES, 2013a). However, while this gap is narrowing, there still exist differences in opportunities available to male and female students, and we have an obligation to support all students of all genders.

Further differences exist between males and females in terms of their social behaviors, some of which are particularly relevant to the context of counseling. Crick, Casas, and Nelson (2002) denote the differences between different forms of aggression that youth and their peers may exhibit toward one another. While some forms of aggression are more physical in nature, more recently Crick et al. (2002) studied relational forms of aggression, such as excluding a victim from a peer social group, withdrawing a friendship, or other forms of affection based upon a perceived slight. With regard to gender differences and how these manifest themselves in aggressive acts, the authors cite that while males tend to be more frequently the victims of physical aggression, females tend to be more frequently the victims of relational aggression. Just as physical forms of aggression are harmful to students, social and relational forms of aggression also deprive the affected victims of peer relationships, feelings of acceptance, and other factors associated with positive well-being for youth. School counselors should be aware of gender differences with respect to different forms of aggression and bullying, as negative consequences may be experienced. School counselors can help both the victims as well as the perpetrators of these offenses be more understanding toward one another and create an overall more positive school climate for students of all genders.

Children and adolescents may also experience other forms of discrimination related to their gender, particularly for those who do not conform to societal expectations of their expected and perceived gender identity and expression. Wyss (2004) qualitatively explored the experiences of gender queer, transgender, and other gender non-conforming high school youth. Through this research, Wyss elicited common themes of experiences of homophobia and transphobia. For example, Wyss provides the examples of the discrimination experienced by biologically female teens who do not fall into societal expectations related to dating males, who present with more of a "tomboyish" image, and wear clothes inconsistent with dominant culture views of beauty. Similarly, for biological male teens, those who may display more feminine forms of self-expression (such as clothing) may experience discrimination as well. Be aware of the pressures faced by gender non-conforming youth and help advocate for their well-being and acceptance by others.

Students Who Are Lesbian, Gay, Bisexual, Transgender, and Queer (LGBTQ)

In January 2005, White County High School junior Kerry Pacer made national headlines from the small town of Cleveland, Georgia. She asked the administration of her high school if she could form a Gay-Straight Alliance (GSA) club. The organization, named Peers Rising in Diverse Education (PRIDE), was initially allowed to meet but quickly drew controversy and protests (Yoo, 2005). Soon afterward, the county school board passed a ruling that all non-academically related clubs, including Pacer's, would not be allowed to meet, although other non-academic clubs such as a dance club and a shooting club were still permitted to meet at the school. The American Civil Liberties Union (ACLU) represented Pacer and other students in a lawsuit against the school board that stated that the students' rights had been violated and that the club should be allowed to meet (Ghezzi, 2006). In July 2006, a federal district judge ruled in the ACLU and Pacer's favor, allowing the organization to meet (Scott, 2006).

The preceding example from recent news headlines illustrates LGBTQ students may experience institutionalized discrimination in the schools. The Gay, Lesbian and Straight Education Network (GLSEN, 2008a) noted that 73.6% of LGBTQ students often or frequently heard homophobic remarks at school. The majority of the students expressed being verbally harassed due to their sexual orientation (86.2%) or gender expression (66.5%). Unfortunately, the report also stated that 22.1% of the students reported being physically assaulted due to sexual orientation, and 14.2% due to gender expression. Even more disturbing is that the report found that even after such students reported incidents of harassment or assault to school staff, almost one third said that the staff did nothing to respond to their complaint. The report also found higher levels of school absenteeism and lowered pursuit of postsecondary education among LGBTQ students compared with a national sample of students.

School counselors are often reluctant to work with this population of students (Pollock, 2006), and training in counseling programs is sparse to nonexistent (Pearson, 2003). These students have a higher rate of victimization, mental health disorders, suicide, and dropping out (Callahan, 2001; Varjas et al., 2007), and school counselors are in a unique position to provide services to LGBTQ students but often recoil from the opportunities (Callahan, 2001). Some explanations may include: (a) incongruence with personal, religious, and political beliefs; (b) concerns with legal age, parental notification, and consent; and (c) lack of professional development (Ziomek-Daigle & Singh, 2008). However, the ethics, professionalism, and efficacy of school counselors might be called into question if they are not advocating for and providing services for all youth, including those identified as LGBTQ.

You should be aware of the discrimination and difficulties that face LGBTQ youth in schools, and discuss this issue with your site supervisor. Such issues may present themselves in terms of difficulty with "coming out," increased class absences, negative self-esteem, increased bullying, and issues related to school disengagement and dropping out. The ASCA's position statement on working with LGBT youth (ASCA, 2014) calls for professional school counselors to support students of all sexual orientations and gender identities as well as to recognize how their own views of these subjects may affect their work with students. In addition to working with individual students, the position statement describes the role of professional school counselors as advocates against discriminatory policies (such as those presented in the introduction of this section) as well as educators for faculty and staff in schools about the importance of diversity in schools, including that of LGBTQ students.

Legal Implications of Working (or Not Working) with LGBTQ Students (Adapted from McFarland & Dupuis, 2003)

As noted in the introduction to this section, several instances of legal action have taken place against administrators and schools that have failed to protect the rights of LGBTQ students. Legal precedent has shown that school administrators must provide equal access and protection to students regardless of gender or sexual orientation. For example, in the 1996 case of *Nabozny v. Podlesny*, a student named Jamie Nabozny was subjected to verbal and severe physical abuse by other students and sued the principals and school district. In his suit, Nabozny stated that the school had treated him differently from other students who had been sexually harassed by failing to take action against the perpetrators of the abuse. The principals settled the suit, costing them nearly $1 million. In 1997, the Office of Civil Rights of the Department of Education specified under its Title IX guidelines that gay and lesbian students should be protected from sexual harassment. The guidelines were used in the 1998 court case of *Wagner v. Fayetteville Public Schools*, in which the school district was mandated by the Department of Education to integrate policies around sexual harassment related to sexual orientation. The Lambda Legal Defense and Education Fund (a link to its website is provided at the end of this chapter) is an organization dedicated to legal issues for LGBTQ persons, and monitors these and many other cases. School counselors, then, must be aware of the legal implications for unfair treatment of and failure to protect LGBTQ students, particularly with regard to sexual harassment in schools.

Conceptual Application Activity 13.7

Answer the following questions and discuss your responses with your peers in small groups.

1. In light of the introductory story of a high school student trying to start a Gay-Straight Alliance at her school, what would be your reaction if one of your students approached you about starting such an organization at your school?

   _____

   _____

2. What unique concerns do you think LGBTQ students of color face in terms of their multiple identities (e.g., a black lesbian or a person with a disability who identifies as transgender)?

   _____

   _____

3. How do you think the coming out experience of a transgender student would differ from the coming out experience of a gay student?

   _____

   _____

4. How appropriate do you think it is for a school counselor to self-disclose his or her own sexual orientation or gender expression to an LGBTQ student he or she is counseling?

   _____

   _____

Language and terms are important, as they help people communicate complex ideas in mutually understood words and phrases. Within the LGBTQ community there are a number of terms and acronyms used to communicate aspects unique to that subculture. As a school counselor-in-training, it would be beneficial to familiarize yourself with some of these terms. Table 13.3 provides an alphabetical list of terms and definitions that may help you get started.

Table 13.3 Commonly Used Terms in LGBTQ Community

Term	Definition
Ally	A person who advocates for or supports LGBTQ people; many allies often identify themselves as straight/heterosexual
Biological sex	Sex as determined by chromosomes, hormones, internal/external genitalia
Bisexual	A person who is attracted to both men and women
Coming out	A lifelong process of declaring one's identity to another individual, to a group of people, or in a public setting
Gay	A person who is attracted only to people of the same sex; this term can be used for both men and women, although the term *lesbian* is typically used for gay women, and the term *gay* by itself typically refers to gay men
Gender identity	How we perceive or call ourselves as "male" or "female"; gender identity may or may not correspond with a person's biological sex
Gender queer	A person who identifies his/her gender to be either between or outside of the male/female dichotomy
Intersexual	A person born with biological aspects of both male and female; about 1.7% of the population can be defined as intersexual
Lesbian	A woman who is only attracted to other women
LGBTQ	An acronym for lesbian, gay, bisexual, transgender, and queer
LGBTQQI	An acronym for lesbian, gay, bisexual, transgender, queer, questioning, and intersexual
Queer	Although this term was historically considered a negative used against LGBTQ people, it has been reclaimed as an umbrella term to refer to people who do not conform to traditional gender or sexual identities or roles; this term frequently appears in a political context
Questioning	Refers to people who are questioning or unsure of their sexual orientation or gender identity
Sexual identity	What we call ourselves or how we perceive ourselves to be; may include gay, lesbian, bisexual, bi, queer, etc.
Sexual	A person's orientation as related to his/her sexual and emotional attraction; may include homosexual, bisexual, heterosexual
Transgender	A person who expresses his/her gender differently from the way that society would traditionally identify that person; transgender is an umbrella term for several other terms, which may include transsexuals, drag kings, drag queens, cross-dressers, etc.
Transsexual	A person who surgically/hormonally changes sex to match gender identity

Source: Adapted from *The 2007 National School Climate Survey: Executive Summary* (GLSEN, 2008b) and *LGBT Definitions* (GLSEN, 2008c).

Conceptual Application Activity 13.8

Read and respond to the following scenario and discuss your answers with your peers in small groups.

Ms. Johnson is a second-semester school counseling intern at Anytown Middle School. She has recently attended a diversity training seminar at her university that focused on LGBTQ issues among university students. The seminar is part of the university's Safe Space program in which participants identify themselves as LGBTQ allies by placing a rainbow-colored sticker in their rooms or offices. Ms. Johnson is very excited about the program and decides to put one of the stickers in the window to her office at Anytown Middle. Her supervisor, Mr. Hood, says that he is supportive of this decision. Ms. Johnson is pleased that several of her students who come in for individual counseling appointments notice the new sticker and ask her what it means. One day, Ms. Johnson arrives at school and finds a note on her door from the principal, Dr. Smith. In the note, Dr. Smith requests that Ms. Johnson remove the sticker from her window, stating that the parents of some students had called the office saying that "the school is no such place for controversial displays." As she finishes reading the note, Dr. Smith enters the counseling suite. What should Ms. Johnson do?

Students Who Are English Language Learners

The National Center for Education Statistics of the U.S. Department of Education estimates that during the 2010–2011 academic year, approximately 10% (approximately 4.7 million) of U.S. public school students were English Language Learner (ELL) students (NCES, 2013b). This represents an increase from an estimated 4.1 million (9%) ELL students in 2002–2003. Geographic and other considerations are also correlated with the relative percentages of ELL students that are served in various regions of the U.S. For example, the NCES (2013b) provides data that western states (such as Oregon, Hawaii, Alaska, Colorado, Texas, New Mexico, Nevada, and California) have higher percentages of ELL students relative to other regions of the country. ELL students may also be clustered within other areas of the U.S. based upon where their families have settled. For example, in Barrow County, Georgia (a rural area east of Atlanta), Hmong students represent the second largest ELL student population in the district after Hispanic students (Barrow County Schools, 2007) and it is believed that this may be the case due to refugee resettlement efforts that sponsored Hmong families to move to this part of the Southeastern U.S. (Hatcher, 2003; Poole, 2004). As such, school counselors-in-training should be aware that potentially a significant number of their students may be ELL students and that depending upon the geographic location of their field placement, they may be working with a particularly concentrated number of ELL students.

Several factors are important for school counselors and school counseling trainees to take into account when engaging in counseling work with both ELL students and their families. For example, family context may be of particular importance to working with these students. Thompson and Henderson (2007) discuss that counselors should familiarize themselves with the "customs, styles, symbols, and standards of behavior of these diverse group" (p. 378). Therefore, working with ELL students and their families should take into account the roles that the students and their family members may play within their own families and within the larger community, and understand the stressors that these students may face in light of balancing maintenance of their native culture while acculturating to the dominant culture. Or, as the authors write in the example of working with immigrant parents, "the key is to reframe the situation with respect to the clients' roots and solve the problem without molding the couple to behave like the dominant culture" (p. 379).

In addition to the roles that may be played by students' parents and other members of their families, be aware that oftentimes students who are English Language Learners may find themselves placed in leadership roles within their families, particularly with respect to interfacing with and translating information between the students' families and the English-speaking communities they live in based upon their own relative proficiency in English compared with their families'. Be sensitive to these roles and recognize that ELL students placed in the role of translators for counseling purposes may create issues related to role confusion, power differentials, and potential ethical concerns with respect to confidentiality (Council of National Psychological Associations for the Advancement of Ethnic Minority Interests, 2003). Furthermore, even when school counselors and their trainees have access to professional translators or outsourced language translation resources such as telephone language line services, it is important that such translators be fluent in counseling-related topics, as otherwise the "nuances and intensity of psychological symptoms and concerns" may be lost (p. 20). Also, keep in mind that ELL students may express their verbalizations of emotions differently in English than in their native language. For example, Santiago-Rivera and Altarriba (2002) write that individuals in counseling may feel less anxiety in expressing potentially embarrassing or taboo subjects in their non-dominant or second language than in their native language because this gives these clients a means of distancing themselves from topics that they may otherwise choose to avoid or feel uncomfortable expressing in their native language. The authors also cite the viewpoint that bilingualism should be considered "a client strength rather than a deficit" (p. 30). As such, school counseling trainees may benefit from honoring the experience of ELL students to utilize both English and their native language in counseling work, knowing that in some situations the student may find it more comfortable to use English and in other situations the student may prefer to express him/herself in the native language.

Other considerations to take into account when working with ELL students include adjustment issues that these students may face with respect to living in a new geographic environment, particularly if they and their families have recently immigrated to the country. School counselors may also wish to explore with these students their expectations for themselves in terms of academic achievement, maintaining contact with their relatives in their native country, how they typically ask for help with social or emotional concerns, and what resources they perceive are available to them in their schools and communities (J. Wu, personal communication, September 21, 2013).

Socioeconomic Differences

Forms of diversity arise not only from racial, ethnic, and other forms of identity but also from economic and financial differences among students. Legal legislation and federal forms of assistance such as Title I, Part A (Title I) of the Elementary and Secondary Education Act (U.S. Department of Education, 2011a) provide funding for schools which have a significant number of their students coming from low-income families. Despite such forms of assistance, school counselors and school counselors-in-training must recognize that their students from low-income families may have special challenges and opportunities. For example, data demonstrate that certain ethnic groups have higher levels of poverty than the national average. For example, U.S. Census data from 2011 described an overall poverty rate (that is, an annual household income below the poverty threshold at the time for a family of four of $23,550) of 15% for the entire U.S. population but that several racial/ ethnic groups, such as blacks and Hispanics, had significantly higher rates of poverty. Furthermore, data suggest that youth with low socioeconomic status tend to be associated with higher levels of mental illness, stress, unemployment, and less education compared with peers who do not grow up in impoverished homes (Macartney, 2011). In the case of students in the school setting, this may mean not only that the students from low-income families may experience higher rates of mental illness but that they are also more likely to have family members or an extended family history of mental illness. Awareness of the socioeconomic context of students and how this may affect the way other students perceive them, the effects of poverty on the student, and the student's family is a critical consideration.

Box 13.2

School counselors have a responsibility to work with all students and to recognize students who are not receiving the services they deserve. Unfortunately, although there have been many initiatives to provide equitable services to students, inequities still exist. Classes in STEM (science, technology, engineering, and mathematics) are considered critical for today's global economy. Yet, there is a significant lack of access for minorities in these core classes. Furthermore, minority students are more likely to attend schools with teachers with less experience than are their more privileged peers.

Source: Hefling, 2014

Students With Multiple Exceptionalities

Finally, with student populations becoming increasingly diverse, school counselors and their trainees are more likely to encounter students who have not only one form of exceptionality or minority identity but multiple forms of exceptionality with respect to their identities. For example, school counselors may work with a student who identifies as both lesbian and black. A trainee may work with a student with a learning disorder who is from a family of low socioeconomic status. Or a school counselor may encounter a student with a physical disability who identifies as gender queer and is also gifted.

Constantine (2002) discusses the limitations for counselors who view various forms of identity such as race, ethnicity, gender, and social class individually and in isolation rather than developing an integrated sense of the counseling client. She proposes that these various aspects of identity are to be perceived in a dynamic, interactive context rather than in isolation. As Constantine (2002) states, "Current models of mental health care often do not allow for the processes by which individuals with multiple oppressed identities arrive at a positive overall sense of cultural identity" (p. 211).

Models of incorporating multiple aspects of a person's identity are available which may help one better understand how to integrate the various forms of identity claimed by a student. For example, Ridley (2005) provides a model of integrated identity that resembles a flower of which each petal represents an aspect of identity (e.g., race, ethnicity, socioeconomic status, gender, sexual preference) with the individual at the center.

Such models also suggest that at various times in a students' educational careers, certain aspects of their identity may be more salient than others. For example, a student who identifies as both lesbian and black may find herself being more discriminated against by others for her lesbian identity in certain settings and in other settings may be more discriminated against for her more physically

Figure 13.1 A flower with aspects of identity displayed on petals is one model for recognizing an integrated identity.

Source: Shutterstock

visible black identity. Therefore, take into account the complete picture of your students' identities and understand where the intersectionality of these various aspects of identity may create challenges for students, but may also be understood to create unique forms of strength and personal identity for these same students.

CONCLUSION

In this chapter you explored student differences. Although the focus of this chapter was specifically students, it is important to remember that many of these differences also apply to administrators, staff, faculty, parents, and other stakeholders in the school. You assessed your diversity competency, looked at components of a school profile to better understand your school's students, reviewed differences among students in your school, and used various scenarios and activities to practice developing your counseling competence. Multicultural competence begins with understanding that there is always more to learn, understand, and respect when considering all of your counselees—those who share similarities and those who are different from you.

WEBSITES

Multicultural Differences

- "Diversity and Complexity in the Classroom: Considerations of Race, Ethnicity, and Gender." Strategies are provided by Charlotte Reed, Ed.D to help work with the wide range of students present in today's schools: http://suu.edu/ed/fso/resources/general-strategies-for-dealing-with-diversity.pdf

Students With Disabilities

- "Teaching Special Kids: Online Resources for Teachers." This link will take you to online information about resources that can help you better understand students with disabilities: www.education-world.com/a_curr/curr139.shtml
- "Adaptations and Modifications for Students with Special Needs." This link provides easy modifications to incorporate into the curriculum for students with disabilities: www.teachervision.com/special-education/resource/5347.html
- "RTI Action Network." This link provides information, resources, and example forms that may be used for understanding and implementing Response to Intervention: www.rtinetwork.org/
- "National Center for Learning Disabilities." This link provides information for parents and educators regarding learning disabilities, IEPs, and Section 504 plans: www.ncld.org/

Students Who Are Gifted

- "Working with Gifted & Talented Students." This webpage provides a list of traits that are frequent indicators of students who are gifted, strategies and ideas that can be utilized to ensure that students who are gifted use their abilities to the greatest potential, and a list of resources: www.teachersfirst.com/gifted.cfm
- "Gifted Children." This webpage provides links to articles and resources for working with students who are gifted: www.educationworld.com/parents/special/gifted.shtml

Gender Differences Among Students

- "Gender Differences and Student Engagement." A white paper that discusses biological and physical factors accounting for gender differences in student engagement: www.leadered.com/pdf/Student%20Engagement%20and%20Gender%20white%20paper.pdf

Students Who Are Gay, Lesbian, Bisexual, Transgender, and Queer

- The Gay, Lesbian and Straight Education Network (GLSEN) provides research and statistics on LGBTQ students: www.glsen.org
- PFLAG (Parents, Families, and Friends of Lesbians and Gays): www.pflag.org
- ASCA Position Statement on Gay, Lesbian, Bisexual, Transgender, and Questioning Youth: www.schoolcounselor.org/files/PS_LGBTQ.pdf
- The Human Rights Campaign is an organization dedicated to political advocacy for LGBTQ people: www.hrc.org/ .
- Lambda Legal is an organization dedicated to LGBTQ legal issues: www.lambdalegal.org/
- The Georgia Safe Schools Coalition (GSSC) is an organization that advocates against LGBTQ oppression in school systems in Georgia: www.georgiasafeschoolscoalition.org

Students Who Are English Language Learners

- "Helping English Language Learners in the Classroom" provides information, strategies, and considerations in working with ELL students: www.glencoe.com/sec/teachingtoday/subject/help_ELL.phtml

Students of Various Socioeconomic Statuses

- "American Psychological Association Factsheet on Education and Socioeconomic Status." This article describes various facts and statistics for consideration regarding the effects of socioeconomic status on education: www.apa.org/pi/ses/resources/publications/factsheet-education.aspx

Students of Multiple Exceptionalities

- "Multiple Disabilities." This article explores strategies for working with students who may have more than one disability: http://specialed.about.com/od/multipledisabilities/a/multiple.htm

REFERENCES

ASCA [American School Counselor Association]. (2012). *The ASCA National Model: A framework for school counseling programs* (3rd ed.). Alexandria, VA: Author.

ASCA. (2013). *The professional school counselor and students with disabilities.* Retrieved from www.schoolcounselor.org/asca/media/asca/PositionStatements/PS_Disabilities.pdf

ASCA. (2014). *The professional school counselor at LGBTQ youth.* Retrieved from www.schoolcounselor.org/asca/media/asca/PositionStatements/PS_LGBTQ.pdf

Barrow County Schools. (2007). *Primary languages of barrow county students 2007–2008.* (Report). Winder, GA: Barrow County Schools.

Callahan, C. (2001). Protecting and counseling gay and lesbian students. *Journal of Humanistic Counseling, 40*(1), 5–10.

Clarke County School District. (2013). *Georgia's gifted eligibility rule.* Retrieved from www.clarke.k12.ga.us/offices.cfm?subpage=47

Constantine, M. G. (2002). The intersection of race, ethnicity, gender, and social class in counseling: Examining selves in cultural contexts. *Journal of Multicultural Counseling and Development, 30*(4), 210–215. doi:10.1002/j.2161–1912.2002.tb00520.x

Council of National Psychological Associations for the Advancement of Ethnic Minority Interests. (2003). *Psychological treatment of ethnic minority populations.* Washington, DC: Association of Black Psychologists.

Crick, N. R., Casas, J. F., & Nelson, D. A. (2002). Toward a more comprehensive understanding of peer maltreatment: Studies of relational victimization. *Current Directions in Psychological Science, 11*(3), 98–101. doi:10.1111/1467–8721.00177

Delisle, J., & Gailbrath, J. (2002). *When gifted kids don't have all the answers: How to meet their social & emotional needs.* Minneapolis, MN: Free Spirit Publishing.

Dykens, E. M. (2006). Toward a positive psychology of mental retardation. *American Journal of Orthopsychiatry, 76*(2), 185–193.

Ghezzi, P. (2006, February 28). ACLU files suit vs. district over school clubs rule; gay support group seeks right to meet. *Atlanta Journal-Constitution*, 3B.

GLSEN [Gay, Lesbian, and Straight Education Network]. (2008a). *GLSEN Safe Space: A how-to guide for starting an allies program*. New York: GLSEN. Retrieved from www.glsen.org/binarydata/GLSEN_ATTACHMENTS/file/000/000/294–3.PDF

GLSEN. (2008b). *The 2007 national school climate survey: Executive summary*. New York: The Gay, Lesbian and Straight Education Network. Retrieved from www.glsen.org/binary-data/GLSEN_ATTACHMENTS/file/000/001/1306–1.pdf

GLSEN. (2008c). *LGBT definitions*. Retrieved from www.glsen.org/cgi-bin/iowa/all/library/record/2335.html?-state=media

Gysbers, N., & Henderson, P. (2012). *Developing & Managing Your School Guidance Program* (5th ed.) Alexandria, VA: American Counseling Association.

Hallahan, D.P., & Kauffman, J.M. (2006). *Exceptional learners: Introduction to special education* (10th ed.). Boston: Pearson/Allyn & Bacon.

Hatcher, B. (2003, November 10). Diversity abounds in Barrow County. *Athens* [Georgia] *Banner-Herald*.

Hefling, K. (2014, March 23). New data show gaps in education for minorities. *Knoxville Sentinel*, 19A.

Holcomb-McCoy, C. (2004). Assessing the multicultural competence of school counselors: A checklist. *Professional School Counseling, 7*, 178–186.

Holcomb-McCoy, C., & Chen-Hayes, S.F. (2007). Multiculturally competent school counselors: Affirming diversity through challenging oppression. In B.T. Erford (Ed.), *Transforming the school counseling profession* (2nd ed., pp. 98–120). Upper Saddle River, NJ: Pearson Merrill Prentice Hall.

Klotz, M.B., & Canter, A. (2006). *Response to intervention (RTI): A primer for parents*. Bethesda: National Association of School Psychologists. Retrieved from www.nasponline.org/resources/factsheets/rtiprimer.aspx

Lapan, R.T., Tucker, B., Se-Kang Kim, & Kosciulek, J.F. (2003). Preparing rural adolescents for post-high school transitions. *Journal of Counseling & Development, 81*(3), 329.

Lee, C.C. (2013). *Multicultural issues in counseling: New approaches to diversity* (4th ed.). Alexandria, VA: American Counseling Association.

Lee, C.C., & Hipolito-Delgado, C. (2007). Counselors as agents of social justice. In C.C. Lee (Ed.), *Counseling for social justice* (pp. xiii–xxviii). Alexandria, VA: American Counseling Association.

Lockhart, E.J. (2003). Students with disabilities. In B.T. Erford (Ed.), *Transforming the school counseling profession* (pp. 357–409). Upper Saddle River, NJ: Merrill Education/Prentice Hall.

Macartney, S. (2011). *Child poverty in the United States 2009 and 2010: Selected race groups and Hispanic origin. American community survey briefs*. Retrieved from http://search.tb.ask.com/search/SNdns.jhtml?searchfor=www.resourceli%adbrary.gcyf.org&cb=UX&pg=GGmain&p2=^UX^fox999^YYA^us&n=780bfdde&qid=a97fccfcbddd424997e452235928bcc7&pn=1&ptb=A87A9C93–327F-488A-BC1C-CDA6970BDC70&tpr=&si=CD15543&st=dns

McFarland, W.P., & Dupuis, M. (2003). The legal duty to protect gay and lesbian students from violence in school. In T.P. Remley, M.A. Hermann, & W.C. Huey (Eds.), *Ethical & legal issues in school counseling* (2nd ed., pp. 341–357). Alexandria, VA: American School Counselor Association.

National Association for Gifted Children. (2008). *Characteristics checklists for gifted children*. Retrieved from www.austega.com/gifted/characteristics.htm

NCES [National Center for Education Statistics]. (2012). *Percentage of 3-, 4-, and 5-year-old children enrolled in preprimary programs, by attendance status, level of program, and selected child and family characteristics*. Washington, DC: National Center for Education Statistics.

NCES. (2013a). *Fast facts: Title IX*. Retrieved from http://nces.ed.gov/fastfacts/display.asp?id=93

NCES. (2013b). *English language learners*. Retrieved from http://nces.ed.gov/programs/coe/indicator_cgf.asp

National Center for Learning Disabilities. (2013). *What is RTI?* Retrieved from www.rtinetwork.org/learn/what/whatisrti

Pearson, Q.M. (2003). Breaking the silence in the counselor education classroom: A training seminar on counseling sexual minority clients. *Journal of Counseling and Development, 81*, 292–300.

Peterson, C. (2006). *A primer in positive psychology*. New York: Oxford University Press.

Pollock, S.L. (2006). Counselor roles in dealing with bullies and their LGBT victims. *Middle School Journal, 38*(2), 94–102.

Poole, S.M. (2004, August 4). Hmong refugees to settle in area; an old war debt is being repaid to the Laotian ethnic group, which has been exiled in Thailand for decades. *Atlanta Journal-Constitution*, 1F.

Ridley, C.R. (2005). *Overcoming unintentional racism in counseling and therapy: A practitioner's guide to intentional intervention* (2nd ed.). Thousand Oaks, CA: Sage Publications.

Santiago-Rivera, A., & Altarriba, J. (2002). The role of language in therapy with the Spanish-English bilingual client. *Professional Psychology: Research and Practice, 33*(1), 30–38. doi:10.1037/0735–7028.33.1.30

Scott, J. (2006, July 15). Judge rules gay group can use school. *Atlanta Journal-Constitution,* 3E.

Shepard, J.M., Shahidullah J.D., & Carlson, J.S. (2013). *Counseling students in levels 2 and 3: A PBIS/RTI guide.* Thousand Oaks, CA: Corwin.

Thompson, C.L., & Henderson, D.A. (2007). *Counseling children* (7th ed.). Belmont, CA: Thomson/Brooks/Cole.

Tilly, W.D. (2013). *What are the differences between an IEP and RTI?* Retrieved from www.rtinetwork.org/index2.php?option=com_content&task=emailform&id=366&itemid=202

U.S. Department of Education. (2011a). *Improving basic programs operated by local educational agencies (Title I, Part A).* Retrieved from www2.ed.gov/programs/titleiparta/index.html

U.S. Department of Education. (2011b). *Transition of students with disabilities to postsecondary education: A guide for high school educators.* Retrieved from www2.ed.gov/about/offices/list/ocr/transitionguide.html

Varjas, K., Graybill, E., Mahan, W., Meyers, J., Dew, B., Marshall, M., Singh, A., & Birckbichler, L. (2007). Urban service providers' perspectives on school responses to gay, lesbian, and questioning students: An exploratory study. *Professional School Counseling, 11*(2), 113–119.

Wood, S. (2008, March). *Counseling gifted students.* Paper presented at the meeting of the American Counseling Association, Honolulu, Hawaii.

Wyss, S.E. (2004). 'This was my hell': The violence experienced by gender non-conforming youth in US high schools. *International Journal of Qualitative Studies in Education, 17*(5), 709–730.

Yoo, C. (2005, May 8). Gay teens seek support and safety; White county has become center of emotional clash over equal rights. *Atlanta Journal-Constitution,* 1C.

Ziomek-Daigle, J., & Singh, A.A. (2008, June). *Beyond safe zones: Setting new standards by making schools safer for LGBTQ youth.* Paper presented at the meeting of the American School Counselor Association, Atlanta.

Zirkel, P.A. (2009a). Section 504: Student eligibility update. *Clearing House, 82*(5), 209–211.

Zirkel, P.A. (2009b). What does the law say? New Section 504 student eligibility standards. *Teaching Exceptional Children, 41*(4), 68–71.

14 Developmental Issues of Students

Robin Wilbourn Lee and Jennifer Jordan

CACREP Standards

Counseling, Prevention, and Intervention

C. Knowledge

1. Knows the theories and processes of effective counseling and wellness programs for individual students and groups of students.

Assessment

B. Knowledge

1. Understand the influence of multiple factors (e.g., abuse, violence, eating disorders, attention deficit hyperactivity disorder, childhood depression) that may affect the personal, social, and academic functioning of students.
2. Know the signs and symptoms of substance abuse in children and adolescents, as well as the signs and symptoms of living in a home where substance abuse occurs.

The purpose of this chapter is to:

-   review human development as it relates to school counseling
-   introduce developmental themes and concepts
-   discuss major developmental theories
-   consider the impact of basic forces in human development
-   provide scenarios to help the reader consider strategies for working with counselees in the schools.

INTRODUCTION

School counselor training programs are required to teach concepts surrounding human growth and development. Although you have probably taken a course that highlights life span developmental issues, this chapter is intended not only as a review of conceptual considerations, but also to present ideas to consider while assisting school-aged youth with issues that they bring to your counseling setting.

Developmental Themes and Concepts

Because human development addresses every aspect of the life span, the concepts and themes discussed in the literature play a particularly important role in understanding those with whom school counselors work. The themes of nature versus nurture, continuity versus discontinuity, universal versus context specific, and normative influences are a few developmental concepts for you to review as you apply these concepts during your practicum and internship experiences.

Nature Versus Nurture

Nature versus nurture involves the degree to which genetic or hereditary influences (nature) and/or environmental influences (nurture) determine personal attributes and characteristics. For years, a multitude of research has been conducted to determine which of these influences most directly impacts development. It has been consistently found that development is not due exclusively to either; rather, it is shaped by both, and therefore both are considered interactive influences. For example, a student may be predisposed to heart disease based on heredity and genetics (nature), but with healthy lifestyle choices, proper diet, and exercise, heart disease may be prevented.

Continuity Versus Discontinuity

Continuity is a concept indicating that development is a smooth progression throughout the life span. Continuity indicates that if a person develops certain characteristics early in life (e.g., a student who is shy or timid), these characteristics will continue throughout life (e.g., student becomes a shy and timid adult). Discontinuity indicates that development has a series of abrupt shifts, which influence changes that may occur. For example, a shy, timid child is taught social skills by parents and provided opportunities to utilize these skills. As a result, changes can occur to the child's personality, and he or she may become more social and outgoing.

Universal Versus Context Specific

The field of human growth and development considers the path of development as either universal (one similar path for all people) or context specific (different paths related to environmental factors). Many developmental tasks occur similarly and in the same time frame (e.g., language development across different cultures); however, context or environment still can have an impact (e.g., the fact that the child learns the language[s] to which she is exposed) on development.

Normative Influences

Many developmental tasks are normative, or what are considered typical or average. However, developmental tasks can be affected by age, history, and atypical occurrences. When considering age-graded normative influences, developmental tasks are affected by events that are related to particular age groups, generations, or cohorts (i.e., birth group). Living generations and cohorts include GIs, Baby Boomers, Generation Xers, Millennials, and a yet-to-be-identified generational group (suggestions include the Homelanders or Generation Z). Normative history-graded influences describe the impact that historical events can have on development. For example, the tragic events of September 11, 2001, will have a major impact on the development of future generations.

Keep these developmental themes and concepts in mind when you work with students. They provide constructs from which to view and understand student temperament, behavior, and characteristics. They can also be used as reframing tools when counseling students; counselees can be taught these development ideas to better understand their own journey and the journey of their peers.

THEORIES OF DEVELOPMENT

From a human growth and development perspective, a theory is defined as "an interrelated, coherent set of ideas that help to explain phenomena and make predictions" (Santrock, 2012). Theories of development can be divided according to perspectives. Some of the broader perspectives that are more pertinent to school settings include psychodynamic, learning, cognitive, and systems theories. Although there are numerous additional developmental theories, each of the aforementioned perspectives is briefly reviewed next.

Table 14.1 Erikson's Eight Stages of Psychosocial Development

Developmental Task/ Interpersonal Challenge	Age	Positive Outcome	Negative Outcome
Trust vs. mistrust	Birth to 1 year	Hope	Fear and mistrust of others
Autonomy vs. shame and doubt	1–3 years	Self-sufficiency if exploration encouraged	Doubts about self, lack of independence
Initiative vs. guilt	3–6 years	Discovery of ways to initiate actions	Guilt from actions and thoughts
Industry vs. inferiority	6 years to adolescence	Development of sense of competence	Feelings of inferiority, no sense of mastery
Identity vs. role confusion	Adolescence	Awareness of uniqueness of self, knowledge of role to be followed	Inability to identify appropriate roles in life
Intimacy vs. isolation	Early adulthood	Development of loving, sexual relationships and close friendships	Fear of relationships with others
Generativity vs. stagnation	Middle adulthood	Sense of contribution to continuity of life	Trivialization of one's activities
Ego integrity vs. despair	Late adulthood	Sense of unity in life's accomplishments	Regret over lost opportunities of life

Psychodynamic Theory

According to Seligman and Reichenberg (2014), the roots of present problems are a result of incidents in the past, and exploration and interpretation of these incidents are essential for understanding these problems. Psychodynamic theories are typically stage based, in that development is based on sequences of stages. Erikson (1950, 1968) developed a theory that explained human development in terms of the impact of social demands on the person. Erikson's psychosocial theory is composed of eight stages, with each stage emerging at a particular age. Within these stages, the person is met with a developmental task or interpersonal challenge, with the outcome dependent on whether the person meets the challenge successfully. If the person is successful at each stage, there is a positive outcome; if not successful, then there is a negative outcome (see Table 14.1 and Table 14.2). Remember that each person accomplishes the task somewhere along this continuum.

Conceptual Application Activity 14.1

Consider some of the students you have met and counseled in your practicum or internship. Identify which of Erikson's stages best fits each student. Describe the student and the stage you chose, and discuss your reasoning with your peers. How might you use this information when counseling these students?

_____

_____

Learning Theory

Whereas psychodynamic theories focus on the influence of motives and drives, learning theories focus on the influence of learning on the person's development. According to social learning theory, the emphasis includes the importance of modeling, or the person's ability to learn from others. Albert Bandura's (1977, 1986) social cognitive theory integrates both cognitive and social influences.

Table 14.2 Various Developmental Aspects

Life Span	Cognitive Development	Social Development	Moral Development	Emotional Development	Play	Gender Roles and Concerns
	Early Childhood					
Stage characteristics	Preoperational: Egocentric, lack ability to be empathic, have difficulty following rules.	Shame and doubt: Begin to understand they are autonomous. Initiative vs. guilt: Work on gaining autonomy, develop intentionality, begin to understand they are responsible for their own behavior.	Preconventional: Child's view is based on the outcome of pain or pleasure in the consequences.	Emotions are not socialized. Children need to learn how to interpret emotions, control them, and learn how and when they are appropriate.	Pretend play helps with problem solving and cognitive and social development. Daydreaming is normal at this stage. Solitary play, parallel play, onlooker play, associative play, and cooperative play.	Understand gender and begin to conform to sex-appropriate patterns. Those who differ are often rejected by peers.
Implications for school counselors	Do not assume children know why they have done something. They look at things from one point of view; this causes difficulty understanding what teacher wants. Children now have a new tool for making sense of the world through questioning.	Important to allow for exploration and independence. do not overprotect.	Authority figures are seen as the ones who determine the consequences; therefore, children react primarily to them. Understand the motivation for misbehavior using Dinkmeyer's theory: Undue attention, power, revenge, and assumed inadequacy.	Children who are a product of insecure attachment to parents or caregivers in the first years of life may show signs of manipulation, aggression, disrespect, and deceitfulness. Help teachers to understand where the behavior stems from, encourage empathy and understanding, and know children will push the envelope as far as possible to test for trust. Do not give up on these children.	Play is the child's language; there are short-term play techniques that can be much more effective than talk therapy to solve school problems.	Gender differences in bullying. Boys tend to be more physically aggressive to solve conflict; girls tend to use more relational aggression.
Age-appropriate actions	Make age-appropriate contracts and give children a prize for completion.	Allow children to create their own games and rules; allow them to create rewards and consequences; use strategic games like checkers, Sorry, Trouble, or Connect Four; you can let the kids win because it is about the process of learning self-regulation by taking turns.	Talk with the teacher; understand the reaction and consequences given to the child. Explore the child's perception of the teacher's consequences to see where they fit into the theory above. Work with teacher to change consequences if they are not getting the reaction that they want.	Play the feeling word game. Play a game to show you can have more than one feeling at a time (put each emotion on a separate piece of paper to tell a story that involves several emotions; have the child identify them and put the appropriate amount of poker chips on the feelings chosen to show the different intensity levels of each feeling). Self-control techniques can be taught with the games Pickup Sticks and operation.	Use fun games that allow laughter and silliness to build rapport, like catching bubbles before they hit the floor, or using bubbles to teach breathing techniques to calm themselves. (Show how to blow very large bubbles; it takes a deep breath that must be exhaled slowly.) Use ask-the-expert game: Pretend the child is the expert and you are interviewing the child with pretend questions from other children who have similar issues as the child; this is great for developing problem-solving skills.	Develop an antibullying school policy. Intervene immediately. Increase adult supervision at key times.

Middle Childhood

Life Span	Cognitive Development	Social Development	Moral Development	Emotional Development	Self-worth	Friends and Peers
Stage characteristics	Concrete operational: have a more logical thought process, base knowledge on things they have seen or can imagine easily.	Industry vs. inferiority: Need to feel successful in school; failure results in feeling insecure and inferior. Self-worth and esteem come from acknowledging how others act toward them, how they perceive themselves in comparison to others, and how closely they feel they are who they want to be. Emotions are often strongly tied to feelings of worth. Happy children express more happiness than sad children. Friendships become very important and selective.	Conventional: Progress from obeying rules of others to understanding others' perspectives to wanting to maintain social order.	Parental authority is questioned, emotions become regulated.	Friendships become very important and selective. Reciprocity is key. Social skills determine the ability to make friends.	Relational regression peaks in middle school girls. Relationships become more intimate and are used to gain power. Boys gain power through physical means.
Implications for school counselors	Conversation has advanced; children's primary mode of expression is no longer through play. Cognitive behavioral, solution-focused, and choice theories become applicable. Play can still be incorporated to help process from the preoperational stage to the concrete stage.	This is time for children to be given every chance to be successful. They need to be exposed to many activities to find their niche.	Intentions matter more than consequences. They know not all negative behavior will be immediately punished or even detected.	Regulation of feeling often masks true feelings. Shame may be associated with negative feelings; fear for self or those who have been emotionally abusive are hidden. Societal taboo limits expression of emotion regarding sexual abuse. Emotional issues become a hidden secret that affects socializing, trusting, self-worth, and many other aspects of emotional development.	Many children in middle childhood do not have friends. Friends influence behaviors of others in their peer group (peer pressure).	Interpersonal relationships differ between boys and girls. Children are developing physically at different rates, causing more awareness of body image and potential self-esteem issues related to body image. Be aware of subtle relational exclusion from girls.
Age-appropriate actions	Use groups to focus on the here and now, which leads to the development of empathy for others. Use creative activities that are age-appropriate. Apply short-term objectives to academic and behavioral objectives.	Encourage students to find a niche in school as well as outside school. Run groups that include social skills training. For those with developmental disorders, it is especially needed in the middle school years. Guidance lessons can concentrate more heavily on issues that children are going to face this now or in the future. Smoking, drinking, drug use, and sex are some examples of topics needed for guidance or group activities.	Punishments must fit the crime or these children become angry. They depend on a fair consequence, which shows that wrongs need to be righted.	Activities that promote self-worth and self-esteem are important. Programs include Girls on the Run.	Implement social skills training; have a plan set up for new children to adjust to school and meet other children. Peer mediation applications are successful with this population.	Incorporating gender roles into your lessons becomes important. The issues the sexes face are now more complicated and diverse. Guidance lessons including sexuality should be split between the sexes. Friendships with the opposite sex are explored including dating rituals.

(Continued)

Table 14.2 (Continued)

Life Span	Cognitive Development	Social Development	Moral Development	Emotional Development	Self-worth	Friends and Peers
		Adolescence				
Stage characteristics	Formal operational stage: Can now understand hypothetical concepts; they begin to ponder the meaning of life, feel others are always passing judgment, and at the same time feel they are special and are not susceptible to the same risks as others: "It won't happen to me."	Identity vs. role confusion: Need to develop a strong sense of self-understanding; what one's own beliefs and values are. Staying closely in line with this creates a strong sense of self, whereas those that stray from this struggle with themselves have a low sense of worth and are more susceptible to peer pressure. Social learning theory suggests suicide is linked to the child's social system.	Postconventional: Can understand moral versus legal implications and can take perspective of mankind as a collective whole.	Emotional distancing from caregivers. Suicide rates soar. Isolation leading to depression.	With independence comes the ability to make their own decisions.	Freedom is a primary value. More independence. Relationships with more intense intimacy are coveted. For some, becoming more comfortable with self, showing more of the values they believe instead of those from parents or others in their lives. Being shunned from a peer group can cause many psychological stressors.
Implications for school counselors	High-risk behavior is more prevalent.	Understanding how one differentiates from others is important. Those with a lack of clarity in themselves will struggle with career choices and experimentation of the choices available to them.	Fictitious dilemmas are not very powerful. Often students do not progress past a stage two orientation without guidance.	Be aware of isolated students, who do not display outward problems, as they may be more at risk for depression.	Those without social groups feel isolated and think, "If I weren't here no one would even notice."	Peer interactions are imperative.
Age-appropriate actions	Plan events such as bringing in a wrecked car to campus, bringing in speakers whom the kids can relate to, and programs to show the impact of pregnancy and parenthood.	Use more group activities to foster the need for socialization.	Encourage debates using real moral dilemmas. Challenge the students by incorporating thoughts consistent with next developmental level.	Help identify goals, create a sense of belonging.	Help others get kids connected.	Volunteer and become part of the greater whole.

Source: Adapted from Lefrancois (1996)

Bandura believed that people attempt to understand the world around them, as well as their place in the world (cognitive). In addition, Bandura considered the influence of others an important force of development (social). For instance, consider the influences of parents/guardians on the social process to better understand the students with whom you are working.

Conceptual Application Activity 14.2

Read and respond to the following scenarios and discuss your answers with your peers.

Angela is a second grader at a local elementary school. Over the years, she has shown tremendous anxiety whenever a thunderstorm occurs, often crying uncontrollably and demanding her mother be called to take her home. Her teachers and the school counselor are very puzzled by her behavior. Angela is upset by her reaction and does not understand why she reacts this way. After a brief meeting with the school counselor to discuss Angela's situation, Angela's mother reports that as a child, her family home was destroyed by a tornado, and whenever there is a report of inclement weather, Angela's mother insists they all get in the closet to protect themselves. How may have Angela's mother's previous experience affected Angela's thinking (cognitive) and reaction (behavior) to thunderstorms?

How might you work with Angela to calm her fears?

_____

_____

Kim is a sixth grader at a local middle school and made an appointment to see the school counselor. During the visit, Kim reveals she has recently been diagnosed with diabetes and is having to take daily shots for her condition. With Kim's permission, the school counselor schedules a consultation with the school nurse to learn what she can do to help Kim. The school nurse reports that Kim has not been diagnosed with the condition. After meeting with Kim again, the school counselor learns that Kim's parents were recently divorced. Kim attended a school assembly where an eighth grader recently diagnosed with diabetes was joined by her parents on stage to help the school understand how to deal with diabetes. Kim believes that by having an illness, her parents will reconcile.

How did the eighth grader's condition and the assembly influence Kim's beliefs about her parents' divorce? How can you assist Kim?

_____

_____

Parent/Guardians and Other Social Influences

Parents or primary caregivers are the most influential social models for children. Working alongside and supporting parents or primary caregivers is one way you, as a school counselor, can greatly impact a student. Parenting style has a deep impact on the social and emotional well-being of children. Positive parenting styles have been linked to high self-esteem, self-regulation of emotions, academic achievement, prosocial skills, and friendship development, as well as low levels of aggressive behavior and negative social skills (Santrock, 2012). Negative parenting styles have been linked to low self-esteem, aggressive behavior, anxiety, anger, poor social skills, and possibly being more susceptible to bullying.

Baumrind (1971) developed four parenting styles based on the quality of parenting: (a) authoritative, (b) authoritarian, (c) permissive, and (d) rejecting–neglecting. The authoritative style is considered the most positive form of parenting in that this style provides both nurturing and discipline, and children are given freedom while adhering to consistent rules and limits. Authoritarian parents are inflexible, rigid, and often cold, establishing rules which require unquestionable obedience. Children of authoritarian parents may have difficulty expressing emotions due to the fact that a negative emotional environment is the norm. Permissive parents are the exact opposite of authoritarian parents and are typically very loving but provide few rules. Discipline is not a priority with these parents. Children of permissive parents may have high self-esteem but may be less self-reliant than other children. These children may exhibit impulsive and aggressive behavior. Rejecting–neglecting parents are the most flawed type, providing little nurturing and discipline. These parents spend little time with their children and tend to be less affectionate. Children of rejecting–neglecting parents are neglected and ignored, often leading to significant aggression and depression.

Conceptual Application Activity 14.3

Two scenarios are offered in the following. Read each scenario and respond to the questions. Compare your answers with those of your peers.

Jackson has recently been getting in trouble with other classmates. He is easily frustrated and takes out his frustration on the other students. When talking to you as the school counselor-in-training, he reveals that his father beats him almost every day and never lets him make decisions for himself. He also says that he is criticized for everything he does and is often threatened to be sent away if he does not do what his father says.

What kind of parenting style is Jackson's father using? How would you intervene in this situation?

_____

_____

Tonya's parents recently divorced after her mother caught her father cheating. Tonya and her two younger brothers are in her mother's custody, but Mom does not take the time to care for the three children because she has lost the initiative and ability to do so. Mom often sits in her room, depressed because of how her life has turned out. When Tonya and her brothers try to spend time with her, she tells them to go away. What might Tonya be experiencing and what kind of parenting style is Tonya's mom using? How is this impacting Tonya and her two brothers? How might you respond to Tonya and the family?

_____

_____

Although awareness of parenting styles can help school counselors understand the dynamics between children and their parents, we must acknowledge that other factors may affect children's development, including genetics, gender, different beliefs of mother and father, culture, and child temperament. It is expected that school counselors will encounter each of these parenting styles in their careers. Parent education may be an appropriate activity for you to consider during your clinical experiences while learning about the school counselor's role in working with parents/guardians.

Cognitive Theories

Cognitive theories focus on the influence of thought processes on development; particularly on how people think and how their thinking changes over time. Piaget (1926, 1929, 1972; Piaget & Inhelder, 1969) developed one of the most influential cognitive theories, known as cognitive development theory. Piaget's theory focused on cognitive development in childhood and adolescence, focusing primarily on the construction of knowledge and changes that occur over time. Piaget believed that it is the natural inclination of children to try to understand their world, and that significant cognitive changes occur three times in a person's life: at 2 years old, at 7 years old, and right before adolescence. Each change is based on children's ability to understand and organize their environment as cognition becomes increasingly more sophisticated. Piaget's theory is based on four stages—sensorimotor, preoperational thought, concrete operational thought, and formal operational thought (see Table 14.3).

Table 14.3 Piaget's Four Stages of Cognitive Development

Stage	Age	Description
Sensorimotor	Birth to 2 years	Infants know the world through their senses and through their actions. For example, they learn what dogs look like and what petting them feels like.
Preoperational	2–7 years	Toddlers and young children acquire the ability to internally represent the world through language and mental imagery. They also begin to be able to see the world from other people's perspectives, not just from their own.
Concrete operational	7–12 years	Children become able to think logically, not just intuitively. They now can classify objects into coherent categories and understand that events are often influenced by multiple factors, not just one.
Formal operational	12 years and older	Adolescents can think systematically and reason about what might be as well as what is. This allows them to understand politics, ethics, and science fiction, as well as to engage in scientific reasoning.

Conceptual Application Activity 14.4

Read and respond to the following situation. Compare your answers with those of your peers.

Cassie, a high school freshman, is shown a glass of water by her teacher. The teacher then pours the water into a shorter, wider container and asks which glass has the most water in it. Cassie responds that both glasses contain the same amount of water but that they appear to have different amounts only because the glasses are shaped differently. She is asked to arrange sticks on her desk from shortest to tallest, a task she completes without difficulty. She can also give the teacher directions from her classroom to the lunchroom.

What stage of Piaget's cognitive development is Cassie likely in?

_____

Consider some strategies school counselors can use to engage students who are in this stage of development.

_____

_____

Box 14.1

Neurologists have discovered that the brain is continually adapting to new input. Meditating daily improves the area in the brain that is essential for focus, memory, and compassion. School counselors can teach students meditation and mindfulness strategies to alter the physical structure of the brain (Weaver, 2014).

Sociocultural Perspective

A Russian psychologist and theorist, Lev Vygotsky (1934/1986), developed the theory of human cultural and biosocial development, in which several important concepts are helpful to understanding how children learn. Parents and school personnel use Vygotsky's concept of scaffolding quite frequently. Scaffolding is the process by which a more accomplished learner (parent, teacher, or peer) provides direct instruction via prompts and cues to assist learning, and then slowly provides less instruction as the child's knowledge increases. Scaffolding requires the advanced learner to enter the child's *zone of proximal development*, defined as the difference between the child's ability to solve problems and the ability to be taught by another person. These two concepts can be particularly significant for you to remember as a school counselor-in-training, since you are involved in the direct instruction of social/emotional knowledge and problem-solving skills related to personal situations. Or, you may assist teachers in the instruction of study skills within the academic domain. You can enter the child's zone of proximal development and use scaffolding to help the child learn how to deal with peers, adjust emotional reactions, and deal with problems such as attention-deficit hyperactivity disorder (ADHD). Or, as a supervisee, you may consider applying this concept by creating a mentorship program in which older students who understand and can model concepts are paired with younger students to enhance academic and social skills.

Conceptual Application Activity 14.5

As a school counselor-in-training, what are some other strategies that can be used to apply the concepts of scaffolding in your school setting?

_____

_____

Systems Theories

Systems theories are often referred to as ecological theories due to the environmental focus on development. Bronfenbrenner's (1979) ecological systems theory is based on the fact that development stems from the interaction of various systems in the person's life. According to Bronfenbrenner's theory, the environment is divided into four systems: microsystem, mesosystem, exosystem, macrosystem. The microsystem is defined as the person's immediate environment (e.g., parents, children, daycare, schools, church), which has significant influence on development. The mesosystem refers to the interaction between the person's microsystem and any modification that can occur based on this interaction. The exosystem is defined as the social settings that influence the person, either directly or indirectly (e.g., extended family, media, job/work environment, neighbors). The macrosystem is considered the broadest of the systems and involves cultural influences (see Figure 14.1).

Conceptual Application Activity 14.6

Lydia is an 8-year-old girl who lives with her mother and grandmother. She and her mother moved in with her grandmother after Lydia's father died. Lydia's father was a soldier who was killed during combat in Afghanistan. There are two cousins who live with Lydia's grandmother as well as her uncle Bob, Lydia's mother's brother. Because of the death of her father, Lydia's family has been attending church regularly to deal with their grief. Her mother also takes Lydia to a local support group for children who have lost a parent. The family recently attended a memorial

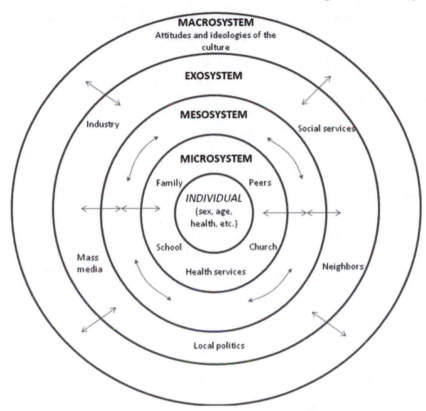

Figure 14.1 Four systems, according to Bronfenbrenner's theory.

Source: Hchokr

service held by the community to honor soldiers from the community who died while serving in the military. Lydia is very proud of her father and believes that serving in the military is very noble. She is considering joining the military when she is older.

Which system can you, as a supervisee, access to assist in Lydia's development? How can the various systems influence how school counselors or school counselors-in-training work with their students?

In working with students at various age and grade levels, consider how each of the developmental theories and concepts impacts students and how change occurs. Further considerations include your values and perspective in relation to those values and perspectives of the individuals you are counseling. For instance, consider Lawrence Kohlberg's (1976) theory of moral development adapted from Piaget's work to explain the development of moral reasoning as you work with children and adolescents.

Moral Development

Kohlberg (1976) extended Piaget's theory by considering moral development as a continual process occurring throughout the life span. Whereas Piaget described a two-stage process of moral development, Kohlberg's theory of moral development outlined six stages within three different levels. Preconventional, the first level, begins with making moral choices to avoid punishment and progresses into a hedonistic stage in which moral judgment is based on self-indulgence (if it feels good, it must be the right thing to do). Conventional, the second level, begins with interpreting the reactions of others and how they would view the person as a result of decisions made. As this stage progresses, values of honor and duty motivate conduct. Postconventional, the third level, moves away from social acceptance to the rights of individuals and the societal responsibility to uphold those rights to principles of justice for everyone (see Table 14.4).

Table 14.4 Kohlberg's Stages of Moral Development Chart

Level 1: Preconventional
Stage 1: Obedience and punishment. No respect for the underlying social order that is supported by punishment and authority. There is a concentration on avoiding punishment.
   Stage 2: Reward seeking, self-benefit. Self-interest motivates any good deeds or favors provided to others.

Level 2: Conventional
Stage 3: Avoidance of disapproval. Recognition sought for being "good." Desire to please other people in order to gain their approval. One is concerned about the opinions of others.
   Stage 4: Law and order. Belief in the value of society's rules, not just the avoidance of punishment. Law is enacted to protect the rights of the individual. Laws are important.

Level 3: Postconventional—Decisions Based on Personal Ethics
Stage 5: Contract fulfillment. A belief in the rights of individual. If laws are not good, they should be changed, since one need not obey a bad law. There is an awareness of personal opinions and values.
   Stage 6: Individual principles, conscience. Reliance on abstract ethical principles with an emphasis on value of human life.

Conceptual Application Activity 14.7

Read and respond to the following scenario. Compare your answers with those of your peers.

Cara is an 18-year-old girl who is a senior in a private high school. Recently she has gotten a facial piercing and a visible tattoo, although both are against school rules. Her parents discouraged her from getting the piercing and tattoo because they knew it was against school policy; however, because Cara is of legal age, she went ahead and got them anyway. She is currently suspended and faces possible expulsion from school if she does not remove the piercing and cover the tattoo while at school. Cara refuses to do either and references the Constitution and its statement of "freedom of choice" as her justification.

At which stage of Kohlberg's moral development theory is Cara? How would you, as a school counselor-in-training, use Kohlberg's theory to assist you in addressing this situation?

_____

_____

BASIC FORCES IN HUMAN DEVELOPMENT

Developmental tasks are typically examined in terms of what is happening to the student biologically, physically, cognitively, and psychosocially. By considering and combining the effects of these variables, we can begin to better understand the development of the student. The interaction of these forces is referred to as a *bio-psycho-social framework*. Biological forces are defined as aspects of development pertaining to genetics and heredity, physical development, and overall health-related issues. Psychological forces include cognitive development, as well as emotional and affective issues and personality characteristics. Social–cultural forces describe the impact of social issues and culture on the person's development. By using the bio-psycho-social framework, each stage of development and age group can be understood better, helping you to apply these concepts in counseling.

ELEMENTARY SCHOOL–AGED CHILDREN AND DEVELOPMENTAL ISSUES (GRADES K–5)

Biological Development

In general, elementary school–aged children are typically healthy and self-reliant. Growth is fairly steady at this age, with the greatest growth occurring in the legs and trunk. Growth can be affected positively or negatively by nutrition, genetic factors, and gender. Brain size development reaches adult size by age 7, and both boys' and girls' brain sizes tend to be the same, although individual differences may exist based an environmental factors. Middle childhood is a period of time when chronic illness is less common than at any other time in life. Changes in fine and gross motor development become apparent. For girls, there is a focus on fine motor skills with improvement in dexterity, flexibility, and balance. For boys, the focus is primarily on gross motor skills, with improvement in strength.

Common contemporary issues in early childhood include childhood obesity, asthma, autism spectrum disorders, ADHD, and learning disorders. School counselors-in-training should be aware of concerns that can develop in childhood, understand treatment, and know how to discuss these issues with parents when necessary.

Childhood Obesity

Childhood obesity is currently being considered by the medical community as an epidemic in the United States. Children may either be overweight (20% above ideal weight for height) or obese (30% over ideal weight for height). According to the Centers for Disease Control and Prevention (CDC, 2014a), the rate of overweight children has doubled over the past 30 years; however, the good news is that the obesity rate among youth between the ages of 2 and 4 who are from low socioeconomic backgrounds is falling in 19 states, which is considered a sign of progress. Overweight children may have psychological, physical, and medical problems, low self-esteem, and difficult peer relationships. Childhood obesity can occur due to genetic factors; however, it may also occur due to environmental issues such as cultural values, lack of exercise, poor-quality food, and sedentary lifestyle (e.g., watching excessive television and playing video games).

Box 14.2

Conventional wisdom states that obesity is a result of a sedentary lifestyle. However, recent information indicates that it is not just a matter of Americans eating more higher-caloric food, but that food has become cheaper and easier to obtain. Food is less expensive in our society today than at any other point in history, but there has been a 20% increase in calories in the past 40 years. The solution is to make fruits and vegetables less expensive than junk food.

Source: Health Scare of the Week, 2014

Asthma

Asthma is the most common medical problem causing school absences and is the third leading cause of hospitalization among children under the age of 15 (American Lung Association, 2012). Asthma, three times more prevalent today than 20 years ago, is defined as a chronic inflammatory disorder of the airways, which affects between 10% and 20% of school-aged children in North America. The rate of asthma is expected to double again by 2020. Although the school nurse will likely be the staff member to deal directly with any medical concerns, the school counselor may be the entry point for students who are dealing with physical issues. School counselors can be aware of the early warning signs of a child developing asthma or asthmatic children who are at risk of an attack. Children who appear or act differently from the norm, even with something relatively minor like asthma, may be teased or ostracized. As a school counselor-in training, you can use the clinical experiences as an opportunity to learn more about the emotional toll a physical condition like asthma may cause.

Autism Spectrum Disorder

In the *Diagnostic and Statistical Manual of Mental Disorders*, fifth edition (DSM-5) (American Psychiatric Association, 2013), autism spectrum disorder (ASD) is defined as "persistent deficits in social communication and social interaction across multiple contexts" (p. 50). Autism spectrum disorder is characterized by persistent impairment in reciprocal social communication and social interaction (Criterion A) and restricted, repetitive patterns of behavior, interest, or activities (Criterion B, p. 53). Other developmental disorders include Rett's disorder and childhood disintegrative disorder. According to the Centers for Disease Control and Prevention (CDC, 2014b), approximately 1 in 68 children has been diagnosed with ASD, and it is five times more common in boys. However, these disorders are still less common than other conditions, such as speech and language impairments, learning disabilities, and ADHD. Early intervention is key to helping children diagnosed with autism or other related disorders. Because symptoms usually can be observed by 18 months of age, children with autism may already be diagnosed by the time they enter school. However, as a school counselor-in-training, you can learn more about this disorder and hone skills to help children diagnosed with autism improve their social and communication skills, provide information to parents, and act as a support for teachers of autistic students.

Box 4.3

Autism has previously been diagnosed in children by the age of 3, but more recently, there is evidence that a simple name test when the child is 1 year of age could present a clue to potential difficulties. It is possible that a potential developmental difficulty may exist if a child does not respond to his/her name on a consistent basis.

Source: Detecting autism, 2013

Attention-Deficit Hyperactivity Disorder (ADHD)

According to the National Institute of Mental Health (n.d.), ADHD is one of the most common disorders of childhood, which may continue through adolescence and even into adulthood. The DSM-5 (American Psychiatric Association, 2013) states that the essential feature of ADHD is "a persistent pattern of inattention and/or hyperactivity-impulsivity that interferes with functioning or development" (p. 61). In addition, the DSM describes three subtypes of ADHD. First, the predominantly inattentive type focuses primarily on inattentive behaviors such as not paying attention to details; poor listening and organizational skills; not following instructions; failing to complete work, chores, and so forth; avoiding tasks requiring mental effort (e.g., schoolwork, homework); losing items such as toys and school materials; and forgetting daily activities. Second, the predominantly hyperactive/impulsive type focuses on behaviors such as fidgeting, squirming, running, or climbing excessively when inappropriate; having difficulty focusing on leisure activities or playing; talking excessively; blurting out answers; difficulty awaiting turn; and often interrupting others. The ADHD combined type has criteria of both inattention and hyperactivity/impulsivity. Although the causes of ADHD are unknown, possible causes include neurological problems and genetic vulnerability. The primary treatment of ADHD includes medications such as Ritalin or Adderall. In some cases, the most appropriate treatment is a combination of medication and counseling to help the child develop coping skills for dealing with the impact the condition may have on school and learning. As a school counselor-in-training, you can learn about special accommodations that assist these individuals, provide individual and group counseling, consult with teachers, and observe and participate in an Individualized Education Plan (IEP) team.

Learning Disabilities

In childhood, cognitive ability rapidly develops and is typically reflected in improved test scores, including aptitude and intelligence quotient (IQ, measuring the potential to learn or achieve in the future) and achievement (measuring what the child has already learned). Although the school psychologist may be the helping professional most likely to conduct intelligence testing, school counselors are often asked to participate in the testing process. Although IQ testing is a common assessment in schools, this type of testing comes with criticism because it does not consider achievement and the influence of other environmental factors such as culture, family, strength of school, and rate of development.

One specific use of IQ testing is to determine if a student has a learning deficiency. Some students experience learning disabilities that, if identified early, can be addressed to enhance the student's ability to be successful in school. A learning disability is defined as a marked delay in a particular area of learning that is not associated with any physical handicap, mental retardation, or any significant stress in the home environment. A common type of learning disability is dyslexia, which is typically manifested by reading difficulty. Once a student has been identified as having a learning disability, schools are legally required to provide special accommodations for those students. Refer to Chapter 13 for more information on children with exceptional needs.

Memory is another concept important to understanding the cognitive development of children. *Working memory* is defined as the part of memory that holds information currently being used or to be accessed at a specific time. Changes occur in early childhood through an expansion of the capacity to hold information. In addition, *executive functions*, referring to skills related to managing memory, controlling cognitions, planning behaviors, and inhibiting responses, increase significantly after age 5. *Rehearsal* is an example of an executive function that helps students remember new information through repetition. *Selective attention* is defined as the student's ability to attend to information from several areas of the brain at one time while attending to the most important elements. Although selective attention improves with age, younger children face the challenge of being distracted by irrelevant information. As you train for the school counseling profession, helping children focus on the more important aspects of information may be crucial to successfully overcoming problems.

Automatization is defined as the process by which thoughts and actions are repeated in sequence until they become routine or automatic; therefore, *automatic* thoughts and actions require very little conscious thought. Reading is an example of automatization. Automatization affects how children maintain appropriate and desirable behaviors, whether in the classroom or with peers, and is helpful for you to remember as you work with school-aged youth.

Figure 14.2 Reading is an example of automatization.

Source: Shutterstock

Janet Belsky, author of *Experiencing the Lifespan* (2007), offers information processing tips that are beneficial to any adults, including school counselors. Some of her tips for students in early and middle childhood include:

Early Childhood

1. Do not expect a child to remember, without considerable prompting, regular chores such as feeding a pet, the details of a movie, or the name of the person who telephoned that afternoon.
2. Expect the child to have a good deal of trouble with any situation that involves inhibiting a strong "prepotent impulse," such as not touching toys, following unpleasant rules, or keeping a secret. Instead, tell the child what you want (e.g., keep your hands to yourself, raise your hand and wait to be called on before speaking).

Middle Childhood

1. Do not assume that the child knows how to best master school-related memorization tasks. Actively teach how to rehearse information, selective attention strategies (such as underlining important points), and other studying skills.
2. Scaffold organizational strategies for school and life. For example, get the child to use a notebook for each class assignment and to keep important objects, such as eyeglasses, in a specific place.
3. Expect that problems may occur with situations that involve many different tasks, such as getting ready for school. Also, expect activities that involve ongoing inhibition to give children trouble, such as refraining from watching TV or using the Internet before finishing their homework. Try to build in a regular structure for mastering these difficult executive-functioning tasks: "The rule is that at 8 or 9 p.m., it's time to get everything ready for school for tomorrow," or "Homework must be completed by dinner time or the first thing after you get home from school."
4. To promote selective attention (and inhibition), have a child do homework or other tasks that involve concentration in a room away from tempting distractions such as the TV or Internet.

Psychosocial Development

Psychological and social development for elementary-aged children tends to focus primarily on establishing independence and developing stability for future emotional life. Much of psychological development and socialization begins with the parents and cultural influences. Children, who are trying to master abilities and cultural values, often judge themselves as either competent or incompetent, productive or failing, winners or losers. Competence increases are related to emotional regulation and the understanding of self and others. However, this self-awareness has consequences, which can include lowered self-esteem and more self-criticism and self-consciousness. *Social comparison* among peers emerges. Social comparison is the tendency to assess abilities, achievements, social status, and other attributes by comparison with others such as peers. Friendship building and relating to peers are the most important aspects of the psychosocial developmental tasks at this age. Children begin to develop peer groups that are usually composed of the same age, ethnicity, and socioeconomic status who play, work, or learn together. Children depend on each other for companionship, advice, and self-validation. Children who are willing to assume the best about other children are successful with friendship development and therefore are typically well adjusted and prosocial. Well-adjusted children often display behaviors such as altruism, empathy, and sympathy. In contrast, children who have difficulty connecting with peers often feel rejected, which could lead to other psychological problems later in life.

Conceptual Application Activity 14.8

Read and respond to the following scenario. Compare your answer with those of your peers.

Andre often gets in trouble for fighting at school with his classmates. He claims they make comments to disrespect him, and he is not going to let anyone run over him. Many of the students are scared of him and think he is a bully.

What types of strategies will you, as his school counselor-in-training, implement to help Andre learn more effective social skills?

_____

_____

ADOLESCENTS AND DEVELOPMENTAL ISSUES (GRADES 6–12)

Biological Development

When discussing the biological development of adolescents, the first and most critical aspect is puberty. Puberty is the time in life when children become more mature sexually, based on hormonal and physical changes. Puberty is a period of rapid physical growth and sexual maturation and is typically completed 3 to 4 years after the first visible signs.

Puberty cannot be discussed without acknowledging the extreme emotional reactions associated with biological changes that occur in adolescents during this time. G. Stanley Hall (1904) referred to the difficulty adolescents experience during puberty as *storm and stress*. Due to the rapidly increasing hormone levels, extreme emotional shifts occur, and increased hormone levels produce visible signs of sexual maturation, which often leads adults to think of the adolescents as adult-like, with an expectation of maturity. School counselors-in-training can help adolescents entering puberty by normalizing what is happening and recognizing that they are not alone in that it is a universal development task that happens to everyone.

Normally, body changes begin to appear between ages 8 and 14, a wide span of years. With puberty comes a growth spurt, defined as rapid changes in size, shape, and proportions of the body.

There is an average increase in height of about 8 inches in boys and about 4 inches in girls. Boys may gain an average of about 40 pounds, while girls may gain an average of about 35 pounds. Facial features change dramatically, with the nose and ears growing before the skull, causing disproportional facial features that are corrected when the head growth catches up to the rest of the face. This pattern may create emotional distress for youth who are already coming to grips with self-concept in relation to their peers. For girls, the growth spurt typically begins 2 years before boys, with adult height often reached by age 12.

Although puberty is considered a universal developmental task, it is also context specific. All individuals go through puberty (universal), but the timing of puberty can vary (context specific). Factors that can affect puberty include genetics, culture, ethnicity, nutrition, body weight, family stress, and socioeconomic status.

The stress experienced by most adolescents in puberty can manifest in a variety of ways. Early-maturing girls may be embarrassed by their early development. Late-maturing girls can have equal embarrassment due to their childlike appearance when their peers are becoming more adult-like. Both can be subjected to teasing. Early-maturing boys often excel in sports, making them more popular than their late-maturing counterparts. Late-maturing boys may be shunned and ostracized. Early-maturing adolescents may experience unrealistic expectations from adults who expect them to demonstrate more adult-like thoughts and feelings than they are capable of. Early-maturing girls may begin to choose friends who are older, thereby exposing themselves to more risky behaviors such as sex and taking drugs and alcohol. For both boys and girls, another problem that can cause stress is an overproduction of oil and sweat in the skin, causing acne. Due to the tremendous changes in physical appearance during puberty, dissatisfaction with body image can become a stressful part of adolescence. Many adolescents become very critical of their bodies, often leading to extreme measures such as dieting, exercising, or developing an eating disorder.

Helping the prepubescent adolescent, rather than focusing on the adolescent already experiencing puberty, is an ideal approach for you as a counselor-in-training. In the years from 2006 to 2008, most teens received formal instruction on sexually transmitted diseases (STDs), HIV, and abstinence, yet approximately one third had not received instruction on contraceptives (Guttmacher Institute, 2012). For schools that do provide sex education classes, the focus is typically on what not to do (avoid sexual contact, STDs, teen pregnancy), rather than on having an open discussion about these issues and strategies to handle the significant changes that adolescents are experiencing or are about to experience. Educating parents about how to deal with their prepubescent adolescents can also be an important school counselor function. Parents can be encouraged to talk to their children about puberty, and when possible, parents can be reminded about the pros and cons of talking to their same-sex child. Specifically, it is important for mothers to remember to avoid negatively discussing menstruation in front of their female children (Rembeck & Gunnarsson, 2004), and both parents can also avoid teasing their children about their changing bodies.

Cognitive Development

During adolescence, many intellectual advances occur in logical and intuitive thinking. Brain maturation continues, helping in the areas of planning, analyzing, and being able to pursue goals. Language mastery also improves. According to Piaget (1972), adolescents are in the fourth and final stage of his model—formal operations, which begins around 12 years of age. In this stage, Piaget believed that adolescents are able to think logically, abstractly, and hypothetically and are better able to see the various aspects of a problem. Determining the cognitive level of your counselees is helpful in determining a theoretical counseling approach and techniques that would work best for each individual you counsel. For instance, a youth at the concrete cognitive level may benefit more from physical movement as opposed to theories that rely on higher-level cognition.

One of the positive aspects of this improved adolescent thinking is the ability to self-monitor and self-regulate; however, with this improved thinking comes other challenges that rival only puberty in terms of difficulty. Elkind (1978) applied Piaget's theory to help understand adolescent emotional states. He developed the term *adolescent egocentrism* to describe adolescents' focus on self to the exclusion of others and the belief that their personal thoughts, feelings, and experiences are unique.

Elkind (1978) described three types of adolescent egocentrism: (a) invincibility fable, (b) personal fable, and (c) imaginary audience. The *invincibility fable* is defined as adolescents' belief that they are immune to the laws of mortality, probability, and nature. This belief can explain why adolescents tend to engage in risky behavior without recognizing the consequences of their choices. The *personal fable* describes when adolescents imagine their own lives as unique, mythical, or heroic and destined for fame or fortune. The *imaginary audience* is characterized by adolescents fantasizing about how others will react to them. They tend to be very concerned about the opinions of onlookers, often assuming that others are judging their appearance.

Although adolescents may be able to think logically, they may often be challenged with decision making; they tend to think about possibilities, not practicalities. Because of this, they may be less likely to consider important matters rationally. This may cause parents and other involved adults to spend a great deal of time and effort trying to protect teenagers from experiencing consequences resulting from poor judgment.

School counselors can be influential when adolescents are learning to make thoughtful, wise, and healthy decisions. Adolescents will be challenged with many aspects of life. Some of these aspects that relate more closely to the school counselor include the school environment; decisions about sex, drugs, and alcohol; establishing a healthy independence; depression; and suicide.

Conceptual Application Activity 14.9

Read and respond to the following scenarios. Compare your answers with your peers.

While at a school-sponsored swimming party, Jody decided to jump off the roof of the nearby pool house into the pool. Despite being cautioned of the risks by some partygoers, Jody dismissed their concerns and listened to those who were encouraging his antics.

How will you, as a school counselor, work with Jody or other individuals who exhibit these types of behaviors?

_____

_____

Naomi is a talented high school basketball player. Her coaches and others encourage her to pursue playing for a college basketball team. Although Naomi accepts this encouragement to pursue college basketball, she believes she is destined to play basketball in the major leagues (WNBA). She emails the manager of the Los Angeles Sparks, requesting a tryout.

What are some strategies that school counselors can utilize to assist adolescents to develop a realistic outlook on self and others?

_____

_____

School Environment

Some of the challenges that adolescents face are decisions about school. When adolescents graduate from high school, they are exposed to many benefits, including healthier lives, living longer, a likelihood of financial stability, stronger possibility of marriage, and owning a home. However, there are also numerous reasons for dropping out of high school. According to the report *The Silent Epidemic* (Bridgeland, DiIulio, & Morison, 2006), adolescents across the country reported reasons for dropping out such as classes being uninteresting, being unmotivated to work hard, getting a job, becoming a parent, or caring for a family member. In addition, some reported failing in school as a major factor. Another important factor discovered by the survey was that 70% reported feeling confident they could have graduated, despite having lower grades. A majority of teens reported they would have stayed in school if classes had helped prepare them for real-world experiences, if higher expectations were required from school personnel and parents, and if more supervision were provided.

Another very interesting aspect of our schools today is that the school schedule may create difficulties for the adolescent. According to Berger (2007), our school structure was established in the early 1900s when only 8% of teens completed high school, and today this structure may not meet the needs of today's students. For example, despite often very large schools, there is little supervision, minimal interaction between teachers and students, and a schedule that does not match the needs of the adolescent.

Researchers have recently investigated developmental factors and contributions to delinquency; however, the amount of sleep adolescents get has not been investigated. Sleep deprivation has been associated with lower stress management, deficiencies in problem solving, and increased health problems. Furthermore, youth who receive 6 hours of sleep or less also report greater violent delinquency (Clinkinbeard, Simi, Evans, & Anderson, 2011). With these negative associations to fewer sleep hours, schools that begin early may contribute to this problem. In a study by Boergers, Gable, and Owens, (2014), beginning school as few as 25 minutes later may more closely align with adolescents' sleep needs. Basically, the biological clock of teens is working against them, with alertness coming at night rather than during the day when school is in session.

Decisions About Sex

Sexual activity is one of the most difficult decisions teens have to make. According to the CDC (2014c), among high school students who were surveyed in 2011 regarding their sexual activity, approximately 47% stated that they engaged in sexual intercourse. But with decisions about sex come other risks such as STDs and teen pregnancy. Sexually active teenagers are at greater risk of getting an STD (i.e., gonorrhea, genital herpes, syphilis, and chlamydia) due to biological susceptibility, not getting the recommended STD tests, not having insurance or transportation, and difficulty in talking about sexual behaviors (CDC, 2014c).

Although teen pregnancy rates have been declining for years, recent reports indicate that they are rising again. Over the past few years, the definition of what teens consider sexual activity has changed because most teens do not believe that being sexually active includes sexual behaviors other than penile–vaginal penetration. For example, most teens believe that oral or anal sex is not considered sex.

Drugs and Alcohol

Tobacco, alcohol, and marijuana are three drugs that are known as *gateway drugs* due to their potential to lead to abuse and addiction, as well as other socially significant problems. Tobacco, the most physically addictive of the gateway drugs, can decrease food consumption, interfere with absorption of nutrients, and reduce fertility. Alcohol is harmful in adolescence due to its effects on the teen's physical, sexual, and emotional development. Marijuana seriously slows thinking processes, especially memory and abstract reasoning, and can create a lack of motivation and indifference toward the future.

Depression

The self-esteem of children tends to drop at around age 12, and adolescents without support from family, friends, or school are more vulnerable to self-esteem issues than others. A loss of self-esteem may push the adolescent toward depression, which can affect 1 in 5 teenage girls and 1 in 10 teenage boys. It is possible that hormonal changes can account for depression, but various stress factors experienced by adolescents also can play a part. Teens can experience internal and external emotional problems. Internalizing problems are manifested inward to inflict harm on oneself (depression or suicide), while externalizing problems are "acted out" by injuring others, destroying property, or defying authority.

Suicide

According to the CDC (2014d), suicide is the third leading cause of death among adolescents. Although suicidal ideation appears to be common enough among high school teens that it may be considered the norm, the act of suicide is rare. According to the CDC (2012a), suicide rates for males are highest for those aged 75 and above. So why do we believe suicide is a common occurrence during this time? First, the rates of suicide have tripled in the last 40 years. Second, although these figures may be alarming, it is important to note that these statistics typically include young adults (ages 20 to 24), who tend to have much higher rates of suicide than adolescents. Third, when adolescents commit suicide, the media is more likely to focus attention on it than on adult suicides. Last, although suicide may not be common, suicide attempts are very common, thus affecting the perception of others.

Establishing a Healthy Independence

The antithesis of establishing a healthy independence can be adolescent rebellion. As discussed previously, adolescents do not have the cognitive ability to recognize what is considered to be risky behavior. According to the CDC (2012b), "motor vehicle crashes are the leading cause of death for U.S. teens. In 2010, seven teens ages 16 to 19 died every day from motor vehicle injuries" (para. 1). Drinking alcohol excessively is associated with approximately 75,000 deaths per year. Youth violence (homicide, physical assaults, extreme sports injuries, exposure to guns at school, etc.) is the second leading cause of death for adolescents.

Based on these alarming statistics, it is crucial that the adults in the lives of teenagers are aware of the risks and are prepared to help them make better decisions. You can be a strong voice to encourage teens to choose wisely. According to Belsky (2007), there are certain factors that can alert school counselors and others to adolescent risk factors, including emotional problems early in life, adolescents with poor family relationships, and adolescents who engage in risky behavior (drinking, doing drugs, being truant, and exhibiting aggressive behaviors) in middle school. She offers six questions to consider when working with at-risk teens (p. 285):

1. Does the child have close family relationships?
2. Does the child have nurturing relationships with other competent and caring adults?
3. Does the child live in a community with good schools and good after-school programs for teenagers?
4. Does the child have close friends who are prosocial?
5. Is the child religious?
6. Does the child have a life passion or special talent?

Answering no to any of these questions does not mean the adolescent is destined to have problems, but the responses may serve as a guide when making decisions about teens who may need some type of intervention.

Psychosocial Development

The primary focus of psychosocial development for adolescents is based on developing *self* and *identity*. The primary question they must answer is "Who am I?" According to Erikson (1968), the developmental struggle for the adolescent is identity versus role confusion. Identity can be defined as unique individual beliefs based on roles, attitudes, values, and aspirations. Erikson believed that unsuccessful teens will develop *identity confusion*, marked by an inability to develop a positive path toward adulthood. Until they are able to integrate all aspects of their identity, they may try out *multiple or possible selves*, various possibilities of who they are or who they wish to become in the future.

Through the process of engaging in multiple or possible selves, teens come closer to integrating all aspects of their identity, and they begin to reach identity achievement. This process occurs when they are successful in establishing their own identity by accepting or rejecting the values, beliefs, and goals they have been or will be exposed to through parents, community, and culture. However, this is a challenging process, with some adolescents being successful and others not. James Marcia (1966) developed four types of identities to help understand the process of identity development, *identity achievement* being the first type. *Identity foreclosure* describes an adolescent who adopts values and goals of parents and culture without questioning. Basically, the process of identity development closes before it actually begins. *Identity diffusion* describes the most troubled adolescent, who lacks commitment to goals or values and is apathetic about taking on any role. *Identity moratorium,* the healthiest approach to identity, describes an adolescent who experiments with different identities, by trying them out in order to make decisions about the future.

Conceptual Application Activity 14.10

Read and respond to the following scenarios. Compare your response with those of your peers.

Tim is a 13-year-old, late-developing boy and physically small compared with the other boys. Tim's father is a large man, who won an Olympic medal in wrestling. Tim's father has always talked about how good he was at wrestling and how disappointed he is with Tim's size. Upon entering middle school, Tim joined the middle school wrestling team. He is not successful and is often hurt during matches. He becomes withdrawn and depressed.

How will you assist Tim in reflecting on his own strengths and weaknesses to determine future sport or career choices?

_____

_____

One of the key aspects of successfully navigating adolescence is a strong support system that consists of family, friends, and positive relationships. This support system helps the adolescent through both good and bad times, and you may be a significant part of that support system.

Considering the impact of developmental issues on children and adolescents is an important aspect of a school counselor's work. Because of the comprehensive nature of human growth and development, a tremendous amount of knowledge can be gained by understanding developmental concepts and how these can be applied in a school setting.

Conceptual Application Activity 14.11

Read and respond to the following scenario. Compare your response with those of your peers.

Michelle is a 16-year-old female who is failing her classes. In middle school, Michelle was a good student who reported wanting to be a doctor. She has become very withdrawn and is associating with a new peer group that is not interested in school and spends most of its time at the local mall. The school has reported to Michelle's parents that she has been absent from school multiple times for the past few weeks. Michelle appears content with following her new peer group rather than considering her future goals. She reports having no career goals or interest in her future.

How can you help Michelle develop a sense of who she is in relation to others?

_____

_____

CONCLUSION

Throughout this chapter you have reviewed many theories and concepts related to human development. Your task is to understand how developmental constructs influence your counseling relationship with your students. Not all the students with whom you work will be at the same developmental stages biologically, cognitively, or socially. School counselors have the responsibility to work with all students in the school and to facilitate an understanding of developmental issues with other educators and parents/guardians so that each counselee will have the opportunity to develop his or her potential to be a contributing member of our society.

WEBSITES

Social and emotional development issues in middle childhood are found on this website: http://psychology.about.com/od/early-child-development/a/social-emotional-development-in-middle-childhood.htm

Cognitive developmental issues are discussed on this website: http://psychology.about.com/od/early-child-development/a/social-emotional-development-in-middle-childhood.htm

Many developmental issues that impact adolescents are found in this website: http://childdevelopmentinfo.com/child-development/teens_stages/

REFERENCES

American Lung Association. (2012). *Asthma & children fact sheet*. Retrieved from www.lung.org/lung-disease/asthma/resources/facts-and-figures/asthma-children-fact-sheet.html

American Psychiatric Association. (2013). *Diagnostic and statistical manual of mental disorders* (5th ed.). Washington, DC: Author.

Bandura, A. (1977). *Social learning theory*. Englewood Cliffs, NJ: Prentice-Hall.

Bandura, A. (1986). *Social foundations of thought and action*. Englewood Cliffs, NJ: Prentice-Hall.

Baumrind, D. (1971). Current patterns of parental authority. *Developmental Psychology, 4*(1), 1–103.

Belsky, J. (2007). *Experiencing the lifespan*. New York: Worth.

Berger, K.S. (2007). *The developing person through the life span*. New York: Worth.

Boergers, J., Gable, C.J., & Owens, J.A. (2014). Later school time is associated with improved sleep and daytime functioning in adolescents. *Journal of Developmental and Behavioral Pediatrics, 35*, 11–17.

Bridgeland, J. M., DiIulio, J. J. Jr, Morison, K. B. (2006). *The silent epidemic: Perspectives of high school dropouts*. Retrieved from www.ignitelearning.com/pdf/TheSilentEpidemic3-06FINAL.pdf

Bronfenbrenner, U. (1979). *The ecology of human development*. Cambridge, MA: Harvard University Press.

CDC [Centers for Disease Control and Prevention]. (2012a). *Suicide: Facts at a glance*. Retrieved from www.cdc.gov/violenceprevention/pdf/Suicide-DataSheet-a.pdf

CDC. (2012b). *Teen drivers: Fact sheet*. Retrieved from www.cdc.gov/MotorVehicleSafety/Teen_Drivers/teen drivers_factsheet.html

CDC. (2014a). *Childhood obesity facts*. Retrieved from www.cdc.gov/HealthyYouth/obesity/facts.htm

CDC. (2014b). *Data and statistics: Prevalence*. Retrieved from www.cdc.gov/ncbddd/autism/data.html

CDC. (2014c). *Sexually transmitted diseases*. Retrieved from www.cdc.gov/std/life-stages-populations/STDFact-Teens.htm

CDC. (2014d). *Prevention*. Retrieved from www.cdc.gov/ViolencePrevention/suicide/index.html

Clinkinbeard, S.S., Simi, P., Evans, M.K., & Anderson, A.L. (2011). Sleep and delinquency: Does the amount of sleep matter? *Journal of Youth Adolescence, 40,* 916–930. doi: 10.1007/s10964–010–9594–6

Detecting autism at age 1. (2013). Health secrets. *The Week Magazine,* p. 29.

Elkind, D. (1978). Understanding the young adolescent. *Adolescence, 13,* 127–134.

Erikson, E. (1950). *Childhood and society.* New York: W.W. Norton & Co.

Erikson, E. (1968). *Identity: Youth and crisis.* New York: W.W. Norton & Co.

Guttmacher Institute. (2012, February). *Facts on American teens' sources of information about sex.* Retrieved from www.guttmacher.org/pubs/FB-Teen-Sex-Ed.html

Hall, G.S. (1904). *Adolescence.* New York: Arno Press.

Health Scare of the Week. (2014, June 14). *The Week Magazine,* p. 18.

Kohlberg, L. (1976). Moral stages and moralization: The cognitive-developmental approach. In T. Lickona (Ed.), *Moral development and behavior* (pp. 31–55). New York: Holt, Rinehart & Winston.

Lefrancois, G.L. (1996). *The lifespan.* Belmont, CA: Wadsworth.

Marcia, J. (1966). Development and validation of ego-identity status. *Journal of Personality and Social Psychology, 3,* 551–558.

National Institute of Mental Health. (n.d.). *Attention deficit hyperactivity disorder (ADHD).* Retrieved from www.nimh.nih.gov/health/topics/attention-deficit-hyperactivity-disorder-adhd/index.shtml

Piaget, J. (1926). *The language and thought of the child* (M. Worden, Trans.). New York: Harcourt Brace Jovanovich.

Piaget, J. (1929). *The child's conception of the world* (J. Tomlinson & A. Tomlinson, Trans.). New York: Harcourt Brace Jovanovich.

Piaget, J. (1972). Intellectual evolution from adolescence to adulthood. *Human Development, 15,* 1–12.

Piaget, J., & Inhelder, B. (1969). *The psychology of the child.* New York: Basic Books.

Rembeck, G.I., & Gunnarsson, R.K. (2004). Improving pre- and postmenarcheal 12-year-old girls' attitudes toward menstruation. *Health Care for Women International, 25,* 680–698.

Santrock, J.W. (2012). *A topical approach to life-span development* (6th ed.). New York: McGraw Hill.

Seligman, L., & Reichenberg, L.W. (2014). *Theories of counseling and psychotherapy* (4th ed.) New York, NY: Pearson.

Vygotsky, L.S. (1986). *Thought and language* (A. Kozulin, Trans.). Cambridge, MA: MIT Press. (Original work published 1934)

Weaver, F. (2014, April 11). The mainstreaming of mindfulness meditation. *The Week,* p. 9. http://theweek.com/article/index/259351/the-mainstreaming-of-mindfulness-meditation

Section IV
Completing the Clinical Experiences

15 Transitioning Forward

From Clinical Experiences to a Professional School Counselor

Michael Bundy

CACREP Standards

Foundations

A. Knowledge

4. Knows professional organizations, preparation standards, and credentials that are relevant to the practice of school counseling.

    The purpose of this chapter is to:

- present ideas on how to successfully terminate the clinical experiences,
- provide tools to self-assess your competencies as a school counselor with regard for knowledge, skills, and attitudes,
- suggest strategies for interviewing for a position as a professional school counselor,
- offer ways to enhance professional identity and to obtain professional development once employed.

INTRODUCTION

The time has come for you to plan how to leave your practicum or internship site. Your site supervisor has encouraged you and has provided you with positive guidance. Teachers and administrators at your clinical sites gave you support and assistance when you needed it. Many students were changed by the individual and small-group sessions you held with them. By showing your appreciation to them, future counselors-in-training who follow you to this school will be warmly received too. So, give careful consideration to how you separate from your students, teachers, site supervisor, and others with whom you have worked closely.

Terminating Relationships With Students

The process of terminating a counseling relationship can be a stressful time for students, but it can also be an opportunity to affirm their growth and see ending as a new beginning. Students who have received special attention from you may become uneasy when you begin to discuss terminating their counseling sessions. They may need help considering what it will be like to function without you as part of their support system. Seeing the end of one relationship or event as a natural time to redefine and begin new relationships and activities is a healthy way to perceive change. Here are a few tips on closing your relationships with students and some examples of what you can say to implement the suggestions in a session with them:

- *Give students advance notice.* You should begin talking with students about ending their counseling at least two sessions before their last one. *What to say:* "Jill, in two weeks my time at Jefferson

School will end because my internship training with your school counselor Ms. Jones will be completed. I would like for us to talk a bit about what we have done together to help you with the goals you wanted to work on."

- *Have students self-assess their progress.* Allow students to express the progress they think they have made as a result of their relationship with you. You should help them acknowledge their accomplishments in terms of how they changed their behaviors, their thoughts, and/or their emotional responses. *What to say:* "I'd like to hear what changes you think you have made since we have been meeting. You had some goals you wanted to accomplish. What progress do you think you have made toward them?"

- *Offer your observations.* Be prepared to provide students with your assessment of their progress. Students often need to hear what you think of what they have done. This can be an encouraging and confidence-building time for them. The more specific your observations, the more powerful and meaningful they will be to your students. *What to say:* "Jill, would you like for me to tell you what I think you have done these past few weeks toward achieving your counseling goals? I have noticed that you no longer say things like 'I must do what Bill tells me to do or he won't like me anymore.' "

- *Anticipate future challenges.* Help students identify potential stumbling blocks they may encounter. It is quite likely that students will continue to face challenges when their counseling sessions with you are over. Talk about those potential hurdles and how students might overcome them. This could be another confidence builder for students as you help them realize how resourceful they have become. *What to say:* "Jill, what will you think if Bill says that he wants to spend time apart? What will you say to him? How will you control your emotions?"

- *Identify student resources.* Help students utilize resources within their support systems for times when they may need extra assistance to overcome difficulties. Those resources could be the adults they respect and with whom they have a good working relationship (e.g., school counselor, favorite teacher, trusted relative, youth minister). *What to say:* "Jill, should one of those 'stumbling blocks' begin to give you a big hassle, what can you do? Is there someone you can talk to about it?"

- *Create a picture of the future.* In order to help students feel confident and build resiliency to cope with the challenges to come, it is usually effective to have students think and talk about what they would like to have happen, new relationships they may want to develop, or activities they want to start. If this is too difficult, have students try to imagine how they would like things to be for them. This could give them a positive image and provide motivation to continue moving forward along the path of successful change they found in counseling with you. *What to say:* "Jill, where would you like to be in six months when it comes to having or not having boyfriends?"

- *Write notes to students.* Recording your goodbyes in handwritten notes can be powerful and can give meaningful messages to students. Students have been known to carry these treasured thoughts with them for months. Your note should express appreciation for what you have learned from them, and it should communicate encouragement to them to continue growing, learning, and moving forward. The following notes were written by a school counseling intern to significant people at her internship site.

Janna,

You are truly a very special person. Your mom would be so proud of where you are. That first day you made me feel at ease. I looked forward to seeing your smiling face every day. I will miss our talks. Remember to give your dad a break; he loves you very much and you are still his baby. Study hard in college and you will do well. People who deal with you will see that you are genuine and honest. You are a great role model. Watch over Vicki and please continue your friendship with her. You will be a tremendous school counselor one day. You have already changed lives . . . including mine . . . you will always have a place in my heart.

Debbi

Conceptual Application Activity 15.1

Think about one of your past or current students. To make this activity more challenging, think of a student with whom you had difficulty. Write a brief note to this student. In your note, review resources available and create a positive picture of the future.

_____

_____

Terminating counseling groups should be another growth experience for students and can be a fun activity as well. Most counselors-in-training give their groups a 2-week notice so the students have ample time to process their feelings and plan for the future. The following are a few suggestions that counselors-in-training have found to be effective closing activities:

- *Have refreshments at the last group session.* Food always makes for an enjoyable time. Be sure that your refreshments are consistent with any dietary restrictions of group members or school rules. Popcorn and juice boxes are usually safe for elementary students. Older students could be responsible for bringing their own tasty treats to the final group meeting. Put some limits on what can be brought; food can become a distraction to your final group agenda. Have some group process activities planned so closure is focused and meaningful.
- *Have group members acknowledge their progress.* This would be a time for group members to proudly announce changes they have made as a result of group support. Expressive art activities or open letters written to the group provide structured approaches for sharing retrospective observations.
- *Give feedback to group members.* Upon terminating the group, give each group member your assessment of his/her progress in specific terms before you leave. Follow a similar approach to that which is given above for individual students; offer your observations to the group as a whole and/or to members in individual sessions.
- *Write notes to group members.* These notes should offer specific observations and encouragement. Your message could be to the whole group allowing them time to respond, or you could give notes to individual members outside the group session. If the notes are read to the whole group, it could make a powerful closing session that builds cohesiveness among group members or assists members to see their peers from a different perspective. If your note contains content to a specific student, provide that student with positive pragmatic feedback to help him/her continue improving upon the growth already started in the group. Imagine how a group member would be affected upon receiving the note below.

Emilie,
  How can I ever put in words how proud I am of you? You never missed a group session and always kept up with the other students. You now have the confidence to keep a smile on your face. I know how hard it is, but just remember that we talked about how we can control what we think and how we act, and as a result our feelings will follow. I have seen you do this for the past five weeks. Your teachers have noticed how much easier you are to get along with and how your anger doesn't boil over so quickly. YOU are the one who chooses these actions, you made your own decisions and you can continue on. I will miss you, but know that all the lessons we talked about are still in your head and you can pull out your group notes and use them when you feel stressed. Please don't forget to be as proud of yourself as I am of you!!!

                                                                              Debbi

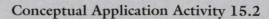

Conceptual Application Activity 15.2

Consider the same student you identified in the previous activity or think of a different student. Review the student's progress and provide feedback specific to him/her. Be encouraging and be honest.

_____

_____

Terminating With Colleagues

Bringing relationships with your new colleagues to a close requires a heartfelt expression of appreciation for the mentorship and collaboration they provided. Throughout your experience, your site supervisor offered you wisdom and encouragement. Teachers in your school site worked with you to meet student needs, resulting in confidence in your counseling and consulting competencies. It may seem that a simple 'thank you' note would be insufficient to communicate your feelings toward them, but it carries special meaning to those who receive one. Shortly, you expect to be employed as a professional school counselor, and when this dream becomes your reality, these folks who helped you during your training may now be meeting with you as new colleagues in professional meetings or conferences. The impression you leave them with will be carried over into new professional relationships. Give them something extraordinary to remember about you. Try writing a note similar to the following:

> *Bruce,*
>
> *The words 'Thank you' can hardly express how I feel about all I have learned and experienced in school counseling this semester. Your training has been exemplary, and I have learned so much. Seeing CT (Choice Theory) in action is so much more powerful than just reading about it. You taught me how to teach others but never criticize them. You taught, by example, how to empower students to find the answers for themselves. You have shown me what school counselors are doing on a daily basis. You truly made a difference in so many lives; just add me to the list. Thank you so much for allowing me to be your student! I hope someday to make you proud. I will never forget this time and what a truly great mentor you are! You're really the best!*
>
> *Debbi*

Terminating With Administrators

You must not avoid or forget to say goodbye to administrators who approved your placement and supported your clinical activities. Central office supervisors and building-level principals may not have worked as closely with you as your site supervisor or the teachers, but their support was certainly critical to your success. Moreover, they will be important to your future job plans. When you apply for a counselor position, the employing principal will likely call the principal where you conducted your clinical experiences to ask about your performance. You will certainly want to leave the principal at your sites with a positive impression of your maturity, independence, and competencies as a school counselor.

Here are two things you should consider doing: (1) make an appointment to debrief the principal of the things you accomplished before you leave, and (2) send a note of thanks to the principal and any central office personnel involved in your placement. The following is a note written by a school counseling intern to her site principal after she met with him before she left her internship experience in his building.

Mr. Schneitman:

Thank you so much for the opportunity of completing my internship at Jefferson County High School. You are a multi-talented administrator who has put together an awesome staff. I also know that I would not want your job for love or money.

Thank you for allowing me the pleasure to put together a program using the peer counselors already in place as mentors for special-needs children and helping them learn social and emotional skills. You allowed me time for group counseling during school and gave me a place in the media center to conduct my sessions. You have allowed our program to have some great successes and for that I will be forever indebted. I wish you, your staff, and your students continued success.

Debbi

Conceptual Application Activity 15.3

Write a thank you termination note to either a colleague or an administrator. Express your sentiments and provide specific examples of how this person assisted you. Keep in mind that this person may provide a reference or recommendation letter for you or even be your future employer.

_____

_____

SELF-ASSESSMENT AS A TRANSITION ACTIVITY

With your clinical experiences almost finished, and as you continue your transition from student to professional school counselor, it can be both an anxious and an exciting time for you. At this point, you should reflect upon the development of your competencies as a future professional school counselor. You will want to approach this new challenge with the same intensity and determination that you exemplified during your training program. But where do you begin the process?

Because counselor preparation programs provide ample opportunities for students to examine themselves and to facilitate personal growth, most counselors-in-training know themselves fairly well at this stage of their training. The information you have accumulated from your counseling coursework should be used to help you identify your strengths and areas that may need further development. Most recently, you have (or will have), feedback from your site supervisor and from your program supervisor. They have objectively assessed your readiness for assuming the responsibilities that come with organizing a comprehensive school counseling program as an appropriately credentialed professional. You should take these data and develop a plan to maximize your strength and overcome your relative weaknesses; however, a more systematic self-assessment would be most beneficial to your planning.

The American School Counselor Association (ASCA) has a long history of providing vigorous leadership in articulating a professional identity for counselors who work primarily in school settings. As needs of pre-K–12 students have changed and as society's expectations have changed for schools, the ASCA has been at the forefront in promoting standards for counseling training and for the practice of counselors. As you have already learned, the ASCA developed the School Counselor Professional Competencies document that lists the knowledge, abilities and skills, and attitudes counselors should possess in order to implement a comprehensive school counseling program. In addition, school counseling program faculty can use these competencies to assess how well their counselors-in-training are meeting identified proficiencies. These competencies were formatted in Chapter 6 to assist you in identifying tasks to perform during your training, and can be revisited each year to identify knowledge, abilities and skills, and attitudes that you still need to attain. With this information, develop a self-improvement plan that includes long-term goals and short-term goals that reflect the degree to which you need to acquire certain competencies. For example, suppose you expect to be employed as an elementary school counselor and you consider that you need more experience in classroom management. If so, then this is a high priority and you will need to identify short-term goals to gain competency in this area. Completing this self-assessment will also give some points to consider when preparing to apply for and interview for a counseling position. Interviewees will certainly wish to highlight their strong points and acknowledge a plan to address relative weaknesses. For example, in completing an application or during an interview, prospective employees are often asked what they consider to be their strengths for the job and what they believe are weaknesses. The self-assessment provides an informed position from which you can confidently respond.

Box 15.1

U.S. News and World Report (2014) ranked the 100 best jobs based on growth volume, growth percentage, median salary, job prospects, employment rate, stress level, and work-life balance. School counselor ranked number 86 out of jobs in all areas, and number 17 in the best social services jobs.

THE APPLICATION PROCESS

Searching for a job as a professional school counselor can be a daunting process. Here are a few tips to assist you with this journey.

Searching and Applying for Job Openings

- *Use technology to accelerate the search.* As the old commercial said, "Let your fingers do the walking." Using the Internet, research all of the school systems where you wish to apply. Go to the Human Resources link and complete the online application. You will find that almost all school systems now prefer applicants to submit electronic applications. Even though surrounding area school systems may not currently have a school counseling position posted, it is advisable to complete an application for each of your desired locations anyway. You will soon learn that school principals know of their staff vacancies long before they are announced and generally begin a search to fill the opening long before the position is officially posted. Therefore, it is better to have your application on file for principals to review as soon as they begin their search.
- *Proofread online applications.* A word of caution: It would be prudent for you to complete a hard copy of the application before you enter it online. Before you hit the 'submit' key, you should make a copy of your online application and proofread it. Proper grammar and spelling are essential!
- *Attend monthly meetings of the local counselor association.* You should attend these meetings, especially during your clinical experiences. It is here that you will develop your professional network and hear of potential job openings. This will give you advance notice to begin developing your strategy for applying. You can 'pick the brains' of your new colleagues to assess the counseling needs of the schools where vacancies will be. You can begin to shape your application and start to prepare for the interview for those schools.
- *Request letters of recommendation.* Ask professors who know the quality of your work best, especially internship and practicum professors, as well as your school site supervisors, to write a recommendation. Give them something in writing that describes some points about yourself and some activities you conducted well at your sites (such as a résumé). Express your passion for school counseling, but do not use too much hyperbole. You may also provide them with a list of your strengths and skills (see your self-assessment results) for them to use.

- *Prepare a portfolio.* This professional portfolio can be taken to a job interview to show examples of your class work applicable to developing a school counseling program. For example, you could include a career lesson plan you wrote for one of your classes. Your practicum and internship will also provide excellent opportunities to add to your portfolio. Include counseling activities, group lesson plans, pictures of students, notes from people you helped, and the like. Make it well organized and visually attractive. Or, you may prefer electronic portfolios that contain artifacts of your work. A link to this electronic portfolio can be sent to the building principal in advance of your interview. For more information about electronic portfolios, go to the Teacher Tab website: http://eduscapes.com/tap/topic82.htm
- *Develop a strong résumé.* Prepare a one- or two-page résumé that is concise, organized, and professional. It must present you as the outstanding candidate that you are! See Figure 15.1. Email it to principals who have or will have counselor positions available.
- *Have others review your materials.* Ask your classmates, professors, site supervisors, and others to review your résumé and portfolio. They may have some great suggestions to add or other change materials that will enhance your image.

Conceptual Application Activity 15.4

Prepare or revise your résumé. Give it to three people and request written feedback. Make revisions based on this feedback. Be prepared to continue to update and revise your résumé on an ongoing basis.

Preparing for an Interview

Once you have received an appointment for an interview, you want to be overprepared. Visit that school's website and thoroughly research the school. Also, visit websites of the school district and the state department of education. Analyze the school's testing results and its No Child Left Behind status. Pay particular attention to the disaggregated data of subgroups. Ask yourself, "What can I do as a school counselor to support the academic development of *all* students in this school? What special challenges does this student population have that I as a school counselor can address?" Note any special successes this school announces on its homepage. Take time to visit websites of teachers that are linked from the school's homepage. What feelings about the school climate, its staff, and students do you glean from the homepage? This information can provide you with possible issues within this school that may indicate possible questions that you could be asked during the interview. They could also indicate questions that you wish to raise to your interviewer.

Box 15.2

"I am wondering if anyone has any suggestions for getting hired as a school counselor." This question was recently asked by one of my student trainees at a local counselor's meeting. Practitioners offered the following answers:

a. *Continue to attend the professional development meetings to network.*
b. *Substitute teach or volunteer in the schools. This helps make you visible and school personnel will have an opportunity to know who you are.*
c. *Work with as many different populations as you can. When I applied for a job I was asked about my work with "at risk" youth.*
d. *Always follow up interviews with a phone call or email thanking administrators for the interview. If you don't get the job, don't be shy about calling the interviewers to ask how you can improve your interviewing skills.*

William Robert Woods
46 Volunteer St.
Big Orange, TN 37830
(865) 326-3333
woodswr@utk.edu

Career Goal

To develop, implement, and lead a comprehensive school counseling program aligned with ASCA National Model.

Education

The University of Tennessee-Knoxville
MS in School Counseling (2014)
GPA (4.0 Scale): 3.95
BS in Psychology (2012)
GPA (4.0 Scale): 3.825
Dean's List, Phi Beta Kappa

Professional Association Membership

American School Counselor Association
Tennessee School Counselor Association
Smoky Mountain Counseling Association

Experiences

School Counseling Practicum at Modesto Middle School, Modesto, CA

- 60 hours of providing individual counseling
- 20 hours of conducting group counseling
- 10 hours of teaching classroom guidance lessons
- 15 hours of supervision

School Counseling Internship at Excel Elementary School and at Above Average High School, Oak Ridge, TN 37830

- Completed over 600 hours
- Counseled students individually and in small groups
- Consulted with teachers and parents
- Collaborated in IEP & RTI meetings and parent–teacher conferences
- Taught classroom guidance lessons

Volunteer at GREAT KIDS Summer Program, High Achievers School, Oak Ridge, TN

- Worked with special needs students in small group as teacher assistant

Accomplishments

- Created a career information webpage for middle school students
- Presented research paper at Smoky Mountain Counseling Association conference, entitled "Effective use of peer counselors in high school"

Skills

- Computer Skills: Proficient in word processing and data management, multimedia production, webpage development
- Foreign Language Skills: Spanish

Figure 15.1 Sample résumé.

School Counselor Interview Questions

1. Tell us about yourself—what experiences have prepared you for the position of professional school counselor?

2. Explain the national standards in school counseling and how you would use them to plan your counseling program.

3. Talk about how you would develop our classroom school counseling program.

4. How will you establish relationships with outside school resources?

5. Tell us about a small-group counseling series you have conducted.

6. Our population is unique—what strengths do you have to work with our students and their families?

7. We have kindergartners who cry every day for weeks into the school year. How would you help beginning kindergartners and parents adjust to school?

8. Tell us how you would help a teacher who is highly frustrated and feeling overwhelmed by the behavior of a student.

9. What are some of the best practices in school counseling you have come across?

10. How can you help us analyze and interpret test data to guide our instruction and curriculum decisions?

11. As a school counselor, how would you facilitate parent involvement in our school and in our classrooms?

12. How would you use technology as part of your counseling program?

13. What do you love about school counseling?

14. How would you show that what you are doing is effective?

15. Do you have any questions for us?

Figure 15.2 Interview questions.

A drop-in visit to your interview school may be a turn-off to the busy principal and staff; however, it could be beneficial for you to drive around the community it serves. If you get a chance to talk with parents or students, you might gather information that you may be able to use during your interview (perception data). For example, what are some needs of this school's student population? What are some strengths of this teaching staff? How does (or could) the counselor contribute?

With the data you have collected about this school, you are now ready to prepare for your interview. Think about the questions that may be asked and consider your responses. Figure 15.2 lists actual questions asked during a school counselor interview.

The interview process has been such an important part of the transition from training to employment that suggestions have been made to counselor educators to add this component to their training programs (Nichter & Nelson, 2006). Administrators who want a counseling program that is aligned with the ASCA National Model are seeking school counselors who can deliver such a program, and are receiving suggestions on interview questions to ask (Meyers, 2006). They can visit the ASCA website where they will find a link tab especially for "Administrators" and a link called "Interviewing School Counselors." As a counselor applicant, you may wish to review these questions as well.

Figure 15.3 School counselor applicant discussing her educational background and her portfolio with the school principal.

Source: Shutterstock

Conceptual Application Activity 15.5

After you have considered other questions that may be asked during your interview and you have considered your responses, role-play an interview with your classmates. They may have other questions and suggestions on how to respond. While practice may not make you 'perfect,' in this instance practice will certainly help you fill gaps and build your confidence.

The Interview

The following are some tips on conducting yourself during the interview. By now you are fully prepared, and you want to make an outstanding impression that will remain with interview committee members long after you have departed the meeting.

- *Dress appropriately.* Business professional is considered clothing du jour.
- *Arrive early for your interview.* You might have an opportunity to chat with staff members before you go into the interview room.
- *Have several copies of your résumé printed on quality paper.* An intern who interviewed for a job made a good impression when she was able to distribute a copy of her résumé to each committee member.
- *Bring an attractive portfolio.* Have it available to show illustrations of your work during your training. For example, in response to a question, you might mention that you have an example in your portfolio of something similar you did during your practicum and internship. Or, you may provide a link to your electronic portfolio.
- *Remember to use good non-verbal skills.* Lean forward slightly and maintain good eye contact with *each* committee member when answering each question. Don't just focus on one person or the committee member asking the question. This shows confidence.

- *Speak clearly and confidently.* Use a strong voice that reflects your assurance in what you say. Talk at your normal pace to show comfort and command of a comprehensive school counseling program.
- *Answer the questions directly and succinctly.* Principals like interviewees to keep their answers to the point. However, you want to ensure that you demonstrate sufficient knowledge and enthusiasm for school counseling.
- *Relax and believe in yourself.* Rely upon your training in human relationship and your preparation. You will do well!

PROFESSIONAL CREDENTIALS

Professional credentials are required at the state and district levels in order to be employed to practice school counseling. They are also a way of promoting professional identity and of demonstrating a higher level of counseling competency. Three areas of professional identity are presented in this chapter: (1) the basic requirements for employment, (2) ways to continue professional development, and (3) paths to obtain national credentials.

Qualifications Vary by State

Requirements for credentialing professional school counselors differ from state to state. Some states issue a license to practice school counseling, while other states issue a certificate. In addition, states change their criteria for issuing credentials from time to time. You likely already know the qualifications to practice as a school counselor in the state in which you are receiving your training, but if you wish to apply for a school counseling position in another state, you will need to know the requirements in that state. Some states have a reciprocity agreement with neighboring states to allow a counselor with credentials in one state to practice in another state. Another resource is the ASCA homepage, www.schoolcounselor.org, where you search at the "State Certification Requirements" link, or call the ASCA at (703) 683-ASCA if you need further assistance. A state-by-state description of requirements and a link to the department of education of each state will have more specific information.

The Praxis Exams

Most states require the Praxis Professional School Counselor (0421/5421) in order to earn licensure or certification. Test code 0421 is a 2-hour, 120 multiple-choice, paper and pencil test, whereas the 5421 is a 2-hour, 120 multiple-choice, computer-based exam. The Praxis Exams are developed and administered by the Educational Testing Service (ETS). The exam covers approximately 22 questions in foundations, 54 questions in delivery of services, 18 questions in management, and 26 questions in accountability. For more information regarding this test, go to www.ets.org/s/praxis/pdf/0421-5421.pdf

To register for the Praxis, go to its website at www.ets.org/praxis/ or call ETS at 1-800-772-9476. You can purchase study guides from ETS to help you prepare for the exam.

Continuing Education Requirements

Once you obtain your state certificate or license, you will be required to renew it periodically. Each state has a specific time frame in which school counselors and teachers must apply for renewal of their credentials. To renew state credentials, successful completion of a given amount of continuing education activities is required. This continuing education requirement could be called continuing education units (CEUs), professional development, in-service education, professional growth activities, or accredited institution credits. Ongoing professional training may be in-service programs hosted by your school district or it could include professional conferences held by your local, state, or national counseling association. The amount and type of continuing education you must complete within the given period varies from state to state. Check with your state department of education or your school district's human resources director for the specific requirements of re-credentialing. On its website, the ASCA has a general overview of each state's requirements and contact information.

National Credentials

Once you have fulfilled the requirements for a school counselor credential at the state level, you may wish to seek additional qualifications. There are two organizations at the national level where you can obtain additional credentials: the National Board of Certified Counselors (NBCC) and the National Board of Professional Teaching Standards (NBPTS). The benefits of national certification are three-fold: By participating in the certification process, you will be acknowledged for your competencies and accomplishments as a nationally certified counselor; you will be elevating your professional identity, which could be important to your building principal and your community stakeholders; and you may receive financial incentives from your state and/or local school board.

National Certified School Counselor

The NBCC was founded in 1982 to develop an examination of counseling competencies for practitioners to obtain national certification. In the late 1980s, working with the American School Counselor Association and the American Counseling Association (ACA), the NBCC developed a specialty credential for school counselors called National Certified School Counselor (NCSC). In 1991, the first NCSC was awarded to a school counselor. At the present time, there are approximately 2500 certificated school counselors nationally (NCSC, n.d.).

The application process involves documenting a master's degree or higher from a school counseling program accredited by the Council for Accreditation of Counseling and Related Educational Programs (CACREP) or regionally accredited; a state credential in school counseling; at least 3 academic years of postgraduate counseling supervision and work experience as a school counselor in a pre-K–12 school setting; and a passing score on the National School Counselor Examination (NCSCE). The NCSCE format includes seven simulated counseling cases and 40 multiple-choice questions. The exam covers the following content areas: School Counseling Program Delivery, Assessment and Career Development, Program Administration and Professional Development, Counseling Process Concepts and Applications, and Family-School Involvements. You can receive more information about the NCSC application process and the NCSCE test by visiting the NBCC website at www.nbcc.org.

The NCC is the basic certification for all NBCC specialty areas, such as the NCSC. NBCC provides school counselors with the opportunity to earn two credentials with a single exam and application process. For counselors who do not hold NCC credentials, NBCC offers a combination NCC/NCSC application. By completing this combined process for the NCSC, counselors cover two credentials, NCC and NCSC. Counselors who already hold NCC credentials can apply for NCSC.

These certifications are issued for a period of 5 years, during which you must complete 100 clock hours of counseling-related continuing education, of which 25 hours must be in the area of school counseling. Check the NCC website for current costs of exams and annual maintenance fees.

Some states provide financial incentives to NCSC-certified counselors. In addition, some local school districts award salary supplements to school counselors with NCSC certification. For more information about NCC/NCSC advantages and the application process, see the National Board for Certified Counselors at www.nbcc.org/ or call 1-336-547-0607.

National Board for Professional Teaching Standards

Founded in 1987, the National Board for Professional Teaching Standards (NBPTS) is dedicated to advancing quality instruction by recognizing teachers, school counselors, and others who distinguish themselves through accomplishing certain performance standards. There are eleven standards in which school counselors must show evidence of meeting. They include: School Counseling Programs; School Counseling and Student Competencies; Human Growth and Development; Counseling Theories and Techniques; Equity, Fairness, and Diversity; School Climate; Collaboration with Family and Community; Informational Resources and Technology; Student Assessment; Leadership, Advocacy, and Professional Identity; and Reflective Practice. These are very similar to the School Counselor Competencies as identified by ASCA.

Applicants for NBPTS must hold a state school counselor credential and have practiced school counseling for at least 3 years. Interestingly, a master's degree is not required for this credential. The application process for NBPTS involves a performance-based assessment with two key components: a portfolio of counseling practice and an examination of counseling knowledge. The portfolio includes student work, video recordings, and other counseling examples.

NBPTS certification for accomplished school counselors is for a 10-year period. Check the NBPTS website for current application and recertification fees. There is no annual fee to maintain the certification, but the Profile of Professional Growth must be completed within the 10-year period. The Profile of Professional Growth documents the three areas of continuing education that accomplished school counselors have completed. The recertification process involves a video recording of performance.

All 50 states offer some financial incentives to offset the application costs involved in the NBPTS certification process; however, those funds are limited. Each state has specific guidelines and deadlines, so counselors seeking to request these funds to help with the cost of NBPTS should contact their respective state departments of education as soon as possible. An increasing number of local school districts are electing to provide increased pay to accomplished school counselors certified by NBPTS. You should check with your local human resources director and/or your state's department of education for details *before* you begin the application process. For more information about the application process and possible financial support available to assist with the application costs, visit the National Board for Professional Teaching Standards at www.nbpts.org or call 1-800-228-3224.

Comparison of NCC/NCSC and NBPTS

Both the NCC and the NBPTS offer opportunities for school counselors to grow and be acknowledged professionally through the demonstration of competencies beyond state credentialing requirements. Both afford school counselors a higher level of professionalism when they earn national credentials, and both require additional assessment of knowledge and skill in implementing comprehensive school counseling programs (Milsom & Akos, 2007).

Each approach has advantages and limitations, as you can see in Table 15.1 below. Should you prepare yourself to earn national certification? If so, which path to national certification should you choose? Both require 3 years of experience before one can obtain national certification, which gives a beginning counselor ample time to prepare for the rigors of an evaluation based upon national standards. The NBPTS assessment is heavily weighted in performance and written measures, while NCC/NCSC is rooted in a multiple-choice examination. While NBPTS is initially more expensive, limited financial assistance is available from some local districts, state departments of education, and national resources.

Table 15.1 NCC/NCSC vs. NBPTS

	NCC/NCSC	*NBPTS*
Minimum educational requirement	Master's degree	Bachelor's degree w/state license
Supervision experience requirement	100 hours over 3 years	3 years
Written examination	Yes	Yes
Portfolio of work	No	Yes
Period of certification	5 years	10 years
Required continuing education	100 clock hours	Complete *Profile of Professional Growth*
Salary supplements	Yes	Yes

It is believed that pursuing either one or both certifications will make one a better school counselor (Milsom & Akos, 2007). Nationally certified counselors are perceived as more professional and competent and are likely to be more respected by their principals. This typically means more support for their counseling programs. The bottom line is that a growing number of states and local school districts are providing additional compensation to nationally certified teachers and counselors.

MEMBERSHIP IN PROFESSIONAL ORGANIZATIONS

As you complete your final preparations to become a professional school counselor, it would be prudent for you to consider membership in professional organizations. Associating with other counselors will help you to maintain your enthusiasm and your passion for your work and will provide opportunities to engage in professional activities and resources specific to the field.

The American School Counseling Association is the ACA counselor division that supports and advocates for school counselors; however, only one in nine school counselors belong to ASCA (Hatch, 2008). This is unfortunate in that many school counselors are missing out on the personal and professional growth activities that the ASCA promotes through its many workshops and conferences and the tremendous resources available to *members only* at its website. The following are some professional materials and information members can access at the ASCA website:

- *ASCA Resource Center* contains links, publications, sample articles, sample documents, and journal articles on almost 50 topics, ranging from abuse to war/deployment.
- *ASCA Legal & Ethical* includes ASCA's Ethical Standards for School Counselors, journal archives on legal and ethical issues, and a forum where members can submit ethical questions.
- The *Publications* link enables members to search the archives of ASCA publications such as *Professional School Counseling*, *ASCA School Counselor*, and *ASCA Aspects*.
- *Professional Development* provides a comprehensive listing of state conferences, site-based training, upcoming conferences, and training opportunities on the ASCA National Model.
- The *Online Store* offers professional books and materials at discounted prices to members.
- The *ASCA National Model* link gives detailed information about the four quadrants of the model and how to become involved in the Ramp Program.
- *ASCA Scene* is a social networking site that gives school counselors a method to connect and to communicate using blogging, discussion forums, and the like. This is an excellent service for soliciting suggestions to issues and concerns school counselors typically face.
- *ASCAway* is a podcast service to provide members with information about school counseling issues, trends, and interviews. You can hear relevant information presented in a timely and portable manner.

The ACA is the umbrella organization dedicated to promoting counseling as a profession. Its mission is more global and its scope is broader than that of ASCA and provides a very useful service to school counselors. There are additional resources ACA provides that are of mutual interest to school counselors that can be accessed on the ACA website.

- *Resources:* The *Ethics* link provides Ethics and Professional Standards services and promotes ACA online learning opportunities to receive continuing professional education.
- The *Publications* link allows ACA members to search articles among its publications. This tool is valuable when a counselor needs to find critical information in a timely manner.

As education reformers rapidly revise the educational landscape on which school counselors must tread, it is important to be astute on proposed changes. The combined numbers of school counselors and other counseling professionals can have an impact on state laws and regulations that affect our counseling practice and professional image. It would be important for beginning school counselors to join forces with others to provide new approaches and fresh energy to association work. Collaboration with counseling colleagues can be highly rewarding work for new school counselors who wish to use their leadership and advocacy skills to make a difference on a larger scale.

CONCLUSION

This chapter began with a few suggestions on how to conclude your counseling and collaborating work at your clinical school sites in a manner that is both personal and professional. Taking a little extra time to plan positive closure activities with students and staff will not only help establish effective future behavior patterns, but it will enhance your professional reputation as well.

As you prepare to leave your counselor training program and begin the transition into the world of a professional school counselor, you will want to improve your emerging knowledge and skills. Use the self-assessments provided in this chapter to annually monitor your professional development in order to focus on your career goals and provide reassurance in what you do.

Be mindful of your identity as a professional school counselor. You possess unique knowledge and skills that are greatly needed in schools today. The vision you have for developing a comprehensive school counseling program requires the support of significant others in your school, community, and state, but you will want to follow the advice of the Chinese philosopher Lao-tzu, who wisely stated, "The journey of a thousand miles begins beneath your feet." Build your school's counseling program component by component, and let data guide your journey.

This is the best time in history to be a well-trained and prepared school counselor. Whether you are hired in an elementary school, a middle school, or a high school, challenging and rewarding work awaits you there. What better calling can there be than to have a dream to build a comprehensive school counseling program and to have the abilities to design and deliver it for our nation's future generation?

WEBSITES

- Microsoft Office Online provides various templates that you can use to build your résumé: http://office.microsoft.com/en-us/templates/CT101448941033.aspx
- This link provides you with tips for a successful job interview: http://jobsearch.about.com/od/interviews/tp/jobinterviewtips.htm

REFERENCES

Hatch, T. (2008). School counselor beliefs about ASCA National Model School Counseling Program Components using the SCPCS. *Professional School Counseling, 12*, 34–42.

Meyers, P. (2006). Finding the perfect match. *ASCA School Counselor, 44*(1), 31–32.

Milsom, A., & Akos, P. (2007). National certification: Evidence of a professional school counselor? *Professional School Counseling, 10*, 346–351.

NCSC [National Certified School Counselor]. (n.d.). *National Certified School Counselor (NCSC)*. Retrieved from www.nbcc.org/specialties/NCSC

Nichter, M., & Nelson, J. (2006). Educating administrators. *ASCA School Counselor, 44*(2), 15–20.

U.S. News and World Report. (2014). *Best jobs 2014*. Retrieved from http://money.usnews.com/careers/best-jobs/rankings/best-social-services-jobs

Index

academics, domain 26, 51, 66, 94, 95, 97, 110, 119, 122, 128, 130, 131, 142, 144, 151, 163, 188, 220, 221, 242
Achievement Orientation Model (AOM) 97–8
action plans 143, 171
administrators, school: role of 28; terminating relationships with 262
adolescent egocentrism 251
advisement 155–7, 164; supervision 82; students 155–7, 164
advisory council 140
advocacy 119–21
American Counselor Association (ACA) 4
American School Counselor Association (ASCA) 4
anxiety performance 155
application process: interview 268; letters of recommendation 264; jobs, searching for 264; resume 266
appraisal, 155, 178
art, in counseling 49–51; materials 48
ASCA National Model 66, 94–6, 108, 116, 129, 167
ASCA Mindsets and Behaviors for Student Success 66, 94, 131–2, 140
ASCA National Standards for Students *see* ASCA Mindsets and Behaviors for Student Success
assessments: instruments to measure 171; peer 178; program 138–9; retrospective 175; school counselor 177–8; self 180–1; student 178
asthma, childhood 246
Attention-Deficit Hyperactivity Disorder (AD/HD) 216, 247
Autism Spectrum Disorder 245–6
automatization 247
autonomy, in supervision 77–9

Bandura, Albert *see* Learning Theory
beliefs, foundation 128
biological development: adolescents 249–50; school-aged youth 245
board, school 27
bookkeeper/treasurer, school 37
Bronfenbrenner, Urie 242–3
Buckley Amendment *see* FERPA
bullying *see* Safe School Initiatives

calendars 147–8
career: domain 66, 94, 98, 128, 130, 144, 156

case notes 178–9
challenges, in supervision: anxiety 85–6; dual roles 86; multicultural 81, 85; parallel process 86; resistance 85–6
Choice Theory *see* Reality Therapy
classroom instruction 151–3
classroom management 24, 151–3
clinical experience 5
cognitive theories, of development 241, 250
collaboration 113, 122, 164
Common Core State Standards Initiative 22
communication: prompt 23; regarding job 23; website 32, 72
community agencies 35, 191
competencies: school counselor 99, 132; student *see* ASCA Mindsets and Behaviors for Student Success
Comprehensive Developmental School Counseling (CDSC) Program *see* ASCA National Model
conceptualization skills, in supervision 80, 81
confidentiality 124, 163, 179, 187, 189, 244
consultation 82, 163, 185
continuity versus discontinuity 254
coordination 82, 113
Council for Accreditation of Counseling and Related Educational Programs (CACREP) 4–6
counseling: crisis 158; group 158, 188; individual 41–7, 158
counselor identity, 20/20 vision 4–5, 95, 113
creative counseling approaches *see* specific theories
credentials, professional 269–70; continuing education 269–70; national requirements 269–70; state variations 269
culture, school *see* school culture
curriculum 151
custodians, school 34

data: school profile 167, 213; uses of 141; *see* specific types
depression 252
developmental supervision models: basic structures 76–9; levels of 76–9
developmental theories, 245; biological development 245, 249; cognitive development 241, 247, 250–1; independence, establishing *nature versus nurture*, debate 234; psychosocial 249, 253–4; *see* specific developmental theories

Dewitt Wallace-Reader's Digest Fund 113
DIRT suicide acronym 160
disclosure statement 12, 62
Discrimination Model, of supervision: roles 80–1
drugs and alcohol 252
dual roles 86
Dufour, Richard 27

Ellis, Albert 43
Epston, David 47
Erickson, Milton 45
Erikson, Erik *see* psychodynamic theory
ethical decision making models: apply standards 185;
   colleagues, responsibilities to 190; consequences of
   action 186; considering 186; determining actions
   185; evaluate 186; identifying problem 185;
   implementing actions 186; *see also* confidentiality
ethics: ASCA Ethical Standards 187–93; *autonomy*
   184; *beneficence* 184; decision making; *fidelity* 184;
   group work 188; *justice* 184; maintenance of 193;
   nonmaleficence 184; parents/guardians, responsibilities to 190; principles 184–4; profession, responsibilities to 192; records 189; school and community,
   responsibilities to 191; self, responsibilities to 192;
   standards, maintenance of students, responsibilities
   to 187; *veracity* 184; *see also* ethical decision-making
   models
evaluation 82,176
experimental, action research 169–70

Federal Education Rights and Privacy Act (FERPA)
   11, 25

gateway drugs 252
Glasser, William 42–3
goals: program 130, 181; SMART 130

Hall, Stanley G. 249
Health Insurance Portability and Accountability Act
   (HIPPA) 11

identity, adolescents: *achievement* 254; *audience*
   251; *confusion* 253; *diffusion* 254; *foreclosure* 254;
   moratorium 254; *self* 253
independence, healthy establishment 253
informed consent 12, 187
internship: practicum, *versus* 5–6; purpose of 6
intervention skills, in supervision 80–1
interview 268
invincibility fable 251

Kitchener 184–7
Kohlberg, Lawrence 243–4

laws 18, 185, 198
leadership: shared 116; transformational 117
learning disabilities (LD) 247
learning theory 235–8

lesson plans 144, 147
LGBTQ students 223–4; legal implications 223

management agreements 140
Marcia, James 254
MEASURE system 169–71
moral reasoning, development of 243–4
motivation, in supervision 77–9
motivational interviewing (MI) 39–41
multiculturalism: assessment 210; cultural/ethnic
   diversity 214; English language learners 226; gender
   differences 222; multiple exceptionalities 227–8;
   School Counselor Multicultural Competence
   Checklist 210–12; socioeconomic differences
   227; supervisor-supervisee relationship 85; *see
   also* LGBTQ students; students with disabilities;
   students who are gifted
music, in counseling 53–4

narrative therapy: *dominant plot* 47; *externalization*
   47; multicultural perspective 47; overview of 47;
   sparkling moments 47; *unique outcomes* 47
National Board of Certified Counselors, Inc. (NBCC)
   270
National Board for Professional Teaching Standards
   (NBPTS) 270–1
National Center for Transforming School Counseling
   (NCTSC) 4–5, 113
National Certified School Counselor (NCSC) 270–1
nature versus nurture 234
needs assessment 142
No Child Left Behind (NCLB) 18
nonprofessional interactions. *see* dual roles
normative influences 234
nurse, school 34

obesity, childhood 245
observations 172
outcome data 143

parenting 239–40
parents/guardians 31, 190
parallel process 86
Partnership Process Model *see* collaboration
peer: assessment 178; facilitation 161; mediation 24,
   161; person centered counseling 41; personalization
   skills, in supervision 80–1; multicultural
   perspective 41
perception data 141–2
Piaget, Jean 241, 250
play: in counseling 52; materials 53
portfolio 181
Positive Behavior Intervention Support (PBIS) 19–20
practicum: direct *versus* indirect hours 7; internship
   versus 5–6; purpose of 5; supervision aspects 6
PRAXIS 269
pre-post test 173
process data 141–2

Professional Disclosure Statement 12
Professional Learning Community (PLC) 27
professional organizations 272
program focus 128
program placement coordinator 4
psychodynamic theory 235
psychologist, school 34
psychosocial development 249

Rational Emotive Behavior Therapy (REBT):
    multicultural perspective 44; overview of 44
Reality Therapy: multicultural perspective 42–3;
    overview of 42–3; *see* Choice Therapy
referrals 162, 188
reframing 31, 226
response to intervention (RTI) 21, 217
responsive services 157
resume, sample of 266
Rogers, Carl 41

safe school initiatives 19; bullying 19
SAMI²C³. 42
school: board 27; climate, defined 17–18; contextual
    aspects 39; culture 18, 96, 114; environment 19,
    39; improvement plans 18–19
School Counseling Supervision Models 82
school counselor: discipline 24, 137; division of
    responsibilities 23; office 137; professionals,
    interactions 33; school related personnel 33; special
    education 26; testing 25
School Motivation and Learning Strategies Inventory
    (SMALSI) 98
secretaries, school 34
security resource officer (SRO), school 35
School Wide Intervention Supports (PBIS). *see*
    positive behavior
Second Step 19
Self-Directed Search (SDS) 98
self-other awareness in supervision 76, 78–9
self-reflection, readiness for supervision 64
sexual activity 252; pregnancy 250, 252; STDs 250,
    252
SLAP suicide assessment 160
Social Cognitive Career Theory (SCCT) 98
social/emotional, domain 98, 187
social role models *see* Discrimination Model
social workers, school 34
sociocultural perspective 242
solution-focused brief counseling (SFBC) 45;
    multicultural perspective 45
students: building relationships 30, 61–3; disabilities
    26, 216, 247; gifted 219; individual planning 155
Student Success Skills (SSS) 98
study skills strategies 153–4
suicide 158–60, 253

supervisees: anxiety 85–6, 155; attendance 61;
    contracts 9, 66–7, 96; dress 60; goal setting 65;
    introducing self 61–2; initial contact 59–60; policies
    and procedures 61; safety plan 68–9; school site,
    choosing 13; self-care 70–1; wellness 69, 73
supervision: anxiety 84–5; challenges 75, 83–4; concep-
    tualization skills 80–1; evaluation 82, 84; experiences
    5, 15, 59, 263; goal setting 9, 59, 66–7, 123; group 9;
    individual 4, 8, 82; motivation 7; multicultural influ-
    ences 85; personalization skills 80; policies/procedures
    61; relationship 66, 83–5; resistance to 85–6; roles 82,
    87; school-site, choosing 12; technology-mediated 10,
    71; triadic 4, 8–9; working alliance 83
supervision models *see* specific models
supervisor: choosing 13; doctoral-student 6, 8; pro-
    gram faculty 4, 8; site supervisor 4, 9–10, 63, 134,
    178; *see also* supervisees
surveys 174
systemic change: knowledge of change 114; organiza-
    tional understanding 114; perspective of education
    114; stakeholder ownership 114; systems design 115
systems theories of development 242–3

taping counseling sessions: confidentiality 10–11, 179;
    equipment 10; issues with 11
teachers 29–30
technology: application, jobs 264; counseling 71–2;
    supervision 10, 71–3; *see also* taping counseling
    sessions
termination: administrators, with 262–3; colleagues,
    with 262; students, with 259–60
testing, high stakes 25, 155
themes, of ASCA National Model *see* specific themes
theories, counseling *see* specific models
time: direct 108; indirect108; percentage of 108, 139,
    168
tools 140
TRAINER model 119–20
Transforming School Counseling Initiative 4, 5, 116,
    125

universal versus context specific 234

values 78, 127, 132, 185, 243
vision and mission 129
Voyager Learning 21
Vygotsky, Lev *see* Sociocultural perspective

Wagner v. Fayetteville Public Schools 227
WDEP system 42
White, Michael 47
working memory 247

zero-tolerance policies 19, 52
zone of proximal development 242

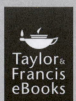